Issues in Management

Issues in Management

Articles from SAGE Business Researcher

SAGE Business Researcher

Los Angeles | London | New Delhi
Singapore | Washington DC | Melbourne

FOR INFORMATION:

SAGE Publications, Inc.
2455 Teller Road
Thousand Oaks, California 91320
E-mail: order@sagepub.com

SAGE Publications Ltd.
1 Oliver's Yard
55 City Road
London EC1Y 1SP
United Kingdom

SAGE Publications India Pvt. Ltd.
B 1/I 1 Mohan Cooperative Industrial Area
Mathura Road, New Delhi 110 044
India

SAGE Publications Asia-Pacific Pte. Ltd.
3 Church Street
#10-04 Samsung Hub
Singapore 049483

Acquisitions Editor: Maggie Stanley
Editorial Assistant: Alissa Nance
Production Editor: Kimaya Khashnobish
Typesetter: C&M Digitals (P) Ltd.
Proofreader: Annie Lubinsky
Cover Designer: Michael Dubowe
Marketing Manager: Amy Lammers

Printed in the United States of America

Library of Congress Cataloging-in-Publication Data

Names: Sage Publications, issuing body.

Title: Issues in management : articles from Sage business researcher.

Other titles: Sage business researcher.

Description: Los Angeles : SAGE, [2018] | Includes bibliographical references.

Identifiers: LCCN 2017045102 | ISBN 9781544316086 (pbk. : alk. paper)

Subjects: LCSH: Management.

Classification: LCC HD31.2 .I87 2018 | DDC 658—dc23
LC record available at https://lccn.loc.gov/2017045102

This book is printed on acid-free paper.

SFI label applies to text stock

17 18 19 20 21 10 9 8 7 6 5 4 3 2 1

BRIEF CONTENTS

DETAILED CONTENTS

PART III • TRENDS IN MANAGEMENT

Chapter 12 • Failure 277

Vickie Elmer

THE CHANGING NATURE OF WORK

THE GIG ECONOMY
Are Millennials failing to develop important work skills?
Damon Brown

EXECUTIVE SUMMARY

Many Millennials are gravitating toward the gig economy of temporary and freelance jobs, enabled to do so by the rise of sharing-economy companies such as Uber and the advent of powerful social media. Many who have taken this route say they enjoy being untethered from the traditional workplace and have little interest in permanent full-time jobs. Some observers say the 2007–09 recession and the soft economy that followed have pushed Millennials in this direction. Whether because of choice or necessity, the increasing prevalence of gig work raises the question of whether these younger workers are failing to learn the communications, leadership and teamwork skills that come from functioning in a more conventional work setting.

Some key takeaways:

- The number of those working in the gig economy increased 60 percent between 1997 and 2014.

- Millennials who expect to leave their jobs within two years exceed those who plan to stay for at least five years.

- A wealth of social media apps and websites has sprung up to facilitate life in the gig economy.

OVERVIEW

Author and motivational speaker Simon Sinek argued recently that Millennials are spoiled—and this is wrecking U.S. workplaces.

"I keep meeting these wonderful, fantastic, idealistic, hardworking, smart kids, they've just graduated school, they're in their entry-level job," Sinek, who is 43, said in a December television interview. "I go, 'How's it going?' They go, 'I think I'm going to quit. . . . I'm not making an impact'. I'm like, 'You've been here eight months!' "[1]

From *SAGE Business Researcher*,
June 26, 2017

Uber and its ubiquitous app have come to symbolize the gig economy, with all its strengths and drawbacks.

Source: Adam Berry/Getty Images

Sinek's argument: A perfect storm of internet-fueled impatience, a soft U.S. economy and poor interpersonal communication skills have made the generation born between 1982 and 2004 unfit for the traditional workplace.[2]

But there is another possibility: Because they came of age during the rise of major startups that earned billions of dollars by disrupting entire industries, Millennials don't *want* to be in that traditional workplace.

The Millennial workforce and the biggest startups are so intertwined because high-flyers such as the ride-sharing company Uber, valued at $69 billion, and hotel-alternative Airbnb, worth $31 billion, don't rely on traditional employees.[3] Uber is powered by independent contractors using their own vehicles to ferry customers around, while Airbnb asks people to rent out their homes (or their apartments, creating a matryoshka doll of renters renting a place they don't own).

The trend has a catchy name, coined at the height of the financial crisis in 2009 and derived from an earlier term applied to jazz musicians: the gig economy.[4] And it's a growing phenomenon. The number of these nontraditional workers—defined as the self-employed, sole proprietors, contractors and freelancers—increased from 15 million in 1997 to nearly 24 million in 2014, according to a study by the Brookings Institution, a Washington think tank.[5]

The growing prevalence of these young gig workers is reshaping the American workplace by changing the expectations people have about their work, the way they communicate with each other on the job and the competencies they develop. It also raises the question of whether Millennials will possess the skills in communication, leadership and teamwork needed to function in a more traditional corporate environment, should they choose to make that transition.

Why Millennials Are Turning Down the 9-to-5

A wealth of data demonstrates that large numbers of Millennials, although perhaps not the majority, are uninterested in traditional jobs. A 2017 survey by the Deloitte consulting firm found that nearly one-third of Millennials worldwide prefer freelance work to full-time employment. It also found that the number of Millennials who anticipate leaving their current jobs within two years exceeded those who expect to stay for at least five years (although the gap has shrunk from last year).[6]

Millennials themselves cite three primary, correlated reasons for turning down traditional work: the soft economy, growing freelance opportunities and technology-enabled freedom.

"The Millennial struggle is definitely unique to our economy," says Katasha Kay, a self-described "recovering broke Millennial" who created the financial website Broke Girl Rehab. "When my mother was my age, she was able to walk into an office—with no degree and no experience—and land a middle-class job as an IT professional. That's impossible now."

Instead, many Millennials are looking to create stability through a patchwork of jobs. Kay says she utilized the freelancing platform Upwork to make a living while traveling abroad, while other Millennials who shared their perspective discussed using online freelance marketplaces Fiverr and TaskRabbit to get revenue.

Morissa Schwartz, who created the online publishing site GenZ and authored a book on the gig world, says the economy is pushing her generation to go independent. "People are interning to get jobs, but that doesn't guarantee an opportunity as much as my mom's generation. Some of us would actually like to get jobs."

Simon Sinek: Millennials' elders didn't prepare them for today's economic realities.

There is a fascinating parallel between the Millennial take on an American Dream deferred and non-Millennial Sinek's view of the younger generation. In the TV interview, Sinek said that the older generation bears responsibility for the current Millennial challenges because it didn't prepare Millennials for the new economy of instability and disruption.[7]

Schwartz voices a similar thought: "My high school counselors said, 'You need a 9-to-5 to be a success,' but I don't. My counselors and advisers said, 'You need internships, you absolutely need to do this and that to succeed.' It virtually brainwashed us into thinking this was the only path."

It is no coincidence that the gig economy took off as the Internet increased ways to generate revenue and boosted freelance job opportunities. Once-costly websites could now be launched for free, Web domains bought for under $10 and social media profiles set up as virtual storefronts within minutes. And, of course, there were the Millennial role models, entrepreneurs such as Facebook co-founder Mark Zuckerberg and Snapchat CEO Evan Spiegel, who banded together with others in their generation and created their own economic weather just by using a computer.

"I have the entrepreneurial spirit to do what I want when I want," Schwartz says. "I think many of us have that independent spirit being part of the Internet generation."

The road is still steep, however. At tech incubator Y Combinator, the original business accelerator, fewer than one out of 10 startups attained a value of at least $40 million. In other words, even at one of the most successful entrepreneurial organizations in Silicon Valley, most entrepreneurs did not achieve significant success.[8]

The Communication Gap

Apple unveiled the first iPhone in 2007, just months before the U.S. economy tanked, and at a moment when many Millennials were coming of age. The launch of the now-ubiquitous smartphone changed the way people communicated, spawning a host of apps ranging from Slack and iMessage to Instagram and Snapchat, as well as nomenclature such as text abbreviations and Japanese emoticons.

Devices like the iPhone have contributed to a communication gap that impedes some Millennials' abilities to thrive in a traditional work environment.

Source: Vyacheslav Prokofyev/Getty Images

It also created a generational communications gap in the workplace, between Millennials raised on e-conversations through tech venues and older employers accustomed to face-to-face or at least telephone talks. And that gap may be short-changing Millennials by leaving them wanting in some important communication skills, says Jodi Raymond, founder of People Matters, a Michigan-based human resources firm.

"Building and maintaining effective relationships over time is an essential part of day-to-day life in the corporate world," says Raymond, speaking about where she believes gig-economy Millennials may need to improve their skills. "Welcoming and acclimating new team members, listening deeply, sharing ideas without alienating teammates, working with challenging personalities, valuing and bringing together diverse perspectives, managing conflict and handling criticism are all aspects of being part of a team."

Raymond adds that another valuable skill is "the ability to quickly understand a corporate culture and the ability to effectively operate within it. It includes identifying and interpreting formal and informal structures, building allies and relationships across departments, and behaving professionally. Being in an organization grows patience for bureaucracy and knowing how to still make an impact while staying within the written and unwritten boundaries."

Kay says that having—or lacking—such skills can really matter. "I've noticed that for people who don't have experience working in an office, they operate at a level that's cute when you're just a solopreneur," she says. "But when you're managing a team and landing $100,000 contracts, that lack of professionalism makes everything fall apart fast."

As for Schwartz, she's finishing work on a master's degree in communication at Monmouth University in New Jersey. "I need to make sure my communication is down pat," she says.

The Dark Side of the Gig Economy

Few pop-culture moments resonated as powerfully among Millennials as the publication of "The 4-Hour Workweek" by Tim Ferriss. The book, destined to become a bestseller, arrived in April 2007, just two months before the iPhone launch.

The essence of Ferriss' book is that it *is* possible to have it all: A life of freedom, leisure time and significant profits. "From using Jedi mind tricks to disappear from the office to designing businesses that finance your lifestyle, there are paths for every comfort level," he wrote. "How does a Fortune 500 employee explore the hidden jewels of China for a month and use technology to cover his tracks? How do you create a hands-off business that generates $80K per month with no management? It's all here."[9]

The book's philosophy is superficially appealing but ultimately misleading, according to Ferriss' critics. What his book underestimates, they say, is time: the time it takes to build a reputation within a job to earn a promotion; the time required to master a particular skill; the time needed each day to create a bond with co-workers. Ferriss seems to argue that things previous generations took years to do can be done swiftly with the right "hack" (shorthand for a quick work-around).

One such critic, author/entrepreneur Penelope Trunk, asserted that Ferriss' own experiences undermine his argument. "The week that Tim actually works a four-hour work week will be a cold week in hell," Trunk wrote in 2009. "Tim got to where he is by being an insanely hard worker. I don't know anyone who worked harder at promoting a book than he did. But the thing is, he didn't call it work. . . . His four-hour work week is merely semantic."[10]

Most Expect Workers Will Moonlight in the Future

In a similar vein, Jia Tolentino, a writer for The New Yorker, has argued that there is a fundamental disconnect in the gig economy between appearance and reality.

"The contrast between the gig economy's rhetoric (everyone is always connecting, having fun, and killing it!) and the conditions that allow it to exist (a lack of dependable employment that pays a living wage) makes this kink in our thinking especially clear," Tolentino wrote recently."[11]

At the heart of this contradiction, she wrote, "is the American obsession with self-reliance, which makes it more acceptable to applaud an individual for working himself to death than to argue that an individual working himself to death is evidence of a flawed economic system."[12]

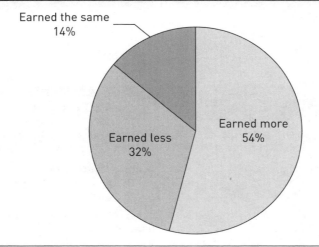

Office professionals predict most people will have multiple jobs

Earned the same
14%

Earned less
32%

Earned more
54%

Most people in the future will hold multiple jobs simultaneously, a majority of more than 1,000 U.S. office professionals surveyed in 2016 predicted. Majorities in the United Kingdom and India held the same view.

Source: "Work in Progress," Adobe, May 2016, http://tinyurl.com/yays4wwk

And gig-economy workers are at the mercy of the startups, lacking the benefits and legal protections of permanent employees, even those who can be terminated for any reason. Tolentino tells the story of a pregnant Lyft driver who felt so compelled to keep driving, perhaps because of the low pay rate, that she picked up a fare even as she was driving herself to the hospital, in labor, to give birth.[13]

Lyft's biggest competitor, Uber, has faced its own controversies. Critics accuse it of using psychological techniques, such as an algorithm that sends another fare opportunity before the current trip is finished, to manipulate drivers into working longer hours. In May, Uber said it had mistakenly underpaid its New York City drivers and agreed to reimburse each one an average of $900.[14] Uber announced in June that it was accepting a series of recommendations by former Attorney General Eric Holder Jr. stemming from his investigation of the company's internal culture.[15] Later in the month, a shareholder revolt forced co-founder Travis Kalanick to resign as CEO.[16]

What's Next?

Millennials, particularly younger ones, often do not have the same familial or outside responsibilities faced by older generations. While the insecure gig economy may fit a twentysomething's lifestyle, it's less certain it will work for that person a decade later.

Both Kay and Schwartz say they are passionate about the gig economy, but also are aware that corporate-level skills will be necessary tomorrow, even if the gig economy is feeding them today. HR expert Raymond says the transition isn't something to be too concerned about: "These skills are harder to learn and obtain, but not impossible."

For Millennials such as Kay, keeping all options open feels like the smartest move. "This week, [my day job] informed me that layoffs were not beyond the realm of possibility," she says. "I figure, this is the best opportunity I have to finally take the plunge and become a full-time freelancer."

Chronology

1982	The earliest Millennials are born, according to researchers William Strauss and Neil Howe, who define the generation as those born between 1982 and 2004.
2007	Apple launches the iPhone, initiating a major change in interpersonal communications. . . . Tim Ferriss publishes The 4-Hour Workweek, which becomes a best-seller.
2008	A severe recession boosts the U.S. jobless rate to 7.3 percent by year's end and sends shock waves throughout the global economy.
2009	Uber starts operating in San Francisco, initially with contractors driving black town cars owned by the company, but shortly afterward by utilizing independent contractors who use their own cars and are not compensated for fuel or wear and tear. . . . The U.S. unemployment rate hits 10 percent in October.

2010	The Patient Protection and Affordable Care Act becomes law, enabling millions of Americans to get health insurance coverage without having a full-time job.
2011	The number of men and women ages 25 to 34 moving in with their parents rises 5 percent and 2 percent, respectively, over 2005 levels, according to the U.S. Census Bureau. . . . Billionaire Peter Thiel creates "The Dropout Fund" fellowship to pay college students $100,000 each to drop out and found startups.
2012	Facebook executes an initial public offering (IPO), immediately making Millennial co-founder and CEO Mark Zuckerberg a billionaire and one of the youngest self-made rich people in the world.
2014	The number of Americans employed in the nontraditional gig economy—defined as the self-employed, sole proprietors, contractors and freelancers—reaches nearly 24 million, an increase of 60 percent from the 1997 level, the Brookings Institution reports.
2017	Among Millennials, 38 percent anticipate leaving their current job within two years, according to a Deloitte survey.
2020	For the first time, five different generations will be together in the workplace: Traditionalists, Baby Boomers, Generation X, Generation Y/Millennials and Generation Z.

RESOURCES

The Next Step

Gig Economy Globally

D'Cunha, Suparna Dutt, "Why the Gig Economy Could Reinvent the UAE Workplace for the Better," Forbes, June 9, 2017, https://tinyurl.com/yd99gsh3.

The United Arab Emirates' expanding and diversifying economy could generate a gig economy because of the country's massive infrastructure and energy projects. Such projects need highly skilled independent contractors, and new service-based apps have helped introduce the sharing economy concept to the region.

Lowrey, Annie, "What the Gig Economy Looks Like Around the World," The Atlantic, April 13, 2017, https://tinyurl.com/y7kjo3g6.

A three-year study of workers in the online gig economy in sub-Saharan Africa and Southeast Asia by researchers at the University of Oxford and the University of Pretoria finds patterns, both positive and negative, that resemble the situation in the United States.

Price, Rob, "Sleepless nights and hospital runs: The struggles of parenthood in the gig economy," Business Insider, June 6, 2017, https://tinyurl.com/y8ftkl2w.

Three couriers and an Uber driver in the United Kingdom share stories of taking care of their families while working in the gig economy. While some would like benefits and possible recognition as full-time employees, others do not want to compromise the freedom their jobs afford.

Protections for Gig Workers

Gutman, David, "Judge temporarily blocks Seattle law allowing Uber and Lyft drivers to unionize," The Seattle Times, April 4, 2017, updated April 17, 2017, https://tinyurl.com/kotovmp.

A federal judge has put on hold a 2015 Seattle law—the first of its kind in the United States—allowing Uber, Lyft and taxi drivers to unionize. The U.S. Chamber of Commerce and a group of Uber and Lyft drivers is challenging the law.

Heller, Nathan, "Is the Gig Economy Working?" The New Yorker, May 15, 2017, https://tinyurl.com/ly7cwou.

The yin and yang of the gig economy: It may be the future of the U.S. workforce, especially for independence-seeking Millennials. But it favors the better educated, and it comes with burdens: higher economic risk and a dearth of benefits.

Knibbs, Kate, "Will Gig-Economy Workers Ever Have Benefits?" The Ringer, June 7, 2017, https://tinyurl.com/y9akdlf7.

Sen. Mark Warner, D-Va., has proposed legislation to address the problem of lack of benefits for gig-economy workers: portable benefits that are linked to the employee rather than the job.

Organizations

American Civil Liberties Union
125 Broad St., 18th Floor, New York, NY 10004
1-212-549-2500
www.aclu.org
Twitter: @aclu

Legal organization that represents the concerns of independent contractors in the gig economy.

Brookings Institution
1775 Massachusetts Ave., N.W., Washington, DC 20036
1-202-797-6000
www.brookings.edu

Nonprofit public policy institute that conducts extensive research on the U.S. economy.

Deloitte
30 Rockefeller Plaza, New York, NY 10112
1-212-492-4000
www.deloitte.com

International consulting firm focused on financial growth.

GenZ Publishing
1-732-306-5995

www.genzpublishing.org/
Twitter: @genzpub

Millennials-oriented online publishing house run by author Morissa Schwartz.

Upwork

441 Logue Ave., Mountain View, CA 94043
1-650-316-7500
www.upwork.com/

A freelance-hiring platform.

U.S. Bureau of Labor Statistics

Postal Square Building, 2 Massachusetts Ave., N.E., Washington, DC 20212
1-202-691-5200
www.bls.gov

The federal agency that tracks job trends.

U.S. Census Bureau

4600 Silver Hill Road, Suitland, MD 20746
1-800-923-8282
www.census.gov

The government organization that collects and analyzes population statistics.

Y Combinator

320 Pioneer Way, Mountain View, CA 94041
www.ycombinator.com/

The original accelerator, it has funded more than 1,200 startups since 2005.

2

THE SHARING ECONOMY
Is it really different from traditional business?

Patrick Marshall

EXECUTIVE SUMMARY

What's called the sharing economy—peer-to-peer transactions conducted via the Internet and smartphones—has changed how people arrange car rides, find vacation lodging and more. Revenue is projected to soar in the coming years, although profitability remains untested. But as businesses such as Uber, Lyft and Airbnb flourish, regulation and collection of taxes, primarily by state and local authorities, have become more difficult to enforce. Traditional businesses such as taxis and hotels complain that these newcomers are gaining an unfair advantage by ducking oversight that's meant to protect consumers. Additionally, debate has grown over whether service providers in the sharing economy are independent contractors or employees. Some of the key issues under debate: Is the sharing economy more efficient than traditional markets? Should regulators treat the sharing economy the same way as conventional competitors? Are sharing-economy companies platforms for independent contractors, or are they employers?

OVERVIEW

The "sharing economy"—in which consumers connect with service providers using Internet applications instead of relying on traditional providers—is booming. On a typical day, an estimated 247,000 items are sold on Etsy, 140,000 people rent accommodations through Airbnb and 1 million people ride with Uber.[1]

Because very few sharing-economy companies are publicly traded, it's unknown whether they are profitable. But many sharing-economy companies are attracting major investments and have quickly become players in the economy. Based on venture capital funds raised, The Wall Street Journal estimated Uber's value at more than $40 billion and Airbnb at $25 billion.[2]

In fact, according to the Federal Trade Commission, sharing-economy transactions totaled about $26 billion globally in 2013.[3] And PricewaterhouseCoopers (PwC), an

From *SAGE Business Researcher*,
August 3, 2015

auding and consulting firm, estimates that in 10 years, the biggest sectors of the sharing economy could see $335 billion in global revenue. PwC projects that by 2025, sharing-economy companies will account for about half of the business in their market sectors, up from only 6.25 percent in 2013.[4]

What's more, sharing-economy companies are emerging in numerous niche markets. It's not, in short, just about renting apartments and hailing cars. There is a platform that cities can use to share heavy equipment (MuniRent), a platform that skiers, bicycle and surfboard owners can use to rent their recreational equipment

A Lyft car, marked with a bright pink mustache, lines up next to a traditional taxi in San Francisco traffic. Ride-hailing services such as Lyft are among the most visible players in the sharing economy. The taxi industry charges that these new firms compete unfairly.

Source: Justin Sullivan/Getty Images

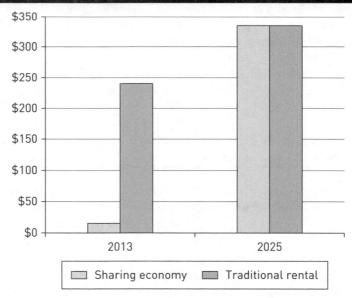

Sharing Economy to Match Rental Revenue by 2025
Projected revenue for rental services, by sector, in $U.S. billions, 2013 and 2025

Legend: Sharing economy — Traditional rental

Internet-based sharing businesses will generate an estimated $335 billion in revenue by 2025, the same amount projected for five traditional rental sectors (equipment rental, B&B and hostels, car rental, book rental and DVD rental).

Source: "The sharing economy—sizing the revenue opportunity," PricewaterhouseCoopers, 2014, http://tinyurl.com/ophtwcf

Note: 2025 estimates based on historical data and projected growth rates and economic outcomes for 10 industry sectors.

(Spinlister) and a platform that musicians can use to share their equipment (GearLode). There is also a robust group of platforms that connect investors to individuals and small businesses seeking funding (Funding Circle, LendingClub, Prosper, TransferWise).

"It's clear that consumers are embracing it," says John Breyault, vice president of public policy at the National Consumers League, a consumer advocacy group in Washington, D.C.

Chicago taxi driver Keith Williams joins a February 2015 protest against smartphone-hailed car services. Cities across the world are wrestling with how to regulate such sharing-economy companies.

Source: Scott Olson /Getty Images

Of course, the sharing economy—which has also been described as a peer-to-peer economy—is not actually new.

"Peer-to-peer businesses were around long before the Internet," Philip Auerswald, associate professor of public policy at George Mason University, told a House hearing on the sharing economy last year. "Indeed, there was a time in this country and elsewhere in the world (roughly until the end of the 19th century) when the peer-to-peer economy *was* the economy. Large corporations providing consumer services simply did not exist. Regulation governing consumer services was minimal. People provided services on a personal basis to other people who were very much like them."[5]

While peer-to-peer transactions may not be new, analysts say, how those transactions occur is. The Internet and smartphones have allowed transactions to take place around the block or around the globe, almost instantaneously. "It's these different technologies that are making things easier," says Dean Baker, an economist and the cofounder of the Center for Economic and Policy Research, a Washington, D.C., think tank.

Indeed, the Internet has fundamentally changed the nature of peer-to-peer transactions. Where previously those dealings involved only the buyer and seller of goods or services, now they are mediated through a software platform, which is owned by a company or, in some cases, a nonprofit organization. That change has led to two developments. First, regulation and collection of taxes, primarily by state and local authorities, have become more difficult to enforce. Second, there is growing debate over whether service providers in the sharing economy are really independent contractors or employees.

The stakes involved are high. If regulators require sharing-economy companies to conform to laws governing employers' treatment of employees, the prices of their goods and services will likely rise and their competitive advantage against traditional companies will be reduced.

Corporate involvement in the sharing economy, some analysts say, means that much of this economy has little or nothing to do with sharing. "Make no mistake about it, today's sharing economy is big business, involving lots and lots of money and all kinds of players motivated powerfully by financial gain," said Nancy Koehn, a professor at Harvard Business School.[6]

Although the Internet has enabled the sharing economy to blossom, other factors also have contributed. "While some of these sharing models might have resulted from a need for frugal spending after the global economic recession of 2008," wrote entrepreneurship professors Boyd Cohen and Jan Kietzmann, "their success was also driven by a growing environmental consciousness combined with the ubiquity of Internet and associated information and communication technologies which make sharing possible at scale."[7]

Koehn speculated that deeper aspects of consumer psychology may explain the booming popularity of many sharing-economy companies. "There is a directness about calling a limo ride yourself on Uber or Lyft and then rating the driver and car after you get to your destination that is both empowering and seemingly more transparent than calling a car service or hailing a taxi," she said. "Individuals from all walks of life, particularly younger consumers, simply do not have much trust in established business, governmental, and other large-scale organizations. Against this backdrop, many consumers—and sellers—find peer-to-peer buying and selling to be more appealing because it is not so closely associated with a big business that may (or may not) have a mixed track record in their minds."[8]

The relatively new technologies that power the sharing economy have put many transactions outside the purview of regulators. While cities issue taxi medallions to a limited number of service providers, they have little control over the drivers who connect to passengers using Uber, Lyft or Sidecar. And while cities license and tax hotels, they haven't yet developed a way to manage and monitor homeowners and companies renting through sharing-economy companies such as Airbnb.

As a result, although consumers generally seem happy with the savings and convenience delivered by sharing-economy companies, many of those companies are beginning to feel pressure from several directions. Those include their contractors (or employees) unsatisfied with wages and the lack of benefits; government agencies and competing businesses that claim sharing-economy companies are dodging needed regulation; municipalities that accuse service providers of failing to pay taxes; and consumer groups that say some companies are underserving certain groups of people.

Not surprisingly, the greatest amount of attention has focused on the most successful sharing-economy companies: Uber and Airbnb.

"The growth of illegal hotels is rapidly becoming one of the biggest obstacles in the struggle to protect and expand New York City's stock of affordable housing," Democratic New York state Sen. Liz Krueger told the Federal Trade Commission in May. "Online platforms like Airbnb lure individuals into breaking the law with promises of more income from operating illegal hotels, leaving residents with an increasingly scarce supply of affordable housing."[9]

Krueger also charged that the lack of effective regulation over Airbnb exposes consumers to drawbacks of which they may not be aware. "Most illegal hotels fail to meet federal, state and city accessibility requirements for people with disabilities," she said. "Far from being a harmless service that promotes 'sharing,' companies like Airbnb threaten public safety and make it more difficult for everyday New Yorkers to find an affordable place to live."

Airbnb did not to respond to repeated requests for comment. In a blog post in 2013, however, CEO Brian Chesky argued that the company actually helps New Yorkers stay in their homes. "In New York, our 15,000 hosts are regular people from all five boroughs. Eighty-seven percent of them rent the homes in which they live," wrote Chesky. "On average, they are at the median income level and more than half of them depend on Airbnb to help them stay in their home."[10]

Ride-sharing companies have drawn even greater criticism from competitors and regulators. "The thing with Uber and Lyft, what they're doing is they are cutting corners on safety and responsibility under the guise of the sharing economy," says Dave Sutton, a spokesman for the Taxicab, Limousine & Paratransit Association, which represents 1,100 taxicab companies. "Their insurance has gaps, which has come to light, and more and more will be revealed. Their background checks are not conducted by law enforcement and don't involve fingerprinting. And those are truly undercutting public safety."

Uber declined requests for interviews and responded to questions only by providing links to materials on the company's website. The materials do not indicate that Uber's background checks include fingerprints and reviews by law enforcement agencies.

The reaction to Uber by taxi drivers in some other countries has been even more dramatic. In early July, for example, Uber was forced to suspend its UberPop service in France after taxi drivers violently protested.[11]

Because sharing-economy companies are using new technologies that transform the way business is conducted, analysts say, a period of adjustment is inevitably needed to balance the competing interests of companies, regulators and consumers. "It is no surprise that Uber, Airbnb and other new companies find themselves operating in an area where the application of existing laws is potentially unclear," said Koehn. "It is also not surprising that these companies are fighting efforts by regulators to apply government rules and standards to their growing market."[12]

As the market presence of the biggest sharing-market companies has surged, friction with regulators—particularly at the state and local levels—has grown more pronounced in recent months.

For example, in the wake of an October report by the New York State Office of the Attorney General, which found that 72 percent of units booked via Airbnb in New York City appeared to violate state and local laws, city officials have begun filing suit and imposing fines on property owners.[13] The day after the report was released, the New York Daily News learned that New York City had filed suit against two property owners.[14]

In fact, many cities have long banned rentals of fewer than 30 days for properties that have not been inspected and licensed. And several cities have successfully pressed Airbnb to collect appropriate taxes from hosts for payment to the cities.

For its part, Uber has been banned by several communities and airports and has been sued by drivers who say that the company should be treating them as employees rather than independent contractors. In June, in a ruling that could be portentous, the California Labor Commissioner's Office determined that an Uber driver should be classified as an employee, not an independent contractor. Uber was ordered to reimburse the driver, Barbara Ann Berwick, $4,152.20 in expenses and other costs for the eight weeks she worked as an Uber driver. While the ruling applies only to Berwick and Uber is appealing it, the case could significantly affect Uber's competitive pricing if other courts agree that drivers are employees.[15]

"The explosion of sharing or on-demand services like Uber and Airbnb is the beginning of an economic upheaval every bit as significant as the Industrial Revolution," warned Frank Shafroth, director of the Center for State and Local Government Leadership at George Mason University. "The on-demand economy promises to radically reshape the cost of services and change the face of the workforce. These upheavals, in turn, are altering state and local government policies—imposing unforeseen fiscal risks."[16]

Specifically, Shafroth wrote, in addition to the challenges of recovering lost tax revenue and ensuring public safety, policymakers will have to deal with an upsurge in the number of temporary or part-time workers in the economy. "These workers are providing on-demand services at rock bottom prices. They are not working in downtown or suburban office buildings or for traditional employers, nor are they eligible for traditional health-care or pension benefits," he said. "Leaders will need to be part of a discussion about changing rules for 'contract workers,' and of an even larger federalism and governance discussion about how pensions and health-care benefits are delivered in the future."

Number of Part-Time Workers Peaked During Recession

Additionally, the expansion of the sharing economy may have a lasting impact on other industries, such as automobile manufacturing. As consumers come to rely increasingly on sharing-economy transportation services, car ownership could decline. Indeed, a 2012 report by the U.S. Public Interest Research Group and the Frontier Group found that between 2001 and 2009, the average annual number of vehicle-miles of driving by young people (16 to 34-year-olds) decreased from 10,300 miles to 7,900 miles per capita—a drop of 23 percent. The report cites the rise of services such as Zipcar as a major factor in the trend. [17]

Shafroth said, "It's not for nothing that the on-demand economy is simultaneously dubbed the disruptive economy."[18]

As the controversy around the sharing economy grows, here are some of the questions being debated:

Weighing the Issues

Is the sharing economy more efficient than traditional markets?

Sharing-economy supporters say that the companies and the platforms they offer are using technology not only to offer savings and convenience to consumers but also to make more efficient use of resources and to expand income opportunities for service providers.

The sharing economy, the staff of the House Committee on Small Business wrote in a January 2014 memo, more efficiently allocates "resources which in turn results in new consumption leading to new production."[19]

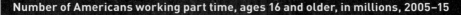

Number of Americans working part time, ages 16 and older, in millions, 2005–15

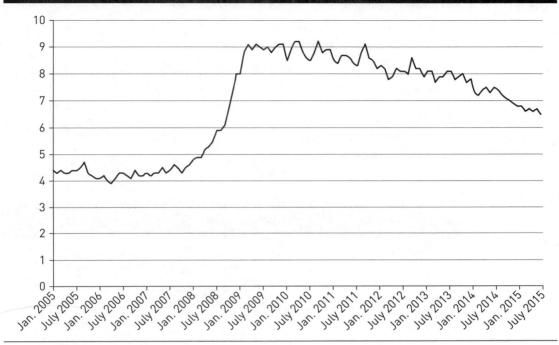

About 6.5 million Americans work part time for economic reasons, even though they say they would prefer to work full time, a number that experts say could rise with a growing sharing economy. The number of these part-time workers jumped from 4.3 million in October 2007 to 9.1 million by March 2009 during the recession, hovering there for about two years before gradually declining.

Note: Part-time workers are those who indicated they would like to work full time but were working 1 to 34 hours per week for economic reasons, such as being unable to find full-time jobs.

Source: "Labor Force Statistics from the Current Population Survey," U.S. Bureau of Labor Statistics, downloaded July 20, 2015, http://tinyurl.com/m6996nd

"Peer-to-peer marketplaces can have very different roles in an existing service industry," explains Chiara Farronato, an economist who is researching peer-to-peer Internet platforms. "They can actually take a thin local market and make it 'thick' and very global." She cites eBay's creation of global markets for goods that previously were difficult to sell locally. "And you can create new markets," she says. "For example, Instacart delivery options are creating a new [grocery] market that was not previously available."

Even Airbnb, which may divert some customers from traditional hotels, has expanded the market, especially in locations where the supply of hotel rooms is constrained by either regulations or geography, Farronato says. "In San Francisco, for example, there is a limit to expansion and demand is high," she continues. "So the entry of Airbnb has actually not led to people substituting away from hotels. It's possible for more people to come to

San Francisco to visit the city." Farronato says her research has shown that hotels didn't experience a large reduction in mean price and occupancy.

Peer-to-Peer Markets Growing More Quickly Than Traditional Sectors

Similarly, while Uber has no doubt diverted some riders—and drivers—from other transportation providers, at least one study has found that the company has expanded jobs and ridership overall. "The availability of modern technology, like the Uber app, provides many advantages and lower prices for consumers compared with the traditional taxi cab dispatch system, and this has boosted demand for ride services, which, in turn, has increased total demand for workers with the requisite skills to work as for-hire drivers, potentially raising

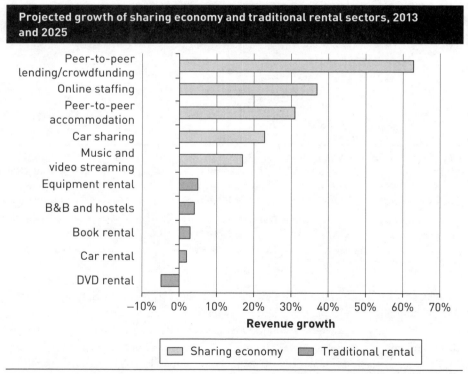

Projected growth of sharing economy and traditional rental sectors, 2013 and 2025

Sharing-economy sectors are expected to grow rapidly from 2013 to 2025, with the largest revenue growth in peer-to-peer lending/crowdfunding (up 63 percent) and online staffing services (up 37 percent). Forecasters project marginal or negative revenue growth for comparable traditional rental sectors.

Note: Growth estimates based on historical data and projected economic outcomes for industry sectors.

Source: "The sharing economy – sizing the revenue opportunity," PricewaterhouseCoopers, 2014, http://tinyurl.com/ophtwcf

earnings for all workers with such skills," write Princeton economist Alan B. Krueger and Jonathan V. Hall, head of policy research at Uber Technologies.[20]

The study has been questioned by some economists, who note that it is based on selected Uber data. "Krueger's study looks at gross income for Uber drivers and compares it with ostensibly net income for cab drivers in the same cities," Baker of the Center for Economic and Policy Research says. "The reason he doesn't have an estimate of the net for Uber drivers is that he doesn't know how many miles those Uber drivers drove. Uber has that data. They just chose not to give it to him."

Sarah Cannon, Google Capital manager, and Lawrence H. Summers, former U.S. Treasury secretary, defend the sharing economy. "These firms bring significant economic, environmental, and entrepreneurial benefits, including an increase in employment," they argued in a Harvard Business Review article. They added that car-sharing services should reduce carbon dioxide emissions, benefiting the environment.[21]

Some analysts have estimated that for every shared vehicle, between nine and 13 private vehicles are removed from the roads, either by members selling a personal vehicle or postponing a planned purchase.[22] According to Susan Shaheen, an expert in innovative mobility research at the University of California, Berkeley, car sharers report reducing the vehicle miles traveled by 44 percent.[23]

While acknowledging that sharing-economy companies have had positive effects on markets, some analysts—as well as competitors—say that in some cases sharing-economy companies simply move jobs from existing industries to the new companies. They charge that these companies gain their competitive advantage by evading taxes, regulations and the cost of providing employee benefits.

"There are obviously some efficiencies there, using the technologies to connect buyers and sellers," Baker says. "And I'm sure there is some net job creation. But I suspect that for the most part it is displacement, that you have lost jobs in the traditional cab industry, and you're replacing them with Uber drivers."

Ride-sharing services, Baker says, are also evading regulations, and consumers may not even be aware of the hidden costs. "There are hidden costs in the sense that people are maybe getting a car that's not safe, or a driver who is not safe." Baker acknowledges that Uber has begun to take steps to ensure the safety of drivers and cars. "But they originally were trying to evade that," he says. "It remains an ongoing issue."

Some analysts say that while consumers may like the low prices that companies can offer by avoiding costly regulations, the overall impact on jobs is to drive wages down.

"There are a lot of articles coming out saying that these sharing-economy companies are turning people into mini-entrepreneurs, but in many cases, the way some people look at it, they are exploiting people," says Giana Eckhardt, professor in the School of Management, Royal Holloway, University of London.

Eckhardt notes that independent contractors not only often work for lower wages but also don't receive benefits, such as health insurance and sick leave. What's more, independent contractors must make their own payments for Social Security and Medicare, costs that are normally paid by a worker's employer.

Of the growing chorus of complaints by Uber drivers, Joseph De Wolf Sandoval, an Uber driver and the president of the California App-Based Drivers Association, told a reporter, "It's not just a small group of disgruntled or unprofessional drivers, as Uber would like to cast us. It's a nationwide feeling of general unhappiness and unease with policies and programs that are being promulgated by Uber without the drivers' input whatsoever."[24]

When Uber lowered fares in July, some drivers took exception. "Since Uber implemented the 20 percent off discount on all Uber rides, I've been losing $200 a week," Oris Fortuna, an Uber driver, said. "To make up for it, you have to work 20 percent more. That means more mileage and more gas. An $8 trip is not worth it."[25]

Should regulators treat the sharing economy the same way as conventional competitors?

Sharing-market companies, along with free market advocates, argue that the new platforms driving the sharing economy have features that make the old regulatory frameworks unnecessary.

"While some regulators are tempted to regulate sharing economy companies like their competitors, to do so would be a mistake that betrays a misunderstanding of how the sharing economy works," wrote Matthew Feeney, a policy analyst at the Cato Institute, a libertarian think tank.[26]

According to Feeney, the online customer ratings that sharing-economy companies such as Uber and Airbnb have made a central part of their business models are more effective than regulations at stopping misbehavior. "Badly behaved providers and consumers in the sharing economy do not last long, and the lack of anonymity means that anyone who does commit a crime is unlikely to escape justice," Feeney said.

As for dealing with bad actors, Arun Sundararajan, professor of information, operations and management sciences at New York University's Stern School of Business, says that the platforms can deal with them more efficiently than can regulators. "The interests of the platforms are well aligned with facilitating safe and profitable peer-to-peer trade (since their revenues are directly linked to the volume and continued growth of such trade)," Sundararajan told a House hearing in written testimony in January 2014. "The platforms are also better positioned to 'take action' against infringing entrepreneurs and consumers (for example, by simply disconnecting them from the platform)."[27]

Even in the absence of formal regulation, the review tools offered by sharing-economy platforms are not the only options for keeping bad actors in check.

"We have to remember there are always civil and criminal protections that will keep people safe," says Christopher Koopman, a research fellow at the Mercatus Center at George Mason University. "Just a few mistakes by these firms could sink one of these companies before they really have a chance to take off."

Other analysts point out the review system poses several problems, starting with the possibility that sharing-economy companies can manipulate the process.

Asked what assurance consumers have about the integrity of companies' review systems, economist Farronato says simply, "It's their word." She notes that historically 15 percent of reviews on Yelp proved to be fake. "The peer-to-peer platforms are very different in how they handle fake reviews," she says. "Some are working much harder than others. My take is that large companies are probably doing a very good job of weeding out the fake reviews."

Koopman says, in fact, that companies have a vested interest in earning consumers' trust. "If people are not trusting the rating systems, they're no longer trusting the companies," he says. "If they are no longer trusting the companies, they're not going to want to do business with them anymore."

A second problem, some analysts say, is that a negative consumer review doesn't appear until after something bad has happened.

"Unfortunately it takes a tragedy and then people become aware," says Sutton of the Taxicab, Limousine & Paratransit Association.

Ideally, advocates of regulation argue, regulators require behaviors that prevent abuses from happening in the first place.

Uber has begun running background checks on drivers, which Baker calls "wonderful." But unless there's a regulatory framework that requires those checks, he adds, "there's no guarantee they will always be doing it."

Baker says the need for regulations is just as great for hostelry services like Airbnb. "With hotels we have a set of regulatory structures that ensure they're not fire traps, that they are not a nuisance to their neighbors," he says.

And regulations often go beyond simple safety issues to require companies to meet societal goals. "There are important services that we expect people to have access to, and that means all people," says Baker. He notes that because of the Americans with Disabilities Act, cab companies must have a certain number of handicapped-accessible cabs. "That is a totally legitimate public purpose," he says. "But Uber is not bound by that and as long as we have the two systems side by side, Uber is essentially dumping off the cost on the traditional cab companies."

Free market advocates say the problem is regulation itself—and that the solution is to remove the regulations that apply to traditional companies. "Rather than pursue legislation that seeks to regulate sharing economy companies like their traditional competitors," Feeney wrote, "lawmakers ought to deregulate these competitors in order to make the regulatory playing field as level as possible while allowing for innovative disruptors to enter markets."[28]

Are sharing-economy companies platforms for independent contractors, or are they employers?

Sharing-economy companies that connect service providers with customers say they are simply providing a convenient platform to help the two parties connect. An Uber spokesperson, talking on background, described Uber as a technology company that matches riders with drivers. The company classifies drivers as "partners," not employees.

As long as service providers are considered independent contractors, companies aren't bound by minimum wage and overtime laws, nor do they incur expenses for such things as unemployment insurance, workers' compensation and health insurance.

However, service providers have sued some sharing-economy companies—including Uber and Lyft—saying they are really employees and should receive benefits. Those lawsuits are pending, and neither company responded to requests to discuss them.

The initial indications are that the companies may face a tough sell of their argument that the companies are just platforms and not transportation companies with driver employees. Judge Edward Chen of the federal District Court in San Francisco called that argument "fatally flawed," noting, "It is clear that Uber is most certainly a transportation company, albeit a technologically sophisticated one."[29]

As for the argument that the drivers are independent contractors and not employees, Chen said that the issue will have to be decided at trial under California law.

The California Labor Commission's determination in early June that at least one Uber driver was, in fact, an employee, will likely be taken into consideration.

"Defendants hold themselves out as nothing more than a neutral technological platform, designed simply to enable drivers and passengers to transact the business of transportation," the Labor Commissioner's Office wrote in its decision. "The reality, however, is that defendants are involved in every aspect of the operation."[30]

While several other states—including Georgia and Texas—have ruled Uber drivers to be contractors, Florida authorities decided in May that a former Uber driver had been an employee for purposes of claiming unemployment benefits. Uber is appealing that decision.

There is no federal law defining the difference between independent contractors and employees, nor have states been consistent in defining the terms. But, according to Kai Falkenberg, senior legal counsel at the New York City Department of Consumer Affairs, there are a number factors the courts tend to consider in making such determinations, including the amount of control the company exerts over the service provider's activities.

For its part, the Internal Revenue Service applies "the usual common law rules" in determining employee status for tax purposes. This involves determining the extent to which the company exerts behavioral control and financial control over the service provider, as well as factors such as contract obligations, if any, and provision of benefits, such as health insurance.[31]

"One of the reasons that Uber drivers might be considered as employees is the degree of control that the companies are exerting," Falkenberg says. "And one of the manifestations of that is, interestingly, through the rating system. That seems to be a significant degree of control."

Falkenberg explains that Uber relies on its customer review system to cultivate trust in the service. If drivers get bad reviews from customers, they are likely to be let go.

"The companies really want to provide the best caliber service, and they want the people using the service to trust them," she says. "There's a tension between providing a high level of service but without changing your status from basically being a platform that provides a matchmaking service to a company that is actually employing people who are providing a service."

"For all practical purposes they are employees and if we're just going to play a semantic game here then there is no point in the regulations in the first place," Baker says of Uber drivers. "Obviously if you have the option to define someone as an independent contractor rather than an employee, and evade all of the regulations, then you've given companies enormous incentive to classify people as independent contractors."

Some analysts say the real problem is with the way important benefits are tied to employed positions vs. independent contractors.

"The sharing economy in a lot of ways is putting a spotlight on weak spots in public policy," says Koopman. "One of those is why we continue to insist on tying health insurance to employment."

Sundararajan of the Stern School of Business agreed. "The dichotomy of employees and independent contractors is out of date," he wrote. Sundararajan called for labor laws to "be updated to provide a social safety net to people whose chosen form of work is something other than full-time employment. Health coverage, insurance against workplace injuries, paid vacations and maternity leave: these have long been universal entitlements in many economies. They should not become exclusive perks for a dwindling band of salaried employees."[32]

BACKGROUND

Out of the Shadows

Before the development of effective monetary systems, nearly all economic activity took place within sharing economies that relied upon either barter or gifting to exchange goods and services. After the Industrial Revolution and the rapid spread of capitalism in the mid-1700s, the exchange modes of the sharing economy were relegated to an unofficial shadow economy in industrialized countries.

Some sources point to Harvard law professor Yochai Benkler as the first person to articulate the modern concept of the "sharing economy." Benkler coined the term "commons-based peer production" to describe activities in which numbers of people work together, primarily over the Internet, to create value. Benkler further developed the concept in his 2004 paper, "Sharing Nicely: On Shareable Goods and the Emergence of Sharing as a Modality of Economic Production."[33]

Benkler was describing a trend that had been developing for several years. Increasingly, individuals and companies were taking advantage of the emerging capabilities of the Internet to connect people to information, products and each other. As early as 1995, when a person had something to sell, she could simply post it on eBay or Craigslist and instantly reach thousands of people instead of having to take out a relatively expensive ad in the local newspaper that might reach a small number of people.

Not surprisingly, different sectors of the sharing economy developed independently and at different times as new technologies enabled more complex interactions.

The earliest companies in the modern sharing economy were those focused on connecting individual buyers of products and services with individual sellers.

Person-to-Person (P2P) Markets

"It's hard to believe now, but until 1991, commercial enterprise on the Internet was strictly prohibited. Even then, the rules favored public institutions and forbade 'extensive use for private or personal business,'" wrote Wired executive editor Keven Kelly.[34] In the eyes of the National Science Foundation (NSF), which at the time was the primary authority governing Internet activity, "the Internet was funded for research, not commerce," he said.

The NSF didn't officially lift its prohibition on commercial activity until 1995.[35] Even before then, however, e-commerce had begun. In 1992, Book Stacks Unlimited in Cleveland opened one of the first commercial sales websites that supported credit card processing. Only two years later, what would become a dominant e-commerce site—Amazon.com—was founded.[36]

Book Stacks Unlimited and Amazon were, of course, e-commerce sites rather than sharing-economy platforms. But they pioneered the technologies that would drive the emergence of online services that allowed consumers to share products through the Web.

And in 1995, two companies that would evolve into two of the largest drivers of the sharing economy appeared.

In early 1995, Craig Newmark began an email distribution list to inform his community of Internet developers in the San Francisco area about local events. The service proved popular—especially for its job listings and listings of items for sale—and as the mailing list grew others began to contribute items. By 1996, Newmark converted the mailing list to a website, craigslist.org.[37]

EBay, also founded in 1995, was intended from the start by its founder Pierre Omidyar to be a commercial site for selling goods and services. Unlike Amazon, however, eBay aimed at connecting individual sellers with individual buyers through online auctions.[38]

In 2008, Shelby Clark, then a graduate student at Harvard Business School, realized that the P2P model didn't have to be limited to individuals buying and selling products. It could also be used for sharing things like personal cars. On Thanksgiving Day in Boston that year, Clark wanted to visit his cousins but he didn't have a car. "It was a frickin awful winter day in Boston," he recalled in an interview. "It was snowing and the freezing wind was coming from every direction and I'm biking through the snow and sleet to get this damned car. Meanwhile, I'm passing all these cars that are covered in snow. They clearly hadn't been driven in weeks."[39] That's when he got the idea to develop a platform on which car owners could offer their vehicles for rent.

Clark couldn't find any such service online, but he did discover the major hurdle he had to clear: insurance. Existing policies didn't cover car rentals between individuals. It took Clark 18 months to arrange appropriate coverage, after which he started RelayRides.

Also in 2008, Joe Gebbia and Brian Chesky were inspired to apply the model to another underused resource: living space.

"Joe Gebbia and Brian Chesky were two jobless friends living together when they received a terrifying letter from the landlord," wrote Alex Stephany, author and CEO of a European sharing company called JustPark.[40] The letter informed them that their rent was increasing by 25 percent. Chesky didn't have the money. "He had days to find a solution when the two noticed all the unused space in their living room," wrote Stephany. "What if someone would pay to sleep there? Gebbia had just been camping and had an airbed. They blew it up . . . and came up with the concept of 'airbed and breakfast': cheap accommodation on your beds with a no-frills breakfast of Pop-Tarts."

Two days later, www.airbedandbreakfast—later to be known as Airbnb—was born. The company grew so quickly that, in 2015, it has 1.2 million listings in 190 countries.[41]

But the power of the Internet-powered sharing economy isn't just about big markets. It also allows smaller communities to connect across great distances.

Poshmark, a platform founded in 2011 that runs on a mobile application, connects women who want to buy and sell used clothes with each other. Sellers take photos of their items to offer for sale. When an item is sold, the Poshmark app emails the seller a shipping label addressed to the buyer.[42]

Product Sharing and Renting

While P2P markets connect individual buyers to individual sellers, Robin Chase's idea in 1999 was to provide a platform and products that individuals could easily share.

She had met a friend at a café in Cambridge, Mass., Chase recalled. The friend had just returned from a vacation in Germany and mentioned that she had come across a car being rented to people by the hour or by the day. Chase, who would become a cofounder of Zipcar, wondered if that idea might work in Cambridge.

"My husband drove our car out to his suburban office every morning, where it would sit in the parking lot all day," Chase wrote. "And while I definitely needed a car sometimes, there was absolutely no way I wanted to buy another, park it on the street in our city neighborhood, maintain it, and shovel it out after snowstorms."[43]

Zipcar began with an initial investment of $50,000. "Four months later, Zipcar had $68 in its bank account and three days before going live," Chase said. "The plan was to place four cars in four reserved parking spaces, one near each of four consecutive subway stops in Cambridge and Boston."[44]

According to Chase, the company's goal was to make renting a car "as easy and convenient as getting cash from an ATM."[45] Chase and her team accomplished this by creating a website for making reservations, then placing devices in the cars that could read members' cards for unlocking, enabling the ignition and tracking distances.

At the same time as major sharing-economy companies were launching, so too were scores of nonprofit grassroots efforts that, collectively, have greatly affected the economy and communities' use of resources.

In May 2003, for example, Deron Beal started the Freecycle Network to connect his friends and a few nonprofits in Tucson, Ariz., so that they could exchange goods they no longer needed without charge. Freecycle Network now has 5,000-plus groups and more than 7 million members worldwide.[46] It's a grassroots and entirely nonprofit movement of people who are giving (and getting) stuff for free in their own towns and keeping good things out of landfills.

Peer-to-Peer Loans

As companies were helping people share goods and services, some companies turned to the Internet to allow people to loan each other money instead of going through banks and other financial institutions, which generally charge higher rates of interest.

The first such peer-to-peer lending service was Zopa, begun in Great Britain in 2005. Since then, Zopa has made more than $1.4 billion in loans with reserves pooled from more than 51,000 people.[47]

The next year, the first peer-to-peer lending company in the United States—Prosper Marketplace—launched in San Francisco.

According to a Federal Deposit Insurance Corp. report, however, early peer-to-peer lending platforms had few qualifications for borrowers, which led to defaults and high loss rates. The report noted that the major peer-to-peer services have tightened borrower requirements.[48]

Some platforms gave a twist to the peer-to-peer lending model by combining it with features of eBay-like auctions to create "crowdfunding." The best-known of these platforms—Kickstarter—was founded in 2009. Kickstarter provides a structured means for individuals or companies to pitch their products and services in order to enlist contributions. As of July 27, Kickstarter says it has funded 89,000 projects since 2009, with 9.1 million contributors pledging $1.8 billion.[49]

Fee-for-Service Markets

The preeminent example of fee-for-service firms are transportation network companies (TNCs), including Uber, Lyft and Sidecar. With TNCs—which offer rides to consumers, booked via websites or mobile apps—the vehicles aren't actually shared or rented. Instead, drivers with their own vehicles share the TNC platform to offer their services to consumers.

While car-renting companies such as Zipcar and car-sharing companies such as RelayRides had established themselves years earlier, TNCs, which deliver services on a moment's demand, had to await the development and ubiquity of smartphones and the apps that run on them.

That technological hurdle was cleared by 2009 when Uber was founded as "UberCab" by Travis Kalanick and Garrett Camp.

The Beginnings of Regulation

Regulators have struggled to find ways not only to regulate the various types of sharing-economy companies but also to monitor their activities and collect appropriate taxes. For the most part, such efforts have taken place at the local level.

The TNCs have drawn the greatest attention, because they compete in an industry that has long been heavily regulated for public safety reasons and because governments want to control their effects on communities and public facilities, such as airports. This process of fitting TNCs into the existing regulatory frameworks has been a challenge that has resulted in a patchwork of requirements.

In June 2014, Colorado became the first state to pass legislation creating a statewide regulatory framework for TNCs.[50] The legislation specifies necessary levels of insurance and details requirements for regular background checks. The state Public Utilities Commission is empowered to revoke or suspend a company's permit, but penalties against drivers are prohibited. Other measures include yearly safety inspections of drivers' vehicles and exterior markings signifying them as vehicles for hire. In addition, the TNC cannot discriminate against riders based on their location or destination, nor can it charge additional fees for passengers with disabilities.

CURRENT SITUATION

Regulatory Pressure Grows

The sharing economy is filled with companies that have as many differences as similarities. In fact, the only thing they have in common is that customers access goods or services through the Internet.

Most of these businesses—such as Etsy, MuniRent and Zimride (a ride-sharing service for companies and universities)—pose few, if any, problems for consumers or regulators. That's because they simply connect providers to consumers and are not engaged in the types of activities that require safety regulations to protect the public. Most sharing-economy companies are also generally free of controversy because they are not directly competing with traditional companies. And most don't rely extensively, if at all, on service providers who might press claims for employee benefits.

Other companies—most notably, Uber, Lyft and Airbnb—are facing increasing pressure from regulators, employees and competitors.

In the last five months alone, legislatures, city councils, regulators and others have been active on numerous fronts:

- In early March, the Vermont Department of Financial Regulation issued a consumer alert, "Be aware before you share." The alert warned residents wanting to drive that participation in sharing-economy businesses could expose them to major liabilities if they lack appropriate insurance. The state labor commissioner announced she was investigating Uber in Vermont to determine whether its drivers are employees or independent contractors.[51]

- On April 21, the Portland, Ore., City Council voted 3-2 to end a prohibition on ride-sharing companies by allowing them to operate under a 120-day pilot program. The two dissenting council members indicated that they still have concerns about minimum insurance coverage and Uber's business practices.[52]

- On May 4, California Democratic state Sen. Mike McGuire introduced legislation that would require companies such as Airbnb to adhere to local laws with regard to vacation rentals, including paying occupancy taxes. The legislation also calls for data reporting on room rates and the number of nights stayed by renters.[53]

- On May 5, Uber announced that it was ceasing operations in Kansas after the state Legislature overrode the governor's veto to pass legislation with stricter insurance requirements and background checks for drivers.[54]

- On May 12, the Santa Monica, Calif., City Council adopted a home-sharing ordinance that prohibits the rental of an entire unit for less than 30 days. The ordinance also requires hosts to obtain a business license and to pay a 14 percent hotel tax. Proceeds from the tax will help pay for enforcement officers and staff to search online for illegal rentals.[55]

- On May 26, San Francisco International Airport and the San Francisco Municipal Transportation Agency petitioned the California Public Utilities Commission to impose tighter regulations on ride-sharing companies. Specifically, the agencies called for mandated vehicle inspections, a limit of 375,000 miles on vehicles, the use of permanent "trade dress" markers on vehicles and training for drivers.[56]

- On May 29, Republican Nevada Gov. Brian Sandoval signed legislation providing a regulatory framework for ride-sharing services in the state. The framework includes a 3 percent tax on fares.[57]

- On June 18, Lyft agreed to pay the state of New York $300,000 to settle claims that it was in violation of state and municipal laws. The agreement also placed tighter requirements on insurance for Lyft drivers, and required the company to comply with state and local laws covering for-hire car services.[58]

Companies Responding

One of the major challenges facing sharing-economy companies is that to do business nationally, they must conform to not just one regulatory authority but potentially hundreds of state, municipal and port authorities.

"It's a problem for the companies," says John Browning, a Southern Methodist University adjunct law professor who also works with tech start-ups. "They have lobbyists going to 50 different state legislatures."

Browning says federal legislation could simplify things, although no bill has been introduced. "Are there companies, particularly in the tech sector, that have an interest in getting some sort of federal legislation? Absolutely," he says. "That would give companies some measure of predictability, reliability and, to a certain extent, protection."

Perhaps in anticipation of, or to fend off, regulation, many of the larger sharing-economy companies, in addition to stepping up lobbying efforts, have been introducing or increasing their own insurance coverage and taking other steps, such as performing background checks for relevant service providers.

"Generally, these companies want to at least have the appearance that they are in line with consumer expectations," says Breyault of the National Consumers League. "By and large, I think they are implementing these because they want to avoid more onerous regulations that could harm their business model."

Uber, for example, instituted background checks for drivers in 2014 that cover:

- County courthouse records going back seven years for every county of residence.

- Federal courthouse records going back seven years.

- The multistate criminal database going back seven years.

- A National Sex Offender Registry screen.

- A Social Security trace, which ensures the number is valid and confirms names and addresses.

- Checks of existing motor vehicle records, as well as regular future checks.[59]

Critics, however, charge that the background checks aren't thorough enough because they do not include fingerprinting and processing through law enforcement agencies.

In July 2014, Uber also announced it had obtained a commercial insurance policy to provide $1 million of liability coverage per incident, as well as contingent comprehensive and collision insurance.[60] The new coverage applies to Uber's most widely used service, called UberX. (Commercial insurance already covered the company's other more specialized services such as black-car limo rides.)

In March 2015, Uber and the Property Casualty Insurers Association of America (PCI) announced model legislation for consideration by states that they jointly developed; 18 states have already passed laws that mirror the model, according to Robert Passmore, PCI's senior director for personal lines.

"Auto insurance is based on years and years of track records and loss history," says Passmore. "We don't have a lot of loss history behind these folks." Thus, says Passmore, it's especially important to have clear rules about what kinds of coverage are required.

Airbnb, too, has moved to provide insurance. As of January 2015, the company's Host Protection Insurance provides up to $1 million in coverage in the event a guest is injured on a host's property during a stay. The insurance applies only in the United States.[61]

Airbnb has also made agreements with some localities—including the District of Columbia, San Francisco, Phoenix, Portland, Ore., San Jose and Chicago—to collect taxes owed by hosts and pay them directly to the local government. While Airbnb did not respond to requests for comment, its website notes that these agreements make "the tax collection process easier for all parties involved."

"In many cases, these taxes were designed for hotels and folks with teams of lawyers and accountants, and the reality is that the person who's renting out his basement in Cleveland Park [in D.C.] once a month probably doesn't have tax experts on payroll," Nick Papas, an Airbnb spokesman, told a Washington Post reporter. "You shouldn't need a lawyer and a tax specialist if you want to rent out your house."[62]

According to Stephen Cordi, the deputy chief financial officer in the Office of Tax and Revenue in D.C., it was Airbnb that approached the city about making the arrangement to pay taxes.

"It's undoubtedly true that people particularly at the bottom end of this probably didn't know what to do," Cordi told The Washington Post. While individual Airbnb hosts should have been registering with the city and paying the taxes all along, he said, "this will eliminate the need for them to do that."

Still, according to Norton Francis, senior research associate at the Tax Policy Center, which provides research on taxes for the Urban Institute and the Brookings Institution, cities and states are "losing tax revenue because of these new forms" of services in the sharing economy. "The product isn't any different; it's the delivery," he said. "States are one step behind commerce in an effort to try to maintain their tax bases."[63]

LOOKING AHEAD

Rivals Need to Adapt

The technologies that define the sharing economy—the Internet-enabled applications that allow consumers to connect directly to service providers—are clearly not going to disappear.

"I think this is the beginning of the second-order issues of the sharing economy," says Koopman of the Mercatus Center. "The first-order issues were whether the sharing economy should exist at all. That debate is settled. The sharing economy is here to stay. Now comes the second wave of issues for sharing economy firms: How are the regulators going to treat them?"

Because the technologies driving the sharing economy are new, the old regulatory frameworks are no longer appropriate, most analysts agree. Even those who maintain the need for strong regulatory structures acknowledge that in some areas changes are warranted. "You can make plenty of arguments, and there is some truth to them, that a lot of the regulations that we have in place are excessive," says Baker of the Center for Economic and Policy Research.

"Do you apply old regulations to new innovations or try to adapt and evolve the regulations to fit the market over time?" Koopman asks. "I think when you try to apply the old laws and the old rules to new innovation and new entrepreneurship, you end up hamstringing innovation. This should be an opportunity for everyone to critically reevaluate the regulations on the books."

In the meantime, say some analysts, it's time for traditional companies to adapt to the new technology environment. "The entry of these new platforms has put pressure on existing suppliers," economist Farronato says. "From the point of view of innovation, it is pressure for the better." She adds that as traditional companies adopt the new technologies—such as online review—old regulatory frameworks may no longer be needed. "It might be the case of the industry will actually evolve in a way that the regulatory environment will be more lax," she says.

While free market advocates worry about regulators stifling innovation, former Clinton administration Labor Secretary Robert Reich warns about the ramifications of an unfettered sharing economy.

"In effect, on-demand work is a reversion to the piece work of the nineteenth century—when workers had no power and no legal rights, took all the risks, and worked all hours for almost nothing," Reich wrote in an article on his website. "Uber drivers use their own cars, take out their own insurance, work as many hours as they want or can—and pay Uber a fat percent. Worker safety? Social Security? Uber says it's not the employer so it's not responsible."[64]

Of course, how consumers and investors will respond to higher costs caused by increased regulation of the sharing economy is unknown.

With respect to investors, they seem undeterred so far. "There have been very high investment levels within these areas where regulation hasn't been settled," says Eckhardt of the University of London.

Consumers' response, she says, may be more problematic. "When you start to see that competitive advantage eroding away, and prices rise, consumers may perceive [the companies] to be gouging," she says. "These so-called sharing-economy companies are, in a way, responsible for this because the way they tend to position themselves as, 'Oh, we're doing better for the world. We're somehow different than all of these regular companies.'"

Chronology

1990s	**Technologies that will power the sharing economy appear, and pioneer e-commerce companies take advantage.**
1991	The National Science Foundation (NSF), which controlled the Internet backbone, allows commercial access to the formerly government and academic network.
1992	E-commerce begins when Book Stacks Unlimited in Cleveland opens a website that supports credit card processing.
1994	Amazon is founded and would soon grow into a dominant e-commerce site.
1995	Craig Newmark launches an email distribution list that will be converted the next year into a website that allows people to buy and sell goods and to find jobs: craigslist.org. . . . eBay is founded as an online platform to connect individual sellers with individual buyers through online auctions. . . . NSF formally lifts its prohibition on commercial activity on the Web.
1999	Zipcar—an online car rental service—appears, with four cars stationed near subway stops in Cambridge and Boston, Mass.
2000–2007	**Early sharing-economy companies are founded.**
2003	The Freecycle Network goes online, allowing individuals and nonprofits to exchange goods they no longer need.
2004	Yochai Benkler, a Harvard law professor, publishes, "Sharing Nicely: On Shareable Goods and the Emergence of Sharing as a Modality of Economic Production," the first analysis of the modern sharing economy.
2005	Zopa, the world's first online peer-to-peer lending platform, debuts in London.
2007	Zimride, which became Lyft, begins offering on-demand rides; its drivers are independent contractors who own their own cars.
2008–Present	**Recession spurs growth of the sharing economy as regulators begin to take action.**
2008	Harvard Business School graduate student Shelby Clark launches RelayRides, a service that allows individuals to rent their personal cars to others. . . . Joe Gebbia and Brian Chesky, needing money to pay their rent, offer their living room online as a place for someone to sleep. A few days later, they launch www.airbedandbreakfast.com, which will soon become known as Airbnb.
2009	Kickstarter, a crowd-sourced platform for funding projects, opens. . . . UberCab, which will soon change its name to Uber, is founded in San Francisco.

(Continued)

	(Continued)
2014	Colorado becomes the first state to pass legislation creating a statewide regulatory framework for "transportation network companies," such as Uber and Lyft. . . . In June, the California Labor Commissioner's Office rules that an Uber driver should be classified as an employee, not an independent contractor. . . . In October, the New York State Office of the Attorney General releases a report that finds that 72 percent of units booked over Airbnb in the state appeared to violate state and local laws. Within days, New York City files suit against two property owners.
2015	On May 5, Uber announces it is ceasing operations in Kansas after that state passes legislation with stricter insurance requirements and background checks for drivers. . . . On May 12, the Santa Monica, Calif., City Council adopts a home-sharing ordinance that prohibits the rental of an entire unit for less than 30 days. The ordinance also requires hosts to obtain a business license and to pay a 14 percent hotel tax. . . . On May 26, San Francisco International Airport and the San Francisco Municipal Transportation Agency petition the California Public Utilities Commission to impose tighter regulations on ride-sharing companies. . . . On May 29, Nevada Gov. Brian Sandoval announces passage of a regulatory framework for ride-sharing services in the state; the framework includes a 3 percent tax on fares. . . . On June 18, Lyft agrees to pay the state of New York $300,000 to settle claims that it was in violation of state and municipal laws. The agreement also places tighter requirements on insurance for Lyft drivers, and requires the company to comply with state and local laws covering for-hire car services.

RESOURCES

The Next Step

Niche Markets

Goel, Vindu, "Start-Ups Clamor to Be the Airbnb of Boats," The New York Times, June 10, 2015, http://tinyurl.com/ndy7hu3.

Boat owners find a niche market in peer-to-peer boat rentals, but face new challenges due to insurance and safety requirements.

Sharam, Andrea, and Lyndall Bryant, "An Uber for apartments could solve some common housing problems," The Conversation, July 20, 2015, http://tinyurl.com/p2wy2v4.

Two-sided matching markets, commonly used in the sharing economy, could create a housing market that encourages quality and affordability by pairing consumers with developers.

Zhuo, Tx, "5 Lessons Entrepreneurs Can Learn From Niche Marketplaces," Entrepreneur, May 14, 2015, http://tinyurl.com/nj9ltuu.

Successful niche markets employ multiple tools, including partnerships with potential competitors, specialized services and an interest in consumer needs.

Regulation

Badger, Emily, "Who millennials trust, and don't trust, is driving the new economy," The Washington Post, April 16, 2015, http://tinyurl.com/p9hjp78.

While trust in individuals has declined over the past 40 years, trust in crowds has increased, allowing for the rise of an industry with fewer regulations, according to a survey by PricewaterhouseCooper.

Peltz, Jennifer, "Cities keen on 'sharing economy' but concerned about safety," The Associated Press, June 3, 2015, http://tinyurl.com/pqsok5y.

Officials in U.S. cities support growth in the sharing sector, but question the safety of an unregulated industry, according to a National League of Cities survey.

Popper, Ben, "Uber can't be stopped. So what's next?" The Verge, July 27, 2015, http://tinyurl.com/ppvl35j.

New York City becomes the latest locale to try to regulate Uber, but fails.

Technology

Bahceli, Yoruk, "Netherlands to make room in rules to stimulate 'sharing economy,'" Reuters, July 20, 2015, http://tinyurl.com/ou9xobv.

Officials in the Netherlands are adapting rules to meet the demands of new services, promising "technology-neutral" regulations that will not discriminate against less-savvy companies.

Howard, Alex, "Open data, crowdsourcing, and sharing economy tech take on new roles in disasters," Tech Republic, Aug. 8, 2015, http://tinyurl.com/q56uomg.

Some peer-to-peer companies are attempting to expand services to crisis response, offering "disaster technology" to those seeking information, aid and even housing during emergencies.

Kerr, Dara, " 'Sharing economy' apps to boom with their lure of cheap and easy," CNET, April 14, 2015, http://tinyurl.com/p7alnxb.

User-friendly apps and simple digital transactions help to engage a growing number of customers and entrepreneurs in the sharing economy.

Worker Treatment

Lapowsky, Issie, "A Sharing Economy Star Shuts Down As Labor Issues Simmer," Wired, July 17, 2015, http://tinyurl.com/ovqkeug.

One start-up specializing in home cleaning services closed after failing to supply workers with basic benefits.

Macmillan, Douglas, "Sharing Economy Workers Need 'Safety Net,' U.S. Senator Says," The Wall Street Journal, June 8, 2015, http://tinyurl.com/ngn4xcj.

Sen. Mark Warner, D-Va., is calling for new programs that would protect independent contractors in the United States, providing insurance and other basic employee benefits to freelance workers.

Manjoo, Farhad, "Start-Ups Finding the Best Employees Are Actually Employed," The New York Times, June 24, 2015, http://tinyurl.com/q46u73l.

One tech company classifies its workers as employees, not contractors, arguing that valued employees provide better service.

Organizations

Airbnb

888 Brannan St., San Francisco, CA 94103
415-800-5959
www.airbnb.com

Company that provides a platform for peer-to-peer rentals of living spaces.

Cato Institute
1000 Massachusetts Ave., N.W., Washington, DC 20001-5403
202-842 0200
www.cato.org

Libertarian think tank that explores the impact of government policies, including regulation.

Center for Economic and Policy Research
1611 Connecticut Ave., N.W., Suite 400, Washington, DC 20009
202-293-5380
www.cepr.net

Think tank that focuses on the effects of economic policies.

Federal Trade Commission
600 Pennsylvania Ave., N.W., Washington, DC 20580
202-326-2222
www.ftc.gov

The U.S. commission that is charged with preventing business practices considered anticompetitive, deceptive or unfair to consumers.

Lyft
2300 Harrison St., San Francisco, CA 94110-2013
866-292-2713
www.lyft.com

Company that offers on-demand transportation network services.

Mercatus Center, George Mason University
3434 Washington Blvd., 4th Floor, Arlington, VA 22201-4508
703-993-4930
www.mercatus.org

Describes itself as "the world's premier university source for market-oriented ideas—bridging the gap between academic ideas and real-world problems."

Property Casualty Insurers Association of America
8700 W. Bryn Mawr, Suite 1200S, Chicago, IL 60631-3512
847-297-7800
www.pciaa.net

Trade association for property casualty insurers.

Uber
1455 Market St., 4th Floor, San Francisco, CA 94103
877-223-8023
www.uber.com

Company that offers on-demand transportation network services.

Pro/Con: Dean Baker on Regulating the Sharing Economy

YES SHOULD SHARING-ECONOMY COMPANIES BE BROUGHT INTO THE SAME REGULATORY FRAMEWORKS AS THEIR COMPETITORS?
Economist, Co-founder of the Center for Economic and Policy Research

Written for SAGE Business Researcher, August 2015

Over many decades we have developed a long series of regulations that apply to taxi companies, hotels and other businesses that compete with upstart sharing-economy companies. These regulations cover a wide range of areas, including consumer protection, safety, worker protection and restrictions on discrimination based on race, gender and disability.

In some cases, these regulations are excessive, imposing unnecessary costs on business, which are in turn largely passed on to consumers. Some of the regulations were designed to protect the incumbents in the industry, most notably restrictions on the number of cabs that can be on the road. But most of these regulations do serve a public purpose. For this reason, it does not make sense to give the sharing-economy companies a pass, even if people order their service over the Internet.

In the case of Uber, there should be guarantees that Uber's cars are safe, that passengers are covered by insurance in the event of an accident, that the drivers have good driving records, and that the drivers are not dangerous criminals who pose a threat to their passengers. This may not require the same sort of strict rules that are imposed on the traditional cab industry in most cities, but it does mean a mechanism should be in place to ensure that Uber meets basic standards.

Similarly, Uber drivers need the same sort of protections as other workers. This means they should be covered by minimum wage laws, overtime rules, workers' compensation and be insured not only when they have a rider in the car but also on their way to and from cab pick-ups. If this is too complicated for Uber to deal with, then they can be replaced by companies that are more computer-savvy.

Uber should be required to have a certain percentage of its cars handicap-accessible; the company also needs to either develop a mechanism for payment by customers without access to credit cards or to pay a fee to ensure that such people have access to taxi service.

Similarly, Airbnb facilities should not be fire traps and should comply with building and neighborhood rental codes. Airbnb must also take responsibility for ensuring that people have access to facilities it rents regardless of their race and ethnicity. We expect this of traditional hotels; Airbnb should be held to similar standards.

Pro/Con: Christopher Koopman, Matthew Mitchell and Adam Thierer on Regulating the Sharing Economy

NO

SHOULD SHARING-ECONOMY COMPANIES BE BROUGHT INTO THE SAME REGULATORY FRAMEWORKS AS THEIR COMPETITORS?
Research Fellows, Mercatus Center at George Mason University

Excerpted from testimony before the Federal Trade Commission, May 26, 2015

As the debate surrounding the sharing economy moves forward, policymakers must keep in mind that merely because regulations were once justified on the grounds of consumer protection does not mean they accomplished those goals or that they are still needed today.

Markets, competition, reputational systems and ongoing innovation often solve problems better than regulation when they are given a chance to do so. There are two reasons for this. First, market imperfections create powerful profit opportunities for entrepreneurs who are able to find ways to correct them. Second, regulatory solutions too often undermine competition and lock in inefficient business models.

Exempting newcomers from traditional regulations could place incumbents at a disadvantage. Such regulatory asymmetries represent a legitimate policy problem. But the solution is not to discourage new innovations by simply rolling old regulatory regimes onto new technologies and sectors. The better alternative is to level the playing field by "deregulating down" to put everyone on equal footing, not by "regulating up" to achieve parity.

By trying to head off every hypothetical worst-case scenario, preemptive regulations actually discourage many best-case scenarios from ever coming about. For that reason, ex post remedies are often preferable to ex ante regulation. Private insurance, contracts, torts and product liability law, antitrust enforcement and other legal remedies can be utilized here when things go wrong, just as they are used in countless other segments of our economy.

The Internet and the information revolution have given rise to new online feedback mechanisms that have made it easier than ever for honesty to be enforced through strong reputational incentives. This has, in turn, alleviated many traditional concerns about informational deficiencies. With the recent growth of the sharing economy, even more robust reputational feedback mechanisms now exist that help consumers solve information problems and secure a greater voice in commercial interactions. These mechanisms have been integrated into the platforms connecting buyers and sellers and have become an essential feature of these sectors.

The Internet and real-time reputational feedback mechanisms should force a reevaluation of traditional regulations aimed at addressing perceived market failures based on asymmetric information. Such regulations have typically failed to improve consumer welfare and have undermined innovation and competition. This may explain why, when recently surveyed by PricewaterhouseCoopers, 64 percent of U.S. consumers said that in the sharing economy, peer regulation is more important than government regulation.

TECHNOLOGY AND BUSINESS ETHICS

3

Can companies resist wrongdoing in a digital world?

Patrick Marshall

EXECUTIVE SUMMARY

Rapidly advancing technologies such as big data analytics offer potentially great benefits to companies and consumers, but experts warn that modern technology also has a downside: It can give companies seeking a competitive edge the tools to engage in illegal or unethical practices. Because digital devices—from the sensors and computers that control the inner workings of automobiles to code that tracks individuals' activities on the Internet—are powered by software that is inherently invisible, consumers and regulators are often in the dark about the data that companies are collecting and how they are using it. Industry groups and outside observers disagree about what should be done. The former argues self-regulation is sufficient while the latter seeks tough regulation and increased ethics training in business schools and companies. Among the questions being debated: Should the uses of big data be more tightly controlled? Should there be limits on employers' monitoring of employees? Is software too open to abuse?

OVERVIEW

Months after Volkswagen publicly admitted in August 2015 that it had installed software in 11 million diesel automobiles designed to deceive emissions tests, the public remains in the dark about just who was responsible.

Michael Horn, head of Volkswagen's American division, told Congress on Oct. 8 that neither Volkswagen's supervisory board nor its top executives ordered the installation of devices that could sense when they were being tested and then change the vehicles' performance to improve results. "This was not a corporate decision," Horn said. "This was something individuals did."[1]

While it is not yet known who was behind the decision to deploy deceptive software, it is growing clear that the company is paying a huge price for the scandal.

From *SAGE Business Researcher*,
February 15, 2016

Volkswagen, which admitted last year that it had installed software in 11 million diesel automobiles designed to alter emissions tests, faces fines and lawsuits that could run into the billions of dollars.

Source: Adam Berry/Getty Images

Indeed, as a result of sharply lower sales, in late October Volkswagen reported its first quarterly loss in at least 15 years.[2] And even though the company has denied the involvement of upper management, its CEO was forced to resign and five high-ranking executives have been suspended. Volkswagen reportedly has set aside $7.3 billion to bring affected vehicles into compliance with emissions standards, and the company faces an uncertain amount of fines and lawsuits that experts expect to run into the billions of dollars.[3]

Volkswagen is not alone in embedding legally or ethically questionable practices in complex technologies. The Internet is riddled with software with hidden functionality. For example, AVG, a company that offers users free antivirus protection, recently acknowledged that it tracks users' browsing and search activity and that it may sell that information to advertisers.[4] AVG defended the practice by noting that it is disclosed in the consumer contract that users accept—even if they don't read it—when installing the software.

The power and opacity of modern technology—from software to surveillance tools and big data analytics—is both a boon to business and a temptation to companies to engage in illegal or unethical practices to gain an edge in a competitive global economy. The growth in these practices has occurred so rapidly that it is outpacing the law. At the same time, because digital devices are powered by software that is inherently complex and non-transparent, consumers and regulators alike generally are in the dark about just what data is collected and the purposes to which it is being put.

"What happens behind the screen is unknown to almost everyone," says Penny Duquenoy, a principal lecturer at Middlesex University, London, who specializes in the ethical implications of information technology (IT). "The fact that technology is opaque gives people the opportunity to exploit it."

According to Duquenoy, digital technologies present a special challenge for business ethics because they are opaque not only to consumers but also to managers and corporate executives. "The IT people are coming from a different place and use a different language," she says. "You need some technical people at the board [of directors] level to get across what happens with technology."

Kirsten Martin, assistant professor of strategic management and public policy at George Washington University's School of Business, agrees. "I do think there is a problem in that the number of people who know how to code is very small," she says. "I do think that impacts how many questions an executive or an account manager will ask because they feel stupid."

The situation puts an extra burden on companies—rather than lawmakers or regulators—to follow ethical practices in implementing new technologies, says Arthur Schwartz, general counsel of the National Society of Professional Engineers.

"I don't think the laws and regulations ever keep up," Schwartz says. "We need to train engineers and other learned professions about the ethical implications of their activities. And it's not just something to study in college. It needs to be ongoing."

The Volkswagen situation illustrates how technology allows unethical and illegal actions to occur almost invisibly and "with comparatively few people being in the accountability line," says Ken Goodman, director of the University of Miami's Miller School of Medicine Institute for Bioethics and Health Policy and co-director of the University of Miami Ethics Programs.

"In the next business ethics seminars [after the Volkswagen scandal], we are going to say, 'Why did they do it? Do they not think they would get caught? Were they not concerned?'" Goodman says.

Whether it's in the board room or the engineering labs, digital technologies present hurdles for ethical business practices, says Tony Wasserman, professor of software management practice at Carnegie Mellon University. "There have always been people who live on the edge of ethics and propriety," he says. "It's just that now we have created a whole new set of opportunities for the people who want to push the boundaries."

Possibilities for abuse abound. "Sophisticated monitoring software and hardware allow businesses to conduct basic business transactions, avoid liability, conduct investigations and, ultimately, achieve success in a competitive global environment," according to Corey Ciocchetti, professor of business ethics at the University of Denver. At the same time, Ciocchetti wrote, "This trend is problematic because excessive and unreasonable monitoring can: (1) invade an employee's reasonable expectation of privacy, (2) lead employees to sneak around to conduct personal activities on work time, (3) lower morale, (4) cause employees to complain and, potentially, quit and (5) cause employees to fear using equipment even for benign work purposes."[5]

Despite the challenges, surveillance technologies have been used widely. A survey by the American Management Association found:

- 45 percent of companies track employees' keystrokes, and time spent at the keyboard.

- 43 percent of companies store and review computer files.

- 12 percent of companies monitor the blogosphere for comments about the company.

- 10 percent of companies monitor social networking sites.[6]

Business ethicists and privacy advocates also are concerned about the need to establish standards for appropriate uses of consumer data that companies collect.

"The ongoing collection of personal information in the United States without sufficient privacy safeguards has led to staggering increases in identity theft, security breaches, and financial fraud," Marc Rotenberg, executive director of the nonprofit Electronic Privacy Information Center (EPIC), told Congress in April 2014.[7]

Nearly Half of U.S. Companies Track Employees' Browsing

And big data analytics—the use of software to analyze huge amounts of collected data to reveal hidden patterns—has led to privacy incursions. One often-cited example of the unexpected consequences of such data analysis was Target's use of data about one customer's purchase patterns to determine that she was pregnant. The retail chain began sending her coupons for baby products. The problem was that she had not yet told her family that she was pregnant.[8]

According to EPIC, "By 'connecting the dots' between different, disparate datasets, or even by analyzing data from the same dataset that on its face does not seem to have any connection, companies can infer characteristics about people that they might not otherwise wish to be made public, or at least not wish to share with certain third parties."[9]

In fact, in light of the power of big data and its potential for abuse, an analyst for Gartner, a technology consulting firm, told a conference in October 2015 that by 2018, half of business ethics violations will result from improper use of big data analytics.[10]

At least some experts are hopeful that companies are coming to realize the importance of taking steps to ensure the ethical use of digital technologies.

Percentage of employers that . . .

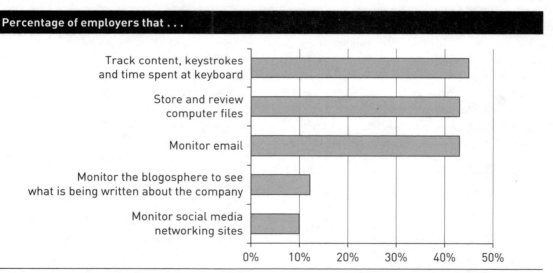

Forty-five percent of American companies track employees' browsing content, keystrokes and time spent at the computer, according to a 2007 survey by the American Management Association. At that time, while about four in 10 companies stored and reviewed employee computer files or monitored their email accounts, only about one-tenth monitored blogs or social media for coverage of their companies.

Note: Based on survey of 304 U.S. companies from 2007.

Source: "The Latest on Workplace Monitoring and Surveillance," American Management Association, updated Nov. 17, 2014, http://tinyurl.com/guk2q3k

"Some companies are beginning to realize that there is a benefit to trying to encourage transparency and being forthcoming," Schwartz says.

In 2012, the Business Roundtable, an influential Washington, D.C.-based group of corporate CEOs that advocate for pro-business policies, formed a new effort on innovation and technology as part of the group's Institute for Corporate Ethics. The goal of the effort, the Business Roundtable said on its website, was to develop "leading thinking and practices for managing the ethical challenges that emerge from technological advancement and innovation."[11]

According to George W. Reynolds, professor of business at Strayer University and author of a textbook on information technology ethics, one way to respond is an increased focus on ethics training, both in business schools and in companies. He cited research that "86 percent of the employees in companies with a well-implemented ethics and compliance program are likely to perceive a strong ethical culture within the company, while less than 25 percent of employees in companies with little to no program are likely to perceive a culture that promotes integrity in the workplace."[12]

Others have proposed increasing professionalization of IT workers, including certification that requires adherence to ethical codes. "The IT industry is not regulated in the same way as lawyers and doctors," notes Duquenoy. "If lawyers or doctors transgress, they lose their license and are not allowed to practice. That doesn't apply when it comes to information technology engineers or software engineers."

Some experts have argued that whistleblower protections for private-sector employees need to be improved. Employees are more likely to take a stand against unethical behaviors if they don't fear losing their jobs as a result. [13]

"I think we definitely need a culture of whistleblowing," says Karen Sandler, executive director of the Software Freedom Conservancy, a nonprofit organization based in Brooklyn that advocates the use of open-source software.

As technologists, managers and ethicists consider the implications of information technology for businesses, here are some of the issues under debate:

Weighing the Issues

Should the uses of big data be more tightly controlled?

Big data is big business. IDC, a market research firm, estimates that the big data technology and services market will grow by more than 26 percent a year to reach $41.5 billion by 2019.[14]

The amount of data collected on U.S. citizens by private-sector companies is also huge. According to a 2014 report by the Federal Trade Commission, one data broker—a company that collects, combines and analyzes data—by itself has information on 1.4 billion consumer transactions. Another data broker cited by the commission adds 3 billion records each month to its databases. Yet another data broker has 3,000 data "segments"—individual categories of data—on nearly every consumer in the United States.[15]

"The scale of the Big Data Revolution is such that all kinds of human activities and decisions are beginning to be influenced by big data predictions, including dating, shopping, medicine, education, voting, law enforcement, terrorism prevention, and cybersecurity," wrote law professor Neil M. Richards and CenturyLink executive Jonathan H. King. "Many of the most revealing personal data sets such as call history, location history, social network connections, search history, purchase history, and facial recognition are already in the hands of governments and corporations. Further, the collection of these and other data sets is only accelerating."[16]

At the same time, the data brokerage industry remains largely unregulated, and most consumers have little idea about the types and amount of data being collected about them.

"Since consumers generally do not directly interact with data brokers, they have no means of knowing the extent and nature of information that data brokers collect about them and share with others for their own financial gain," according to a recent staff report for the Senate Committee on Commerce, Science and Transportation. [17]

As a result, some legislators and privacy groups have been calling for legislation to limit what data companies can collect and what they can do with it after collecting it.

Among others, the Center for Democracy & Technology, a Washington, D.C.-based nonprofit research and advocacy group, has called for passage of general national privacy legislation to regulate companies' use of data. "Most industrialized democracies, except the United States, have such a law," says Chris Calabrese, CDT's vice president for policy. However, because the Republican-controlled Congress generally takes a dim view of imposing limits on business in such a fashion, he acknowledges, "It's a tough road at the federal level."

"Far too many organizations collect detailed personal information and use it with too little regard for the consequences," wrote the Electronic Privacy Information Center in response to a request for information from the federal Office of Science and Technology Policy. "The current Big Data environment is plagued by data breaches and discriminatory uses of predictive analytics."[18]

Tracking of information by data brokers is more worrying than surveillance by the U.S. government, according to now-former Sen. Jay Rockefeller, D-W.Va., who in 2013 chaired a Senate committee that looked into the brokerage industry.[19]

The committee's report found that data brokers "operate behind a veil of secrecy," and concluded, "It is important for policymakers to continue vigorous oversight to assess the potential harms and benefits of evolving industry practices and to make sure appropriate consumer protections are in place." [20]

The FTC has gone further, calling for legislation that would, among other things:

- Require data brokers to give consumers access to their data.

- Require opt-outs, so that consumers can prevent use of their data.

- Require retailers and other "consumer-facing entities" to provide prominent notice of data sharing, as well as an opt-out.

However, any such legislation will need to have teeth, because the FTC has long made such recommendations, according to Nate Cardozo of the Electronic Frontier Foundation, a San Francisco-based civil liberties advocacy group. "The FTC says that we should have choice about whether to be tracked and about what companies do with the information," Cardozo says. "If that was the way the world actually worked, consumer privacy advocates around the country would be out of a job. But that's not the way the world works."

Data brokers stress the benefits of the data and analytic tools they deliver to companies and to consumers.

"Marketing data, in particular, brings lower prices and greater convenience to consumers by strengthening competition," Tony Hadley, Experian's senior vice president for government affairs, told Rockefeller's committee. As one of the three big credit reporting companies, Experian is an active data brokerage. "Both large and small businesses rely on data to make their marketing efforts more efficient and to identify new customers. . . . Consumers also benefit from receiving relevant advertising offers that they are more likely to value and use."[21]

Additional restrictions are unnecessary, Hadley said. "Experian shares data responsibly—by carefully safeguarding compliance with all privacy and consumer protection laws and industry self-regulatory standards, advancing and observing industry best practices, and establishing and monitoring adherence to our own corporate policies and practices," he told the committee.

Jerry Cerasale, senior vice president of government affairs at the Direct Marketing Association, a New York City-based group that represents marketing companies, also argued to the committee that industry self-regulation is sufficient. "Some policymakers have raised concerns that data collected for advertising purposes could be used as a basis for employment, credit, health care treatment, or insurance eligibility decisions," he said. "In fact, these are hypothetical concerns that do not reflect actual business practices. Nevertheless, industry has stepped forward to address these concerns by expanding its codes of conduct to clarify and ensure that such practices are prohibited and will never occur."[22]

Experian and the Direct Marketing Association did not respond to interview requests for this report.

Should there be limits on employers' monitoring of employees?

Companies have monitored employee telephone and computer use for as long as there have been telephones and computers. But recent advances in digital technologies have made it possible to monitor employee behavior, and even attitude, to an unprecedented degree.

The New York Times last year highlighted a situation involving Jim Sullivan, a waiter at a Dallas restaurant whose actions came under scrutiny "not by the prying eyes of a human boss, but by intelligent software. The digital sentinel, he was told, tracked every waiter, every ticket, and every dish and drink, looking for patterns that might suggest employee theft. But that torrent of detailed information, parsed another way, cast a computer-generated spotlight on the most productive workers."[23]

Four in 10 Data Scientists Support Ethical Standard

The monitoring worked out well for Sullivan, who was recognized as a stellar employee and promoted to manager. Although the surveillance was legal, the article provoked angry comments on The Times' website from readers complaining that it was overly intrusive.

Sullivan's workday was scrutinized by NCR's Restaurant Guard, a program that monitors restaurant transactions in real time, using artificial intelligence to detect patterns of fraud and to spot performance bottlenecks. Using software that detects specified keywords, many employers monitor telephone calls and network traffic, including even emails sent from an employee's private email account. Some companies also employ video cameras to watch employees and geolocation tools to track employees with company cars or cellphones.

Internet and email monitoring is most prevalent, but 12 percent of businesses in a recent survey also acknowledge monitoring blogs and 10 percent track social networking sites to see what is being written about the company.[24]

The public's suspicions about Restaurant Guard's intrusiveness led Andrew McAfee, co-director of the Initiative on the Digital Economy at the Massachusetts Institute

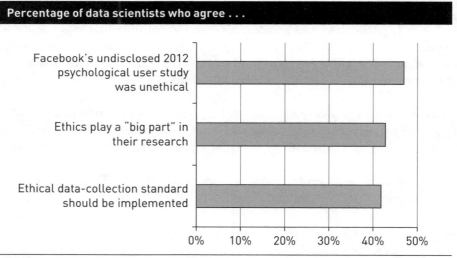

Percentage of data scientists who agree . . .

Almost half of data scientists surveyed at an American Statistical Association conference in August 2014 said Facebook's undisclosed 2012 psychological study of almost 700,000 users' profiles was unethical. (Users were not told the study was being conducted; it was disclosed later.) Forty-two percent of respondents said the big data industry should develop and implement an ethical standard for data collection.

Note: Based on survey of 144 data scientists at the American Statistical Association's Joint Statistical Meetings conference in Boston from Aug. 2–7, 2014.

Source: Survey data from Jeff Bertolucci, "Data Scientists Want Big Data Ethics Standards," InformationWeek, Sept. 17, 2014, http://tinyurl.com/jwsnqpy

of Technology's Sloan School of Management, to write a Harvard Business Review column in defense of the software. He argued that it "doesn't engage in surveillance of employees' personal electronic communications, or any other activity they might reasonably consider private. Instead, it monitors their on-the-job performance, which is exactly one of the things that managers are supposed to do."[25] Other business professors and consultants cite specific reasons for employers to monitor employees.

Using software that detects specified keywords, many employers monitor telephone calls and emails sent from an employee's private email account.

Source: Thomas Trutschel/Getty Images

"Most of this monitoring is perfectly legal and even prudent in today's employment arena," wrote Ciocchetti of the University of Denver. "While employee monitoring remains a contentious issue, employers have good reasons for checking in on their employees' activities. Sexual or pornographic e-mails and Web pages, containing pictures or merely sexually explicit language, can form the basis for a harassment lawsuit. Excessive personal use of company broadband capacity or e-mail accounts will lead to decreased productivity, storage shortages and slower network operations. Failing to monitor is also likely to allow rogue employees to steal trade secrets or send out confidential information in violation of various federal and state laws."[26]

Nancy Flynn of the ePolicy Institute, an electronic policy consulting firm based in Columbus, Ohio, agrees. "In the United States, employers have a legal right to monitor all of the content and activities that take place on the organization computer system, accounts and devices," Flynn says. "So all employers as a best practice should take advantage of their legal right and monitor everything that is taking place on their computer systems."

Flynn also advises clients to monitor social media sites. "You want to see what people are saying," she says. She concedes, however, that monitoring employees' personal social media is "trickier." First, she notes that 17 states have laws preventing employers from asking for employee login information.

For employers in the other states, Flynn cautions against going on "fishing expeditions." She says, "You only want to do this if you have legitimate suspicion that, for example, confidential company information has been posted online or consumers' personal financial or health information has been exposed online."

While most academics and privacy advocates are not against all monitoring, many say there should be legal limits that enforce ethical boundaries.

"The American legal system's effort to protect employee privacy is a patchwork of federal and state laws combined with the common law tort of intrusion upon seclusion," wrote Ciocchetti. "This regime is not properly equipped to defend against excessive invasions of privacy that come from increasingly sophisticated monitoring practices."[27]

"Most employees know that their employer has the ability to conduct surveillance but they have no idea how much surveillance is really happening or the circumstances under which it happens," says Lewis Maltby, president of the National Workrights Institute, a worker advocacy group based in Princeton, N.J. For example, Maltby notes that many employees think that their boss looks at their email or Internet traffic only when there's a reason to do so. "But that's not how it works," he says. "It's an open secret that IT techs read other employees' emails for fun. And many employers don't even have a paper policy against this."

Majority Doubt Companies, Agencies Will Protect Records

Maltby says that while he thinks legislation is needed to protect worker privacy rights at work, adoption of best practices by companies is at least as important. "There are companies that do it right," he says. He cited one hotel chain that conducts monitoring, but only when a manager gets clearance from the chief privacy officer after demonstrating a specific need.

"We're not saying don't do it," Maltby says. "We're saying do it right."

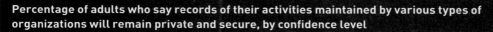

Percentage of adults who say records of their activities maintained by various types of organizations will remain private and secure, by confidence level

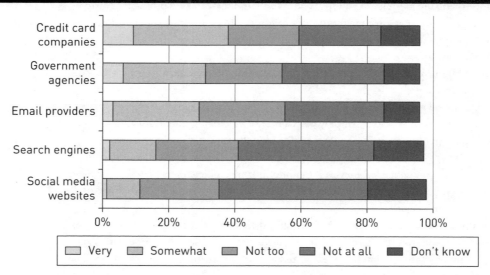

Nearly 70 percent of U.S. adults say they are "not too" or "not at all" confident that social media websites will keep their activity records private and secure, according to a summer 2015 Pew Research Center survey. Two-thirds say they are just as unsure about search engine companies protecting their activity records, and more than half say the same of government agencies and email providers.

Notes: Based on online survey of 498 U.S. adults from Aug. 5–Sept. 2, 2014. Totals do not add to 100 percent because those who refused to respond are not shown.

Source: Mary Madden and Lee Rainie, "Americans' Attitudes About Privacy, Security and Surveillance," Pew Research Center, May 20, 2015, p. 7, http://tinyurl.com/j6lmk7m

Is software too open to abuse?

In 2000, Wells Fargo bank offered a "community calculator" to visitors to its website that purported to help homebuyers find the right place to live. To use the calculator, visitors were prompted to enter the ZIP code of their current residence, along with other data. The calculator used demographic data to determine the visitor's likely race and then steered whites to white neighborhoods and blacks to black neighborhoods.[28]

The company eventually dropped the calculator, after the Association of Community Organizations for Reform Now (ACORN), a now-defunct community activist group, filed a lawsuit. While it was impossible to tell what was going on under the hood of the calculator, ACORN was tipped off to the bias by the use in Wells Fargo documents of racial descriptions to categorize neighborhoods depicted as downtrodden.[29]

Whether deceptive code, unintended bugs or vulnerabilities, in most cases it's impossible for outsiders to know what actions software actually performs.

Because of the inherent opacity of software, some experts are calling for the widespread adoption of open-source software—software for which the underlying source code is made freely available for inspection and even modification by anyone. That, say open-source advocates, is the best way to deter companies from burying unrelated unannounced functionality in code. For their part, while several companies declined interviews on this issue, they have generally argued that their source code is a trade secret and essential to their competitiveness.

"Software has vulnerabilities in it, whether it's free or proprietary," says Sandler of the Software Freedom Conservancy.

Open-source software, because it can be examined by outside programmers, is more resistant to bugs, vulnerabilities and deceptive code, advocates say. "Free and open software is better and safer over time," Sandler says. "And if there is a problem, it can be fixed very quickly."

Wasserman at Carnegie Mellon University agrees. "Transparency is a good thing," he says. "The ability to see what is actually going on in any piece of software is beneficial."

Others—especially software vendors—argue that open-source software often doesn't match the standards of proprietary software, particularly when it comes to security and new features.

"Security mechanisms must walk a careful balance between being open for review and being secret to protect specific information," wrote Jim Allchin, group vice president for platforms at Microsoft Corp., in testimony during a 2002 court case. "It is generally a good practice not to disclose specifics of the implementation of a security mechanism. By analogy, a jewelry store might show off its safe to customers, with thick steel walls and complicated locks. However, the jewelry store would not post safety inspection schedules, fire alarm tests, or similar information relating to its safe."[30]

Only one year after Allchin's testimony, anxious for sales in China and under pressure from the Chinese government, Microsoft agreed to disclose source code for its Windows operating system, but only to certain government clients, including the Chinese.[31]

Microsoft did not respond to interview requests for this report.

Some analysts note that proprietary software delivers one thing that open-source software does not—profit. "Proprietary software exists for one simple reason: as a means of enabling software as such to generate revenue," wrote tech journalist John Carroll. And besides gratifying shareholders, profit can drive development of new features and products. "When software generates profit, it enables companies to grow, attracts investment (as investors prefer profitable companies as a place to put their money) and enables those companies to grow into tremendous sources of innovation and local employment," Carroll wrote. [32]

Rather than pushing for the demise of proprietary software, some experts have proposed a compromise: Require disclosure of source code in return for software receiving patent protection. That would allow companies to keep their code proprietary and protected from competitors, but also would provide regulators an opportunity to detect deceptive code, thus deterring the practice.

According to Martin at George Washington, even if the disclosure was not made publicly available, it could deter patent applicants from including hidden functionality. "If we require them to disclose, then we could get them for lying about it in addition to whatever bad practices or unethical practices they were doing in the algorithm," Martin says.

It would be more practical to amend current laws that prevent researchers from examining the inner workings of software, said Cardozo at the Electronic Frontier Foundation.

Cardozo notes that the 1998 Digital Millennium Copyright Act (DMCA), which governs digital intellectual property rights, makes it a crime to circumvent access control measures on digital devices.

"The DMCA prevents researchers from digging into code to see what it is actually doing," Cardozo says. "The Copyright Office will enforce this and will allow companies to bring copyright infringement claims against, for instance, a researcher who wanted to dig into the Volkswagen engine control unit to see what it was doing."

According to Section 1201 of the DMCA, researchers who examined the working of protected software would be violating the law even if they did not appropriate or change the software.

Cardozo argues for reform or outright repeal of Section 1201. "That would rebalance the table and allow consumers to open the hood and see what is going on in products they already own," he says.

According to Cardozo, automakers are lobbying against such changes. "They're pushing back pretty hard on the grounds that allowing people to look under the hood of their own cars poses a safety and environmental risk," he says. "This, despite the fact that Volkswagen's behavior shows that not allowing people to look under their hoods actually posed a risk."

In written comments to the U.S. Copyright Office, arguing against a proposal that would partially exempt automobiles from Section 1201 protections, General Motors contended, "While proponents such as Electronic Frontier Foundation characterize the exemption as merely allowing the vehicle owners to 'tinker' with their vehicles 'in a decades-old tradition of mechanical curiosity and self-reliance,' if granted, the proposed exemption could introduce safety and security issues as well as facilitate violation of various laws designed specifically to regulate the modern car, including emissions, fuel economy, and vehicle safety regulations."[33]

BACKGROUND

Early Issues

Each advance in technology presents new opportunities and new challenges for company interactions with the public, with regulators and with employees.

When the nascent nation's postal service was established in 1775, for example, no law barred anyone from opening mail in transit. And while many considered opening mail to be unethical, it was routinely done until Congress in 1782 made opening mail in transit illegal.[34]

"While the Constitution's Fourth Amendment codified the heightened privacy protection afforded to people in their homes or on their persons (previously principles of British common law), it took another century of technological challenges to expand the concept of privacy rights into more abstract spaces, including the electronic," according to a 2014 report from the President's Council of Advisers on Science and Technology. "The invention of the telegraph and, later, telephone created new tensions that were slow to be resolved. A bill to protect the privacy of telegrams, introduced in Congress in 1880, was never passed."[35]

The introduction of inexpensive portable cameras—marketed to the masses after the founding in 1888 of what became the Eastman Kodak Co.—gave rise to the first real push for a general privacy law. In their seminal 1890 article, lawyers Samuel Warren and Louis Brandeis, a future Supreme Court justice, wrote, "Instantaneous photographs and newspaper enterprise have invaded the sacred precincts of private and domestic life; and numerous mechanical devices threaten to make good the prediction that 'what is whispered in the closet shall be proclaimed from the house-tops.' For years there has been a feeling that the law must afford some remedy for the unauthorized circulation of portraits of private persons."[36]

As the President's Council of Advisers on Science and Technology noted, it took another 75 years for the Supreme Court to determine—in Griswold v. Connecticut (1965)—that citizens have a constitutionally protected right to privacy. The advisory council cited several specific meanings of "privacy" that have subsequently been derived from the ruling, including the individual's right to keep secrets or seek seclusion and the ability to control access by others to personal information after it leaves one's exclusive possession.

Only two years later, however, the Supreme Court specifically established in Katz v. United States that a conversation is protected from unreasonable search and seizure under the Fourth Amendment only if it is made with a "reasonable expectation of privacy." According to Reynolds of Strayer University, subsequent decisions soon made it clear that employees have no reasonable expectation of privacy in most circumstances at work. "The Fourth Amendment cannot be used to limit how a private employer treats its employees," wrote Reynolds.[37]

Big Data

Arguably, the first major private-sector big data effort was that of consumer credit reporting agencies, which first appeared in the 1950s. Throughout the 1960s, credit reporting companies were industry specific and community-centric. "As such, bank-, retailer-, or finance company-sponsored 'bureaus' did not share loan or inquiry information with each other," wrote Mark Furletti, an analyst at the Federal Reserve Bank of Philadelphia. "This kept banks from knowing about loans or inquiries made by finance companies or retailers and vice versa. The situation limited any creditor's ability to understand a potential customer's entire debt situation."[38] However, there was no assurance that the data collected was accurate, and once one company shared data with another, the errors could be very difficult for consumers to learn about, much less correct.

As credit-reporting companies began to share data, Congress responded with the Fair Credit Reporting Act (FCRA), aimed at ensuring the accuracy and fairness of the data being collected. The act requires that consumers have an opportunity to view, correct and challenge the contents and uses of their credit reports. "The industry stopped reporting things like marriages, promotions, and arrests and focused its efforts on reporting verifiable credit-related information," Furletti said. "This included both positive information, such as a consumer's ability to consistently pay her bills on time, as well as negative information, such as defaults and delinquencies."[39]

Congress followed up in 1996 with another major privacy-protection law, the Health Insurance Portability and Accountability Act (HIPAA), which regulates companies' management of consumers' health-related data.

In 1997, the Federal Trade Commission (FTC)—the primary agency responsible for enforcing the credit-reporting law—turned its attention to examining the activities of data brokers, companies that collect data from a variety of public and private sources for analysis. In response to an FTC-sponsored workshop, data brokers that year voluntarily formed the Individual Reference Services Group to provide self-regulation for the industry.

Self-regulation did not work, according to a 2014 FTC report. What's more, in the wake of that "short-lived" effort, the report said, "data broker practices have grown dramatically, in both breadth and depth, as data brokers have expanded their ability to collect information from a greater number of sources, including from consumers' online activities; analyze it through new algorithms and emerging business models; and store the information indefinitely due to reduced storage costs. Despite the Commission's past recommendations, lack of transparency and choice remain a significant source of concern about this industry."[40]

The FCRA and HIPAA, though limited in scope, remain the primary regulatory authority over private-sector uses of big data. From 2002 to 2014, the FTC initiated more than 50 actions against companies that it alleged engaged in unfair or deceptive practices involving consumer data, with many of the cases resulting in multimillion-dollar fines.[41]

Electronic Privacy

As new and more powerful technologies—computers, email, the Internet, cellphones—delivered more powerful communications and data-gathering tools to companies and consumers alike, they also created new opportunities for invasions of privacy by governments, companies and individuals. The first major legislation specifically relating to abuses involving computer and other digital technologies in the private sector was the Electronic Communications Privacy Act (ECPA) of 1986. Fundamentally, the law extended existing regulations governing wiretaps of telephone calls to include transmissions of electronic data by computers. The ECPA also prohibited some access to stored electronic communications.

While the restrictions of the ECPA apply to private-sector companies just as they do to government agencies, as a result of two statutory exemptions, they do not inhibit employers' actions with respect to employees at the workplace or using company equipment. The first exemption allows "a provider of wire or electronic communication service, whose facilities are used in the transmission of a wire communication, to intercept, disclose or use that communication." In short, if the employer provides the service, interception is allowed. According to some experts, however, it is not clear if that exemption holds up if the employer contracts with an outside service provider.[42]

The second exemption is if the employer obtains the implied or express consent of employees. "If an employee has knowledge of the employer's policy and he or she continues to use the system anyway, this will likely fall under the consent exception. In practice, moreover, many employers routinely require employees to acknowledge—if not explicitly sign away any residual rights—that the employer may monitor computer usage including Internet and email access," according to course materials at the Berkman Center for Internet and Society, a research program at Harvard Law School.[43]

Critics complain that the electronic privacy law not only is too limited in scope but also is seriously outdated. "The ECPA was intended to extend privacy protection from wire communications such as telephone calls to electronic communications such as e-mails and text messages," wrote Ciocchetti of the University of Denver. "The problem is that contemporary technology has advanced tremendously since 1986, and the ECPA is not equipped to keep pace."[44]

Specifically, the act protects messages only while they are in transmission, and once they are stored the wiretap protection provisions do not apply. "This is a major distinction because the vast majority of electronic communications are only 'in transmission' for mere seconds before arriving at their destination," Ciocchetti said.[45]

Finally, Ciocchetti noted that no federal law—and only two state laws—require that notice be provided to employees prior to monitoring. What's more, he added, "for the most part, private employers must intrude into very private places—such as restrooms or locker rooms—in order to face liability for intrusion upon seclusion."[46]

Regulating Software

When software—the instructions that direct a computer to perform specific operations—was introduced in the 1940s, it was not considered eligible for either copyright protection or patent protection. That was a major concern for companies that were investing money in developing software and wanted to protect that investment. Software companies responded in two ways: first, by keeping the source code for the software secret so others would find it difficult to reproduce; second, by lobbying for legislation protecting software.

"In the 1960s and early 1970s, computer programs enjoyed very limited intellectual property protection," wrote Robert M. Hunt, an economist at the Federal Reserve Bank of Philadelphia. "And it was widely believed that patent protection for computer programs was unavailable. This impression was bolstered by a 1972 Supreme Court decision (Gottschalk v. Benson) involving an application to patent a computer program that translated decimal numbers into binary numbers. The court concluded the program was a mathematical algorithm, which, like laws of nature or an abstract idea, does not fall into one of the categories of patentable subject matter."[47]

It wasn't until 1980 that Congress amended the Copyright Act to explicitly cover software. But by then it was already clear to software manufacturers that copyright protection was of little use to them, because all it protected was the specific expression of the coding. There was nothing in copyright law to prevent competitors from examining the code and replicating its functionality.

In 1994, software companies received help from the U.S. Court of Appeals, Federal Circuit, which ruled definitively that a computer program was patentable. And unlike copyrights, patents protected not just the instance of the invention but also the idea of its functionality. The Patent Office had rejected the patent application by three engineers who had created a program to modify the output of an oscilloscope on the ground that it lacked any physical transformation of matter. The court, however, ruled that the software was in essence a machine and was, thus, patentable.[48]

In 1998, the Digital Millennium Copyright Act made it illegal to evade copy protection measures.

In 2014, the Obama administration released a report from a task force that included two Cabinet members and several other senior officials about the ways in which government could enhance the accountability of big data. A year later, the task force issued a second report calling for an array of measures including adoption of a White House-proposed Consumer Privacy Bill of Rights and amendment of the Electronic Communications Privacy Act to ensure the standard of protection for online content is consistent with that afforded in the physical world.

"The declining cost of data collection, storage, and processing, coupled with new sources of data from sensors, cameras, and geospatial technologies, means that we live in a world where data collection is nearly ubiquitous, where data retention can be functionally permanent, and where data analysis is increasingly conducted in speeds approaching real time," noted the task force's 2015 report. "While there are promising technological means to better protect privacy in a big data world, the report's authors concluded these methods are far from perfect, and technology alone cannot protect privacy absent strong social norms and a responsive policy and legal framework."[49]

CURRENT SITUATION

Best Practices

The recent Volkswagen scandal and strings of major data breaches have given rise to calls from advocacy groups, professional organizations and academicians to implement measures to encourage best practices within companies.

Many experts say that expanded training in ethics is needed both in companies and in business schools. Flynn of the ePolicy Institute says companies will be facing increasing ethical quandaries with respect to their own employees.

"I do think that given the fact that we are now looking at a young workforce, coming into business—people who have grown up with electronic devices, and particularly mobile devices—organizations are going to start to face more and more ethical challenges and resistance from employees," Flynn says. "When employers try to impose restrictions on them, they're going to meet more resistance than they have met in the past. So I think employers are going to be finding themselves increasingly in a position . . . where they're wrangling more and more with ethical issues."

While noting that almost all engineering programs have mandatory ethics classes, Martin at George Washington says the same is not true at business schools. "We're not very good at it," she says. As a faculty member, Martin has reviewed dozens of course proposals and has noted that they rarely focus on ethical issues. "For one of my papers I went out and looked at 15 proposals," she recalls. "I figured there must be one program in big data analytics that has an ethics requirement. I looked through the curricula and there was no ethics requirement."

Finally, some experts argue that ethical training isn't just about "doing the right thing." Over the long haul, it's also the smart thing. "Being ethical is good for business, at least for a sustainable business," says Duquenoy at Middlesex University in London, who specializes in the ethical implications of information technology.

Despite Duquenoy's conviction that ethical behavior is good for business, she says it can often be difficult to communicate that in the workplace. "Technology people don't tend to talk in terms of ethics," she says. In the end, according to Duquenoy, the strongest arguments aren't about ethics as much as about potential consequences. "It comes down to a risk analysis and a cost-benefit, and whether doing something is worth the risk," she says.

Current Legislation

Despite calls from the White House, Congress has shown little interest in regulating companies' use of digital technologies. The sole piece of legislation introduced in the current Congress that is related to private-sector uses of technology directly affecting consumers or employees is the Data Broker Accountability and Transparency Act of 2015 (S. 668) introduced by Sen. Ed Markey, D-Mass.[50]

The bill, which was sent to committee in March 2015, would require any commercial entity that collects, assembles or maintains personal information to establish procedures to ensure the accuracy of that information and to provide individuals with a cost-free means of reviewing their personal data. The bill also calls for procedures to allow consumers to dispute data and for an "opt-out" provision that would allow individuals to prevent personal data from being collected and used.

While consumer groups and privacy advocates have generally praised the bill, critics complain that its scope is far too broad. "Time and again, Congress has found that access and correction to consumer data are necessary only when the information is used for eligibility purposes, and marketing is not an eligibility purpose," said Peggy Hudson, the Direct Marketing Association's senior vice president of government affairs, in response to the introduction of almost identical legislation in 2014. "Imposing an access and correction regime on marketing data is not necessary to protect consumer privacy and doing so would make it harder for companies to keep data secure at a time when consumers are more concerned about identity theft than ever before."[51]

The DMA, an industry advocacy organization, declined interview requests for this report.

As of early 2016, the bill had just three co-sponsors—all of them Democrats—and most analysts gave it almost no chance of being approved. GovTrack, a nonpartisan company that monitors and analyzes legislation, gave the bill only a 4 percent chance of passage.[52]

Consumer Bill of Rights Act

The other major proposed legislation, which has not yet been introduced in Congress, is the Consumer Bill of Rights Act. The Obama administration followed up on its 2012 report calling for a Consumer Bill of Rights with draft legislation in February 2015.[53]

Among its provisions, the draft bill would provide:

- **Individual control**: Give consumers the right to exercise control over what personal data is collected and how it is used.

- **Transparency**: Require data collectors to make privacy and security practices accessible and understandable.

- **Respect for context**: Require companies to collect, use, and disclose personal data in ways that are consistent with the context in which consumers provide the data.

- **Security**: Require companies to secure personal data.

- **Access and accuracy**: Give consumers the right to access and correct personal data.

While generally welcomed by consumer groups and privacy advocates as a first step, the proposal has drawn criticism from all sides.

"The administration's concrete legislative proposal is an incredibly important step," noted the Center for Democracy & Technology in its analysis of the bill. "A number of elements need to be improved if this bill is going to offer consumers comprehensive protection. As it is, there are too many loopholes, and enforcement is noticeably lacking."[54]

Data Brokers Rely on Marketing Revenue

The center particularly dislikes that privacy fines would be calculated not by the number of individuals affected by a violation but by the number of days that a violation persisted. "Thus, if a multibillion-dollar company decided to sell millions of records in one day in violation of its promises, under this bill it would face a maximum fine of $35,000—an incredibly perverse result," the report said.

Industry groups were even more critical of the proposal, warning that its provisions are both costly and unnecessary. Gary Shapiro, president of the Consumer Electronics Association, said that such legislation "could hurt American innovation and choke off potentially useful services and products."[55]

Percentage of revenue at data brokers, by product type, 2012

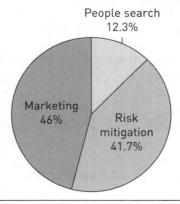

People search
12.3%

Marketing
46%

Risk
mitigation
41.7%

Nearly half the annual revenue at a sample of nine data brokers came from selling data for marketing purposes, according to a Federal Trade Commission study. Risk mitigation—including identity verification and fraud detection—was the second-largest revenue generator, (42 percent), followed by people search products (12 percent), such as consumer directories and search tools.

Note: Based on federal study of data collection practices by a sample of nine data brokers in 2012. Percentages have been calculated from revenue total in $U.S.

Source: "Data Brokers: A Call for Transparency and Accountability," Federal Trade Commission, May 2014, p. 23, http://tinyurl.com/mwury6w

Likewise, a representative of the Internet Association, an industry group that represents Internet companies, including Google and Facebook, said in early 2015 that privacy rules should be "finely tailored to address specific harms," and the proposal in contrast cast "a needlessly imprecise net" that could "create a drag on our economy."[56]

LOOKING AHEAD

"New Generation of Nuance"

Technology has fundamentally changed the nature and extent of the ethical challenges facing businesses, experts say.

"What we are seeing now is a new generation of nuance as regards accountability and responsibility," says the University of Miami's Goodman. And he is not optimistic about preventing such abuses in the near future. "The idea that software can be used daily to deceive people, or government regulators, is a bit of a wake-up call," he says. Given that technology is inherently opaque, Goodman says, trusted entities must serve as watchdogs. "I'm sentimental enough to hope that that might be journalists, but I'm despairing of journalism these days, too," he says.

Ultimately, Goodman says, people have to take personal responsibility for their behaviors. Referring again to the Volkswagen scandal, he says, "It goes straight to the people who wrote the code and the people who ordered it to be used. These are human beings who intentionally used the tools of their trade to deceive."

Martin at George Washington suggests that broadened whistleblower protections and requirements for disclosure of source code may help encourage ethical behavior. "If we require them to disclose [code in a patent] application," she says, "then we could get them for lying about it in addition to whatever bad practices or unethical practices they were doing in the algorithm."

Otherwise, "I don't know how you'd regulate it," Martin says. "I really don't. People with technology just figure out a way to not fall within the scope of the regulation."

Martin says that such measures are unlikely to get through the currently divided government in the United States. As a result, she says, she expects change will only come "either through public shaming or through lawsuits."

Goodman agrees. "It's cases like Volkswagen . . . when people realize that they are not on a level playing field with the businesses that have rigged these games," he says. "I am hoping that the Volkswagen scandal kicks a bunch of people in the butt."

"I hate to say it, but what we are going to need is more failures," echoes Sandler at the Software Freedom Conservancy. She says that ensuring ethical use of technology will require a change in technology cultural values. "We need a culture among the engineers to understand that there is that responsibility to speak out," she says, where whistleblowers are accepted. "I think we need a culture of understanding the social implications around our technology."

The stakes are high, warned law professor Neil M. Richards and Jonathan H. King, vice president at CenturyLink Technology Solutions, a nationwide communications provider headquartered in Monroe, La. "We are building a new digital society, and the values we build or fail to build into our new digital structures will define us," they wrote. "Critically, if we fail to balance the human values that we care about, like privacy, confidentiality, transparency, identity, and free choice, with the compelling uses of big data, our big data society risks abandoning these values for the sake of innovation and expediency."[57]

Chronology

1700s–1900s	**New technologies challenge privacy.**
1782	After complaints about the security of mail in the nation's new postal service, which was established in 1775, Continental Congress passes legislation making the opening of mail in transit illegal.
1890	Shortly after the introduction of the inexpensive and portable Kodak camera, lawyers Samuel Warren and Louis Brandeis, a future Supreme Court justice, warn that "instantaneous photographs and newspaper enterprise have invaded the sacred precincts of private and domestic life; and numerous mechanical devices threaten to make good the prediction that 'what is whispered in the closet shall be proclaimed from the house-tops.'"
1950s–1970s	**Consumer databases attract regulation.**
1965	In Griswold v. Connecticut, the Supreme Court rules that citizens have a constitutionally protected right to privacy.

1967	The Supreme Court holds in Katz v. United States that a conversation is only protected from unreasonable search and seizure under the Fourth Amendment if it is made with a "reasonable expectation of privacy." Subsequent decisions make it clear that employees have no reasonable expectation of privacy in most circumstances at work.
1970	Congress passes the Fair Credit Reporting Act to promote the accuracy, fairness and privacy of consumer information contained in the files of consumer reporting agencies. The act regulates the collection, dissemination and use of consumer information, including consumer credit information.
1972	The Supreme Court decides in Gottschalk v. Benson that computer programs cannot be patented, ruling that mathematical algorithms are abstract ideas like laws of nature.
1980s–1990s	**Legislators tackle computer technology.**
1980	Congress amends the Copyright Act to explicitly cover software, but manufacturers find it of little use because it doesn't protect others from copying the program's functionality.
1986	The Electronic Communications Privacy Act extends existing regulations governing wiretaps of telephone calls to include transmissions of electronic data by computers.
1994	Federal courts hold that computer programs can be patented.
1995	The European Union passes the Data Protection Directive, which puts clear limits on the collection and storage of personal data by companies.
1997	The Federal Trade Commission (FTC) examines the activities of data brokers—companies that collect and analyze consumer data. In response to an FTC-sponsored workshop, data brokers voluntarily form the Individual Reference Services Group to provide self-regulation for the industry. Self-regulation was short-lived.
1998	The Digital Millennium Copyright Act makes it illegal to attempt to circumvent protection schemes in software and digital devices. Critics argue that the act allows bad actors to hide unethical or illegal code. . . . The Environmental Protection Agency announces settlements totaling in the hundreds of millions of dollars with carmakers Honda and Ford resulting from the companies' use of "defeat devices" to get around emissions control systems.
2000s– Present	**Calls for regulation of technologies increase.**
2002	The European Union (EU) adopts the e-Privacy Directive, which extends the protections of the Data Protection Directive to telecommunications, specifically all publicly available telecommunications networks in the EU.
2009	Heartland, a Princeton, N.J.-based payment processor, announces that cybercriminals had penetrated its databases and acquired information on approximately 130 million credit and debit cards.
2012	The Obama administration calls for a Consumer Privacy Bill of Rights that will ensure consumer control over personal data and how it is used; it also calls upon private-sector companies to adopt enforceable codes of conduct.
2014	The Federal Trade Commission urges legislation that would, among other things, require data brokers to give consumers access to their data. The report also recommends mandatory "opt-outs" that would give consumers to right to prevent their data from being collected.
2015	Volkswagen publicly admits that it had installed software in 11 million diesel automobiles designed to deceive emissions tests. (August) The incident renews calls for amending the Digital Millennium Copyright Act to allow regulators and researchers to examine software. . . . The European Court of Justice rules invalid an international pact that governed the movement of data—such as individuals' Internet search histories and social media data—between the EU and the United States. (October) The court concludes that "the law and practice of the United States do not offer sufficient protection against surveillance by the public authorities of the data transferred to that country."

RESOURCES

The Next Step
Big Data

Clover, Charles, "China: When big data meets big brother," Financial Times, Jan. 19, 2016, http://tinyurl .com/ztcmzg2.

The Chinese government has licensed eight companies to collect Web users' data and develop so-called "social credit" ratings that affect eligibility for activities ranging from travel to pet adoption, a practice that some have deemed mass surveillance.

Darrow, Barb, "Coming Soon: Ethics Training for Data Scientists," Fortune, Dec. 4, 2015, http://tinyurl .com/zdw4tg5.

All university data science programs will add classes in 2016 on the human implications of mass data collection, a principal data researcher for Microsoft predicts.

Green, Chloe, "By 2018 big data will be responsible for half of ethics violations in business – study," Information Age, Oct. 7, 2015, http://tinyurl.com/gl2rg2y.

Big data collection will cause up to half of all business ethics violations by 2018, although companies can cautiously invest in advanced analytics and implement clear strategies for their use to reduce future violations, according to a U.S. market research firm.

Employee Monitoring

Melendez, Steven, "The Office Is Watching You," Fast Company, May 22, 2015, http://tinyurl.com/ooor6en.

Technology start-ups are developing software that other companies can use to track employee time spent in meetings and track behavior and workplace engagement levels.

Shockman, Elizabeth, "Gamifying the workplace: is it ethical?" Science Friday, Public Radio International, Sept. 5, 2015, http://tinyurl.com/h4wpl4e.

More companies have introduced software in offices in recent years that track employee health habits to optimize performance, though some say such technologies can be disruptive and disregard the personal interests of employees.

Son, Hugh, "JPMorgan Algorithm Knows You're a Rogue Employee Before You Do," Bloomberg Business, April 8, 2015, http://tinyurl.com/qy5e6qw.

Financial services firm JPMorgan Chase will introduce an employee-surveillance program in 2016 that uses algorithms to track whether workers follow trading rules and complete compliance courses, among other criteria, to reduce legal risks.

Europe

Ashford, Warwick, "EU privacy watchdog to set up ethics advisory group," Computer Weekly, Jan. 6, 2016, http://tinyurl.com/j5wqg6t.

The European Union's independent supervisory data-protection body plans to form an ethics advisory group that will recommend ways for the EU to use new technologies while protecting personal privacy.

Scott, Mark, and Natasha Singer, "How Europe Protects Your Online Data Differently Than the U.S.," The New York Times, Jan. 31, 2016, http://tinyurl.com/zzdtc2p.

The EU grants Web users more data-related protections than the United States, including the rights to request that search engines remove links with personal information from results and that companies share personal data they have collected and how they are using it.

Wagner, Kurt, and Mark Bergen, "Europe's 'Safe Harbor' Ruling: A Headache for Tech Giants, but a Blow to the Little Guys," recode, Oct. 6, 2016, http://tinyurl.com/jcnwx9m.

A 2015 European Court of Justice ruling, which invalidated an agreement that permitted American companies to transmit data gathered in Europe to the United States, will likely mostly harm small- and medium-sized companies that lack other data-collection arrangements with EU nations.

Hiring Discrimination

Lam, Bourree, "For More Workplace Diversity, Should Algorithms Make Hiring Decisions?" The Atlantic, June 22, 2015, http://tinyurl.com/oumx8aw.

A software company that develops algorithms that can analyze job applicants' behavioral data, predict their performance and compare it to that of top employees claims companies using its software would hire 26 percent more blacks and Hispanics on average.

Noguchi, Yuki, "How Startups Are Using Tech To Try And Fight Workplace Bias," NPR, Sept. 1, 2015, http://tinyurl.com/ofpwnk6.

Some software start-ups have developed technology that mitigates racial or gender bias by playing down résumés in favor of skill-based tests, and others have created training methods for managers that identify their hidden biases in evaluations.

Pepitone, Julianne, "Can Résumé-Reviewing Software Be As Biased As Human Hiring Managers?" NBC News, Aug. 17, 2015, http://tinyurl.com/zrpkxvs.

Computer science researchers from the Universities of Arizona and Utah and Haverford College developed a test that they say detects hidden bias in supposedly gender – and race-blind hiring software.

Organizations

Center for Democracy and Technology
1634 I St., N.W., #1100, Washington, DC 20006
202-637-9800
cdt.org

Advocates laws, corporate policies and technology tools that protect the privacy of Internet users.

Direct Marketing Association
1333 Broadway, Suite #300, New York, NY 10018
212-768-7277
thedma.org

Industry organization that represents the interests of marketing companies and data brokers.

Electronic Frontier Foundation

815 Eddy St., San Francisco, CA 94109

415-436-9333

eff.org

Focuses on defending civil liberties in the digital world and lobbies for legislation at state and federal levels.

Electronic Privacy Information Center

1718 Connecticut Ave., N.W., Suite 200, Washington, DC 20009

202-483-1140

epic.org

Research center focused on technology-related privacy and civil liberties issues; also lobbies for privacy legislation.

The ePolicy Institute

2300 Walhaven Court, Columbus, Ohio 43220

614-451-3200

epolicyinstitute.com

Consulting group that offers seminars and webinars to clients seeking to minimize electronic risks, maximize compliance and manage employees' online use and content.

Federal Trade Commission

600 Pennsylvania Ave., N.W., Washington, DC 20580

202-326-2222

ftc.gov

Agency charged with preventing business practices that are anti-competitive or are deceptive or unfair to consumers; also holds workshops, makes legislative recommendations and conducts enforcement actions.

National Society of Professional Engineers

1420 King St., Alexandria, VA 22314

888-285-6773

nspe.org

Professional society that provides education and training, and advocates for measures aimed at protecting engineers and the public from unqualified practitioners.

National Workrights Institute

128 Stone Cliff Road, Princeton, NJ 08540

609-683-0313

workrights.us

Nonprofit spinoff from the American Civil Liberties Union that is focused on protecting human rights in the workplace.

Open Source Initiative

855 El Camino Real, Suite 13A, #270, Palo Alto, CA 94301

opensource.org

Educational and advocacy group that backs adoption of nonproprietary software; also serves as a licensing body for Open-Source Definition compliant software.

Pro/Con: Lewis Maltby on Employee Monitoring

YES

SHOULD GOVERNMENT TIGHTEN REGULATION OF EMPLOYERS' MONITORING OF EMPLOYEES?

President, National Workrights Institute

Written for SAGE Business Researcher, February 2016

Employers have many legitimate reasons to monitor employees. But the reasons are not unlimited. Employers need to be able to monitor work-related email. But your employer doesn't need to read an email you sent to your spouse during lunchtime. Employers need security cameras. But they don't need to put cameras in bathrooms. Employers need to know where employees are during working hours. But your boss doesn't need to use the GPS in your cellphone to track you in your private life.

While most employers don't spy on employees, some do. There are many documented cases of employers installing hidden cameras in bathrooms, including Atlas Cold Storage in Georgia, where the cameras were pointed directly into the stalls of the women's bathroom. The Boston Sheraton was caught installing a hidden camera in the men's locker room. The Lower Merion school district in suburban Philadelphia turned on the webcams of every laptop computer it issued to its employees and students during the evening when the computers were in the employees' and students' homes.

Some abuses are very common. A survey by the Bentley Center for Business Ethics found that 25 percent of employers allow IT employees to look at other employees' personal email and Internet activity for any reason they choose, including their own amusement.

Even responsible employers rarely do anything to protect employee privacy. Employers could easily program email monitoring software to look at only work-related email and not employees' personal email or Yahoo accounts. But almost none of them do so.

Some argue that people shouldn't do anything personal on workplace computers. But private life and work life are no longer different worlds. People routinely send work-related email during the evening. They make business calls on their cellphones on the weekend. They even take their laptops on vacation to keep up with work. There's nothing wrong with them occasionally taking care of a personal matter at work. Employers recognize this; most permit employees to make reasonable personal use of company computers. And even a "no personal use" policy doesn't justify spying on employees during their private lives.

Sadly, our laws do almost nothing to protect us. Wiretapping laws prohibit employers from eavesdropping on personal telephone calls made from work, but they provide no protection from unfair computer monitoring. Most states don't even have laws that prohibit placing cameras in bathrooms or tracking employees off duty.

We need laws that allow employers to monitor work-related behavior but protect the privacy of our personal communications and private lives. Many successful companies, such as Hewlett-Packard and Starwood Hotels, already follow these principles. It's time for other employers to do the same.

Pro/Con: Nancy Flynn on Employee Monitoring

NO

SHOULD GOVERNMENT TIGHTEN REGULATION OF EMPLOYERS' MONITORING OF EMPLOYEES?

Founder and executive director, ePolicy Institute

Written for SAGE Business Researcher, February 2016

To date, 21 states and Guam have enacted laws preventing employers from requesting passwords to employees' personal Facebook and other online accounts as a prerequisite to getting or keeping a job. The state-level privacy push stems from the fact that the United States, unlike some other countries, lacks a federal privacy law.

While government regulations are necessary to ensure the quality of our food and the safety of our savings, regulations designed to shield personal content from professional vetting are shortsighted and potentially damaging to employers, workers and consumers alike. Best practices call for employers to monitor business, personal and public sites as allowed by law.

All organizations face risks when employees communicate electronically. The accidental (or intentional) posting of confidential internal email, consumers' private financial data, students' educational records or patients' protected health information can trigger lawsuits, regulatory audits and public relations nightmares.

If an emergency room nurse comments on a patient's medical condition on a private Facebook account, the hospital could face a six-figure Health Insurance Portability and Accountability Act (HIPAA) fine. Were a broker to discuss a public company on a personal blog, the Securities and Exchange Commission's fair disclosure rule could be violated and the brokerage sanctioned. If an employee disparages a supplier on Twitter, a manager mocks an employee on Facebook or an executive reveals merger plans on YouTube, the results could include litigation, lost revenue and career setbacks.

Fortunately, strategic monitoring enables management to uncover and manage risks.

The federal Electronic Communications Privacy Act grants employers the legal right to monitor company computers. According to the act, content created, transmitted and stored on business systems, sites, accounts and devices (including smartphones) belongs to the boss. Workers have no reasonable expectation of privacy.

Monitoring personal accounts is less clear cut. Before requesting Facebook user names and passwords, visit the National Conference of State Legislatures' site to see if online privacy legislation exists in your state. Consider also whether personal monitoring fits your company's compliance needs and culture.

Here are some of the best practices for legal and ethical monitoring:

Do:

- Establish clear social media, Internet, email and mobile device policies.
- Incorporate content and personal use rules.
- Define monitoring procedures: who, what, when, where, why, how.

Don't:

- Leave compliance to chance. Educate users about risks, policies and procedures.
- Go on fishing expeditions. Monitor only for legitimate business reasons.

MANAGEMENT IN A DIVERSE, DIGITAL WORLD

4

THE WORLDWIDE WORKFORCE

Can companies train the talent needed for a global economy?

Susan Ladika

EXECUTIVE SUMMARY

As multinational corporations expand their footprint abroad, their appetite for workers with global business skills grows apace. Some of the world's best-known brands now base most of their operations and workforces outside their home country, and more employees than ever are being sent abroad. As a result, the ability to manage an international workforce effectively has become a key determinant of success for companies navigating diverse cultural terrain. These businesses face an array of challenges in training, deploying and retaining employees who can operate in an increasingly globalized economy. Among the questions being raised: Does an employee need to spend time abroad to be a successful global manager? Are business schools doing enough to address the training needs of multinational corporations? Can technology help a multinational workforce surmount differences?

OVERVIEW

With a single deal, American insurance giant MetLife Inc. acquired a great opportunity—and a significant problem.

When the company bought American Life Insurance Co. in 2010, it instantly increased its stature as a global force in the industry. Its international presence soared from 17 countries to 64, with new operations ranging from Egypt to Lebanon and Nepal. But it realized something crucial was lacking: leaders with the necessary background to seize the moment. Fewer than 20 percent of its top executives had global experience.

"We needed our more-senior leaders to have international experience as they moved through the management hierarchy so they could really understand the complexity of operating in a global business context," said David Henderson, MetLife's chief talent officer and executive vice president of human resources for its global functions.[1]

To address that concern, MetLife established a global mobility program that sends those who have been identified as high-potential executives to new markets. The program

From *SAGE Business Researcher*,
June 6, 2016

MetLife's iconic blimp. The insurance giant found that it lacked executives with global experience after a 2010 acquisition increased its international presence to 64 countries.

Source: Sam Greenwood/Getty Images

isn't a one-way street. Along with considering what experiences the manager will gain from an international assignment, it takes into account the skills the manager will bring to the assignment. As of mid-2015, about 200 MetLife employees, including 45 senior executives, were on international assignments or waiting to be sent abroad. MetLife's move reflects the new reality that managers need the proper skills to manage a global workforce successfully.[2]

A survey of more than 350 large companies in nine countries found that employers particularly valued employees who could show understanding of different cultural contexts and viewpoints, could demonstrate respect for others and knew a foreign language.[3]

"Our clients increasingly operate seamlessly across borders," said Peter Lacy, a global managing director with the management consultancy Accenture. "Our people need to be able to do the same. That mindset comes from being exposed to new business cultures and experiences that come with international placements."[4]

Managers Increasingly Value International Experience

Being able to manage a global workforce effectively has become paramount for success as the world becomes ever smaller. More than 100,000 multinational corporations employ tens of millions around the globe, up from 40,000 such corporations in 1995.[5]

Some of the world's best-known brands, such as Nestle and Honda, even have most of their operations and workforce outside their home country, and more employees than ever are being sent on international assignments.[6] Many multinationals are finding their greatest growth opportunities in less developed countries, such as India, China and Brazil.[7] Transnational corporations must master a delicate balancing act to manage an increasingly diverse workforce successfully while maintaining their own corporate culture and norms.

But finding talent that's up to the job can be a major challenge. "Global companies are woefully understaffed when it comes to having employees with global experience," says Robert Salomon, associate professor of management and organizations at New York University.

In fact, in a 2014 survey of more than 800 U.S. companies, 43 percent said their overall business would increase "a great deal" if they had more staff with international experience, and another 43 percent said it would increase "some." Just 14 percent said their business wouldn't benefit.[8]

A multinational or transnational corporation operates in more than one country, typically through wholly or partially owned subsidiaries, and nearly three-quarters of

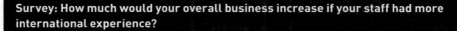

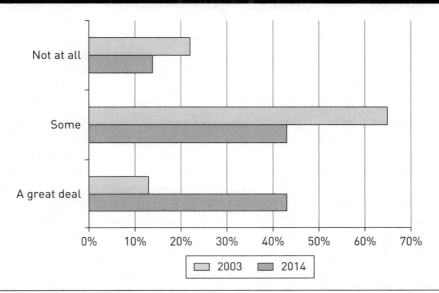

Forty-three percent of management-level employees at U.S. companies said in a 2014 survey that having more staff with international expertise would increase business "a great deal," more than triple the share who said so 11 years earlier. An equal share said increased international expertise would boost business at least "some," while just 14 percent said it would not matter.

Notes: Data for 2014 based on survey of department heads, directors, managers and supervisors at 836 U.S. companies; 2003 data based on survey of managers at 111 U.S. companies. Company types include manufacturing, services, retail, financial services, telecommunications and/or Internet and "other."

Source: Shirley J. Daniel, Fujiao Xie and Ben L. Kedia, "2014 U.S. Business Needs for Employees with International Expertise," the Internationalization of U.S. Education in the 21st Century conference, April 2014, p. 24, http://tinyurl.com/hftpezd

multinationals are based in either North America or Western Europe.[9] Historically, the pattern was to send employees from corporate headquarters to new locations, bringing needed management or technical skills. International assignments often lasted two or three years.

But now employees are moving in all different directions, and short-term assignments are gaining ground.[10] A typical U.S.-headquartered multinational will have American employees based in the United States as well as abroad, and non-Americans working at the corporation's headquarters in the United States, in offices in the country where the employee is from, or in a third country where the company has locations.[11]

If a company gets it right, it can prosper. If not, "at the very least it will result in unforeseen costs," Salomon says. "At the worst you're looking at outright failure. Cultural differences can bring a company down."

Those cultural differences reportedly played a role in undermining the joint venture between vente-privee.com, a French luxury e-commerce company known for its flash sales, and credit card giant American Express. Vente-privee has been a huge hit in Europe, selling fashion and lifestyle products at deep discounts, and now has 30 million members across eight countries.

In 2011, vente-privee and American Express announced the creation of vente-privee USA. The venture lasted just three years. American Express officially said that because the operation was taking longer than expected to become profitable, the companies had decided to part ways and focus on other priorities.

But former employees told Fortune that vente-privee USA botched operations because French officials failed to understand the American market, and the entire U.S. management team ended up leaving the company. Employees said vente-privee's European co-founders disliked efforts to make the American website more user-friendly and didn't understand why the site included a Facebook share button, something typical for U.S. e-commerce sites. And vente-privee CEO Jacques-Antoine Granjon raised eyebrows by commissioning a mural of himself and the board depicted as Jesus and the Apostles at the Last Supper. [12]

Vente-privee didn't respond to a request for comment.

While bringing together two companies from different Western cultures can be challenging enough, it can quickly become even more complex when joining businesses from highly dissimilar cultures, according to Salomon. "It is, of course, trickier to conduct business in a country that varies significantly from your own," he wrote. "Managers often find themselves lost in such situations—struggling to understand local norms, customs, and cultural nuances. They make costly and unnecessary mistakes when they misread or misjudge the local cultural, political, and economic environments." [13]

Salomon cited the example of the Swedish home furnishings retailer IKEA, which has struggled to succeed in Russia since entering the country in 2000. IKEA's woes stem from Russian "corruption, coupled with a legal system that favors local interests over foreign interests," he wrote.

The company's failure to understand this inherent corruption and bias led to a long trail of misadventures. When Moscow's utility company demanded bribes to guarantee electricity to the company's first store in Russia, IKEA refused to cough up the cash and rented generators instead. Then IKEA learned that its employee in charge of relations with the generator provider was involved in a kickback scheme to inflate the price of the service. When IKEA went to Russian civil court over the issue, "the judge not only ruled against IKEA but also slapped the company with a fine for breach of contract with the generator company." [14]

Yet many companies are seeing their greatest opportunities for growth in locations such as China, India and Brazil. These may be countries where they haven't operated before and where business, cultural and political differences can be pronounced.

Walmart, for example, has been unable to generate a profit from its Chinese operations after two decades in the country because of infrastructure limitations, especially outside major cities. "China simply cannot accommodate one of Walmart's greatest strengths: an ultraefficient and technologically advanced supply chain," Salomon wrote. [15]

The United States, Western Europe, Japan and Australia are home to nearly three-quarters of all multinationals. Yet in sheer numbers, China is the leader, with an estimated 12,000 multinationals. The United States is second, with nearly 9,700.[16] As businesses expand to new parts of the world, more employees are on the move than ever before. During the 2000s, the number of international assignments jumped 25 percent, and it is expected to climb 50 percent more by 2020, a survey by the professional services firm PwC found.[17]

As the number has grown, the nature of international assignments has shifted. Instead of two-or three-year stints to another location, assignments that last for a year or less are increasingly common. In some cases, employees are being sent abroad for just a few weeks or months to work on a particular project. Or they may be commuting or taking extended business trips, so they don't need to relocate. Such short-term assignments have become one means to help develop up-and-coming talent.[18]

"Mobility is growing faster than we ever imagined," says Eileen Mullaney, global mobility consulting practice leader at PwC. "It's no longer one-size-fits-all for any organization."

Women remain underrepresented in international assignments. While the number of women sent abroad has doubled over the past decade, they still represent only one-fifth of international assignees.[19]

There also is a growing reliance on contract workers, so organizations can bring in the best person with the best skills for a particular project. And corporations are using virtual teams to allow their top talent to work together on projects from anywhere in the world.[20]

As corporations expand, they need to remain sensitive to employee differences. The relative importance of work, the importance of time and a collective or individual work style are among the factors that can vary greatly among individuals and cultures. Those differences also require corporations to consider varying methods to manage, motivate or compensate employees.

The laws of individual countries also must be taken into account. Standards on hiring and firing, the number of hours worked or vacation days allowed can vary greatly. A company must find a way to observe such laws while not compromising its mission or its corporate culture and norms.[21]

As corporations, managers and educators consider effective ways to manage a global workforce, here are some of the issues under debate:

Weighing the Issues

Must an employee spend time abroad to be a successful global manager?

It's quite clear what Jack Welch, the iconic former CEO of General Electric, thinks of the need for top leaders to have international experience.

"The Jack Welch of the Future cannot be like me," he said in 1999. "I spent my entire career in the United States. The next head of General Electric will be somebody who spent time in Bombay, in Hong Kong, in Buenos Aires. We have to send our best and brightest overseas and make sure they have training that will allow them to be the global leaders who will make GE flourish in the future."[22]

Even as demand grows for managers who have the ability to effectively handle an increasingly international workforce, those skills are in short supply.

In fact, only one-third of corporate leaders rated themselves as highly effective in leading across countries and cultures, a survey by human resources consultant Development Dimensions International (DDI) and the Conference Board found. Of the dozen critical leadership skills considered, those surveyed said they had the greatest lack in cross-cultural skills. Only 45 percent said they could operate effectively in foreign environments, and about 40 percent said they were skilled at intercultural communication. Despite these shortcomings, only 20 percent of organizations emphasize developing global leadership skills.[23]

"It's a very challenging time for people who are in talent management," says William Castellano, associate dean of executive and professional education at Rutgers University.

While some people may be inherently predisposed to navigate successfully across cultures, others might be taught those skills at undergraduate, MBA and executive education programs, or through in-house corporate training programs. But some experts argue that might not be enough.

"I think it's difficult to develop the skills to be truly proficient at managing a global workforce unless you've had a chance to go through all the transformative experiences of having an expatriate assignment," says Julian Dalzell, a lecturer in the Department of Management at the University of South Carolina in Columbia who spent more than 40 years in human resources at Royal Dutch Shell, working in such places as the United Kingdom, Brunei and Malaysia.

Classroom training can have value, Salomon says, "but there is no substitute for experience."

Andrew Walker, mobility leader at the business services firm EY, says certain individuals tend to be predisposed to having a global mindset, but others shouldn't be written off. "If you don't have the predisposition, you can acquire it," says Walker, whose firm was known as Ernst & Young until 2013.

Walker says some senior leaders in his organization "are very effective working across cultures" even though they have never worked outside their home-country office. But others, he says, while successful leaders, "might come across as being too American, or too British, or too German, or too whatever, and they could benefit from having more international experience just to help them develop their global mindset."

Leaders of some of the world's top corporations could be poster children for the value of international experience.

Muhtar Kent, the son of a Turkish diplomat, was born in the United States and went to college and graduate school in London. He landed his first job with the Coca-Cola Co. in Turkey in 1978 after answering a help-wanted ad, and spent time loading trucks. Today he's the company's CEO.

Kent worked throughout the world for the beverage giant and for the Turkish brewer Efes Beverage Group before being named to run Coca-Cola in 2008. "His genes are international," a colleague told Barron's.[24]

Joseph Jimenez's international experience helped him land the CEO job at the Swiss pharmaceutical firm Novartis in 2010. He began his career working in consumer products, including as president of North American and European business for the H.J. Heinz Co.

Jimenez got his start in the pharmaceutical industry in 2002, after being asked to serve on the board of London-based AstraZeneca PLC. Jimenez, an American, said he "was asked to sit on the board of a major pharmaceutical company in Europe, because they wanted somebody with U.S. experience." He then joined Novartis in 2007 as head of its consumer health division.[25]

EY is working to enhance the international skills of early-and mid-career employees through its New Horizons program, which sends hundreds of employees abroad each year. High-performing, highly motivated employees who have been with EY for two years or more are sent on assignment to another country for four to six months, working in a business area that differs from the one to which they are normally assigned so they can broaden their experience.

Even though those in the New Horizon program aren't yet managers, the company sees it as an important investment, Walker says, because "clients want to work with a globally minded company, with a globally integrated company. This helps them develop that global mindset and develop a global network."

But Paula Caligiuri, a professor of international business and strategy at Northeastern University, says that "some of the most culturally agile professionals I've met never set foot out of their home country. Breathing the air of another country doesn't necessarily make someone culturally agile." Instead, she says, it's important for individuals to have the humility to understand the limits of their knowledge, the perspective to be able to operate comfortably without necessarily having complete information, and the resilience to bounce back when things go wrong. "Individuals can have them without going abroad."

A survey of more than 800 U.S. businesses found a strong demand for employees with an appreciation for cross-cultural differences and foreign-language skills. When employees move into management positions, there is a greater need for international work experience and knowledge of various countries or regions.

"These findings have significant implications for U.S. business schools," the authors of a report on the survey's findings wrote. The findings "indicate that undergraduate as well as MBA and executive programs may need a much greater emphasis on assuring that participants achieve a global perspective and an appreciation for cross-cultural differences, political and economic environments and business markets."[26]

Are business schools doing enough to prepare students for careers in multinational corporations?

Although graduates with international skills are a hot commodity, many experts say business schools at American universities could be doing far more to train the upcoming generation of managers.

"I think there's a lot of rhetoric. I think there's a big gap between rhetoric and how they actually do in preparing students" for global careers, says Andrew Molinsky, professor of international management and organizational behavior at Brandeis University in Waltham, Mass.

While Salomon says the situation has improved since he started teaching in 2000, "I still think there's a long way to go." Students have more opportunities to spend time abroad, taking advantage of options such as two-week study trips where they can see firsthand how business is done in various countries. Business schools also may encourage students to study a foreign language and take part in semester-long study-abroad programs.

U.S. Companies Expand International Employee Training

More international students are enrolled in U.S. universities, creating more opportunities for students to interact with those from different cultures. For the 2014–15 school year, almost 975,000 international students were enrolled at U.S. universities, up 10 percent from the previous year. Of those international students, nearly 200,000 were studying business and management—the largest number among all majors. A decade ago, about 565,000 international students were enrolled in U.S. schools, with about 100,000 studying business and management.[27]

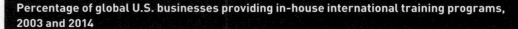

Percentage of global U.S. businesses providing in-house international training programs, 2003 and 2014

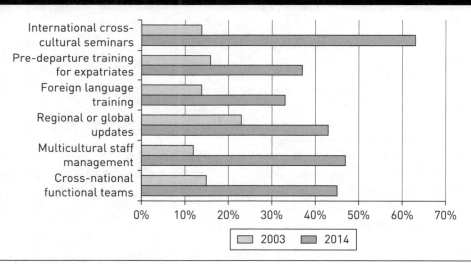

U.S.-based global businesses have expanded offerings of in-house international training programs since the early 2000s. In 2014, six in 10 firms offered their employees cross-cultural seminars; nearly half had training programs for multicultural staff or cross-national team management; and a third offered foreign language classes. Eleven years previously, about one-fourth or less of U.S. companies offered any of these international training programs.

Notes: Data for 2014 based on survey of department heads, directors, managers and supervisors at 836 U.S. companies; 2013 data based on survey of managers at 111 U.S. companies. Company types include manufacturing, services, retail, financial services, telecommunications and/or Internet and "other."

Source: Shirley J. Daniel, Fujiao Xie and Ben L. Kedia, "2014 U.S. Business Needs for Employees with International Expertise," the Internationalization of U.S. Education in the 21st Century conference, April 2014, p. 31, http://tinyurl.com/hftpezd

But that might not be enough. A report by the Association to Advance Collegiate Schools of Business (AACSB) International states: "Present efforts by business schools to globalize typically include a series of independent and fragmented activities. These activities are mostly focused on student and/or faculty diversity and the establishment of cross-border partnerships for student exchange . . . with insufficient emphasis on learning experiences and intended outcomes."

Instead, the AACSB calls for educational experiences that prepare students to perform "competently" and "confidently" in the global business world and suggests accreditation standards of excellence should be established to try to ensure that students are properly prepared for the new global business reality.[28]

The report's suggestions for improving students' preparedness include incorporating global perspectives in the core curriculum, recruiting international students and faculty, requiring foreign language training and providing international experiences, such as study abroad.

"Compared to the business environment, higher education tends to be more tightly rooted in tradition, and tends to encounter more inertia than business in the face of change," the report says.[29]

Businesses themselves could be partially to blame. "What you see is a check-the-box mentality now," says Andrew Spicer, faculty director of full-time MBA programs at the University of South Carolina. "Like everything else on your résumé, people want to know if you have a little international experience—yes or no. If you've taken one of these 10-day trips, they put 'yes.' What we are arguing is that while simple answers provide neat and tailored models, they actually don't deal with the complexities we're talking about. They don't adequately prepare people for foreign assignments."

Spicer says the world isn't converging and becoming one big marketplace. Instead, it is a multipolar world, with differences among locations, such as Asia or the Anglo-Saxon countries, and businesses have to operate accordingly.

He faults U.S. businesses and business schools for being slow to adapt to the new reality. "If you go around the rest of the world, they see the world from this lens. Business schools in the U.S. are a little slower to adopt this."

Spicer heads up an AACSB program to globalize business curriculum, which draws professors from around the world for training. "In my most recent class, the professors from every business school from outside the United States told me that students were required to know two or more languages by the time they graduated," he says. "In contrast, some U.S. participants said that some of their students chose to study business precisely because they were able to opt out of the language requirements that were part of alternative majors.

"Other countries realize that their competitive advantage lies in better understanding and competing in foreign markets. In contrast, the large home market in the United States does not light the same fires and interests in foreign opportunities," Spicer says.

U.S. schools continue to look for a one-size-fits-all model to teach students, Spicer contends. "What we teach and what students actually want is an expert to come forward and tell them what the right answer happens to be. We love models. The truth is when we look beyond a one-size-fits-all model, you see business in China is not the same thing it is in

Russia and is not the same thing it is in Indonesia, and your models might not work. How you figure out when they work and when they don't is a difficult proposition."

U.S. News & World Report ranks the international graduate program at the University of South Carolina's Darla Moore School of Business No. 1 in the country. Yet Dean Peter Brews says that generally, U.S. business schools have much room for improvement when it comes to teaching globalization skills.

Brews, who is a native of South Africa, says the problems faced by U.S. business schools are common among the most developed nations. "Many big, successful countries think global and act American, think global and act French, think global and act German, think global and act British. The challenge is moving students from being ethnocentric to being geocentric, and that's not an easy thing to teach." The only way to overcome it, he says, is to immerse students in situations where they aren't the majority.

He has praise for international business education in The Netherlands—a small country with a rich trading history and a population that is proficient in English—and South Africa. "We're very able to move into other countries," Brews says.

To U.S. businesses, more emphasis on learning about other regions of the world and mandatory foreign language training are considered top priorities. Companies also would like more outreach from U.S. business schools to help them improve their international skills.[30]

"Name" business schools, such as Wharton and Harvard, have had more success expanding their executive education programs than other universities. "Businesses are looking for something they can count on. The brand of the school has a big impact on that," said Lee Maxey, CEO of MindMax, which works with educational institutions to expand their executive education offerings. "Local brands have an easier time and greater success connecting with the local business community, but they can't leverage that online scale that a bigger brand school can."[31]

Corporations are becoming more likely to request custom executive education programs, often tied to the need to develop skills in high-growth business functions. With online technology, it's become easier for schools to modify their curriculum to meet corporate needs.[32]

Can technology help a multinational workforce surmount differences?

Having a diverse workforce spread across the world can make it challenging for corporations to share information or develop a sense of camaraderie and common good. But social media can be useful in drawing together distant workers.

"Social media helps establish an employee brand and culture that attracts Gen Y and multigenerational talent," according to the consultancy Deloitte. "The younger workforce tends to be more accustomed to collaborative social technologies. They view them as a workplace necessity, not a luxury. Because these new workforce members bring tech-savvy skills, global and flexible orientations, and the ability to think in innovative ways, attracting and retaining them will create significant competitive advantage in the coming years."[33]

The French beauty company L'Oreal is among the companies mastering employee engagement through social media. It established #LifeatLoreal as a means to share information on what was happening at the company's various offices and #LorealCommunity so employees could share how they interact with their work colleagues inside and outside the office.

Along with fostering employee engagement, the effort has had an added benefit: helping the company recruit employees as its social media campaigns grabbed attention outside the company.[34]

The Chinese computer manufacturer Lenovo has developed an internal social network called

L'Oreal's headquarters outside Paris. The beauty products company has used social media to foster employee engagement.

Source: AFP/ Stringer/Getty Images

Lenovo Social Champions, where employees share everything from presentations from company events to hardware reviews. "It's about creating connections around a global organization," said Roderick Strother, who previously led the company's global social media marketing.[35]

Google, widely known for its innovative culture, relies heavily on its more than 20 employee-resource groups to forge employee linkages. The groups have been "anchors and havens and think tanks," said Stacy Sullivan, Google's vice president of people operations and chief culture officer. They are used by employees "to build their own community, just for their own support and interactions, within the mass of all Google . . . when you're this big, you can lose sight of being connected to the mass around the world. So this is one way they can all pull together."[36]

Groups cover the spectrum. Women@Google provides mentoring and networking opportunities for women in 27 countries, while Greyglers caters to older workers, and Gayglers supports the lesbian, gay, bisexual and transgender communities.[37]

At Royal Philips Electronics, the company has taken a different tack, using its corporate social network primarily as a work tool. Yet Philips says the network helps to bond employees and bolster collaboration. The Dutch company developed Philips Community, which now has more than 50,000 users. When it was launched as a pilot, Philips drew on its strongest social media users to serve as champions for the group. Within two months it had grown to 7,000 users. Employees turn to the group to find information, ask questions and share ideas.[38]

Initially, "people thought it was an internal Facebook where you posted pictures of your dog and holiday," said Dennis Agusi, communication channels lead at Philips. "But quickly, people realized that it is a business tool built on social technologies that helps us achieve business goals like collaborating and speeding up communications." The company has found more than half of the questions posted to the group are answered within an hour, and 92 percent within 24 hours.[39]

More International Students Studying Business

But Philips' experience seems to go against the grain, as research has shown internal social networks can have a hard time gaining ground. An article in Harvard Business Review states that the networks often fail because corporate leaders don't take part: "Because the top executives didn't see collaboration and engagement as a good use of their time, employees quickly learned that they shouldn't either."

While leaders know it is important to engage with employees, they typically don't. "More than anything else, they fear that engaging will close the power distance between them and their employees, thereby lessening their ability to command and control."[40]

Although groups and technology can be highly successful, Salomon cautions they may not work as well to draw in employees from collectivist cultures, such as those in Asia and Latin America. The reliance on technology may be seen as too impersonal. "With collectivist cultures, I think technology is less effective," he says. "Relationships matter."

Technology can play a vital role in enabling teams to work across borders. Persistent Systems, a software company based in Pune, India, employs almost 9,000 workers across

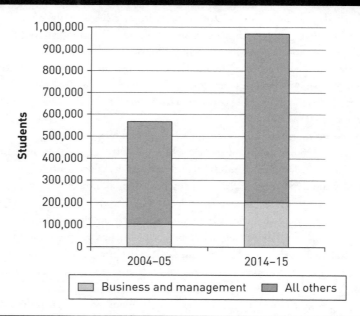

International students studying at U.S. colleges by field of study, in thousands, 2004–05 and 2014–15

About 975,000 international students studied at U.S. colleges during the 2014–15 academic year, a 73 percent increase from 10 years earlier. The share of international students studying business and management at U.S. schools increased slightly during the same period.

Source: "Open Doors Data, International Students: Fields of Study," select years, Institute of International Education, accessed May 23, 2016, http://tinyurl.com/jz5uksb

three continents, including at several locations in the United States. Its team in Boston, for example, frequently works with its counterpart in Kuala Lumpur, Malaysia, says Anagha Vyas, head of Persistent's office in Dublin, Ohio.

"The connection you would make with someone face to face cannot be replicated with a virtual meeting," Vyas says. While it may not totally bridge that gap, "we encourage people to use video because it gives it a more personal touch."

BACKGROUND

Putting Down Roots

The roots of multinational corporations stretch back to the 1500s, when English and Dutch traders began sailing the world looking for commercial opportunities or to acquire territory. Along the way, they set up operations in Asia, Africa and the Americas.[41]

The development of multinationals picked up steam in the late 19th and early 20th centuries, fueled by such developments as the growth of factories, more efficient manufacturing and better transportation. During this era, corporations also sought out natural resources and labor as they expanded their markets.[42]

A company is considered a multinational or transnational corporation when it operates in more than one country, typically through wholly or partially owned subsidiaries.[43] It uses foreign direct investment (FDI) to expand its operations, either by creating a foreign firm, which is known as greenfield investment, or by acquiring an existing one.[44]

Many of today's best known multinational corporations got their start in the late 1800s or early 1900s. For example, Ford Motor Co. was incorporated in 1903, and the following year Ford of Canada was founded. The subsidiary manufactured vehicles and sold them throughout the British Empire.[45]

The history of today's Colgate-Palmolive stretches back to 1806, when William Colgate began selling soap, candles and starch in New York City. The company also turned to Canada to establish its first foreign subsidiary in 1914. The company then spread its reach to Europe, Africa, Asia and Latin America in the 1920s.[46]

American corporations flourished overseas in the wake of World War II. At that time, many Western European and Japanese companies were focused on efforts to recover from the war's destructive force. For U.S. multinationals, it was a time to concentrate on expanding manufacturing and related service industries, and they primarily produced goods that were sold in a host country. Much of the expansion took place in developed countries, as well as in the most advanced of the developing countries. Developing countries were attractive primarily for their natural resources.[47]

But multinationals were often limited in their ability to expand due to economic and political barriers that curtailed trade and foreign direct investment.[48]

Much of the growth of multinational corporations can be attributed to the gradual dismantling of trade barriers. The General Agreement on Tariffs and Trade (GATT), which took effect in 1948 with 23 countries signing on, worked to reduce tariffs and end import quotas.[49] Later rounds of negotiations liberalized trade further. GATT was replaced in 1995 by the World Trade Organization (WTO), which deals with goods, services and intellectual property. By the end of 2015, there were 162 member countries.[50]

On the European front, the desire to prevent a repetition of the destruction from the world wars that had devastated the continent was a principal concern of postwar policy makers. The desire to knit together former enemies economically led to the signing of a treaty forming the European Coal and Steel Community in 1951. France, West Germany, Italy, Belgium, Luxembourg and The Netherlands signed on, agreeing to ensure the free movement of coal and steel.[51]

Six years later, the European Economic Community was formed to create the Common Market, and in 1986 the Single European Act was signed, which led to the creation of the European Union. When the EU was officially launched in 1993, it had a dozen members. Following the end of the Cold War, the EU has continued to expand and now has 28 members.[52]

Meanwhile, the United States, Canada and Mexico signed the North American Free Trade Agreement (NAFTA), which took effect in 1994 and ultimately eliminated all tariffs among the three countries.[53]

Similar agreements have been signed in other parts of the world, including the Association of Southeast Asian Nations (ASEAN), designed to foster economic and political cooperation among 10 member countries in Southeast Asia. Later, free trade agreements were signed with countries such as China and Japan.[54]

The most recent free trade agreement is the Trans Pacific Partnership, signed in 2016 by the United States and 11 other countries, including Australia and Japan. It would strengthen economic ties and reduce tariffs. The partnership now is awaiting ratification by the United States, where it has encountered significant political opposition, and other countries.[55]

As trade barriers have tumbled, market opportunities and multinational corporations have flourished. In 1970, there were 7,000 multinational corporations. By 1995 that number had climbed to 40,000, which had more than 200,000 foreign affiliates. Today, there are more than 100,000 multinationals operating nearly 900,000 affiliates.[56]

Corporations have taken markedly different paths to become multinationals. General Electric, the world's largest transnational corporation when measured in terms of foreign assets, began its foreign expansion only in recent decades, while Royal Dutch Shell, which ranks second, was conceived as a transnational.

Thomas Edison established the Edison General Electric Co. in 1878. It merged with Thomson-Houston Electric Co. in 1892 to form General Electric Co. GE was primarily a U.S.-centric corporation until Welch took the helm a century later. During that time the company made a string of international acquisitions in diverse countries from the United Kingdom to Brazil.[57]

In 2013, GE's total assets topped $685 billion, with more than $338 billion held abroad. Half its sales are outside the United States and 171,000 of its 305,000 employees are outside U.S. borders.[58]

Royal Dutch Shell was created by the merger of two companies that were already international in scope. In the early 1900s, Britain's Shell Transport and Trading Co. was involved in transporting oil from the Far East. Meanwhile, the origins of the Royal Dutch

Petroleum Co. were tied to the development of an oil field in Sumatra in 1890. The two companies began working together in 1903 and merged in 1907.[59]

Now, Shell is the world's second-largest transnational when measured by foreign assets. As of 2014, it had more than $360 billion in total assets, with nearly $308 billion outside The Netherlands. The company also has more than half its sales and 73,000 of its 87,000 employees outside its home country. [60]

Multinationals Flourish Around the Globe

As multinationals have expanded, foreign direct investment has soared. In 1990, FDI inflows were almost $205 billion and outflows were almost $244 billion. Just a decade later, inflows had soared to more than $1.36 trillion while outflows totaled more than $1.16 trillion. During that time, the vast majority of the money came from and went to the developed world.[61]

After 2000, things began to shift, with big inflows to and outflows from developing nations. In 2014, FDI inflows reached almost $1.23 trillion, with less than $500 billion going to more developed economies. FDI outflows topped $1.35 trillion, with almost $823 billion coming from more developed economies. In 2014, both China and Hong Kong received more foreign direct investment than the United States. That same year, the United States continued to lead in terms of outflows of foreign investment, investing almost $337 billion abroad. China, which invested less than $1 billion abroad in 2000, saw brisk growth during the following years. It sent $116 billion abroad in 2014, placing it third, behind Hong Kong.[62]

The majority of multinationals have been, and continue to be, located in the developed world, but a growing number are now headquartered in less developed countries.[63]

Often, Western multinationals set up operations to produce or sell goods in less developed countries, or to take advantage of lower labor costs for factories and call centers. While that continues, corporations from less developed countries are expanding their international operations.

The Indian multinational Tata Group had revenue of more than $100 billion in 2013, with two-thirds coming from abroad, while the Haier Group, a Chinese manufacturer of appliances and electronics, sells its products in more than 100 countries.[64]

That means more employees from less-developed countries are being sent on international assignments across the world. As multinational corporations have expanded their global footprints, demand has soared for employees with international experience.

Initially, multinationals focused on sending managers or those with specialized skills from corporate headquarters in the United States and Western Europe to company offices in other parts of the world.[65]

From the 1970s to 1990s, much of the movement involved sending employees from U.S. headquarters to operations in Europe, while companies that were seeking natural resources were most likely to send employees to remote destinations.[66]

Employees were often sent abroad for several years. Because there was little career benefit from international assignments, companies sweetened the deal by offering generous expatriate packages, which might include benefits such as housing and education allowances and higher pay, says Steve Nurney, a partner at Mercer, a human resources consulting firm.

As multinationals expanded their presence in new markets, costly long-term international assignments soared. But the 2007–09 recession put a major brake on that trend, Nurney says. "It was a catalyst for looking at a segmented approach (to mobility). Organizations recognized not all assignments are the same." Economic improvement has meant an increase in global assignments, but many are for shorter periods, driving down the costs. At the same time, corporations began to view short-term international assignments as an important way to groom promising young talent.

CURRENT SITUATION

"A Tremendous Appetite"

As corporations see a growing need for employees with international skills, employees are increasingly demanding opportunities to work abroad, and more than 70 percent of Millennials say they expect and want to have an international job assignment during their careers. [67]

As a result, overseas opportunities have become a way for corporations to attract and retain top talent.

"There's a tremendous appetite—a greater appetite than we can satisfy—for mobility experiences among our younger talent," says Walker of EY. Employees often are sent on two-week international assignments so they're more prepared for longer assignments when opportunities arise.

A Mercer survey found the main reasons companies send employees to another country are to provide technical skills that are unavailable locally; to transfer knowledge; to provide specific managerial skills; to meet specific project needs; and to foster career management and leadership development.[68]

Companies: Schools Should Teach Communication, Languages

The latter has been embraced by MetLife, which has established the Global Leadership Development Program as a way for the company to build up its bench strength and groom potential general managers. Under the program, top MBA graduates with three to five years of work experience who are hired by MetLife complete three rotations of 18 months each, including an international assignment.[69]

One big concern remains the lack of women on international assignments. Women made up about 46 percent of the U.S. labor force in 2014, and it's a similar percentage for most of the developed world.[70] While the number of women sent abroad has doubled in the past decade, they still represent just 20 percent of international assignees.[71]

"The first hurdle to increased numbers of female expatriates has been selection bias," said William Sheridan, vice president of international human resources services at the Washington, D.C.-based National Foreign Trade Council. Companies may assume a woman wouldn't be interested in an international assignment. They also may believe a

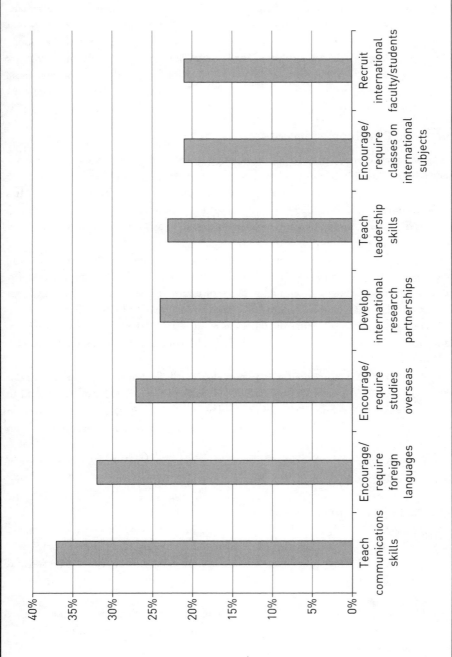

Percentage of large employers that say educational systems could improve students' intercultural skills

Nearly four in 10 human resources managers at large companies say school systems could improve future workers' intercultural skills by teaching communication skills, and about a third say they could do so by encouraging or requiring students to learn foreign languages. About a fourth recommend schools encourage or require overseas studies, develop international research partnerships or teach leadership skills to students.

Notes: Based on survey of human resources managers at 367 large companies in nine countries.

Source: "Culture at Work," British Council, Ipsos and Booz Allen Hamilton, 2013, p. 17, http://tinyurl.com/gktl7pd

woman wouldn't fit in at a male-dominated location or she may have a spouse who wouldn't be able to find a job abroad, according to Sheridan.[72]

It's a brighter picture at EY, where about 40 percent of its expatriates are female. Although the company strives for more gender parity, its overriding aim is to choose the best possible candidate for each international assignment. "That's really what it should be about," Walker says. More women are willing to head abroad, he says, particularly those who are just starting their careers. Unattached women across all age groups also have become more interested in working internationally. On the flip side, Walker has seen more men turn down international assignments because of their spouse's career.

Demand in Developing Markets

Despite their demand for international assignments, Millennials may be picky about where they go. The United States and the United Kingdom top the list of where they want to work. A PwC study found that while more than half said they'd be willing to work in a less developed country, when asked to rank their preferred international destination, only Brazil landed in the top 20. Just 11 percent said they were willing to work in India, and 2 percent in mainland China.[73]

Despite employees' possible reluctance to taken an assignment in a far-away location, that's where there's a growing demand for new assignees. Brookfield GRS, a relocation service company, found the top emerging markets for international assignments were China, Brazil and the United Arab Emirates in 2015. The previous year, India ranked third.[74]

At the same time, Brazil, India and China were rated the most challenging for assignees. The report cited issues such as living conditions, health concerns, pollution, safety and cultural differences.[75]

Those looking for international assignments also may be finding more competition from local employees. "With the onset of globalized education around the world, if you want to find specific knowledge about Brazilian markets, you could probably find a Brazilian who has gone to a U.S. school," Spicer says. "You don't necessarily have to hire an American who is going to Brazil."

From 2005 until 2015, the percentage of corporations on the Fortune Global 500 list from the "BRIC" economies (Brazil, Russia, India and China) and a handful of other emerging economies has soared, from 8 percent to about 25 percent. At the same time, the share of U.S.-based companies on the list dropped from 35 percent to about 25 percent.[76]

Managing a global workforce involves more than just moving employees around a map. It also entails melding corporate culture and norms with an individual's culture. Employers must bear in mind that incentives that motivate employees vary from person to person and place to place, and they may have different reactions to various communication and management styles.[77]

Local laws and cultural norms in areas such as pay, vacation, hiring, firing and other policies also must be taken into account. With more employees than ever moving around the world, equitable systems of compensation must be established.[78]

When Dalzell, the former Shell human resources executive, worked for the petroleum giant, the company set up a system where it paid in the top 75 percent for each country in which it operated. The actual amount paid out would vary from country to country, but the percentage paid always followed the same structure. Few benefits were global; most varied based on local customs or laws.

Multinationals can have a leg up on their local competition when it comes to pay, which may make them more appealing to the best talent, with foreign multinationals paying 40 percent more than local corporations, and even local multinationals paying 15 percent more than their local competition.[79]

LOOKING AHEAD

Shift Toward Developing World

International assignments, which already have been growing quickly, are predicted to pick up in the coming years, increasing by 50 percent by 2020.

Many of those assignments are expected to be in less developed countries, with more than 40 percent of corporations expecting to send more people to remote locations.[80] However, growth is expected at both ends of the spectrum, with the United States, United Kingdom, China Brazil and Singapore predicted to be the top locations for international assignments.[81]

At the same time, there is more diversity in the types of international assignments. While about 55 percent of corporations expect to send employees on short-term assignments, a similar percentage say they expect to do more permanent transfers, and almost half expect to have more locally hired foreigners.[82]

If that diversity isn't enough, corporations are relying more on contract workers; and one effect of this trend is that they can pull together the best talent from anywhere in the world. A U.S. Government Accountability Office (GAO) study found that 40 percent of the U.S. workforce was made up of contingent workers in 2010, up from 30 percent five years earlier. While the GAO definition is quite broad, including part-time workers and shop owners, it also includes independent contractors and similar workers.[83]

With the growing diversity of employees, assignments and contract workers, multinationals "have to be able to manage talent across all buckets," says Castellano, the Rutgers associate dean.

At the same time, the importance of emerging markets for multinational corporations is likely to grow. China has surpassed the United States when gross domestic product (GDP) is calculated in purchasing power parity (PPP). That gap is predicted to widen, and by 2050 India also may have slipped ahead of the United States by that measure. (U.S. nominal GDP, the more commonly cited measure of the size of an economy, remains the highest in the world.)[84]

The distribution of population in the world is also changing, with fast-growing populations in India and various African nations.[85]

EY is working to prepare employees for success in emerging markets, rolling out a new program called the Global Emerging Markets Mobility Program (GEM). Under the program, senior managers in emerging markets will be sent to mature markets for two years. "They go into another market to acquire skills and experience that they can then bring home and strengthen their emerging market location in terms of capacity, knowledge and networking, and also makes them more effective in their own career," Walker says.

At the same time, competition for talent from emerging markets is expected to intensify. With the aging workforce in developed countries, employees from emerging markets may be required to shore up the labor force. The working-age population in developed nations is predicted to decline by 5 percent from 2010 to 2030. "For the first time, more workers retired in Europe in 2010 than joined the workforce," The Economist's Intelligence Unit wrote in a 2015 report. "While this labor gap, at 200,000, is still relatively manageable, it is expected to grow to 8.3 million by 2030."[86]

PwC predicts domestic multinationals in emerging markets will meet or exceed Western multinationals when it comes to career development and compensation by 2020. As a result, employees from these countries who are working abroad will return home. "Local workers with international experience are often far more attractive to domestic employers than foreign workers in the same market; we've already seen Brazilian organizations, for example, that are more than willing to search for the best Brazilian workers overseas and tempt them home," PwC said in a 2012 report.[87]

Chronology

1890s–1920s	**Companies from the developed world begin worldwide operations.**
1892	General Electric, which will grow into the world's largest multinational corporation, is created through the merger of Edison General Electric Co. and Thomson-Houston Electric Co.
1904	Ford Motor Co. opens its first foreign subsidiary, in Canada, which manufactures vehicles and sells them in Canada and the British Empire.
1907	The U.K.'s Shell Transport and Trading Co. and the Royal Dutch Petroleum Co. merge to form the Royal Dutch Shell Group.
1929	Stock market crash wipes out millions of investors, helps push the United States into the Great Depression.
1930s–1940s	**International expansion limited by Depression, protectionist measures and war.**
1930	In reaction to the start of the Depression, the United States enacts Smoot-Hawley tariffs on agricultural and other imports, which trigger retaliation from other countries.
1933	Depression reaches its peak, with 13 million to 15 million Americans out of work. Europe also struggles with steep unemployment.
1939	U.S. economy begins to turn around as demand for manufacturing grows with the start of World War II.
1945	European and Japanese companies focus on rebuilding domestically as World War II ends.
1948	General Agreement on Tariffs and Trade (GATT), which reduced trade barriers, takes effect, with 23 countries taking part.

1950s–1960s	**Companies resume foreign expansion; Europe begins uniting economically and politically.**
1951	Treaty forming the European Coal and Steel Community is signed by France, Italy, Germany, Belgium, Luxembourg and the Netherlands.
1957	European Economic Community formed to create the Common Market.
1967	Conclusion of the Kennedy Round of GATT talks, which began in 1964 and were named after John F. Kennedy, maintains momentum for tariff reductions.
1969	Overseas Private Investment Corp. (OPIC) legislation signed into law, designed to mitigate risks and encourage private investment in developing countries.
1970s–1990s	**Multinationals send personnel overseas as trade barriers fall.**
1970	Seven thousand transnational corporations in existence.
1971	OPIC begins operation.
1979	China opens to foreign investors.
1981	Jack Welch takes helm of General Electric, launching company's unprecedented international expansion.
1993	European Union created with a dozen members after the signing of the Single European Act in 1986.
1994	North American Free Trade Agreement (NAFTA) takes effect, opening up trade among the United States, Mexico and Canada.
1995	The World Trade Organization (WTO) replaces GATT. By the end of 2015 it had 162 member countries.
1999	Foreign direct investment inflows and outflows top $1 trillion.
2000s–Present	**Foreign direct investment booms, multinationals expand.**
2007	Foreign direct investment peaks at almost $1.9 trillion in inflows and $2.1 billion in outflows. . . . United States goes into a deep recession in December. Companies scale back international assignments.
2012	Developing countries receive more foreign direct investment than developed countries for the first time.
2014	More than 100,000 multinational corporations operate almost 900,000 foreign affiliates.
2016	Trans-Pacific Partnership, a trade agreement among 12 nations, including the United States, is signed.

RESOURCES

The Next Step

Business Education

Addo, Koran, "Harris-Stowe begins first-ever study abroad program, sends two students to China," The St. Louis Post-Dispatch, March 3, 2016, http://tinyurl.com/jz9b46w.

Harris-Stowe State University in St. Louis, one of more than 40 historically black colleges and universities partnering with Chinese universities on study-abroad programs, sent two students to study business and Mandarin at Ningbo University in eastern China.

Ortmans, Laurent, "MBA by numbers: US students the least globally mobile," Financial Times, March 13, 2016, http://tinyurl.com/hhurlns.

Few U.S. graduate business school students study overseas or switch careers, industries or countries after completing their degrees, compared with students from other nations, according to an annual survey by the Financial Times.

Redden, Elizabeth, "A Push to Send Students Abroad," Inside Higher Ed, Oct. 2, 2015, http://tinyurl.com/omfvb9p.

Studying abroad can improve students' employment prospects and their knowledge of international business, said university officials during a national summit on expanding study-abroad opportunities for U.S. students.

Expatriate Employees

Carr, Stuart C., and Ishbel McWha-Hermann, "Expat wages up to 900% higher than for local employees, research shows," The Guardian, April 20, 2016, http://tinyurl.com/jkp546e.

Expatriate workers in six low-income countries make far more on average than local workers with similar education and experience, according to the U.K. Economic and Social Research Council, and they also oftentimes receive extra benefits.

Hannibal, Ed, Yvonne Traber and Paul Jelinek, "Tech Tools to Track Your Expatriate Workforce," HR Magazine, April 1, 2015, http://tinyurl.com/jdgnps7.

Human resources departments should factor in cost and necessity when choosing whether to use products that track expatriate employees' activities and the repatriation process, say three employees of a global consulting firm.

Ratanjee, Vibhas, and Andrzej Pyrka, "Fixing the Leadership Gap in Southeast Asia," Harvard Business Review, May 27, 2105, http://tinyurl.com/nlpwvn3.

To increase their share of the global economy, Southeast Asian countries should develop the skills of local executives and rely less on expatriate executives for business leadership, say two Singapore-based employees of global research and consulting firm Gallup.

Technology

Carey, Scott, "Expedia supports global workforce collaboration for 18,000 users with Dropbox cloud file storage, eyes Project Infinite," Computerworld UK, April 27, 2016, http://tinyurl.com/z2jaqbd.

Travel-booking website Expedia implemented a business-oriented version of Dropbox, a cloud-based storage platform, that will allow its global workforce to securely share information through a central system, rather than through individual Dropbox accounts.

Craig, Ryan, "LinkedIn And The Golden Age Of American Education," TechCrunch, Feb. 26, 2016, http://tinyurl.com/jqa6nru.

Web job portals and employee profiles have streamlined the hiring process, say experts, and the CEO of job-centric social networking site LinkedIn expects every company and member of the global workforce to eventually have a tailored profile.

Sweet, Julie, "Access to Digital Technology Accelerates Global Gender Equality," Harvard Business Review, May 17, 2016, http://tinyurl.com/jsuldwk.

Developing countries can broaden the global talent pool for companies and bridge a gender-based skills gap by boosting access to technology for women, according to research by management consulting firm Accenture.

Training

Gordon, Sarah, "On board for Eurostar's journey across cultures," Financial Times, May 23, 2016, http://tinyurl.com/hnrr7zc.

European train operator Eurostar teaches its entire workforce, ranging from senior management to hospitality staff, how to better communicate with guests and colleagues from various cultural backgrounds and also has its own in-house language school.

Molinsky, Andy, "The Mistake Most Managers Make with Cross-Cultural Training," Harvard Business Review, Jan. 15, 2015, http://tinyurl.com/knk2lpv.

Cross-cultural training programs often emphasize cultural differences but do not train employees to adapt to specific situations or give them real-life examples to test their training, says a professor of international management at Brandeis University.

Vollmar, Rick, "Cultural Training: Conference Addresses 'Intercultural Competence,'" Bloomberg BNA, March 17, 2016, http://tinyurl.com/zq9q3op.

Firms entering global commerce must have policies and practices that work effectively across cultural lines, and they are more likely to succeed if they train employees to be culturally competent, said international business experts at a March conference in Washington, D.C.

Organizations

AACSB International
777 S. Harbour Island Blvd., Suite 750, Tampa, FL 33602
813-367-5238
www.aacsb.edu

Global association dedicated to advancing management education worldwide.

Association for Talent Development
1640 King St., Alexandria, VA 22314
1-800-628-2783
www.td.org

Professional association that supports those who develop knowledge and skills of employees in organizations around the world.

The Conference Board
845 Third Ave., New York, NY 10022-6660

212-339-0900

www.conferenceboard.org

Nonprofit business membership and research organization.

Society for Human Resource Management

1800 Duke St., Alexandria, VA 22314

1-800-283-7476

www.shrm.org

World's largest human resources membership organization.

United Nations Conference on Trade and Development

Palais des Nations, 8–14, Avenue de la Paix, 1211 Geneva 10, Switzerland

41-22-917-1234

www.Unctad.org

United Nations body responsible for dealing with international trade.

World Trade Organization

Centre William Rappard, Rue de Lausanne 154, 1211 Geneva 21,Switzerland

www.wto.org

Organization dealing with the global rules of trade.

Worldwide ERC

4401 Wilson Blvd., Suite 510, Arlington, VA 22203

703-842-3400

www.worldwideerc.org

Association for those who manage international employee transfers.

Q&A: Paula Caligiuri on Cultural Agility

"CEOS ARE SAYING THEY ARE DESPERATE FOR PEOPLE WHO HAVE CULTURAL AGILITY"

Paula Caligiuri, a professor of international business and strategy at Northeastern University in Boston, is an expert on how to succeed in a cross-cultural environment. She previously was a professor and the director of the Center for Human Resource Strategy at Rutgers University. Caligiuri is the author of "Cultural Agility: Building a Pipeline of Successful Global Professionals" and co-author of "Managing the Global Workforce." Caligiuri talked with SAGE Business Researcher freelance correspondent Susan Ladika. This is an edited transcript of their conversation.

How would you describe cultural agility?

Cultural agility is the individual ability to quickly, comfortably and effectively work in different cultures and with people from different countries. Cultural agility is the ability to know how to respond in a given cultural context.

For years it has been a belief that adaptation was critical. Actually that's not true. There are times when one does need to adapt—sales, marketing, government relations and the like; and there are times when one needs to hold to the standards of your company—safety, ethics, production schedules. There are lots of reasons to say, "You know what, I understand we're doing it differently here, but we need to maintain the standards of my company or my own ethical standards." And then there are times you need to slow down and integrate: "It's not going to be your way, it's not going to be my way, we're going to have to come up with a new approach. A completely new way of working." What we're finding is that highly effective, culturally agile professionals are able to toggle across those three when needed.

What are important traits of culturally agile individuals?

Individuals who are culturally agile tend to share certain cultural competencies like perspective taking, tolerance of ambiguity, humility, and resilience.

Is cultural agility something you're born with or predisposed to, or is it something you can develop?

What we've found is, there are certain attributes of individuals that tend to help them more readily attain cultural agility. Some of those are dispositionally based, relatively immutable traits. They have a component of them that is heritable. I'm not saying you're totally hardwired for it, but for those who have certain personality traits like openness, emotional strength and social orientation, gaining cultural agility becomes much easier.

What can help someone gain cultural agility?

There are two erroneous assumptions of how cultural agility is built. One is you can train everything. The truth is, cross-cultural training is exceedingly helpful for helping people gain cognitive awareness of what might be different, or how people might see the world differently. There's a value in building that awareness first. But it's a myth to believe that's all that is needed.

The other part of it is really a deeper experiential opportunity. There's a belief that if you send people on an expatriate assignment, uproot an individual and his and her family, put them in another country for a number of years, then bring them back or send them on to other place, they gain cultural agility. The problem with that assumption is that while it is true that living and working internationally can be exceedingly developmental for cultural agility, it's not necessarily the case that just because you're breathing the air of another country means you're gaining cultural agility.

What needs to happen while you're there are very specific elements. Things like having opportunities to receive feedback on your cultural behaviors, having opportunities to work with host nation peers or peers from different countries and cultures, and having the opportunity to see the limits of your own knowledge. Unless you understand the cultural context in which you're operating, you can't be successful. Individuals realize their professional skills aren't enough to be successful. That's when they let humility kick in. When that switch flips is when cultural agility starts building.

Why is it so important for multinational corporations to have people on board who have these kind of skills?

CEOs are having to cancel strategic initiatives because they don't have enough effective professionals to run these

(Continued)

(Continued)

initiatives. CEOs are saying they are desperate for people who have cultural agility. We have CEOs saying they're not very good at cultural agility, and HR saying it's a problem because they aren't very good at building cultural agility.

The challenge for too long has been organizations believing they'll take folks with the best technical skills and then assume everyone can gain cultural agility from international assignments.

Instead, bring the right people in and give them progressively more challenging opportunities in different cultures and with people from different countries. It could be working on a global team, being mentored by someone from a different culture, working on a short-term project and ultimately working on a well-constructed international assignment.

If there's a shortage now and we've got increasing demand for these types of people, will we ever catch up?

There are a lot of people out there in domestic jobs who can be fantastic in global ones. They'll understand the limits of their knowledge and spend more time understanding the context they're operating in. I think we have to do a better job of selection because I believe those folks are out there.

WOMEN IN MANAGEMENT
How can the talent pipeline bottleneck be cleared?

Joanne Cleaver

EXECUTIVE SUMMARY

In nearly every industry, women are well represented in management until they approach the senior echelon. At that point, they begin to fall away. When they leave, companies lose the many documented advantages that women possess as leaders and innovators. The absence of senior women exacerbates the gender pay gap and becomes self-perpetuating when rising women see no further upward path for them. Formal corporate initiatives intended to retain women can be undermined by structural and cultural barriers. Some widely held beliefs about why women leave—such as the assumption that family responsibilities derail career ambitions—have been debunked by recent research. As women and companies seek to address these concerns, here are some key takeaways:

- Research demonstrates that the presence of women in leadership positions correlates with better corporate performance, and investors are taking note.

- Pay inequity and position inequity are closely related, and greater company transparency can help improve the situation.

- Sponsorship is a key element in enabling women to climb the corporate ladder.

OVERVIEW

The young woman stands in front of a restroom mirror, nervously rehearsing talking points she might use to persuade her boss to give her a raise. It's not going well.

Then a toilet flushes, Lucy freezes in embarrassment, and an older woman appears beside her. After a momentary pause, the older woman turns and snaps, "Do it!" Lucy's face morphs from diffidence to determination.

The television commercial for the women's deodorant Secret, titled "Raise," has already attracted 1.3 million YouTube views.[1] It also has generated a robust discussion about a host

From *SAGE Business Researcher*,
October 24, 2016

of issues: the angst that working women feel about advocating for themselves, the power of Baby Boomer women to influence their peers and effect change within companies, and the barriers that hold back women in the corporate world. [2]

The 2016 ad was well-timed, because women's status in the workplace has become top-of-mind in the national conversation, dominating headlines, claiming top billing at events such as the annual Davos gathering of international leaders, generating White House and congressional reports and propelling discussions in nearly every industry.[3] The issue turns on a conundrum: Female advancement helps a company's bottom line as well as its female employees, but progress has been slow to materialize.

A host of recent research reports show that a higher proportion of female leaders correlates with better corporate performance. For example, an International Monetary Fund study of 2 million companies across 34 European countries found that adding a single woman to senior management or a corporate board resulted in a 3 percent to 8 percent increase in return on corporate assets. [4] Researchers and senior executives attribute the performance edge to the power of drawing on diverse perspectives when working through complicated problems.

"If I pick my team from everybody and you pick your team from middle-aged white men, I guarantee I'll pick a better team," JPMorgan Chase CEO Jamie Dimon told a panel discussion audience last month. [5]

Similarly, the Washington-based Peterson Institute for International Economics found a "positive correlation between firm performance and the share of women in upper management." Its study concluded that "a profitable firm at which 30 percent of leaders are women could expect to add more than 1 percentage point to its net margin compared with an otherwise similar firm with no female leaders." [6]

And female-owned and managed hedge funds produced better returns than the overall alternative fund sector, according to the KPMG Women in Alternative Investments Report.[7]

Yet evidence indicates the pipeline that should be supplying companies with talented female candidates for high management posts often hits a bottleneck just before the top level. According to research by Catalyst, a New York-based women's research and advocacy group, women make up 44.3 percent of all employees at S&P 500 companies and 36.4 percent of first-and middle-level managers. But they are just 25.1 percent of senior executives, officials and managers—and only 4.6 percent of chief executive officers.[8]

Things don't get much better when the sample is broadened, according to a report by DiscoverOrg.com, a Vancouver, Wash.-based data-mining company. It surveyed the Fortune 1000—the 1,000 largest U.S. companies, according to Fortune magazine—and found that women made up less than 10 percent of the four most powerful roles: board chair, chief executive officer, chief operating officer and chief financial officer.[9]

This situation persists even at a moment when a woman has been nominated by a major political party for the most powerful job in the world, president of the United States.

"Quite frankly, the numbers are embarrassing," wrote Deborah Gillis, Catalyst's CEO, in a commentary published by CNBC. "This simply isn't good enough if equality is the goal. . . . This isn't about women [versus] men; it's about jointly creating workplaces where everyone can succeed."[10]

Companies have found that there's no easy answer and no single solution to retaining women in the talent pipeline. Training and work-life programs help, but the root problem is that work is misaligned with women's lives, requiring attention to issues such as how children are cared for and how to affect career length and trajectory.

"We don't need to fix women. We need to help men understand the realities that women face and how men can help create a more inclusive environment," says Jennifer Laidlaw, head of gender diversity and inclusion for the Canadian Imperial Bank of Commerce (CIBC), which this year adopted individual performance goals for each manager's progress in advancing women among his or her direct reports.

A 2015 study by the McKinsey consulting firm and the nonprofit women's advocacy group LeanIn.org, championed by Facebook chief operating officer Sheryl Sandberg, concluded that subtle obstacles prevent women from advancing toward the C-suite.[11] It found that women are less likely to have line duties that provide hands-on responsibility for generating profits, a requirement for qualifying for a top-level role.[12] And the study found that because women are still expected to simultaneously carry responsibility for both professional and family success, the escalating stress saps their ambitions, even as they approach the C-level.[13]

Additionally, the study revealed a significant perception gap between genders that may hamper companies' efforts to advance women. It found that 88 percent of men surveyed said they thought women had as many or more opportunities in the workplace as men, while 57 percent of women agreed with that statement.[14]

When women are picked for the top slot, it is often because the company is in trouble, a syndrome that has been dubbed "the glass cliff" because of its high-risk nature. In an 2010 experiment in which researchers from the United States and Germany surveyed a group of college students, 62 percent of the participants picked a male candidate to lead a company that was doing well. For a company in crisis, 69 percent chose a female. The underlying assumption is that women possess characteristics that are important in damage-control situations, such as empathy, problem-solving ability and a high capacity for multitasking.[15]

That can easily set up a female chief executive for failure, said Nyla R. Branscombe, a University of Kansas psychology professor who co-wrote the paper about the experiment. "She will be more likely to fail and we don't see it as due to the conditions she was entering the position under," Branscombe told The Wall Street Journal. "Rather, we'll see it as, 'Well, women just can't do it.'"[16]

Fortune devoted an entire article to this dynamic, citing case after case of women brought in to turn around a company's dire circumstances. It cited a Utah State University study finding that 42 percent of female CEOs were named to their position during a company crisis, compared with 22 percent of males.[17] For example, Mary Barra took the wheel at General Motors in January 2014, and the following month had to announce the recall of 2.6 million vehicles for faulty ignition switches—a problem that had been brewing for years.[18] Meg Whitman, who built eBay into an international peer-to-peer selling platform, was then brought in by Hewlett-Packard to repair a company fractured by a series of failed leaders, among them its first woman CEO, Carly Fiorina.

And old-fashioned misogyny and bias haven't disappeared. A lawsuit by Fox News anchor Gretchen Carlson accusing the network's chairman, Roger Ailes, of sexually harassing her for years triggered a raft of similar accusations and legal actions from other women.[19] Fox apologized to Carlson and settled her lawsuit, and Ailes resigned from the network.[20]

KPMG, a Big Four accounting firm that has a female CEO, Lynne Doughtie, and which won an award in 2015 for being a top workplace for women, was sued the following year by more than 1,000 current and former employees for gender discrimination and lack of opportunity.[21]

Less Than 5 Percent of S&P 500 CEOs Are Women

Female CEOs are far more likely than their male counterparts to be targeted by activist investors because they perceive that women will be easier to influence, according to a study by Arizona State University's W.P. Carey School of Business.[22]

Nearly every industry struggles with the issue of female representation in top-level posts. While the technology industry is chronically under fire for its poor record of advancing women, women are also disproportionately absent from leadership in health care, pharmaceuticals and advertising.[23]

Still, the business advantages of greater female representation at high levels are so compelling that women and companies are exploring new paths. Fresh initiatives are identifying

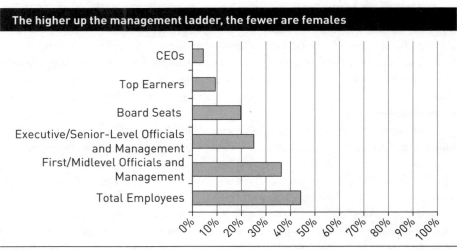

The higher up the management ladder, the fewer are females

Women made up 44.3 percent of all employees at S&P 500 companies in 2016, but only 4.6 percent of CEOs. The higher up the management ladder at these companies, the fewer positions are female-occupied.

Note: Data as of Sept. 19, 2016.

Source: "Women in S&P 500 Companies," Catalyst, http://tinyurl.com/qcnwko5.

specific targets for progress, such as the Rockefeller Foundation's "100×25" effort to pull 100 women into CEO positions at Fortune 500 companies by 2025.[24] Some industries—banking, public accounting, supply chain, cable television—are trying to revise cultural and leadership norms to better align company, industry and women's goals. [25] Corporate leaders are starting to challenge each other to collectively do better.[26]

"You think of it as you do any client problem," says Risa Lavine, chief of staff for CohnReznick, a national accounting firm. "If you had a client experiencing difficulties with a particular market, you'd bring all your brain power to solve that problem, because it's important for your client's success. Why is advancing women any different? It's a business problem."

Katie Bullard, chief marketing officer of DiscoverOrg.com, which did the survey on women in Fortune 100 companies, says that simply defining the problem will help solve it. "As people are conscious that having different perspectives on teams results in different decisions, we'll have more opportunities to live the business case for having more women," she says.

As women and companies alike seek to cope with these concerns, here are the central issues under debate:

Weighing the Issues

Is advancing women a "silver bullet" for pay equity?

Pay equity for women was an issue that had lurked for years on the cusp of public awareness, kept alive by activists and think tanks like the Washington-based Institute for Women's Policy Research. "We've been working on this forever," says Ariane Hegewisch, the institute's program director for employment and earnings.

Then came the 2015 Oscars awards ceremony and the acceptance speech by Best Supporting Actress winner Patricia Arquette.[27] She delivered an unexpected and impassioned call for action for equal pay on behalf, she said, of every working woman. Instantly, Arquette became a leading voice on the much-studied topic, touching off a swell of public policy, corporate and celebrity pledges.

Since then, reports on the issue from think tanks such as Hegewisch's are gaining wider attention. In the current iteration of the debate, the term "pay equity" has rapidly become shorthand for the entire spectrum of issues encompassing working women and their status.

"With a record number of women in the workforce and nearly two-thirds of women functioning as primary or co-bread winners for their families, equal pay for women is critical to families' economic security," said Lisa M. Maatz, vice president of government relations for the American Association of University Women.[28]

Carnegie Mellon University professor Linda Babcock opened a new line of thought in 2007 with the publication of "Women Don't Ask," co-authored with independent researcher Sara Laschever.[29] Based on Babcock's research that found that women hold back from negotiating on their own behalf, they recommended that women become more assertive and that they cultivate negotiation skills for personal and business applications. Babcock says a woman can forfeit more than $500,000 over her lifetime as the consequence of not negotiating. [30]

Actress Patricia Arquette delivered an impassioned call for equal pay as she accepted the Best Supporting Actress Oscar in February 2015.

Source: Robyn Beck/AFP/Getty Images

Pay equity has become such a hot topic partly because Millennial women are surprised it is still a topic at all, says Hegewisch. Women excel in college, which rewards playing by the rules. Then they get a job "and expect the workplace to reward their performance the same way as school, and they find out the world isn't quite like that," she says. "Young women believe that performance is what matters, and that of course employers will recognize that."

Arquette's call for action coincided with Millennial women's dawning realization, fueled by digital media, that the pay gap worsens as they progress in their careers, says Hegewisch.[31]

A key driver of pay inequity is position inequity, according to Maatz.[32]

The much-cited figure that American white women who work full time are paid about 79 cents for every dollar earned by American white male full-time workers is widely debated, partly because it obscures so many factors.[33] An analysis by Fast Company magazine identified several important drivers, including the fact that men occupy more higher-ranking, higher-paying jobs, thus tipping aggregate pay in their direction.[34]

Career data service Glassdoor.com said that in the United States, about 67 percent of the pay gap for various positions was explained by experience, education, performance and other factors, leaving a third of the gap unexplained.[35] Controlling for all those key factors, Glassdoor found residual pay gaps that ranged from 7.2 percent in the health care and insurance industries to 2.5 percent in aerospace and defense.[36]

By occupation, male computer programmers make 28.3 percent more than female programmers, according to the Glassdoor survey, and male medical technicians an additional 14.4 percent. Female social workers, merchandisers and research assistants make more than their male counterparts, while therapists, event coordinators and logistics managers are positions where Glassdoor found pay to be equitable.

Evidence continues to emerge that women are not paid equitably, even when they outperform their male peers. In one case involving such an allegation, a Washington attorney, Kerrie L. Campbell, asserted in a $100 million suit that her law firm systematically paid male lawyers more than female peers through an arbitrary scoring system, even if the males brought in less revenue. (The firm has denied the allegations and said her case is "riddled with falsehoods.")[37]

In April of this year, members of the U.S. women's national soccer team—winners in 2015 of the sport's ultimate prize, the World Cup—filed a complaint with the federal Equal Employment Opportunity Commission (EEOC) contending that they were paid substantially less than the men's team, which was far less successful on the field.[38]

The pay equity debate has spawned a spectrum of initiatives by employers:

- The city of Alexandria, Va., conducted a pay equity analysis of its municipal jobs and announced that it found "substantial gender equity."[39]

- While nonprofits tend to hire female chief executive officers, male CEOs make 23 percent more at larger nonprofits, according to the research group GuideStar USA.[40]

- Amazon found that women at the company were paid 99.9 percent of what men made in identical jobs, based on a staff survey conducted in response to pressure from the Securities and Exchange Commission (SEC) and activist shareholder Arjuna Capital.[41]

- Responding to White House advocacy, 28 high-profile companies had signed on to the White House Equal Pay Pledge by August 2016, and the effort has continued to pick up corporate support.[42]

- The White House itself was found to have a 13 percent gender pay gap, largely attributed to the fact that more male staffers hold higher-ranking, higher-paying positions, according to a Washington Post survey.[43]

- Major employers, including Microsoft and Facebook, announced that they had "achieved gender pay equality."[44]

- The EEOC is considering adopting a regulation requiring employers to report pay data for several "bands" of positions.[45]

U.S. women's national soccer team members Alex Morgan, Lauren Holiday (face hidden), Abby Wambach and Whitney Engen celebrate 2015 World Cup victory. In 2016, some team members filed a complaint contending they were paid less than the men's team.

Source: Christopher Morris/Corbis via Getty Images

As the debate becomes more nuanced, reports and proposed solutions are proliferating. Variable Labs, a California-based virtual reality simulation-design firm, has created a pay equity negotiation simulator that aims to help women sharpen their skills—replicating Lucy's bathroom-mirror practice in the Secret ad. Research sites such as Comparably.com seek to close the transparency gap by providing detailed and relevant pay data, which equips women and minorities to more effectively benchmark current pay levels so they are equipped to negotiate.

Solutions are complex, says Hegewisch, because equity involves drawing women into higher-paying professions, as outlined in her organization's "Pathways to Equity" report, and addressing issues of child care, career longevity and definitions of success.[46] The current intense focus on pay equity might finally catalyze change, she says, especially given that "the discussion is about transparency and about jobs that are substantially equal, and about responsibility. That is exciting."

Is sponsorship the key to keeping women in the leadership pipeline?

Ask and you shall receive. That's the essential dynamic of executive sponsorship, says Lois Frankel, a psychologist who wrote "Nice Girls Don't Get the Corner Office" and has advocated for women in leadership since 1988.

An executive sponsorship can open doors to the executive ranks. But accomplished midlevel women can find themselves in a quandary: They have to know highly influential potential sponsors to get a sponsor. And while many women are familiar with utilizing mentors—confidants who provide behind-the-scenes coaching and guidance—to gain insight into their potential, tapping the power offered by sponsors—powerful high-profile advocates who recommend rising women for specific opportunities—is relatively new.[47]

"Not all career propellants have equal power," according to Sylvia Ann Hewlett, an early advocate of sponsorship.[48] She is a former Harvard Business School professor and now CEO of the Center for Talent Innovation, a New York City-based think tank; founder of her own consulting firm, Hewlett Consulting Partners LLC; and co-director of the Woman's Leadership Program at the Columbia University Business School.

Hewlett identifies what she sees as crucial differences between mentors and sponsors. She defines mentors as experienced leaders acting "as a role model and close adviser to a junior protégé, imparting his/her knowledge and professional expertise."[49] With the 2011 publication of her book, "The Sponsor Effect," Hewlett made a compelling case that mentors were not enough. "While both [mentors and sponsors] are absolutely necessary to career success, they are distinctly different—and so is their ability to significantly change the course of a career."

The opportunities that sponsors can promote women for, writes Hewlett, can break through intended and unconscious barriers that sideline women from responsibilities that qualify them for C-titles.[50]

She wrote that effective sponsors recommend and advocate for their candidates to win "stretch" assignments involving challenges that prove their mettle; major promotions that boost their power, prestige and pay; positions and projects that accelerate career trajectory; and assignments that introduce women to new, highly placed circles of influencers. These can include board members; executives (not functionaries) with key customers and clients; and marquee community leaders.

Sponsorship tends to happen organically for men, as they have opportunities through informal networking (golf, other sports and after-hours pursuits) from which women are often excluded, either because they have conflicting responsibilities or because they aren't welcome in male-dominated settings.[51] A widely cited McKinsey study found that women have to work harder to win the same opportunities as men, and that women choose support roles that offer greater chances of success even while trading away operational experience that might qualify them for the C-suite.[52]

The sponsorship concept has caught on quickly and been adopted by many employers. The World Economic Forum, which runs the annual Davos gathering of A-list leaders, conducted an internal diversity review and in 2016 diagnosed a significant gender gap: 46 percent of its employees, but only 16.5 percent of its senior managers, are women.[53] Its solution: pick a group of high-potential, experienced women and assign them top-level sponsors.

The results of the program are being measured by both the percentage of participating women in "new or broader" jobs and the "amount of interaction" between each participant and sponsor. Since its inception in 2009, the program has resulted in 50 percent of its participating women gaining jobs that are new, broader or more visible, and, four have been promoted to the level that reports directly to the C-suite.

Catalyst, the women's advocacy nonprofit, also identified sponsorship as a differentiating factor for women headed to the top. Sponsors put their own credibility on the line, the report pointed out, and the stakes are high for both sponsor and candidate.[54]

Several of the dynamics Catalyst identified in its research (such as candidates learning inside knowledge about what it takes to succeed) tie in with another missing link—confidence—highlighted by journalists Katty Kay and Claire Shipman.[55] They argued in "The Confidence Code," first published in 2014, that women hesitate to self-promote partly based on society's expectations of gender roles and partly because they believe they must be perfectly suited for a new opportunity. Men tend to plunge ahead even if they think they meet just 60 percent of the criteria.[56]

Even as sponsorship becomes accepted wisdom as a powerful driver of women's success, new evidence continues to emerge that underscores Hewlett's position that the best way to ensure that diverse candidates enjoy the benefits of the power of sponsors is through structured programs.[57]

A Pew Research Center study released in September found that companies often give women less challenging work even at workplaces with specific programs to develop their skills.[58]

A Harvard Business Review article commenting on the Pew research recommended that initiatives intended to help women be accompanied by training and tools to help managers think carefully about how the initiatives are used.[59]Another study found that formal programs are very effective at putting women on leaders' radar screens and cultivating influential relationships.[60]

"Women have to align themselves with potential sponsors and make the relationship a win-win," says Frankel. "You want to make the sponsor a star-maker so that sponsoring you builds their reputation."

White Women Outnumber Females of Other Races on Boards

CohnReznick, the accounting firm, tracks sponsorship relationships to ensure that women are equitably included and that partners and principals are engaged as sponsors, says Lavine. Mutual accountability, she says, is at least as effective as a formal women's initiative, because it shifts culture instead of scheduling opportunity.

"Retention and development is an integral part of leadership competence," she says. "If one gender is leaving or not advancing as much, then you're not living up to your responsibilities as a leader. That's really starting to resonate throughout the firm. The reality is that working together makes that kind of progress."

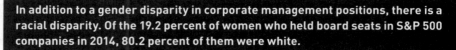

In addition to a gender disparity in corporate management positions, there is a racial disparity. Of the 19.2 percent of women who held board seats in S&P 500 companies in 2014, 80.2 percent of them were white.

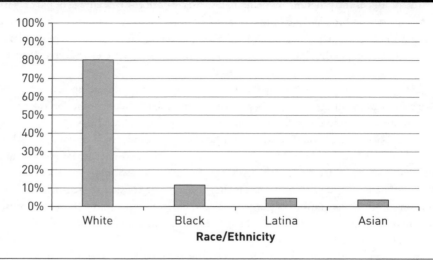

Source: "2014 S&P 500 Board Seats Held by Women by Race/Ethnicity," Catalyst, http://tinyurl.com/zcd3393.

Vivian Moller has seen first-hand much of the recent history of women's striving to reach the C-suite. She is chief financial officer of Hoffman York, a Milwaukee advertising and marketing firm. Female CFOs are a rarity, composing 14 percent of those at Fortune 500 companies.[61]

In the late 1990s, Moller made a midlife career switch from media to finance. She joined Hoffman York as an accounting manager, was promoted to controller and then to CFO. Men mentored and sponsored her, she said, and she now pays it forward by mentoring and sponsoring the next generation.

"Women coming up these days are a lot more open about their expectations," says Moller. "They want to know what their path is to succeed. It's not a checklist: 'Do this and you'll be CFO,' but there's more openness. They want to know, how will you help me succeed? Will it be training or by being a mentor? If I join this company, what will this mean eventually for my career?"

Programs are undertaken because of pressing needs and then fall into irrelevance as conditions and cultures change, Moller says. While focusing on helping the next generation of women, she says she also has come to realize that "part of leadership is not waiting to see everything quantified before you move forward. You need to understand your goals, and the work, and your people, and be flexible along the way."

Will transparency on pay open new doors for women?

Natasha Lamb couldn't believe the timing.

For months, she had been working on shareholder campaigns designed to pressure high-profile, publicly held companies to publicly report the status of gender pay equity among their employees. As managing partner and director of equity research and shareholder engagement at Boston-based Arjuna Capital, she had launched a campaign to call out companies that hid behind what she regarded as outdated excuses for avoiding the issue.

In winter 2015, her overture to eBay's board of directors requesting a pay equity report was rejected. A couple of days later, actress Arquette delivered her speech about pay equity at the Oscar ceremony.

"The timing was amazing," says Lamb. "Here was Patricia Arquette with this amazing limelight. . . . It was reported everywhere, and that cracked open the public conversation about our investor action with eBay, and there has been so much momentum since then."

Another of her wins involved an argument to the Securities and Exchange Commission in March 2016 that helped persuade the SEC to order Amazon to let its shareholders vote on gender pay equity.[62]

As Lamb's campaign escalates—she says seven of the nine companies she has approached have taken action—she has gained a national reputation for her strategy.[63] "Remarkably, nobody had ever approached it from the angle of shareholders. That carries a lot of weight," she says.

Greater transparency is quickly emerging as a powerful force for changing deep-rooted corporate practices and culture that have prevented women from achieving critical mass at the executive level. Invigorated activists—some representing investors, such as pension boards and funds, and some representing specific causes—are challenging companies to build trust by revealing details about their records.[64]

Until recently, companies have seeded presentations, press releases and sponsorships with positive stories; that is no longer sufficient, says Michele Tesoro-Tess, managing director for Italy, Switzerland and the Middle East for the Reputation Institute, which measures the business impact of corporate reputation. The public, investors and business partners want to see proof that a company has good results in advancing women, not just good intentions, he says.

"There is a direct correlation between the presence of women at the top and reputation," says Tesoro-Tess. "It's evidence that the company is investing in its corporate social responsibility role, and that translates to market value."

The Reputation Institute estimates that companies ranked higher by the public on creating equal opportunity for employees can capture greater "intention to buy" and have stronger appeal to potential employees. Overall, corporate social responsibility factors, which also include environmental and sustainability practices, account for 40 percent of a company's reputation capital, says Tesoro-Tess.

Lamb says that just since 2015, the default position has shifted from polite reluctance to disclose, to disclosure as a point of corporate leadership and reputation. For instance, when Intel Corp. decided to disclose its diversity numbers, it did so in the context of its goals and progress toward achieving those objectives.[65] In challenging his tech industry peers to match his company's level of disclosure, Intel CEO Brian Krzanich told National Public

Radio that there's no good reason not to disclose: "There's nothing here [that's] top secret or should not be shared with the rest of the world."[66]

Greater disclosure means companies share their results, for better or worse. A policy of disclosure means that backward steps, such as the fact that Microsoft had a net loss of 2 percent of its female workers in 2015, are released just as regularly as public relations wins.[67] While companies are pivoting to present transparency as a win, the media can pounce on corporate attempts at diversity messaging that are erroneous, incomplete or subject to being interpreted as hypocritical, as in this Vanity Fair headline from April 2016: "Paypal Promotes 'Gender Equality' Panel Without Any Women."

Because there are no national or industry standards for what data companies should release, "the onus is on them to do it right and to do it well, to report factually and accurately," says Lamb. Now that peer pressure is on the side of transparency, the dynamic is starting to turn to companies competing to be the best at telling their stories more completely.[68] Apple's first salary gap was calculated on base salaries; in its 2016 report, the company recalculated to include bonuses and equity ownership, says Lamb. "We are seeing companies more quickly address inequities," she says.

Marc Benioff, CEO of cloud services firm Salesforce, went public when the company discovered a $3 million gender pay gap. Salesforce got media attention at every stage of correcting the gap, turning the potentially embarrassing situation into a bonanza of proactive communication and even a "leadership summit" for women.[69]

Cracking open the "black box" around pay resets the conversation about all kinds of barriers to advancing women and minorities, says Tesoro-Tess. Accountability and transparency are compelling drivers of reputation and trust, he says, and "values drive the value proposition.'"

BACKGROUND

Early Pathfinders

With almost no path to the top of business, a few women at the turn of the last century created their own companies. Cosmetics and hair care were natural categories for launching a company from the kitchen table: Madam C.J. Walker, an African-American, started a hair products company in 1905 that became a powerhouse by 1917. In the same period, Elizabeth Arden started her eponymous cosmetics company.[70]

In the aftermath of World War II, women who had worked in defense industries were encouraged to return to the home. But in 1950, a restless Brownie Wise converted her living room into a sales machine, inventing the party plan model of direct selling and propelling Tupperware (headed by the plastic ware's inventor, Earl Tupper) to national prominence by providing a channel for women's business ambitions.[71]

In the mid-20th century, 35 percent of women were working, including nearly a quarter of married women. Only 6 percent of working women had management positions.[72] One generation and two decades later, feminism was taking root, inflation was ravaging family budgets and women started working en masse for the first time in modern history, accounting for 36 percent of management positions by 1985.[73]

"A Louis Harris poll conducted in 1980 revealed basic differences between the sexes in attitudes toward work," economist George Guilder wrote in The Atlantic.[74] "Unlike the working men surveyed, who overwhelmingly preferred full-time jobs, working women expressed a preference for part-time over full-time work by a 41 to 17 percent margin. The women with the highest earnings capacity—managerial, professional and executive women—preferred part-time work by a 51 to 19 percent margin."

Meanwhile, a milestone was reached in 1972, when Katharine Meyer Graham became CEO of The Washington Post Co., the first woman to lead a Fortune 500 company. It took another 37 years before a black woman—Ursula Burns of Xerox—first ascended to the top spot at a Fortune 500 company. When Burns replaced Anne Mulcahy, it was also the first time one woman had replaced another at such a company.

The 1980s brought big ideas, big hair and big shoulders: John Molloy's "The Woman's Dress for Success Book," first published in 1977, defined a "professional uniform" for women in the corporate world, and Working Woman magazine, founded in 1976, reached its zenith in the '80s.[75] (The magazine folded in 2001.[76])

Impact of the Internet

The 1990s saw the reinvention of work, thanks to the Internet. Women's presence in computer careers peaked in the 1990s and has steadily declined since, according to the U.S. Bureau of the Census.[77] Studies document a hostile culture in STEM workplaces as a primary reason women leave.[78] Women held about 13 percent of engineering positions in 2010. By 2014, about 57 percent of American women worked, and women constituted 5.4 percent of the top bosses at the 1,000 largest publicly held companies.[79]

The 2000s brought the 2008–09 recession, which coincided with shifting expectations as Millennials challenged traditional roles and definitions of success. The advancement of women began to be reframed as a social and economic win for families, companies, countries and women themselves. Companies started to measure the economic effect of retaining women and began to analyze the effects of lost top talent. Human resources managers realized that a talent shortage was in the demographic cards, and that added urgency to retaining women, as they were half of the employee base and half of management talent.

While women had been quietly questioning the payoff for pursuing executive positions, says psychologist Frankel, the discussion finally moved into the open as many women "realized that hard work by itself isn't enough. Women don't want to brag, but then they realize that men who self-promote get ahead, and their hard work doesn't speak for itself," she says.

Women, Men Agree That Workplace Gender Equality Is Important

For a few years in the early part of the 2000s, it was popular for CEOs to claim to be "gender blind" and to treat men and women just the same, Frankel says. That notion crumbled under the reality that "you can't treat men and women the same in the workplace because we as a society put extra expectations on women for childbearing, childrearing and caregiving," she says. "Yet, people who take time off to have children and to care for them aren't seen as committed."

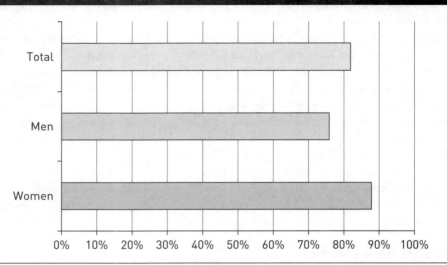

While most Americans of both genders say equality in career advancement opportunities is important, more women than men said it's important for women and men to have the same career opportunities, with 88 percent of women and 76 percent of men agreeing.

Source: "Women in Leadership: Why It Matters," the Rockefeller Foundation, http://tinyurl.com/zlpjuqg.

In the 2000s, rising interest in leadership styles and an emerging body of academic research about gender differences in brain chemistry and communication spawned interest in the unique advantages of a "female" style of leadership.[80]

Collaborative leadership as opposed to the male style of command and control, along with consensus and emotional intelligence, were ascribed by consultants as strengths generally held by women. [81] These strengths were believed to deliver advantages when cultivating new clients, listening carefully to understand clients' and customers' true needs and forging strategies that addressed unspoken needs as well as explicit goals.[82]

Marti Barletta, a marketing consultant who was influential in the late 1990s, introduced insights about how women make decisions (in a spiral, collecting more detail and data as they work toward a decision, compared to a more immediate process supposedly favored by men) that crystallized some of the intuitive strengths that women are believed to bring to corporate leadership.[83]

Babies Versus Bosses

One common view was that women take themselves off the leadership track because they want to spend time with their families. And, in the 1980s and 1990s, Working Mother magazine fashioned itself as the premiere advocate for this group, ranking companies on the basis of benefits that addressed the needs of mothers of young children, such as on-site child care.[84]

But the recession intersected with the shifting expectations of a new generation of parents to change the equation. Millennial parents, lacking both time and money, want career responsibilities to mesh with family life.[85] With stagnant earnings and high student debt, many parents face tough choices about child care, which in 2014 cost 70 percent more than in 1985, adjusted for inflation.[86] Yet, women are the primary or sole breadwinner in 40 percent of American households.[87] Their families count on their earnings, which may help explain McKinsey's 2015 study that found that mothers were 15 percent more interested in being an executive than women without children.[88] About 72 percent of Americans age 40 and older support some sort of child care credit or support, according to an Associated Press-NORC survey done this year.[89]

In 2016, affordable, quality child care—a central issue for working women—became a topic in the presidential election, with Republican nominee Donald J. Trump and Democratic candidate Hillary Clinton both offering programs aimed at easing the financial burden on parents of young children.[90] This prompted The New York Times to declare child care "The Fight Working Moms Won," citing the campaigns' positions as evidence that the issue of whether paid childcare was acceptable—and by extension whether it was detrimental to children to have a working mother—was now moot.[91]

As with pay equity, some states passed their own requirements for paid leave; New Jersey, for instance, adopted in 2009 a law that requires employers to give employees six weeks of partially paid leave.[92]

CURRENT SITUATION

Right Makes Bright?

Is advancing women the right thing to do? The bright thing to do?

It's not a matter of picking a slogan, says Barbara Annis, a consultant on gender issues, member of the executive committee of the Women's Leadership Board at Harvard University's Kennedy School of Government and co-author of the 2014 book "Gender Intelligence: Breakthrough Strategies for Increasing Diversity and Improving Your Bottom Line."

"We've made tremendous progress with women in middle management," she says. "But there are a lot of misassumptions about why women aren't making it to the top levels. The leadership blind spots are, 'Women don't want it, women can't hack it, they are not advancing because of work-life balance.' And the conversation is based on the 1 percent of the population—women who have a choice as to whether they will work." The economic reality, though, means that "women want and need to work. They need the biggest paychecks they can get."

According to ManpowerGroup, a Milwaukee-based staffing firm, 32 percent of U.S. employers are having trouble filling jobs.[93] And companies are well aware that if they lose women, they could close off access to half of their potential leaders, not to mention forfeiting a huge investment in training and in capacity to simply accomplish the current workload.[94]

One deep-rooted obstacle is the dynamic that women are promoted on the basis of past performance while men are promoted on the basis of potential, Annis says.

A widely cited McKinsey study found that women have to work harder to win the same opportunities as men, and that women move into support roles that offer greater chances of success within narrowly defined career paths, even while trading away operational experience that might qualify them for the C-suite.[95]

Underlying these factors is the human tendency to recognize potential in people like ourselves, says Annis. "Men bond with men, so when they are assessing Bob and Carol for promotions, they'll say, 'Oh, Bob is great, he has a huge future.' They see his potential. And about Carol they say, 'She needs a little more experience,' or 'She needs to work in the trenches.' Yet, she has six more years of experience than Bob. He gets promoted based on potential and she gets promoted based on what she has done."

Breaking this nearly universal dynamic is less a matter of programs and more a matter of determination, says Annis. Leaders who question their own assumptions and are genuinely open to others' perspectives are more likely to recognize opportunities for change. "It's about leadership behavior and mindset," she says.

Programs and Culture

Women's initiatives—programs intended specifically to cultivate women—are a mixed bag, say Annis and other consultants. While women often benefit from settings that enable them to speak up without competing with men, programs need to be aligned with business goals and remain fluff-free to achieve their goals.[96] Simply constructing programs doesn't make a difference, and can even foster cynicism when the programs are disconnected from overall company goals, they say.[97] Programs that address positions and pay are most effective when they zero in on very specific problems, such as the circumstances of new mothers, whose earnings are eroded by child care costs and whose work days are complicated by fragmented childcare arrangements.

Annis says the most successful programs concentrate on solving clearly defined problems and measure results. For example, dozens of employers are expanding successful pilots of "returnship" programs that recruit women who have been largely out of the workforce to spend time with young families. The programs blend classes in technical skills with refreshers on workplace culture.[98] Not incidentally, they also create communities for returning midlife women so they can encourage and support their mutual aspirations.

"Appealing to diverse talent requires sensitivity and responsiveness to the particular needs of employees," wrote Nicole Stephens, an associate professor at the Kellogg School of Management at Northwestern University, and Evan Apfelbaum, an assistant professor at Massachusetts Institute of Technology's Sloan School of Management. "In fact, organizations that only take a 'cookie-cutter' approach may be likely to find their diversity efforts are not only ineffective, but counterproductive."[99]

LOOKING AHEAD

Measuring Progress

Victor Dodig, CEO of the CIBC, pledged in 2015 to advocate for more women on boards in the financial services and at Canadian companies.

That was when Jennifer Laidlaw realized that things were going to start changing fast at the bank. She is CIBC's head of gender diversity and inclusion, and she took Dodig's pledge as permission to tackle new ways of drawing more women to upper levels.

"One of the biggest differences is the extent to which we're engaging men," Laidlaw says. "We're no longer focusing on just developing women, but on developing all of our leaders and including men in the conversation about gender inclusion." One major shift is that as of 2016, the retention and advancement of women are now factored into CIBC managers' performances.

Academics and industry groups are coming up with new yardsticks to measure the status of women in industries, positions and professions, the better to detect small differences that can drive major change. For instance, the male-dominated venture capital industry hit a high-water mark in 2014 when 15 percent of early-stage companies had women on their executive teams, compared with 5 percent in 1999, according to a Babson College analysis.[100] The Babson study found that businesses with women on the executive team are "more likely to have higher valuations at both first and last funding (64 percent higher and 49 percent higher, respectively)."

Employers are starting to realize that women take cues—consciously and intuitively—from the ongoing discussion about how women rise and from the stories and career paths of current female leaders, according to Kate R. Salop, senior administrative dean at Brandeis University's International Business School.[101] And with the reality of lower earnings that must stretch over longer lifespans, working women of all ages are realizing that they must pace their careers accordingly, perhaps sticking it out in midcareer instead of assuming that they can step out, according to a Wall Street Journal report.[102]

Partly spurred by Millennials' refusal to take any aspect of workplace culture as is, some consultants are calling for a recalibration of the very definition of success. Perhaps, the consultants argue, women and Millennials together will tip the balance toward a holistic definition of family, personal and career success, from the one-dimensional definition of climbing to the top in terms of power, prestige and pay.[103]

The emerging wisdom is to position the advancement of women as a win-win-win for companies, women and men. Fast Company magazine outlined this as the No. 1 tactic for winning universal buy-in.[104]

CIBC is betting big on this strategy, says Laidlaw. "We have moved away from the concept that women need to change and be 'fixed' to fit into a male-dominated environment," she says. "That's been tried for 30 years, and if you train women not to be women, you lose the advantage of having women."

Chronology

1889–1909	**Women begin building companies**
1889	Anna Bissell becomes America's first female chief executive officer when she takes charge of the Bissell Inc. sweeper company after the death of her husband, the company's founder.
1902	Annie Malone, a daughter of slaves, creates a hair straightener for African-Americans. Peddling it door-to-door, she builds a million-dollar business by 1914.
1905	Madame C.J. Walker launches a hair-care product empire, becoming one of the country's first prominent African-American female entrepreneurs.
1910–1949	**Women defined as a distinct market that women are uniquely qualified to serve.**
1910	Coco Chanel interprets menswear for women, creating a multinational brand that spawns perfume (1921) and accessories.
1919	The First Woman's Bank, created and staffed by women (although its shareholders were men), is founded by Brenda Vineyard Runyon in Clarksville, Tenn. Three years later, the Women's Federal Savings Bank is opened in Cleveland by sisters Clara and Lillian Westropp. These banks are among the first to identify women as financial consumers.
1937	Margaret Rudkin produces the first batch of Pepperidge Farm bread, which she names after her Connecticut farm; her bakery grows during the Great Depression through innovative marketing.
1946	Estée Lauder and her husband create four products in their kitchen and launch an iconic brand and global company of skin care lines.
1950–1971	**Women take unconventional routes to corporate leadership.**
1951	Lillian Vernon, a 24-year-old homemaker, starts a home-based mail-order business monogramming leather goods. Her idea that people would pay for customized products spawns an enterprise that becomes the first female-founded company to go public, in 1987.
1965	The sole supporter for two young children, Ruth Fertel leverages a bank loan to buy the Chris Steak House. The tongue-tying Ruth's Chris Steak House becomes the cornerstone of Ruth's Hospitality Group, a company that owns and operates five restaurant chains.
1972–1999	**Feminism draws women to corporate careers.**
1972	Katharine Meyer Graham becomes the first female CEO of a Fortune 500 company when she takes over The Washington Post Co. . . . Sandra Kurtzig founds ASK Computer Systems, which provides services and software for then-new mini computers.
1979	Marsha Serlin keeps her scrap metal trucking services in Cicero, Ill., running when a blizzard shuts down competitors, and emerges with the basis of a national metal buying and recycling company.
1986	Oprah Winfrey converts her prowess at hosting television talk shows into creation of Harpo Studios, following in the footsteps of actresses Mary Pickford and Lucille Ball as a female studio owner. She subsequently builds a media and branding empire.
1997	Martha Stewart blends her personal sense of style with her stockbroker experience to create an aspirational lifestyle brand both admired and mocked. When Martha Stewart Living Omnimedia goes public in 1999, Stewart's holdings make her a billionaire.
1998	Working Woman magazine publishes the "Top 25 Companies for Executive Women" list, becoming the first publication to chart the status of women at Fortune 500 firms. . . . Meg Whitman sees the potential in digital peer-to-peer auctions and propels eBay to international prominence as the first selling platform of its kind on the Internet. She is now CEO of Hewlett-Packard.

1999	Carly Fiorina becomes CEO of Hewlett-Packard based on her performance increasing revenue at Lucent, another high-tech company. Her tumultuous tenure involves the high-stakes acquisition of Compaq; she is ousted in 2005 after the company's stock price plummeted. She runs unsuccessfully for the Republican presidential nomination in 2016. . . . Carole Black becomes CEO of Lifetime Entertainment, a television network featuring programming geared to women, which until then had been run by men.
2000– Present	**Accelerating research builds the business case for women as leaders.**
2006	Indra K. Nooyi takes the helm at global beverage and food manufacturer PepsiCo. She is the highest-ranking woman of Indian descent at an American corporation.
2007	Angela Braly caps a long career in insurance and health care by becoming CEO of the WellPoint Inc. insurance company.
2009	Ursula Burns becomes the first black female CEO of a Fortune 500 company when she ascends to that position at Xerox. She takes over from Anne Mulcahy, also making it the first transition between female CEOs at a Fortune 500 company.
2012	Marissa Mayer becomes CEO at Yahoo, an early Internet giant that now is floundering in the digital revolution it once led.
2013	Facebook Chief Operating Officer Sheryl Sandberg publishes "Lean In: Women, Work and the Will to Lead," challenging women to push themselves and employers.
2014	Mary Barra rises through the ranks of engineering and operations to take the wheel as General Motors' CEO. . . . Abigail P. Johnson becomes CEO of Fidelity Investments, the global investment and mutual fund firm founded by her grandfather.
2015	Women become CEOs of two of the Big Four international accounting firms: Cathy Engelbert of Deloitte and Lynne Doughtie of KPMG.

RESOURCES

The Next Step

C-Suite

Levy, Rachael, "A bunch of men were asked what they think about diversity on corporate boards—the answer won't surprise you," Business Insider, Oct. 11, 2016, http://tinyurl.com/jpvm5nu.

A majority of men on boards of S&P 500 companies said that women should make up less than 50 percent of public company boards, according to a report from PricewaterhouseCoopers.

Piazza, Jo, "Women of Color Hit a 'Concrete Ceiling' in Business," The Wall Street Journal, Sept. 27, 2016, http://tinyurl.com/guzmfh5.

Although more women of color say they aspire to be top executives, they make up less than 12 percent of first-level managers and 3 percent of the C-suite-level workforce, according to McKinsey & Co.

Winkler, Elizabeth, "The challenges women face in corporate America are curbing their ambitions," Quartz, Oct. 5, 2016, http://tinyurl.com/zmwlfno.

A recent report from McKinsey & Co. and Sheryl Sandberg's LeanIn.Org showed that 40 percent of women want senior leadership positions in comparison to 56 percent of their male counterparts.

Lawsuits

Berthelsen, Christian, and Laura J. Keller, "BofA Settles Gender-Bias Lawsuit With ex-Managing Director," Bloomberg, Sept. 21, 2016, http://tinyurl.com/j43d2jv.

Bank of America agreed to settle a lawsuit with a former managing director who alleged the company was a "bros club" that favored men.

Simpson, Fraser, "Five more women added in gender discrimination lawsuit against KPMG US," AccountancyAge, May 16, 2016, http://tinyurl.com/hqp7cme.

Five more women were added to a $350 million class-action gender discrimination lawsuit against KPMG pursued by more than 1,000 current and former employees.

Soergel, Andrew, "Lawsuit Accuses Yahoo CEO Marissa Mayer of Discrimination Against Men," U.S. News and World Report, Oct. 7, 2016, http://tinyurl.com/zzt8o7j.

A former male Yahoo employee filed a lawsuit against CEO Marissa Mayer, accusing her of encouraging an employee performance rating system that resulted in the ousting of men.

Pay Gap

Bellstrom, Kristen, "Female MBAs Face a $400,000 Gender Pay Gap," Fortune, April 1, 2016, http://tinyurl.com/hsowgsa.

Female MBAs typically make about $400,000 less than their male counterparts in the 20 years after their graduation, according to a study.

Crockett, Emily, "Women negotiate for raises as much as men do. They just don't get them." Vox, Sept. 29, 2016, http://tinyurl.com/jh4u8sh.

Women negotiate for raises and promotions as often as men, but they face a penalty and get denied more frequently, according to a report on women in the workplace.

Weber, Lauren, "Gender Wage Gap Widens at Age 32, Report Finds," The Wall Street Journal, June 21, 2016, http://tinyurl.com/hwheb5r.

The wage gap begins to widen for women around age 32, an age at which they earn approximately 90 percent of their male counterparts' incomes, according to a new report. That share declines to 82 percent by age 40, the study found.

STEM Innovation

Oster, Shai, and Selina Wang, "How Women Won a Leading Role in China's Venture Capital Industry," Bloomberg, Sept. 19, 2016, http://tinyurl.com/znmap9x.

A group of women have risen to the top of venture capital companies in China, and the government estimates women have founded 55 percent of new Internet companies in the country.

Staley, Oliver, "What happened when a global software company scoured its salary data for possible gender bias," Quartz, Oct. 5, 2016, http://tinyurl.com/hdhnpuu.

Software company SAP hired a law firm to examine its employees' pay and discovered that of the 1 percent of workers who were underpaid, 70 percent of those were women.

Zarya, Valentina, "J.P. Morgan Just Made This Woman CIO of Its Corporate and Investment Bank," Fortune, June 20, 2016, http://tinyurl.com/j3wgpgk.

J.P. Morgan added to the names of women in technology in June when it appointed Lori Beer chief information officer of the company's corporate and investment bank.

Organizations

Accounting & Financial Women's Alliance

2365 Harrodsburg Road, A325, Lexington, KY 40504

800-326-2163

www.afwa.org

A group that sponsors research and networks for women in corporate finance and public accounting, two specialties in which women are under-represented.

Anita Borg Institute

1501 Page Mill Road, MS 1105, Palo Alto, CA 94304

650-460-5251

http://anitaborg.org

Named for a pioneering female computer engineer, the institute concentrates on research about and for women in high tech, especially in Silicon Valley.

Catalyst

120 Wall St., 15th Floor, New York, NY 10005

212-514 7600

http://www.catalyst.org

One of the longest-established advocacy and research nonprofits for women, the group is a source of groundbreaking reports.

Center for Women's Entrepreneurial Leadership

Babson College, 231 Forest St., Babson Park, MA 02457-0310

781-235-1200

http://www.babson.edu/Academics/centers/cwel/Pages/home.aspx

A Babson-affiliated group that seeks to empower female leaders through educational programs, events and research.

Forte Foundation

9600 Escarpment, Suite 745 PMB 72, Austin, TX 78749

512-535-5157

http://www.fortefoundation.org/

A nonprofit whose mission is to encourage women to pursue masters of business administration degrees and to stay the course when they are in corporate leadership.

Institute for Women's Policy Research
1200 18th St., N.W., #301, Washington, DC 20036
202-785-5100
http://www.iwpr.org/

An institute that focuses on complex research about interrelated topics relating to women's economic independence; also does in-depth analysis of pay equity trends.

Interorganization Network
1846 Berkshire Road, Columbus, OH 43221
614-203-9115
http://www.ionwomen.org

A consortium of regional and industry-focused women's groups that fosters collaboration on research and programs about women's status at publicly held companies.

Michigan Council of Women in Technology
6 Parklane Blvd., Suite 615, Dearborn, MI 48126
248-218-2578
https://www.mcwt.org/

An organization that connects women in technology across a variety of industries in the STEM-dependent state of Michigan.

National Center for Women & Information Technology
University of Colorado, Campus Box 417 UCB, Boulder, CO 80309
303-735-6671
https://www.ncwit.org

A group that conducts research and constructs advocacy programs for women in IT in tech industries and for women in tech jobs in other industries, such as manufacturing.

Vision 2020
2900 W. Queen Lane, Philadelphia, PA 19129
215-991-8190
http://drexel.edu/vision2020/

This Drexel University-sponsored advocacy program seeks to accelerate the advancement of women in corporate and nonprofit leadership.

Women Presidents' Organization
155 E. 55th St., Suite 4H, New York, NY 10022
212-688-4114
https://www.womenpresidentsorg.com

A group that facilitates networking among women who own companies or run major divisions of corporations, and the mentoring of rising women.

Q&A: Serafina Schorer on Running a Company

"THE BIGGEST MISTAKE WOMEN MAKE TODAY IS, THEY TRY TO BE A WANNABE MAN"

Serafina Schorer is CEO of RIM Custom Racks, a Detroit-based, family-owned manufacturer of shipping racks and gear for getting automotive parts to plants. The company's services and supplies are integral to the supply chain, ensuring that parts arrive intact and on time so that vehicles can be assembled efficiently. She is on the board of the Great Lakes Women's Business Council. In an interview with SAGE Business Researcher freelance correspondent Joanne Cleaver, she discusses the challenges of overseeing a company and offers advice for female managers.

You were thrust into the role of CEO in 2005 when your husband, the company founder, suddenly died. Why did you decide to run the company instead of sell it?

I was a homemaker and the mother of four adult sons. I had no experience in manufacturing or business. I thought, "I'm going to do this." And I did. I found that I loved it. I could understand why my husband was so wound up in the business. It's addictive. There's nothing more exciting than all the things that go into making an automobile.

Shortly after you stepped up to the CEO role, the recession began, and it hit the automotive sector especially hard. How did you get through that?

Here we were, in 2008, with the markets collapsing and the banks weren't supportive of automotive companies; you couldn't get a line of credit, and two of our major customers—GM and Chrysler—declared bankruptcy. It was a very turbulent time. You wear your CEO mask. You say, "We're going to get through this," but secretly, you wonder what's going to happen.

You have your attorneys and your accountants, but there's nobody there to really mentor you. You're going it alone. I went to a conference held by the Great Lakes Women's Business Council and went to a session on how to work with bankrupt customers. I went to that conference very discouraged, but it was a shot in the arm, and I went back to my team and I said, "We're going to make it." Suddenly I had a group of professional women to call on, and I did call them.

How have you reinvested in other women?

I got certified as a woman-owned business in 2010 because I thought I could use all the help I could get, and it changed my whole business. At forums with other women business owners, you meet women from all industries. I always come back with new perspectives.

You had no business experience whatsoever when you took over. What experiences or skills proved to be invaluable, even though you gained them through life experience before becoming CEO?

Women have a collaborative style and that works perfectly with networking and partnering and forming relationships. When you're running a home and a family and you do a lot in the community, you form skills you don't realize you have. But I think the biggest mistake women make today is, they try to be a wannabe man. Instead, be a really talented woman.

What's your best advice for a female mid-manager who wants to be a CEO?

Trust yourself and know that you have a lot to offer. Champion other women and be your own best advocate. Be willing to change direction if need be; look for success in unexpected places.

You have to be able to lead and to inspire. Embrace who you are and be authentic and celebrate your talents and skills. We all have different life experiences and we bring a lot to the table. We can bring a lot to any business if we are who we are.

MEETINGS AND TEAM MANAGEMENT

Are traditional meetings still relevant in today's tech-driven world?

Joanne Cleaver

EXECUTIVE SUMMARY

Not for nothing are so many "Dilbert" comic strips set in meetings. Notorious for wasting time, dulling motivation and draining creativity, meetings are widely seen as a necessary evil—one poll found that 46 percent of Americans prefer almost any "unpleasant activity" over a meeting. Not surprisingly, managers are trying to reinvent meetings to make them more productive and to meet the changing needs of a 21st-century economy. Technology and startup companies are experimenting with meeting formats and lengths, and some established organizations are following suit. And as staffs become more diverse, managers and researchers say meeting dynamics must include more points of view, communication styles and ways of arriving at decisions. Some experts agree that new technologies may help solve many problems associated with routine meetings. Yet others say that changing corporate culture is more important. Among the questions under debate: Is technology fundamentally changing the nature of meetings? Are planned meetings better than spontaneous meetings? Can women be heard in meetings?

OVERVIEW

Are traditional meetings still relevant in today's tech-driven world?

Ask Jeanette Martin about the worst business meeting she ever endured and she will recount her stint at a German auto parts manufacturer. Everybody on the team spoke fluent English, but Martin was the only one who also wasn't a native speaker of German. Every week, the team held a meeting to review the status and progress of ongoing projects. And every week, the meeting opened in English and then quickly transitioned to German. She put up with it for a year, then snapped.

"I said, 'If you don't need all of us in this meeting, because you're speaking German then I've got other things to do.' And they apologized," says Martin, who teaches management at

From *SAGE Business Researcher*,
March 14, 2016

the University of Mississippi School of Business Administration and is co-author of "Global Business Etiquette: A Guide to International Communication and Customs."[1]

Martin also has a happy meeting tale from her days as a staffer at a medical supply manufacturer. Managers were stymied by how to make the most of employees' often excellent suggestions for saving time or money. The suggestion program rewarded the person who came up with a good idea, even though the results often depended on how well others carried out the suggestion.

"One person was getting rewarded while somebody else did all the work," Martin says. A cross-section of executives met to hash out the problem, well aware of the likely repercussions on employee morale and of the potential for blowback. "It was a good meeting because it took on a long-standing company practice—the suggestion box—and we saw people's minds change in the meeting" as participants came up with an innovative solution, Martin says.

Meetings: They're inevitable, inescapable and often intolerable aspects of any organization. Yet the meeting as a form of collaborative energy is so compelling that some meetings have achieved epic status: The Last Supper, the Constitutional Convention of 1787 and the post-World War II Bretton Woods conference on monetary policy, to name a few. In the best cases, the collective minds of meetings hash out agreements, breakthroughs and alliances impossible to engineer in individual conversation.

As the pace of business accelerates, managers are trying to reinvent meetings. Technology and startup companies are experimenting with meeting formats and lengths, and some established organizations are adopting the resulting new practices. The emergence of the flat corporate structure (i.e., few bosses overseeing an army of self-directed, self-managing staff) appears to be diametrically opposed to traditional meeting culture. And as staffs become more diverse in terms of gender, generation and ethnicity, managers and researchers say meeting dynamics must adapt to include more points of view, more styles of communication and more ways of arriving at decisions.

This change is sending stress fractures through long-standing meeting culture and assumptions. From intern orientations to board of directors assemblies, many meetings are happening in different ways, with different players, for different reasons.

Workers typically loathe meetings because they appear to wick away the one thing no one can make more of: time. For 18 percent of Americans, a trip to the Department of Motor Vehicles is a more appealing way to spend time than attending a "status" meeting—a prototypical form of meeting in which attendees update each other on the progress of various projects, according to a survey released in 2015 by software company Clarizen.[2]

The same poll found that 46 percent of Americans would rather do almost any "unpleasant activity" than sit through a meeting. For respondents, death by meeting was not hypothetical: The poll found that staff members spend an average of 4.6 hours weekly preparing for status meetings and 4.5 hours weekly attending such meetings—a full day of each workweek.[3]

A seminal study by University of Southern California (USC) researchers found that status and informational meetings (the latter is where announcements are made) accounted for 45 percent of all meetings.[4] Widespread dislike of these routine meetings has spawned an entire industry dedicated to eliminating them via "virtual collaboration platforms." Only 5 percent of the meetings identified in the USC study were creative or brainstorming meetings—the types, according to organizational psychologists, that are both the most fun and the most productive to attend.

But the USC study also had a cheerier side that validates Martin's best-meeting scenario. Purposeful, well-run meetings that achieve their goals generate high satisfaction among participants and goodwill for those who called and ran them. And a study found that 97 percent of workers consider the collaboration that meetings foster essential "to do their best work."[5]

Many consultants, psychologists and business anthropologists—those who study the underlying dynamics of meetings from a cultural point of view—agree that new technologies may solve or support many aspects of routine meetings, likely for the better. Technology innovators have introduced "collaborative project management systems" intended to eliminate the tedious status meeting. Such software creates online modes of continuously updating team members' progress on projects, eliminating the need to hold a meeting to accomplish that goal. In theory, tech company executives say, the remaining meetings would be productive, enjoyable and mission-driven brainstorming that can focus on idea development and strategy.[6]

Meetings don't just feel like they go on forever—meetings as a ritual actually have been going on forever, says Tomoko Hamada, a professor of anthropology at the College of William & Mary in Williamsburg, Va., who studies cross-cultural business customs.

Humans are hard-wired not just to communicate but to communicate in structured formats that reinforce who belongs to a group and that perpetuate the group's culture, she says. Contemporary business meetings are on the continuum that began with humans gathering to discuss how to stay alive by planning tasks. "We are social animals. From an anthropological point of view, meetings are corporate rituals," Hamada says. "Americans are always saying they're going to eliminate meetings, but they're not going to go away."

Routine meetings are platforms for power players to exercise their authority and for attendees to demonstrate that they are insiders who belong. Newcomers often must go through rituals of "rebirth" to affirm their status as learners, experts say, and to take their proper place (think of the notion that certain chairs are traditionally where certain attendees sit). Communication traditions, such as raising one's hand to signal the desire to speak, also affirm attendees' common culture. The corporate meeting even has a version of the tribal "talking stick": the PowerPoint projector remote.

Inherently, face-to-face meetings include the broadest spectrum of nuance, from side conversations to facial expressions to small gestures and tones of voice. Virtual platforms typically omit pre-and post-meeting rituals because technical requirements dictate the protocols of webinars, virtual meetings and similar formats. These formats are efficient, but the subtleties that reinforce the value of face-to-face meetings are lost, Hamada says. Often, participants make decisions in prior, private discussions so the actual meeting becomes a formality.

Layer on national culture, and it's a wonder that anything is accomplished in meetings that span companies, countries, time zones and generations. In some countries, anxious meeting-goers obsess over small points of protocol, such as when and how to present business cards to Asian colleagues, Hamada says. She once arranged a virtual group meeting between American and Japanese business school students. "The Americans were worried about how formal the Japanese usually are in how they dress, so they all put on neckties for the meeting. The Japanese were worried about how casual Americans are, so they all wore T-shirts and jeans. When they saw each other, they just laughed," she recalls.

Precisely because they are the stage for so much missed opportunity, meetings are ripe for reinvention. "The dilemma of meetings is that you have to invest time to make them more efficient, but then you have to have a meeting about it," says Alok Sawhney, a business psychologist and management consultant in South Florida. And there's no way to agree that a meeting is unnecessary except by having at least a brief virtual meeting to cancel the meeting, he says.

Ironies aside, Sawhney and other psychologists say meetings are prisms into an organization. Observant participants can read company culture, writ small, in a meeting.[7] Who leads, how they lead, how they shepherd the process, how they assign and measure results—all of this, says Sawhney, yields insights into the dynamics of power, influence and action.

Early in his career, Sawhney was excited to be invited to sit in on board and senior-level meetings at the hospital management company where he was a management intern. "It was fascinating," he says. "The most straightforward stuff took on a life of its own, with all the perspectives and conversations, the differences in personalities. That's the beauty of meetings."

"Meetings are a microcosm," says Bill Treasurer, CEO of Giant Leap Consulting, a team development consultancy in Asheville, N.C. He recalls a privately owned company whose leadership team would painstakingly plot meetings without consulting the owner. "They figured they'd show him the agenda for a three-day offsite meeting at the last minute, fearful that he'd change it. . . . And, of course, he changes it the very first time he sees it." That, Treasurer says, is the sign of a corporate culture driven by fear and obedience. "If there is a general dysfunction, you are likely to see it magnified."

As managers, consultants and researchers consider the role of meetings in a changing business world, these are some of the questions under debate:

Weighing the Issues

Is technology fundamentally changing the nature of meetings?

The conundrum of meeting technology is that it makes good meetings better and bad meetings worse.

Now that webinars, conference calls and video conferences are standard formats, managers are realizing that these technologies are best used for transactional discussions: solving relatively routine problems and discussing concrete topics, says Jonathan Lane, managing partner of ProductWorks, a Massachusetts management consultancy that works with technology and startup firms.

In fact, routine meetings seem to generate the most irritation. A 2013 study found that meeting-goers confessed to being late about one time in 20—with the cumulative effect of forcing 37 percent of all meetings to start late.[8] A quarter of meeting attendees reported through the USC study that "irrelevant issues" took up 11 percent to 25 percent of time in status meetings.[9]

Research indicates that new technology doesn't make attendees pay better attention to tedious topics. Standard conference calls have become notorious as gatherings for participants who are doing other things while listening: sending emails, eating and even going to the bathroom.[10] Video conferences command a bit more attention because participants can at least see each other, says Lane.

Conference calls persist for companies and teams that must communicate with workers across

many locations because at least the call officially communicates the same information to everyone at the same time, Lane says. Information published via complementary technology, such as internal social media, intranets, email and digital company communications, might not be read.

But "if the purpose of the meeting is to do real work, the virtual platform degrades terribly," Lane says. A 2015 Boston College study found that telecommuting, while often popular with those working from home or other remote sites, left office-bound colleagues feeling lonely and disconnected. Nonverbal cues and the indefinable value of being together appear to reinforce team understanding and morale in ways not yet fully understood—and not replicated by virtual meeting platforms.[11]

But virtual meetings have their defenders. One is Edward Sturm, a self-employed video and digital marketing content creator in Brooklyn, N.Y., who specializes in collaborating with technology startup companies.[12] He notes that virtual meetings address questions and decisions as they emerge, instead of batching them for resolution at a scheduled later time. In Sturm's experience, this timeliness prevents problems from snowballing.

"Virtual tools give the respondee time to think and time to continue in a flow state if they need it," Sturm says. "Face-to-face meetings are done more for the benefit of the person calling the meeting, so that person can advance in the company or get a connection that he or she needs."

At the same time, though, virtual platforms can undermine the value of face-to-face meetings, says Michael Randel, a Kensington, Md., consultant who specializes in facilitating meetings. "It's a counterintuitive attitude of 'let's *not* meet,'" he says. "People put all this information in shared folders and dashboards so they don't have to have a meeting."

Multitasking by participants during meetings via texting and sharing, often blamed on Millennials, is committed by all generations, says Paul Cooper, a professional facilitator based in Washington, D.C. He has seen many a meeting host struggle with "technology etiquette," with solutions ranging from forcing all attendees to park their devices in a basket that's put to the side, to actually asking attendees to do research during the meeting on their devices.

BeamPro representative in Palo Alto, California chats with attendees at the Consumer Electronics Show in Las Vegas, Nevada. The BeamPro allows users to interact with remote locations by coupling high-end video and audio with the freedom of motion to move about a space. The BeamPro 'Smart Presence System' gives the impression of interacting with a physical person rather than a robot mounted video display.

Source: ROBYN BECK/AFP/Getty Images

But don't blame technology for the easily distracted, Cooper says. The real issue is that the meeting topic and organization aren't interesting enough to hold people's attention. For meeting organizers, hosts and facilitators, "the task is to get people to focus on the here and now, and make it so compelling they don't want to do anything else," he says.

Even though technology itself does not appear to have transformed meetings, others note that management approaches pioneered by some technology companies have been adopted more widely.

For example, "agile project management," which has taken root in software development, is a "spiral process" in which projects are redefined as they progress, partially by ongoing collaboration and many short meetings.[13] (By comparison, traditional project management is linear: Define the project, break it into parts, get the parts done, assemble the parts and complete the project.)

Often, Lane says, agile project team leaders start each day with a short "getting on the same page" meeting. The meetings are intentionally so short—10 to 15 minutes—that everyone can stand, thus sidestepping the usual meeting protocol of sitting around a table. Typically, the team leader organizes the discussion around a board with notes, erasing project tasks just completed and adding tasks and problems to be solved that day. Stand-up meetings are often given nicknames borrowed from sports: "Scrum" and "huddle" are popular.

The concept of a short, stand-up meeting has spread to departments and companies beyond IT, Lane says.

He worked with one established technology services company that felt bogged down by meetings that took too long and accomplished too little. Adopting the agile team management approach, the CEO established a daily 15-minute, 11:45 a.m. standing meeting. "It was about getting visibility into what was happening that day," Lane says. "Everybody has a piece to bring in terms of service challenges, finance, new sales leads, whatever is happening in their departments. The time-boxing . . . moves it along, compared to other meetings where everyone leans back in their chairs with coffee."

The 11:45 meeting has "changed the company culture," Lane says. "It reduces anxiety and 'fire drills,' in which everyone scrambles to find out what's going on with a problem. Everybody knows a problem will be brought up at the 11:45. Over five years, this has become the basic organizing principle of the company."

Are planned meetings better than spontaneous meetings?

Traditional meetings follow a well-worn groove: set a time and agenda; prepare; attend; follow through. Thus, anticipating a meeting forces participants to prepare, clarify their thoughts and validate information, says Dana Ardi, founder of Corporate Anthropology Advisors, a New York City-based consulting firm that works with large corporations. Even short stand-up meetings require participants to bring items to present, she points out.

The collaboration needed to prepare for a meeting is so much a part of emailing, document-sharing and slide-designing that people don't realize how much actual work—analyzing, prioritizing, clarifying—gets done along the way, Ardi says. "It's a whole value chain that surrounds the meeting."

Preparation escalates along with a meeting's importance. When top executives are involved and the stakes are high, including significant decisions about people, money and corporate priorities, attendees prepare more. A "tribal council" meeting involving top leaders usually is preceded by bands of staff preparing research, presentations, charts and briefings. Young managers are often included as observers so they can see what's involved in staging such events.

Most Office Workers Support Meeting Face to Face

The structure of formal meetings, Ardi says, usually ensures that participants have an official chance to make their points.

Organizational psychologists and anthropologists agree that purely spontaneous meetings are valuable mainly for building relationships. By definition, spontaneous meetings don't involve preparation, agendas, research and goals, so the information exchanged is informal and may or may not achieve organizational goals.

In fact, says Cooper, the professional facilitator, a frequent outcome of spontaneous meetings is the decision to call a formal meeting with all the attendant trappings.

How effective or ineffective do you think face-to-face meetings are at your company?

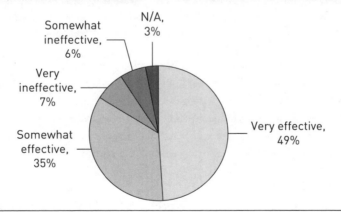

About half of U.S. office workers at companies with 500 or more employees say their face-to-face meetings at work are "very effective," according to a survey conducted by Harris Poll for project-management software company Workfront. Thirty-five percent of workers said such meetings are "somewhat effective," while 13 percent said they are "somewhat" or "very" ineffective.

Note: Based on survey from July 6–24, 2015, of 617 full – or part-time U.S. office workers at companies with 500 or more employees.

Source: "The State of Enterprise Work," Workfront and Harris Poll, 2015, p. 19, downloaded from http://tinyurl.com/hyyo3y6

Somewhere between spontaneous meetings and formal planned meetings sit periodic regular meetings, says Steven Hunt, vice president of customer research at SuccessFactors.

"There are certain people you should meet with on a regular basis, because there's something to talk about, but you don't know what it is until you get together," he says. Successful account representatives, for instance, will check in with key customers "whether or not there's something to discuss," Hunt says. The agenda for such regular meetings is implied: what's going right, what needs attention and what needs are emerging, he says.

Regular meetings also build relationships and trust, banking understanding for times when things might not be going so well. "Knowing the person in real life, you can 'hear' them in emails, read between the lines in emails and have context," Hunt says. "It builds a lot of tolerance into the relationship."

Focusing on *how* meetings are called overlooks the more important issue of *why* they are called, says Cooper. Format is less important than culture, he says. Northwestern University anthropology professor emerita Helen B. Schwartzman came to the same conclusion when she theorized that what the meeting is about is not what the meeting is. Meetings are not propelled by crises and decisions that must be made, Schwartzman says. For most organizations, it's really a case of the meeting "tail" wagging the issues "dog": Meetings are going to be held, thanks to human nature. The only real open question is, what issues are sufficiently important or pressing to justify the inevitable meetings?

Cooper saw this dynamic at a nonprofit where he frequently facilitated meetings. The group had been holding the same type of meeting in the same format, deciding the same types of things, for most of its 90-year existence. Its leaders realized one day during a sleepy meeting that they needed a wake-up call. Aimless meetings indicated a deeper drift of mission and culture. The organization was losing touch with its mission, just as its meetings were losing touch with attendees, he says.

"The meetings used to be easy. People didn't ask big questions," says Cooper. Now, with some new leaders and some reinvigorated old leaders, the meetings are the crucible for the converted culture.

"There used to not be any impatient people in the room. Now, they are more rambunctious," he says. "I have to be attentive to the fact that there are going to be people in the room who think that things are bull——. There's dissent, and energy."

Can women be heard in meetings?

As the only woman in an influential group of nine, a senior professional with several decades' experience, she often felt her views were overlooked in group debate. "When I will say something—and I don't think I'm a confused speaker—it isn't until somebody else says it that everyone will focus on the point," she told a reporter at a conference.[14]

The woman—Ruth Bader Ginsburg, inarguably at the top of her profession as an associate justice on the U.S. Supreme Court since 1993—added, "The same thing can happen in the public setting of oral arguments." She cited instances during which another justice would reiterate the question she had just asked during the oral argument and the lawyer presenting the case would direct his response to the male justice.[15]

If fellow justices don't hear the Notorious RBG, do other women have any hope of being heard in workplace meetings?

Women have a hard time being taken seriously in meetings, according to researchers. Academics at Northwestern and Cornell universities have found that in meetings, women's expertise is overshadowed by female identity and expectations of women in social settings. That makes it harder for the group to hear and use the skills that women offer. The group might not achieve its goals because it didn't make the most of the expertise represented by women—specifically because they were women.[16]

Researchers such as Deborah Tannen, professor of linguistics at Georgetown University and author of several best-selling books on gender communication, argue that it's up to both women and men to consciously negate dynamics drowning out women's voices in meetings.[17]

The stereotypical male style of being direct and straightforward isn't always better in corporate meetings, Tannen told one interviewer.[18] "And in some contexts, men tend to be more indirect than women," she said. "It's true that I have heard from women's groups who tell me that it's very hard sometimes to come to a decision, because people are so committed to consensus that they can never move on and say, 'OK, we're not all going to agree on this point, but we're going to have to do something, so let's do this.'"

"At the same time, though, I would certainly say that there are things men could benefit from by adapting styles more common among women. One is apologizing," Tannen said.

Women's communication style results in better corporate performance, according to a 2013 study of 624 board directors. Researchers, according to one summary, found that "women are more likely to consider the rights of others and to take a cooperative approach to decision-making." Male board members like to follow the rules and trust that their process will result in a valid and defensible decision. Women, though, are more willing to challenge the group, ask outside-the-box questions, request and respond to a broader array of perspectives and collaborate with colleagues more effectively. All of this adds up to impressive results, one study found: Boards with large female representation experience a 53 percent higher return on equity, a 66 percent higher return on invested capital and a 42 percent higher return on sales.[19]

Meetings involving sales and purchasing decisions are especially rife with gender communication problems, say gender communication researchers.

Women tend to examine the major attributes and details of a potential purchase, whether it's for their company or for themselves, according to Marti Barletta, a Winnetka, Ill., consultant who specializes in marketing to women.[20] They often use a time-consuming "discovery process" to get a 360-degree view of what they are considering, looking not just at the essential functions of the item or service but also, for instance, at how much training it might take to get staff to actually use it.[21] Thus, in a sales meeting, other women know they're taking a journey together, while the men grow impatient with the process and wonder when the women will make up their minds, Barletta said.

Perhaps because their views often are discounted and overlooked, even high-ranking women tend to believe they have less influence in their workplaces than men do.[22]

Because so much evidence is accumulating that women's voices are drowned out in meetings, many corporate executives are consciously trying to change the tenor of their meetings, to invite and include more perspectives of all types, says Bernardo M. Ferdman, an organizational psychology professor with Alliant International University in San Diego and a diversity consultant who specializes in working with Latinos and Latinas.

"Top leaders realize the meaning of diversity, but it's the middle who lose power, so they feel threatened," says Hamada of William & Mary. Women often are crowded out of important pre-and post-meeting informal discussions. Astute senior leaders detect these shunnings and step up to advocate for women and other diverse participants, she says.

In a key shift, Ferdman says, executives are starting to recognize that no one person speaks for all people with whom he or she primarily identifies. Market profiles and demographic data often assign common experiences to women—mothering, for example, and the attendant details of caring for small children. But that doesn't mean that any individual woman has that exact experience or represents the statistically average point of view, Ferdman says.

And company leaders are realizing that claiming to be "gender blind" or "race blind"' is misguided. Deliberately ignoring gender or race amounts to dismissing characteristics that have shaped people's life experiences.

The emerging practice, Ferdman says, is to focus on what each individual uniquely brings to discussions and collaboration. "We're all products not just of our own selves, but of our identities, cultures and histories," he says. "Our perspectives are valuable—when we use our perspectives."

BACKGROUND

In Pursuit of the Talking Stick

From North American tribes to medieval guilds to New England town meetings, purposeful gatherings have shaped communication and culture for centuries. Native Americans often used their meetings to decide matters of state—whether to wage war or seek peace—and simply to socialize. In Europe, guild meetings also mixed business and pleasure, not only organizing commerce but formulating funeral and celebration traditions.[23] The famed New England town meeting of the 17th and 18th centuries brought residents together, at which every male citizen not only had the right but a responsibility to speak.[24] Painter and illustrator Norman Rockwell captured this democratic spirit in a painting that depicts a rough-hewn farmer taking the floor at a public forum.[25] The everybody-invited, everyone-can-participate meeting is so entrenched in American culture that even large political and corporate gatherings are often called "town hall" meetings.

One of the most consequential public meetings was the one that established the federal government: the Constitutional Convention, held in 1787.[26] Meeting behind closed doors for three and a half months, a group of male landowners, lawyers and merchants struggled to reach compromises on federalism, presidential powers and other difficult topics. Consensus was elusive, debate was fierce and leaks were common, but this meeting of federalists and anti-federalists, Northerners and Southerners, succeeded in producing a historic document that put the United States on a sound political footing. More prosaically, the convention showed what meetings could do when participants rallied around a common goal and evinced a willingness to compromise.

As the United States grew in the wake of the Constitutional Convention and a manufacturing economy blossomed during the Industrial Revolution, modern corporations emerged, complete with boards of directors, CEOs, marketing departments and products that were sold on international markets. Trailing close behind was the meeting, especially the "status meeting," where goals were assessed and progress was marked. Meetings became a part of corporate culture in the early 20th century and were emblematic of the button-down Eisenhower years in the 1950s, when corporations—and many workers—prospered.[27]

In the "Mad Men" era of the 1960s, committees, task forces, conferences and summits proliferated, each spinning off an orbiting constellation of meetings that were held in time-honored ways. The growing importance of meetings, however, began to produce murmurs of dissent: Midcentury sociologists noted the drain on time and drag on productivity that meetings often produced. And Melville Dalton, a University of California, Los Angeles, professor and author of "Men Who Manage," was among the first to detect submerged purposes to supposedly task-oriented meetings.[28]

Bringing Order to Meetings

"Robert's Rules of Order" for meetings—a formal opening, asserting a quorum, asking that motions be made and seconded and then holding votes—set the basic expectations during much of the 20th century for how gatherings should be run, even though few modern companies strictly follow these guidelines in daily meetings. (Corporate annual meetings are a notable exception.)

There really was a Robert—Henry Martyn Robert, an Army engineering officer who was flummoxed when unexpectedly asked to run a public meeting. Determined to never again be caught by surprise, he created a formal template for how he thought meetings should proceed. Robert's Rules of Order was first published in 1876 and has been continually in print ever since.[29]

In effect, Robert's Rules created a default structure for Western meetings in the same way that tribal societies have default structures for their meetings. Many organizations incorporated Robert's Rules as their de facto legal structure. The Midwestern History Association was typical, referencing Robert's Rules in its constitution and bylaws.[30]

The underlying assumption of the traditional meeting was that everybody accepted the social relationships and structure of the meeting—who will come, the governing protocol and the supporting logistics, according to Schwartzman.[31]

While Robert's Rules provided a common frame of reference for meeting structure, they also served as a handy weapon for those who either wanted to validate every decision "by the rulebook" or invalidate a decision by claiming that the meeting in question did not follow protocol and thus could not produce a valid result. Many a meeting broke down over the technical application of Robert's Rules, to the degree that some public-speaking organizations actually provided cures for Robert's neurosis in the form of specialized training.[32]

Robert's Rules created a consistent way to structure meetings for companies and organizations, but it also created the expectation that simply following the rules would result in an orderly, respectful, productive meeting. In 1989, Schwartzman of Northwestern took this notion on, publishing a seminal work proposing that meetings should drive organizational culture, instead of serving the culture.

Schwartzman's breakthrough was to uncouple the Rules backdrop from what she said was the real purpose of meetings: to reaffirm power structures and relationships.

"The meeting is a specific type of focused interaction," wrote Schwartzman in "The Meeting: Gatherings in Organizations and Communities." "More specifically, a meeting is defined as a communicative event involving three or more people who agree to assemble for a purpose ostensibly related to the functioning of an organization or group, for example, to exchange ideas or opinions, to solve a problem, to make a decision or negotiate an agreement, to develop policy and procedures, to formulate recommendations and so forth."[33] The book is an anthropological field study of the meeting dynamics of one nonprofit organization and is considered pivotal to understanding the dynamics and value of Western organizational meetings.

"Meetings, however, may be most important in American society because they generate the *appearance* that reason and logical processes are guiding discussions and decisions, whereas . . . relationship negotiations, struggles and comments" are, she wrote. "It is this process that can make meetings such frustrating occasions because they appear to be doing one thing whereas, in many ways, they are accomplishing something entirely different."[34]

Reinventing Meetings

While Schwartzman was peeling back the underlying layers of meeting culture, those going to business meetings in the early 1990s started to notice a change: Faster communication, propelled by email and the emerging Internet, was shifting how employees communicated and collaborated.

In their zeal to be No. 1, the initial wave of Internet companies reinvented meetings along with other aspects of corporate culture. They quickly realized the potential of virtual meeting platforms, such as Skype, to solve several problems at once: reducing costly, inefficient travel; minimizing the environmental effects of business transportation; and supporting collaboration among international teams across global time zones.[35] By 2009, consultants and business practitioners debated whether sophisticated meeting platforms could actually replace face-to-face meetings, or whether technology would essentially create a new type of meeting that would co-exist with traditional meeting formats.[36]

Yet, as meeting technology changed, meeting frustration grew, says Schwartzman, now a Northwestern University professor emerita.

Survey: 'Keeping Focused' Is Most Common Challenge

She says there was a profound disconnect between the Robert's-steeped assumptions many people still held about how meetings should operate and what constituted a successful meeting.

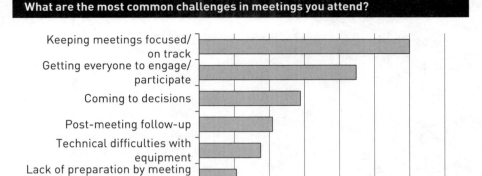

What are the most common challenges in meetings you attend?

Three in five employees say their most common meeting-related challenge is keeping them focused and on-track, while 45 percent highlight participant engagement as the most common challenge, according to a survey by Mersive, a Denver-based collaboration software company.

Notes: Based on survey of 499 workers from Feb. 5–19, 2015. Respondents included workers from customer service, engineering, human resources, information technology, logistics, marketing and sales industries, among others.

Source: "The Truth about Meeting Culture," Mersive, April 2015, p. 4, http://tinyurl.com/pcqy6fs

Formalities such as Robert's Rules, along with defaults for meeting settings (coffee, pastries, a generic room) and courtesies (a bland greeting and bullet-pointed agenda), implied that meetings were a blank slate, an empty stage, that participants animated with personality, conflict, relationships and debate.

"People get frustrated because there's not a recognition that other things are actually happening in meetings," Schwartzman says. "These other things are speaking to issues that are relevant to what the group is doing, but that may not be recognized."

"Say people come together to make a hiring decision, but by talking in a meeting about that decision, they also are talking and enacting, and sometimes commenting on, their own set of relationships with each other," she says. "They may be jockeying, or negotiating, or renewing or underlining what their relationships are. The meeting becomes so important in so many different contexts because so many things are happening. There are a variety of things besides the agenda that are baked into the structure of the meeting."

CURRENT SITUATION

Meeting Spaces Evolve

Office-space planners currently allot about one meeting space for every four to six people, according to Gretchen Gscheidle, director of insight and exploration for Herman

Open office space and exposed, original concrete, inside the leasing office of Rising Realty, representative of 21st-century design trends, and meeting spaces are following suit.

Source: Jay L. Clendenin/Los Angeles Times via Getty Images

Miller, an office design and furnishings manufacturer. "And the spaces are smaller, both enclosed and open. That speaks to how business is done and how fluid collaboration can be," she says.

Smaller spaces, and more of them, indicate how meetings are evolving. They tend to involve fewer people, who are meeting more often. Designers at Herman Miller began seeing this change about 16 years ago. As the 20th century closed, the proportion of meeting rooms to employees started shifting rapidly. Before 2000, the standard was one meeting space for every 20 employees, says Gscheidle. Around 2003, clients started planning more meeting spaces—one for every 10 people—and arranging them throughout each floor of a building.

It's easier to track meeting activity and the space that meetings occupy than it is to monitor the effectiveness of meetings themselves. In fact, meetings are so much the wallpaper of corporate life that they are rarely studied in isolation. One study about meeting effectiveness, widely quoted in blogs, articles and infographics, is "Meetings in America," sponsored by Verizon and published in 1998.[37] A popular study with the same title was published in 2003, a year after the company that sponsored it, WorldCom, filed for what was then the largest bankruptcy in America.[38]

Meeting metrics are slippery. Academics and consultants debate time lost, productivity eroded and morale dampened, yet they have not designed a metric for meeting effectiveness.[39] Meeting participants know a successful meeting when they experience it: a purposeful, inclusive process, focused on a meaningful topic, yielding breakthroughs that individuals could not have reached on their own, and, in many cases, applicable results.

Randel, the consultant who specializes in facilitating meetings, says there is no "overarching method" of measuring meeting effectiveness. "In a simple sense," he says, "a measure of success is, do the sponsors and participants feel that it achieved its objectives? But: Do they share those objectives? It comes back to whether there is an appropriate view of the mission of the meeting." Look no further than the "Dilbert" comic strip for the popular perception of unsuccessful meetings—dispirited, unengaged attendees manipulating what process there is for mutual sabotage, resulting in wasted time, eroded morale and undermined goals.

Part of the problem, says Lane at consulting firm ProductWorks, is that few companies bother to analyze why their meetings work, or don't work. Unlike the military and hospitals, businesses usually don't do postmortems of the underlying drivers of their meetings. Post-meeting discussions "tend to be about blaming, not learning," Lane says. Companies would do well instead to "take a deeper dive, structured as a learning meeting: 'How do we become smarter and better?' "

The chronic tension over the value of meetings is driving both a desire to move routine, repetitive communications to virtual platforms and to make more of the meetings that do need to occur, says Krystal D'Costa, an anthropologist who writes the "Anthropology in Practice" blog for Scientific American.[40]

Most workers, she says, want to be in on meetings, even if they claim otherwise. "You want to be an actor at some point. If you're not, you become ancillary, and they'll look to replace you," D'Costa says. This explains the persistence of status meetings, during which "a leader is rattling off milestones and deliverables. If you don't show up, there's no confirmation that you are fulfilling your role."

Having many meetings to complain about is in some ways a status symbol—especially at the C-level, where executives must meet with their teams and with each other. In 2009, an "Executive Time Use Project" tracked how executives of global companies spent and managed meeting time. It found that the most effective managers spent the most time in meetings with other executives and with clients.[41]

Still, employees and managers often struggle to control their time, especially when they feel they spend more time meeting than they do actually working at specific independent tasks, D'Costa says. Power struggles erupt over planting meetings on others' schedules through online scheduling programs. Gscheidle, the Herman Miller executive, says that many meetings are doomed before they happen when the meeting request barnacles itself on participants' calendars. "People think, 'This is a block of time that has been added to my calendar, thanks to scheduling technology.' And we can't override the tools. So, the default is a tension that you can't control your own time."

Schwartzman says the fact that meetings are so loathed, and thus have become a rich target for satire, parody and platoons of consultants and technologies, only proves that they are not what they seem to be. Modern meetings are in a constant state of reinvention because "we believe that what meetings do or shouldn't do isn't what they actually do or should do," she says.

The more that consultants claim to quantify the ineffectiveness of meetings, the more attention and resources are devoted to transforming something that isn't what most people think it is, Schwartzman says. In fact, she says, those consultants and technology companies on a mission to reinvent meetings have a vested interest in perpetuating the notion that meetings are so bad that they deserve greater investment. Technology is not a solution, she says, if it simply adds layers of meetings in the absence of awareness about why an organization's staffers are chronically frustrated with its meetings.

Space for Thought

Gscheidle says corporate clients still need large, technically equipped rooms for scheduled "show and tell" activity. But her clients also want informal spaces for spontaneous meetings, such as living room-like conversation pits and internal coffeehouses. Many clients specify multiple gathering places for stand-up meetings: a cluster of bar tables (but no bar stools) or slanted, waist-high counters perfect for resting a note-taking tablet.

Managers are paying more attention to how decisions pile up in anticipation of a decision-making meeting, while work coasts in the meantime, Gscheidle says. Some of this is inevitable: "Batching happens," she says. But tolerating bottlenecks and the resulting rush of work is, according to Herman Miller research, giving way to the expectation of ongoing collaboration. "Collaborative events," in Herman Miller parlance, take under 30 minutes, involve two or three people and occur at workstations or in casual settings.[42]

"Meetings are sort of the language of the company. Some companies say, 'We're only going to have 15 minute stand-ups,' or 'It's all open and collaborative.' It's an indication of what they want their culture to be," D'Costa says. "But at the end of the day, that need for face-to-face hasn't been removed. It's still a fundamental part of how we do business. You have to confirm that you belong to the company and to the team."

LOOKING AHEAD

Drilling Down

"I meet. Therefore, I am." That's the existential essence of unnecessary meetings, says Sturm, the video and digital marketing content creator.

But, he says, the hidebound notion of meeting to meet is on a collision course with startup culture. In fast-paced, resource-thin startup organizations, meetings must be worth the time and attention they take away from productive work. Every minute spent in a meeting is a minute lost in getting a product to market.

Established organizations tend to view time as a commodity that they don't want to waste. Startups, in contrast, view time as a resource to be invested, he explains. Startups with such a philosophy find that they must struggle to retain it as they grow and as pressure mounts from within and without to default to the norm.

Sturm experienced this as he started his own company, and he deals with the dynamic daily as he works with clients that are startups. He thinks the startup philosophy of meetings will prevail because other companies want to be like startups.

Paul Graham, a serial entrepreneur, programmer and co-founder of tech investment firm Y Combinator, crystallized the startup philosophy of meetings in his seminal essay "Maker's Schedule, Manager's Schedule."[43] In it, he outlines the difference between "makers"—programmers, writers, designers and other creative or "making" jobs—and "managers," who translate daily operations into short-term and long-term results. Makers and managers have opposite requirements for time and meetings, Graham wrote. Makers need long stretches of uninterrupted "flow" time to stay in their creative grooves. Managers go from one conversation to another. When managers, who usually outrank makers, schedule meetings for their own convenience, it disrupts the creative flow of makers.

In traditional companies, that's just too bad for makers. Job titles such as "individual contributors" or "team members" barely disguise makers' lack of power to protect their most creative periods from meetings that not only take time but also make it difficult to be efficient with the time they do get.

Startup culture, posited Graham, puts makers and managers on the same plane in terms of respect for their process and time. If the makers can't make, the managers don't have much to sell (and investors certainly won't reap returns).

"Each type of schedule works fine by itself. Problems arise when they meet. Since most powerful people operate on the manager's schedule, they're in a position to make everyone resonate at their frequency if they want to. But the smarter ones restrain themselves, if they know that some of the people working for them need long chunks of time to work in," Graham wrote.[44]

In his businesses, he reconciled the maker-versus-manager meeting culture by scheduling meetings in advance so that makers could plan accordingly. Graham also cross-pollinated his meeting approach through the startups that he backed and to other investors and startups through his voluminous network.

Key aspects of Graham's approach include: inviting only employees who must be in the meeting; setting and sticking to a clear, short agenda; and holding brainstorming sessions as separate meetings so free-flowing discussions do not hijack routine meetings.

Startups that grew into large companies, such as Google, have consciously tried to scale Graham-inspired scheduling even as they gain more makers and more managers. Mature organizations attempting to adopt aspects of startup culture are exploring the approach, although it's not easy to retroactively integrate it into settled cultures. "Meetings are still the cockroaches that all companies think they are, but they're slowly dying," Sturm says.

Meanwhile, new technologies have put wheels onto Graham's concept. Sturm doesn't meet with clients face-to-face nearly as often as he used to. Instead, he's constantly in an endless meeting slowly scrolling across a window he keeps open on his computer screen. Virtual collaboration, project management and knowledge-sharing tools have created a new dimension. As with always-on social media, workers are physically in their own space, but virtually together (even if they physically are in adjacent offices).

Project management platforms—such as Slack, Asana, Igloo and Podio—enable workers to check off tasks as they are completed, find experts within their teams for troubleshooting and have quick online "huddles" to change plans or discuss a problem.[45] These are all functions that replace the standard status meeting, say the companies. And, popular virtual meeting platforms, such as Skype and Citrix GotoMeeting, let workers see each others' screens and support webinars and similar forms of virtual meetings.

"It's a constant stream of dialogue," Sturm says of the tools. It's quick and easy to review discussions and decisions, and such tools can be an introvert's best friend, enabling makers (especially) to develop relationships and trust before meeting face-to-face. "You feel smarter," he says. "If you're in a [face-to-face] meeting and you look something up on your phone, it looks like you're not paying attention. But through these tools, you have more resources . . . to look things up. It takes more time, but over the project, it takes less time," he says.

As they adopt technologies that redefine meetings, companies find that work and communication flow differently, forcing a sweeping revision of how work gets done, says Joe Staples, chief marketing officer of Workfront, in Lehi, Utah. Workfront designs, produces and supports cloud-based collaboration tools. And as it has used its own collaboration tool for its own projects, Workfront's own corporate meeting culture has changed, says Staples.

"Eliminating status meetings has allowed us to focus on other types of meetings," he says. For instance, "we'll bring a creative team together to work on a campaign. We'll do some things to structure the meeting, but it wouldn't be reliant on technology. We'd decide on goals and resources, kick around ideas, decide on an idea, and then we'd go into Workfront to assign resources to the campaign."

When everyone knows that the meeting's last phase is slotting work into a new project in the system, the meeting itself is organized around that goal, says Staples. "Now we're thinking about the deliverables that go into the Workfront," he says. "It helps us know what we need to identify, what's the timing, what creative resources do we need. Knowing that we have to define those things sets a structure for what the project looks like. Now, we ask the right questions in the meeting."

Chronology

1600s–1870s	**Formal and informal meetings gain a foothold in American society.**
1630s–1800s	New England towns hold public forums where residents gather to debate tax rates, land policy and other municipal matters—the beginning of so-called town hall meetings.
1787	Influential American landowners, lawyers and merchants convene for the Constitutional Convention in Philadelphia, where, in contentious meetings that last three and a half months, they reach the compromises necessary to frame a constitution for the new nation.
1876	Army engineering officer Henry Martyn Robert writes and publishes "Robert's Rules of Order," a formal guide for meetings that becomes a generally accepted template in American culture.
1880s–1960s	**Industrialization gives rise to modern corporate structures.**
1880s–1920s	As a growing U.S. economy continues to industrialize, corporations featuring boards of directors, chief executives and other departments institutionalize a staple of modern life: the meeting.
1944	Delegates from 44 countries meet in Bretton Woods, N.H., to regulate international financial affairs in preparation for a post-World War II economy.
1950s	U.S. economy thrives and corporations prosper during the presidency of Dwight Eisenhower, further cementing the importance of meetings in American corporate culture.
1960s	A variety of new and more formal meeting types, including summits, conferences and task forces, emerge during an era typified by the male-dominated "Mad Men" of Madison Avenue.
1970s–Present	**New technologies transform American office culture, enabling workers and teams to meet virtually.**
1970s	Researchers invent word-processing software and laser printers and introduce new computer technologies to offices.

1983	Tandy and RadioShack introduce one of the first notebook-style portable laptop computers, the Tandy Radio Shack TRS-80 Model 100—a development that will soon enable employees to work from home or on the road.
1988	Microsoft releases first version of Microsoft Mail.
1989	Northwestern University anthropology professor Helen B. Schwartzman publishes a study of Western meeting culture, proposing that meetings should emphasize organizational communication and decision-making instead of following existing norms and traditional rules from Robert's Rules.
1989	Computer scientist Tim Berners-Lee invents the World Wide Web, which permits users to connect and meet virtually over the Internet. . . . Email becomes popular during the 1990s, led by America Online and other Internet pioneers; the explosive growth of email helps revolutionize the way workers communicate and meet.
1998	Verizon publishes "Meetings in America," a study that proposes ways for companies to reduce meeting costs and improve meeting efficiency.
2001	9/11 terrorist attacks halt international travel, requiring some multinational corporations to forgo face-to-face meetings with their foreign-based employees in favor of virtual ones.
2003	Swedish and Danish entrepreneurs create Skype, one of the first popularized videoconferencing software companies. . . . Meeting spaces begin to grow in number and become smaller, according to designers at Herman Miller, an office design and furnishings manufacturer; the average office goes from one meeting space for every 20 employees before 2000 to one for every 10 beginning around 2003.
2009	A study by Oxford Economics, a global research firm, concludes that face-to-face meetings are making a comeback despite the popularity of videoconferencing and says every dollar invested in business travel adds $12.50 in revenue. . . . Paul Graham, co-founder of tech investment firm Y Combinator, publishes "Maker's Schedule, Manager's Schedule," which calls for a startup approach to meetings in which meetings are structured differently for creative "makers" and managers.
2014–15	A Harris Poll survey finds that more than half of U.S. office workers see "wasteful" meetings as the greatest obstacle to work productivity. . . . Globally, almost 3 billion people have Internet access, as electronic business communication continues to grow and evolve.

RESOURCES

The Next Step

Efficiency

Feloni, Richard, "A Facebook cofounder's productivity startup recommends 5 ways to dramatically improve your meetings," Business Insider, Feb. 8, 2016, http://tinyurl.com/j83jc79.

To increase meeting productivity, companies should impose caps on recurring meetings, designate one "no-meeting" day each week and allow employees five minutes at the end of meetings to ensure everyone is aware of their expected responsibilities, according to a list of best practices by technology company Asana.

Gallo, Amy, "The Condensed Guide to Running Meetings," Harvard Business Review, July 6, 2015, http://tinyurl.com/ohcbwan.

Organizations can make meetings more effective by limiting attendance to seven people, banning mobile devices and setting clear agendas, among other strategies, say two experts on meetings and decision-making.

Ha, Anthony, "Meetings Are Usually Terrible, But YC-Backed WorkLife Aims To Change That," TechCrunch, March 11, 2015, http://tinyurl.com/mcztnwe.

Technology startup WorkLife developed computer and mobile-device software that allows users to update meeting agendas, assign tasks, track time and generate shareable summaries from notes.

Leadership

Joseph, Arthur, "Leadership: Can You Learn to Communicate and Embody It?" Entrepreneur, Oct. 19, 2015, http://tinyurl.com/ordrugw.

Business classes often fail to teach students communication skills required of effective leaders, including how to facilitate and present information at meetings, says a communication strategist and speech coach.

Norton, Steven, "University IT Staff Gets Help Translating 'Geek Speech' to English," The Wall Street Journal, Aug. 25, 2015, http://tinyurl.com/gsh84lf.

A public-speaking group teaches information technology employees at the University of Arizona to improve their leadership and communication skills and has helped many to become more vocal during business meetings, says the university's chief information officer.

Tabaka, Marla, "How a Real Leader Runs a Company Meeting," Inc., Sept. 3, 2015, http://tinyurl.com/p4lto55.

The best leaders establish clear purposes for calling a meeting, respect company hierarchies, manage time and distribute information to staff before the gathering, according to a small-business strategy consultant.

Spatial Design

Gallagher, John, "Office design today embraces flexible workspaces," Detroit Free Press, Aug. 1, 2015, http://tinyurl.com/ptkd2hn.

The increasingly collaborative nature of office work over the past several decades contributed to a shift toward open meeting spaces, say employees of Michigan-based office-furniture maker Herman Miller.

Swanson, Ana, "Fascinating photos show the best and worst office designs for employees," The Washington Post, July 7, 2015, http://tinyurl.com/zeo2kwv.

A principal at architecture and design firm Gensler predicts offices of the future will feature smaller, more numerous meeting rooms—a change from the 1990s, when office layouts began to be more open and collaborative.

Zipkin, Amy, "Conference Centers Offer Companies Meeting Space Without Strings," The New York Times, April 6, 2015, http://tinyurl.com/jc7tdaj.

More stand-alone urban conference centers have appeared since the 2007–09 global recession, offering more flexible and comfortable meeting spaces for companies at cheaper rates than hotel-connected conference centers.

Technology

Segan, Sascha, "At Samsung Unpacked, Zuckerberg Ushers in the Year of VR," PC Mag, Feb. 21, 2016, http://tinyurl.com/jfshtmb.

Virtual-reality headsets will allow business colleagues to hold meetings from around the world, predicted Facebook CEO Mark Zuckerberg at an annual mobile technology conference in Barcelona.

Shah, Agam, "Quick start to meetings saves money, improves efficiency for Intel," CIO, Feb. 1, 2016, http://tinyurl.com/jeeyngm.

Technology company Intel installed wireless tools in more than 500 conference rooms, boosting meetings' efficiency by enabling on-and off-site employees to share information via monitors without having to waste time connecting cables to computers and other devices.

Warner, Kelsey, "Could Microsoft's humongous touchscreen make meetings bearable?" The Christian Science Monitor, June 10, 2015, http://tinyurl.com/zodwcy9.

Microsoft developed the Surface Hub, a touchscreen device available in 55-or 84-inch formats, to serve as a tablet computer, blackboard and TV screen and is marketing it to companies hoping to streamline boardroom meetings.

Organizations

American Anthropological Association
2300 Clarendon Blvd., Suite 1301, Arlington, VA 22201
703-528-1902
www.americananthro.org

Professional association for academic and practicing anthropologists, including business anthropologists, who study group dynamics and cultural history and evolution.

American Society of Association Executives
1575 I St., N.W., Washington, DC 20005
202-626-2723
www.asaecenter.org

Professional association for paid managers of trade, nonprofit and professional associations; provides training and advice on meeting logistics.

International Facilitators Association
15050 Cedar Ave. South, #116-353, Apple Valley, MN 55124

952-891-3541

www.iaf-world.org

Professional association for meeting facilitators.

International Society of Protocol and Etiquette Professionals

13116 Hutchinson Way, Suite 200, Silver Spring, MD 20906-5947

301-946-5265

www.ispep.org

Professional association for experts, trainers and coaches in meeting etiquette, business etiquette, international and cross-cultural etiquette and customs, among other communication and interpersonal dynamics.

Meeting Professionals International

2711 Lyndon B. Johnson Freeway, Suite 600, Dallas, TX 75234-7349

972-702-3000

www.mpiweb.org

Professional association for those responsible for organizing, planning and managing meetings, including nonprofit, business and academic gatherings.

National Speakers Organization

1500 S. Priest Drive, Tempe, AZ 85281

480-968-2552

www.nsaspeaker.org

Professional association for current and aspiring professional speakers.

Q&A: Charles Steinfield on Virtual Meetings

"THESE TOOLS LET YOU DO THINGS YOU CAN'T DO IN A FACE-TO-FACE MEETING"

Charles Steinfield is a professor in the Department of Media and Information at Michigan State University. He talked with SAGE Business Researcher contributor Joanne Cleaver about the respective merits of face-to-face and virtual meetings. This is an edited transcript of their conversation.

Technology companies and many consultants seem to believe that the reviled "status report" meeting can be eradicated through online meeting platforms. Would it be more effective to reinvent face-to-face status report meetings rather than seek to eliminate them?

The value of a meeting is that when there is information to be shared in a group and you bring all those people together, then everyone knows that everyone has been exposed to the same information. It's hard to reliably do that in other ways. You have other tools—posting it on the company intranet—but it's not the same quality of knowledge.

There's also symbolic value that when you bring people together, this is important enough to make everyone stop everything else that they're doing and come to this meeting. Ensuring consistent pickup of information is a historic problem through virtual teams. Say you want to hold a meeting through Skype—it's not a perfect replica of a face-to-face meeting. You have four people in four locations, all on a Skype call; each person still misses some information about what's going on in the other person's context. You have a tiny window through the video camera. You don't know what's happening outside their office, and who else is part of their day. It's a situation that people underappreciate. You're literally not seeing the whole picture. You might not realize that there's someone sitting off camera who's hearing everything.

What are the inherent strengths of virtual platforms versus in-person meetings?

When you have a geographically distributed team, you have to rely on technology. These tools let you do things

you can't do in a face-to-face meeting. You can quickly share things. You can engage in back-channel interactions. Say you're in a Skype meeting, but you're texting in a side conversation through your phone with one person. That's hard to do in a face-to-face meeting or even a traditional video conference. And collaborating virtually is a must for when teams involve self-employed professionals and for smaller companies with geographically dispersed teams.

And what are the inherent strengths of in-person meetings versus virtual platforms?

When people are connecting virtually in real time, the meetings tend to be shorter, and there's less socializing. There's a drive to be efficient. It feels artificial. But in person, there's pressure to do some chitchat and some socializing, and that has a benefit. It strengthens ties among people and has benefits for how teams function. To the extent that that doesn't happen through technology, then teams are a bit less cohesive and less trusting.

Can social media replicate the important informal communication of pre-and post-meetings, creating a more meaningful context for virtual meetings?

Social media can help a lot. With global teams, companies bring in people from different countries for face-to-face meetings, and they will periodically have team meetings virtually, but most companies have implemented their own internal social media platforms, and they provide rich capabilities, like microblogging and status updates. Other networks offer personal profiles that let people share personal information. It helps people build relationships. You can look people up and spark conversation in the meeting that wouldn't otherwise have occurred. Technology doesn't so much replace meetings as complement them. When groups do get together face to face, that meeting is very important, and in between, these other tools keep relationships alive.

7

CYBERSECURITY
Can businesses protect themselves from computer crime?

Pat Wechsler

EXECUTIVE SUMMARY

As fast as Internet use has grown over the past two decades, so too has the cybersecurity challenge for businesses and governments that are fighting to keep their data and networks safe from intruders. Today, they face an unprecedented assault from a powerful global army of sophisticated, well-organized and well-financed hackers who vigilantly seek vulnerabilities to exploit. In the past couple of years alone, these shadowy figures have stolen personal information on hundreds of millions of U.S. customers and employees and have cost enterprises close to $500 billion. With each new device or product connected to the Internet, the possibility of hackers wreaking economic chaos has grown. Despite the mounting threat, most enterprises have failed to implement the kind of rigorous security protocols necessary to keep out even low-tech efforts to penetrate networks. Among the questions being debated: Are companies responding adequately to cybercrime? Should the United States encourage American companies to "hack back" when they think they've been hacked? Can information sharing between businesses and government help fight cybercrime?

OVERVIEW

Larry Ponemon, who has counseled companies for years on how to protect their data and computer systems, remembers a cybersecurity presentation he made not long ago to a major technology company on areas of risk.

"As I wrapped up, some smart aleck—the head of research and development, I think—told me that his company didn't have to worry because 'our security is as tight as Fort Knox,'" the consultant now recalls. "He said, 'No one—not the Chinese, not the Russians, not the Romanians, nobody—would be able to infiltrate the company's network through the Internet.'"

A few months later, the company got in touch to let Ponemon know that the smart aleck turned out to be right—no hacker was able to penetrate the system through the Internet.

From *SAGE Business Researcher,*
February 1, 2016

Instead, cyberthieves disguised themselves as outside contractors, walked into the building and proceeded to steal valuable designs and other data off the network.

"This wasn't unique," Ponemon says. "Companies too often think they have it covered or it will never happen to them."

Ponemon tells the story to reinforce one of the major reasons cybercrime is so difficult to combat: Hackers are numerous, smart, more organized than ever and, above all else, persistent. If they can't penetrate the system using one method on a certain day, they simply keep trying until they find a chink in the corporate armor or a time when a company's guard is down.

For the past two decades, corporations and governments around the world have been fending off intrusions to their computer networks by shadowy figures that may be working in the office next door or thousands of miles away on another continent. The last 10 years, in particular, have been marked by increasingly large and dangerous data breaches—with cyberthieves making off with valuable proprietary information and data from hundreds of millions of personal accounts on corporate and government networks. While these hacks have caused considerable disruption for the corporate and human victims, cybersecurity experts warn that even more dire, even potentially deadly, consequences may lie ahead as almost every aspect of everyday life—from driving a car to operating the national electrical grid—becomes increasingly linked to the Internet or other large "hackable" systems. [1]

The exact dimensions of the economic threat are difficult to quantify. In 2009, security-software seller McAfee warned that the global costs of cybercrime already had topped $1 trillion a year—a figure used subsequently in speeches by President Obama and senators on both sides of the aisle.[2] A more conservative 2014 estimate from the Center for Strategic and International Studies, a Washington think tank, placed the annual cost of cybercrime between $375 billion and $575 billion, making the economic impact comparable to global drug trafficking.[3]

Almost 800 U.S. Data Breaches Reported in 2015

Still, most agree global cybercrime is escalating with the proliferation of both hackable targets and technically savvy and well-financed hackers. A report by Juniper Research contends costs could reach $2 trillion annually by 2019.[4]

Given the increasing sophistication of malware—essentially software designed to disable computer systems—"one of the worries that many of us have in the security industry is the potential for attacks on industrial control systems," says Ponemon, chairman and founder of the Michigan-based Ponemon Institute, who has served on numerous government and corporate Internet security commissions. "In an attack against a power utility, you could cause a brownout for a few minutes, or if it is done well, it could be for months. Those kinds of attacks used to be the stuff of science fiction movies, but they're real."

The escalation of the cyberwar is linked to the increased organization and cooperation among hackers, many of whom operate out of Russia, Eastern Europe and China. Whereas

Number of U.S. data breaches, 2005–15

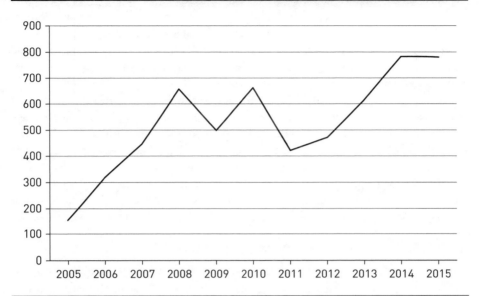

U.S. businesses, government agencies, schools and other organizations recorded 781 data breaches in 2015, just short of a 10-year high in 2014. Before 2015, the number of breaches had risen for four consecutive years. Health and medical record incidents accounted for two-thirds of breaches in 2015.

Note: "Data breach" is defined as an incident in which an individual's name plus a Social Security number, driver's license number, medical record or financial record is potentially put at risk of exposure, either electronically or in paper format.

Sources: Data for 2015 from "Data Breach Reports," Identity Theft Resource Center, Dec. 31, 2015, p. 4, http://tinyurl.com/p8zuqtp; all other data from "ITRC Breach Statistics 2005-2014," Identity Theft Resource Center, 2015, http://tinyurl.com/h4nlmqk

a couple of decades ago hackers tended to be young computer whizzes working alone in their basements, hackers now are part of well-defined, often global enterprises, similar to the syndicates that participate in drug or arms trafficking. Some have even replicated corporate structures, paying salaries to their army of hackers and creating marketing and customer support teams to sell their malware to other hackers.[5]

"Hackers often report to an office every day like the rest of us," says Alan Brill, a senior managing director at investigative risk-analysis firm Kroll. "And they spend their eight hours searching for vulnerabilities in corporate and governmental computer networks. It's organized and relentless."

Because of the global nature of the enterprise, the complicity of some governments and the sophisticated technology hackers use to cloak IP addresses, authorities in the United

States and elsewhere have had only limited success identifying culprits, let alone prosecuting the worst malefactors.

"Upwards of 80 percent of cybercrime acts are estimated to originate in some form of organized activity, with cybercrime black markets established on a cycle of malware creation, computer infection, botnet [networks of infected computers that send out spam and viruses] management, harvesting of personal and financial data, data sale, and 'cashing out' of financial information," a United Nations report stated in 2013.[6]

Increased organization also has changed the nature of hacks.[7] "Early threats were usually hit-and-run," Brill says. "Someone broke in, stole something—perhaps a blueprint or a set of documents—and left, attempting to leave behind as little evidence as possible. Today the goal is to remain inside the network for as long as possible without being detected and do as much damage as possible—either stealing information or causing disruption."

This extended, under-the-radar presence is known within the cybersecurity industry as an Advanced Persistent Threat (APT). Originally a strategy of government-to-government cyberespionage, APT denotes both the attacker and technique. The hack follows a pattern:[8]

- The attackers first research the target organization.

- They then break into the network using social engineering techniques, such as spear phishing, which involves getting people in an organization to open emails and unknowingly infect the system with malicious software.

- Next, they attempt to remain undetected in the network while they gather information and assess where valuable data are stored.

- Finally, the attackers collect the data and extract as much information as possible.

Some of the most infamous recent APTs and spear-phishing assaults included the 2014 attack on the computer networks of Sony Pictures Entertainment, which resulted in dozens of terabytes (each approximately a trillion bytes) of confidential information being stolen—including highly embarrassing emails from the division's top executives.[9] Another was the hack of Target Corp.'s computer network in 2013, when spear-phishing emails were sent to a vendor with access to portions of the retailer's network.[10] Attackers stole information from 70 million customer accounts and 40 million credit and debit card numbers.[11]

A third APT attack, particularly humiliating for the United States, was against the federal Office of Personnel Management (OPM). The attack exposed the personal information of as many as 22 million current and former federal workers, including fingerprints and background checks for classified positions. Although made public in June 2015, the APT began more than a year before. The initial investigation pointed to government-sponsored Chinese hackers. In December 2015, in an unprecedented effort to avoid sanctions and prove innocence, the Chinese government arrested individuals they claimed were responsible.[12]

Experts continue to debate the sources of many recent hacks, sometimes because they involve multiple players simultaneously—and always because hackers have the capability to mask their IP addresses, which would reveal where the attacks originated. In 2011, a politically motivated group called Anonymous attacked Sony's PlayStation Network, the company's online entertainment service for users of its PlayStation video games. The so-called hacktivist group used a distributed denial of services (DDoS) attack, a hacking technique designed to overwhelm a system with traffic from multiple sources. The network was shut down for almost a month. The

Katherine Archuleta, the head of the federal Office of Personnel Management, testifies on Capitol Hill in June 2015 about a data breach at her agency that exposed personal information about millions of government employees. In July 2015, she stepped down from her position.

Source: Drew Angerer/Getty Images

assault was revenge, the group said, for Sony's lawsuit against hacker George Hotz, who was being sued for distributing information on how to break the digital protections on the PlayStation 3 to allow the use of unauthorized programs.[13]

Yet, when it became evident that information on millions of PlayStation accounts, including credit card data, was stolen, Anonymous denied any role. "If an honest investigation into the credit card theft is conducted, Anonymous will not be found liable," the group said in a statement in May 2011. "While we are a distributed and decentralized group, our 'leadership' does not condone credit card theft."[14]

Three people in Spain, reportedly connected to Anonymous, were arrested for participating in the DDoS attack, although no mention was made of any role in the theft of credit cards.[15] Similarly, in the subsequent Sony Pictures hack in 2014, authorities have never been able to pin down whether the culprits were North Korean or Russian hackers or the two working together.[16]

APTs are often associated with a state-sponsored cyberthreat. Cyber investigative group Mandiant, now a subsidiary of security firm FireEye, has published multiple reports outlining the activities of cyberespionage groups working out of China. These groups have conducted hundreds of APT attacks against Western governments and corporations, predominantly in the United States, in an effort to steal confidential data, according to Mandiant.[17]

The plethora of data breaches, particularly since 2013, clearly has alarmed the American public. In a 2014 survey by nonpartisan pollster Pew Research Center, respondents ranked cyberattacks from other countries as the second most serious security threat the nation faces after Islamic extremist groups, such as the Islamic State and al Qaeda.[18] That survey was conducted before the onslaught of cyberattacks in 2014 and 2015.

Yet, despite rising concern, experts say organizations still drag their feet when it comes to instituting rigorous cybersecurity measures. Many recent high-profile APTs succeeded because of sloppy security protocols and the failure to encrypt data or perform timely upgrades.[19]

Some experts say insufficient security measures sometimes reflect the lack of "pain" companies feel because of data breaches or the presumption that only the highest-profile targets need worry. According to the Ponemon Institute, the average breach in fiscal 2015 cost $3.79 million or about $154 per stolen record, but the expense varies dramatically based on location.[20]

The United States tops other nations with a cost of $217 per record, up more than 15 percent since 2013 and 8 percent since 2014. In contrast, a stolen record in India costs only about $56, up from $37 in 2013; in the United Kingdom, the cost is $163, up from $143.

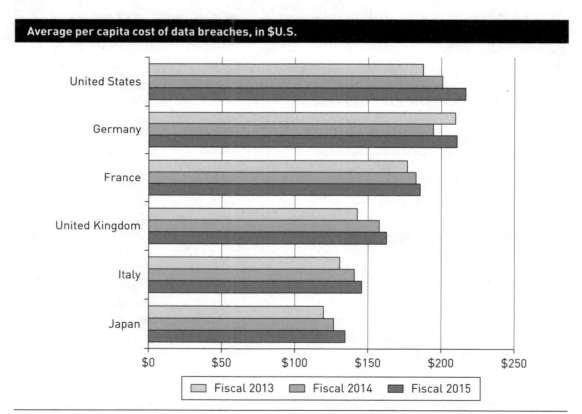

Average per capita cost of data breaches, in $U.S.

The average data breach cost the United States ($217) and Germany ($211) more per stolen or lost electronic record than any other country in 2015. Costs per record increased for each of the last two years in all but one of the six countries with the highest per-capita data-breach costs.

Notes: "Per capita cost" defined as total cost of the data breach divided by the number of lost or stolen records. Estimates are for fiscal years. Graph excludes Canada due to lack of data for 2013 and 2014.

Source: "2015 Cost of Data Breach Study: Global Analysis," Ponemon Institute and IBM, May 2015, p. 5, downloaded from http://tinyurl.com/zjozwe8

Data Thefts Most Costly in United States

While those numbers cause some pain, recent instances of CEOs and high-ranking executives losing their jobs following major breaches may prove to be the greatest incentive for tighter security, some experts contend. Among the high-profile casualties: Gregg Steinhafel, Target's CEO, and Beth Jacob, the company's chief information officer; OPM Director Katherine Archuleta; and Amy Pascal, the co-chairwoman of Sony Pictures.[21]

"What really catches the attention of executives is the sacking of a CEO," says Scott Shackelford, a fellow at the Center for Applied Cybersecurity Research at Indiana University and an assistant professor in business law at the university's Kelley School of Business. "It really makes people sit up straighter in their chairs, the more they see executives held accountable."

With the scope and sophistication of the Internet and computer technology expanding, so too are the threats to privacy, financial stability and physical safety. As individuals, companies and nations grapple with how to meet the growing challenge from hackers, here are some of the issues under debate:

Weighing the Issues

As a favorite target of both politically and economically motivated hackers, Sony has become the poster child for the failure of companies to respond adequately. In 2011, when the PlayStation Network was shut down and more than 100 million accounts compromised in at least two separate breaches, Sony was criticized for storing sensitive customer and employee data unencrypted.[22] Close to a dozen hacks of various Sony divisions occurred during just that year alone.[23]

It didn't end there. In 2014, when hackers attacked Sony's film and television division, the cyberthieves found a folder filled with spreadsheets containing employees' personal information, including salaries and home addresses. Although some of the spreadsheets were password-protected, the passwords—unencrypted—were listed in a document, named "passwords," in the same folder. Not long after that attack, the PlayStation Network was hit again in a DDoS attack that kicked people offline for a couple of hours.[24]

Sony said the PlayStation breach cost it at least $171 million, but some analysts put costs as high as $250 million.[25] The 2014 Sony Pictures breach was expected to cost the company upward of $35 million, significantly less than the 2011 hack because it did not involve customer data.[26]

According to experts, Sony is hardly unique in its inadequate protections against cyberattacks or its failure to learn from its mistakes.

Spending Most Likely for Technologies, Audits

"By any measure, cybersecurity is the biggest common threat organizations face," Bob Moritz, chairman of the accounting and consulting firm PricewaterhouseCoopers (PwC), and David Burg, PwC's cybersecurity practice leader, wrote in an article for Fortune. "It is also the one where we see the largest gap between threat and preparedness."[27]

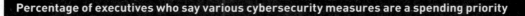

Percentage of executives who say various cybersecurity measures are a spending priority

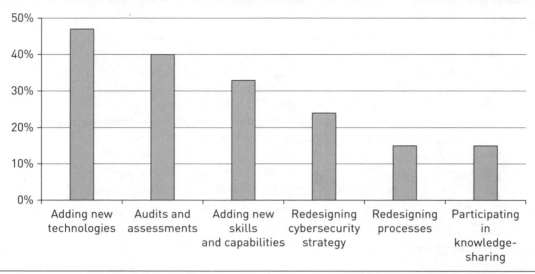

Nearly half of U.S. business, law enforcement and government executives said adding new cybersecurity technologies is a spending priority in a 2015 survey by PricewaterhouseCoopers. About one-fourth included redesigning cybersecurity strategy among their spending priorities, and 15 percent included participating in knowledge-sharing with other organizations.

Note: Based on a survey of more than 500 executives of U.S. businesses, law enforcement services and government agencies.

Source: "US cybersecurity: Progress stalled; Key findings from the 2015 US State of Cybercrime Survey," PricewaterhouseCoopers, July 2015, p. 10, http://tinyurl.com/zfzodqj

While perfect security does not exist, experts agree that most companies fall short of even bare minimums. Some blame the gap in preparedness on a failure to invest sufficiently in technology and personnel, while others see the problem as the lack of a rigorous protocol to keep systems constantly updated and employees well informed about hacking techniques.

"Organizations have not kept their security profiles up to date," says Brill, who founded Kroll's global high-tech investigations practice. "And those enterprises that fail to maintain a reasonable set of controls—recognizing that the standard of reasonable evolves just as technology evolves—are going to find themselves targeted successfully. Failing to put in critical patches, for instance, is something we run into all the time as we work with organizations. It's something that shouldn't happen; it's just too easy to avoid."

Among the slowest adopters of cybersecurity protocols have been small businesses. A survey of 1,016 small-business owners in May 2015 found that almost one-third had suffered a cyberattack and 95 percent lacked insurance to cover such attacks. While 81 percent said cybersecurity was a concern, less than half had invested any money in security measures. Only 11 percent even had an information technology person on staff or an outside consultant to handle cybersecurity.[28]

Cybersecurity Concerns Most Small-Business Owners

That may change as multinational firms with extensive vendor relationships compel their supply chains to meet standards. In several large data breaches—such as Target's and one at Home Depot in 2014 that exposed information on 56 million credit cards—hackers used vendor networks and credentials to get inside the large retailers' systems. [29]

The Federal Energy Regulatory Commission (FERC), regulator of the nation's power supply, has pushed for stricter cybersecurity standards for industry supply chains, particularly as they affect vendors dealing with large utilities and other power generators, which could be appealing targets to hackers. IBM, with its own extensive supply chain, has

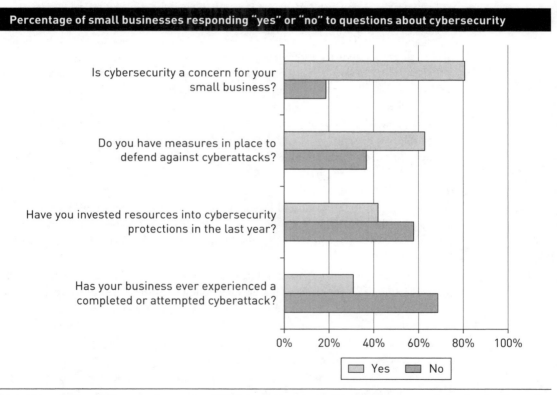

Percentage of small businesses responding "yes" or "no" to questions about cybersecurity

About four-fifths of owners of very small U.S. businesses say they are concerned about cybersecurity, according to a 2015 survey by Web-hosting company Endurance International Group. Nearly two-thirds of respondents said they had measures in place to defend against cyberattacks, although only 42 percent had invested resources into such protections within the last year.

Notes: Based on survey of 1,016 owners of U.S.-based small businesses from April 24–28, 2015. Small businesses are defined as enterprises employing 10 or fewer full-time or part-time workers.

Source: "New Survey Finds A Vast Majority Of U.S. Small Business Owners Believe Cybersecurity Is A Concern And Lawmakers Should Do More To Combat Cyber-Attacks," news release, Endurance International Group, May 4, 2015, http://tinyurl.com/q6tn2mz

started to make meeting federal guidelines on cybersecurity—such as those proposed by the Commerce Department's National Institute of Standards and Technology (NIST)—a requirement for its vendors.[30]

The biggest controversy is not whether companies are doing enough: Most experts agree they aren't. The debate is over the best way to improve that situation.

"Cybersecurity needs to be part of a total risk management strategy," Indiana University's Shackelford says. "Too many companies simply [install] technology and think they have solved the problem. Effective cybersecurity requires businesses to think through possible risks and then test against them. It needs to be proactive."

However, there is no compulsory U.S. or international standard as to what qualifies as adequate cybersecurity. The closest thing is probably the set of guidelines NIST established in 2014, called the Framework for Improving Critical Infrastructure Cybersecurity, or Framework Version 1.0.[31] Although it was developed for sectors considered critical to a functioning nation, such as telecommunications, food production and energy generation, an expanding number of cybersecurity experts contend the framework should be adopted by all industries and then customized to fit the needs of each.

That the framework focuses on "detection, response and remediation instead of just prevention puts [it] ahead of many current IT security strategies that assume attackers can be locked out at the firewall," Kevin Bocek, vice president of product marketing and threat research at security software vendor Venafi, remarked just before the guidelines were announced last year.[32]

In addition, the Federal Trade Commission (FTC), charged with protecting consumers and assessing company accountability in the wake of a data breach, also has suggested that the NIST Framework closely approximates its own enforcement standards. In a speech before the Center for Strategic and International Studies in September 2014 on the role of agencies in cybersecurity, FTC Commissioner Julie Brill noted that the NIST Framework's emphasis on risk assessment and mitigation "is fully consistent with the FTC's enforcement framework."[33]

The FTC's endorsement has prompted many cybersecurity analysts to suggest that companies will risk FTC penalties if they fail to follow NIST and then suffer a breach.[34]

"In effect, the framework may become the de facto standard for cybersecurity and privacy regulation and may impact legal definitions and enforcement guidelines for cybersecurity moving forward," a May 2014 PricewaterhouseCoopers report predicted. "While the NIST Cybersecurity Framework may not constitute a foolproof formula for cybersecurity, its benefits may be missed by those who choose to forgo or postpone implementation of the voluntary guideline, in part or in whole."[35]

But some critics—and they are a minority—point out that the standards are voluntary and therefore toothless.[36] Several experts suggest that the compilation is too vague and leaves too much to each company's interpretation.

"At [a] high level, they got it right," Andrew Ginter, vice president of industrial security at Waterfall Security Solutions, told Reuters after the final framework was issued. "Further down, it gets murky really fast."[37] Waterfall is an Israeli provider of network security products for infrastructure clients, such as power plants and water treatment facilities.

In the end, the debate over too much or too little has left some companies confused. Many executives and cybersecurity experts expect the government to make the NIST Framework compulsory soon for critical infrastructure industries at least. For other companies, the arbiter on whether to adopt NIST may be the legal and regulatory systems and their ability to hold companies accountable if they fail to follow the few guidelines that do exist.

Should the United States encourage American companies to "hack back" when they think they've been hacked?

In November 2015, a bipartisan congressionally appointed panel, the U.S.-China Economic and Security Review Commission, recommended that companies be allowed to "hack back" against unrelenting Chinese cyberwarfare. The commission argued that China's aggressive cyberespionage program has hurt U.S. companies by stealing proprietary designs, technology, trade secrets and other valuable data at a cost of tens of billions of dollars. Given recent high-profile data breaches believed to be perpetrated by Chinese military hackers, there is no other way to stop the Chinese, except to use their own tactics against them, the commission concluded.[38]

"The United States is ill-prepared to defend itself from cyberespionage when its adversary is determined, centrally coordinated, and technically sophisticated," the report stated. "The Chinese government appears to believe that it has more to gain than to lose from its cyberespionage and attack campaign," which "is likely to continue and may well escalate."

Of course, China is not alone in using hacking as a means to an end. Information leaked by former CIA employee and National Security Agency (NSA) contractor Edward Snowden in 2013 showed that the U.S. government has done its share of phone-hacking of allies, foes and U.S. citizens.[39] One major distinction: The United States appears to be searching for information related to national security concerns, while experts claim China steals information to gain an economic edge over other nations and companies.

If hack backs were made legal, private entities would be allowed, even encouraged, to follow infiltrators back into their computer networks and retrieve data that have been taken, or at least wipe the information. Currently, such behavior would be illegal under U.S. law.

A hack-back provision, not solely directed at China, appears in the House version of the cybersecurity information-sharing bill that passed in April.[40] The Senate approved similar legislation with no hack-back provision in October. The two chambers must go to conference to create a third version acceptable to both.

Several cybersecurity experts already think the bills are no longer relevant to the current set of threats faced by companies.[41] And even some supporters of the hack-back approach believe it should not be extended to the private sector.

"Hack back is a great idea because it basically allows the victim to become the attacker," says Ponemon of the Ponemon Institute. "But who should be using that technique? Should it be restricted to the Department of Defense, the NSA? Or should it be extended to commercial organizations that have been the targets? The conversation around this issue can be a very hairy conversation, because you don't necessarily want to start a cyberwar."

Richard Bejtlich, chief security strategist at FireEye, the network security firm, said that hack back is a good idea in the right hands. "We need to get our hackers to go after their hackers to put pressure on them and disrupt their operations," he said. But Bejtlich doubted private companies would be willing to do it or capable of acting. "We need to start with more government pressure, not put the private sector in that role," he said.[42]

Other experts raise additional problems with putting the hack-back option in private hands.

"So, let's say we pass a law in the U.S. that immunizes private companies," says Brill at Kroll. "That doesn't make it legal in other countries. So you may have your IT department here doing a hack back and your manager in another country getting arrested for it. Also, if this law gets passed here, why won't other countries pass a similar one? It could get very messy."

"I think it's a pretty bad idea, frankly," says Shackelford, who teaches business law and ethics at Indiana University. "The argument you hear for it is that companies are in the best position to defend their own networks . . . and if the attribution [the identity of the hacker] were a little more reliable, that might be a valid argument. But it's not—both technically and legally."

Right now, companies and the government often have only suspicions as to which nation or crime group may have pulled off a hack or data breach, based on the IP addresses used and the tactics. To an extent, hackers have signature moves that help identify them to other hackers and the authorities. But given that these are signature moves, it wouldn't be hard for someone to impersonate a known hacker to fool authorities. In the 2011 Sony PlayStation hack, Anonymous claimed that happened to them.

And what if the law allows hacking back against competitors? "I'm not sure how well it's going to go over if a company claims they've been hacked and then happens to see some intellectual property of their competitor in a hack back," Brill says.

To anticipate how hackers may react to legal retaliation, Brill has been working on a scenario in which "the bad guys find ways to pass their data through intermediaries which if attacked in a hack back would cause great embarrassment."

He suggests, "How's it going to look if Company X claims it has been hacked and traces it back to an IP address that turns out to be a pediatric cancer hospital? And your hack back just knocked their radiation equipment offline?"

"The reality is, if hackers have stolen your data, they probably have it in five different places within minutes," Brill says. "The hack back certainly sounds good on paper, but given the globality of the Internet, the real difficulty with attribution, and the low probability of a company getting back its data without it still being out there, it's really holding out a false promise."

Can information sharing between businesses and government help fight cybercrime?

When it comes to the nation's cybersecurity, the Department of Homeland Security (DHS) is an ardent advocate for information sharing. As the lead federal agency responsible for protecting the nation's critical infrastructure and the security of its computer networks,

DHS encourages companies to share any information they have about new malware or new hacking techniques they've had to confront. It's the "if you see something, say something" approach to cybersecurity.

The department already maintains the National Cybersecurity and Communications Integration Center (NCCIC), a 24/7 incident response headquarters, which DHS describes as the "national nexus of cyber and communications integration for the federal government, intelligence community, and law enforcement."[43] The NCCIC shares data to ensure the private sector is aware of potential vulnerabilities, new developments and potential responses.

President Obama in February 2015 signs an executive order promoting private-sector cybersecurity information sharing. Encouraging such sharing has been part of the administration's cybersecurity strategy.

Source: NICHOLAS KAMM/AFP/Getty Images

Information sharing was a major component of the Obama administration's cybersecurity strategy since the president took office in 2009, although hardly the only piece of the puzzle. The administration, through DHS, also had pushed for compulsory standards for company cybersecurity. Mandating cybersecurity standards—a thrust of the proposed 2012 legislation—couldn't make it through Congress.

In theory, sharing information makes great sense—an opportunity to hear about techniques hackers are using so a company can prepare to defend against them. The problem is that information sharing needs to be in real time to keep up with the development of malware and the emergence of new hacker groups. Many experts consider that unlikely, given corporate caution and government red tape.

Still, many security experts say the cybersecurity legislation that has now passed both chambers of Congress represents a significant step forward in the escalating war against hackers.[44] Although the bills fail to set the security standards requested by Homeland Security, proponents believe the collection and exchange of timely data may, in the end, prove useful.[45]

"There has been a lot of caution about government intervention because it can be a bit static and threats to security change pretty rapidly," Ponemon explains. "If you're locked into a particular standard, it may end up working against you.

"Intelligence sharing, on the other hand, informs your strategy and lets you pivot, particularly if that intelligence is timely," he notes. "Right now, the information companies and government share is often months old and therefore essentially irrelevant. To work, the data has to be very, very current for it to make a difference. This new legislation and the administration's commitment to sharing information should make the process ultimately more effective."

But not all experts share Ponemon's optimism about the information-sharing legislation. Lawmakers, the critics say, can't keep up with changes in technology, so new laws are almost always out of date by the time they pass.[46]

"If Congress passes one bill a year affecting technology, you're talking about a lot," says Joshua Goldfarb, chief technology officer for the Americas at FireEye, a California-based network security firm. "Yet, every day there are new intrusion techniques."

The same is true with passing information along, he says. Giving people the most current information won't be helpful if they don't understand it.

"People need to know how to apply the information to the problems and challenges they face," Goldfarb says. "Without that level of understanding, no amount of information in the world—even the best information—will make a difference."

BACKGROUND

Computer Nerds Gone Wild

In the early days of cybercrime, a company or government agency was more likely to be hacked by a 15-year-old boy living with his parents than by a Chinese state-sponsored spy. In the 1970s and '80s—the toddler days of the Internet—hackers seemed less motivated by money than by the sheer challenge of breaking into the sophisticated computer networks of powerful organizations, particularly government agencies or what was then the telephone monopoly, AT&T.

Not to say there wasn't actual criminality afoot. In the 1970s, across U.S. college campuses, little blue "phreaking" boxes began to appear. These devices helped the user hack into automated telephone systems and steal service from the omnipresent Ma Bell.

Phreaking was a kind of training ground for computer geniuses and hackers, who went by names like Captain Crunch, Dr. No and Peter Perpendicular Pimple. These guys—and they seemingly were all guys—used sound frequencies to get the telephone system to make calls for them. Among those who would become the most famous and richest: Steve Jobs, aka Oaf Tobar, and Steve Wozniak, aka Berkeley Blue.[47] Jobs and Wozniak turned selling blue boxes into their first business, when Wozniak was a freshman at the University of California, Berkeley, years before the friends went on to found Apple. John Draper, aka Captain Crunch, who helped Wozniak and Jobs get started, programmed IBM's first word processor by longhand while in prison for phone fraud.[48]

Other famous hackers who got their start phreaking included Kevin Mitnick, aka Condor (after the 1975 movie "Three Days of the Condor"), who was at one point the world's most notorious hacker, breaking into the networks of IBM, Motorola, Nokia and the Pentagon before being arrested in 1995; Kevin Poulsen, aka Dark Dante, who won a Porsche by hacking into a radio station's phone lines to guarantee he would be the 102nd caller; and Mark Abene, aka Phiber Optik, who was a member of the telephone hacking group Masters of Deception, which brought long-distance service to a halt on Martin Luther King Jr.'s birthday in 1993.[49] All three spent time behind bars for their hacking exploits.

Today, Mitnick and Abene are respected computer security consultants, and Poulsen is a contributing editor at Wired magazine.

During the 1980s, there was an explosion of hacker groups like the Masters of Deception. Populated mostly by teenagers and twentysomethings, they went by names such as the Legion of Doom, which became notorious for stealing the technical specifications for BellSouth's 911 emergency telephone network. The 414s, six teenagers from Milwaukee (area code 414), made a name for themselves by breaking into the computer networks of Los Alamos National Laboratory, Security Pacific Bank and Memorial Sloan Kettering Cancer Center.[50]

In response to a rapidly evolving cyberspace and the outbreaks of Internet law-lessness, Congress passed two laws in 1986 to regulate this new frontier: the Electronic Communications Privacy Act, which protected Americans' cellphone and email communications, and the Computer Fraud and Abuse Act, under which almost every breach and intrusion is still prosecuted today.

Rise of the Black Hats

By the 1990s, the exploits of hackers were becoming increasingly dark and motivated by money. One of the best-known hackers of that decade was Vladimir Levin, a twenty-something Russian who, with a team of hackers, stole as much as $12 million from Citibank and then deposited the money in accounts around the world. The hackers were arrested and most of the money was recovered; Levin pleaded guilty.[51]

As the Internet expanded in scope and sophistication, so too did hacking. Hackers no longer were just weird computer geniuses or teenage nerds. They became more systematic and ruthless. In cyber circles, these bad guys became known as black-hat hackers; to purists, they hacked for the wrong reasons. After about 2000, the vast majority of hackers were working for organized crime networks and governments.[52]

Foreshadowing the Occupy Movement, hacking also became the weapon of choice for anti-government, anti-corporate agitators. In 2003, the international organization of hacker activists, or hacktivists, called Anonymous was founded. Known by its signature Guy Fawkes mask, the hacktivist group's message was, "We are legion. We do not forgive. We do not forget. Expect us." Its weapon of choice to bring down its targets' websites and networks was distributed denial of service.[53]

The group attacked the Church of Scientology in 2008 because of the religious group's alleged brainwashing of members and its attempts to force websites to take down a video critical of Scientology and one of its most famous members, Tom Cruise.[54] Later, Anonymous targeted the government websites of Tunisia, Egypt and Zimbabwe. The attacks were in retaliation for alleged censorship by both Tunisia and Zimbabwe and in support of Egyptian protesters.[55]

The most notorious Anonymous hack was carried out by the splinter group Lulz Security, or LulzSec for short, and involved the Sony PlayStation Network.[56] In April 2011, the hacktivists announced plans to take down the network with a DDoS attack. While the assault was in progress, other intruders wiggled in before Sony shut down the network; they stole information on more than 100 million customer accounts and credit cards. Sony suggested in a letter to Congress that Anonymous perpetrated the theft, but experts were not so sure. Although the opportunistic robbers left behind the hacktivist's calling card message, some cyber consultants suspected the DDoS attack merely camouflaged the more insidious breach.[57]

More recently, Anonymous has set its sights on the Islamic State in retaliation for the 2015 terrorist attacks in Paris. In a rare instance of finding common cause with governments, the hacktivist organization claimed on Twitter that it had disrupted the Twitter accounts of more than 4,000 Islamic State followers; it also released those people's personal details online.[58]

Snowden's Impact

The activist-hacker persona was embodied by Snowden, the computer contract worker at the NSA who stole and then leaked classified data in 2013 that showed how the United States was secretly looking into the affairs of American citizens and European allies. Snowden revealed a rabbit warren of government spying that even included hacking of U.S. online giants Google and Facebook.

Snowden's revelations led to some serious reversals of public opinion: A Pew Research Center poll, taken in the spring of 2014, found 54 percent of Americans disapproved of the government's collection of telephone and Internet data as part of anti-terrorism efforts. Three-quarters said protection of their civil liberties was ultimately more important than safety concerns about terrorism.[59]

The disclosures also had financial ramifications: Many U.S. cloud-computing companies—firms that help businesses manage files and applications over the Internet— reported major declines in orders from Chinese businesses and state-owned enterprises, which feared becoming easier targets for U.S. government hacking. In an article, Daniel Castro, director of the Center for Data Innovation at the Information Technology & Innovation Foundation, estimated that the industry could lose as much as $35 billion.[60] Cisco Systems CEO John Chambers told analysts and shareholders in November 2013 that he had "never seen" such a falloff in orders, although the leaks did not seem to interrupt business elsewhere around the globe.[61]

But the United States was hardly the only nation snooping around. North Korea announced in 2004 that it had trained close to 600 hackers who were ready to conduct a cyberwar against three main enemies—South Korea, the United States and Japan.[62] By 2015 the number of North Korean hackers had jumped to close to 6,000, and, according to a defector, they had been trained to go after and destroy critical infrastructure.[63]

In 2005, the SANS Institute, an information-security training firm based in suburban Washington, D.C., made public a series of coordinated cyberattacks on government agencies and defense contractors, including Lockheed Martin, Sandia National Laboratories, the Redstone Arsenal and NASA. Titan Rain, as SANS called its investigation, revealed a three-year-long infiltration by hackers, "most likely" in the Chinese military.[64]

Two years later computer networks of Estonian government agencies, media outlets and banks were shut down by similarly coordinated attacks; investigators believed Russians, and potentially the Russian government, were behind them.[65]

Meanwhile, intrusions and data breaches against multinational corporations also increased in frequency and scope. In 2003, AOL revealed that a list of 92 million of its customers' email addresses had been stolen. Eventually, it was uncovered that the thief was Jason Smathers, an AOL software engineer in his early 20s who sold the list for $100,000 to Sean Dunaway, a 21-year-old who ran an Internet gambling site. After using the list to promote his own site through spam, Dunaway sold it again to spammers who sent out millions of emails peddling herbal penile enhancement products.[66]

Après AOL, Le Déluge

Two years later, the AOL breach looked relatively inconsequential when compared with the damage caused at businesses like TJX Companies, parent of retailers T.J. Maxx and Marshalls, which had credit card data from 94 million accounts lifted by hackers.[67] Almost every year since, there have been high-profile electronic break-ins and thefts, and with each breach the damage done by hackers has increased.

"There are just so many more points to attack today than years ago when you had a mainframe or a single website," says Diana Kelley, executive security adviser for IBM Security. "And there's a lot more to take because as organizations, we collect so many more pieces of information."

In 2009, payment-processing company Heartland Payment Systems discovered it had suffered what is still one of the largest data breaches on record, losing information on close to 130 million credit and debit cards in an attack that started the year before. The data breach turned out to be part of the largest identity theft ever pulled off.

The perpetrator of the data breaches at both Heartland and TJX: Albert Gonzalez, at the time in his late 20s, a resident of Miami and a former Secret Service informant. Gonzalez became an informant after he was caught in New York City using debit cards that he had programmed with stolen numbers. While he helped catch and prosecute a criminal syndicate trafficking a database of stolen credit card numbers, Gonzalez never changed his hacker ways. After resettling in Miami, he teamed with hackers in Eastern Europe and was behind some of the highest profile data breaches in the first decade of the new millennium. He was eventually sentenced to 20 years in prison.[68]

But the bad news on corporate data breaches didn't end there. In fact, the number and severity only intensified. Among the biggest over the next five years: the 2013 theft of 152 million records at Adobe; 145 million at eBay in 2014; more than 100 million at Sony in two 2011 breaches; Anthem's loss of 78.8 million in 2015; and Target's loss of 70 million personal accounts and 40 million debit and credit card numbers in 2013.

"Each year, we say this is the worst," Kroll's Brill says, "but then the next year comes, and we see how much more is possible."

CURRENT SITUATION

Federal Cybersecurity Initiatives

After the avalanche of high-profile, high-impact data breaches in 2014 and 2015—including the intrusion at the federal Office of Personnel Management in which hackers lingered in the network for close to a year without being detected—the stakes for developing an anti-hacking strategy have never been greater.

One problem that vexes companies and regulators: the lack of concrete standards against which to judge the cybersecurity preparedness of an enterprise and assign blame when necessary precautions have not been taken to prevent huge losses. That situation is slowly beginning to be addressed by various agencies, such as the Federal Trade Commission and the Commerce Department's National Institute of Standards and Technology, state governments and the judiciary—each working to set ground rules and protocols, while also establishing jurisdictional lines for cybersecurity oversight.

Probably the most significant development in recent years was the adoption of the NIST voluntary guidelines for critical infrastructure industries. While not the mandatory standards the Obama administration had asked for—and some members of Congress attempted to pass—the Framework for Improving Critical Infrastructure Cybersecurity marks significant progress in laying down essential elements of any digital defense strategy.

"While the Framework targets organizations that own or operate critical infrastructure, adoption may prove advantageous for businesses across virtually all industries," a May 2014 PricewaterhouseCoopers report stated. "The Framework is . . . designed to evolve in sync with changes in cybersecurity threats, processes, and technologies."[69]

The voluntary framework is the result of collaboration among more than 1,000 individuals from industry, academia and government and aims to provide principles and best practices that can be adapted to serve companies regardless of size or industry. Many experts say they expect subsequent versions of the Framework to become enforceable standards. In the meantime, the emphasis on detection and response as well as prevention makes them valuable first steps.

"I think ultimately the NIST guidelines will become the baseline," says Shackelford at Indiana University. "The FTC is using them, and that's a good reason for companies to start."

The PricewaterhouseCoopers report also notes that the Framework provides an assessment mechanism that allows companies to gauge their current cybersecurity capabilities and then set goals for improvement. The NIST guidelines create a common language, which enhances collaboration and information sharing, the report states.

Meanwhile, Congress also is contemplating creating a federal requirement for how quickly companies must alert customers or employees whose personal data have been lost in breaches. Forty-seven states already have legal requirements, and not surprisingly, state attorneys general oppose a federal standard that would supersede these local laws.[70] While a single rule would make compliance easier and cheaper for companies, it would undermine the role of the states in cybersecurity regulation.

Cybersecurity Legal Precedents

Two major legal precedents caught the attention of corporate counsels nationwide in 2015. The first and probably most important is a U.S. Appeals Court ruling that established the FTC's jurisdiction to protect consumer interests in cybersecurity cases.[71] In August, the 3rd U.S. Circuit Court of Appeals in Philadelphia ruled that the FTC could pursue a lawsuit against Wyndham Worldwide for failing to safeguard consumer information. In three breaches in 2008 and 2009, hackers stole credit card data and personal information for 619,000 customers.

"If you look at the surveys, there [are] still a large number of companies that are really motivated by the threat of regulation," Shackelford says. "We're starting to see a lot more of those kinds of enforcement actions and the FTC is leading the way. So that ruling is a big deal, and eventually it's going to start hurting the bottom line."

The second major cybersecurity ruling involved the 2013 Target data breach. In September, U.S. District Judge Paul Magnuson gave class-action status to several small banks seeking $30 million in damages from the retailer to cover the costs of reissuing stolen credit cards. Ultimately, Target agreed to pay almost $40 million to banks, credit unions and other MasterCard issuers. Earlier the retailer agreed to pay Visa member banks $67 million. Individuals are usually protected against fraudulent charges, so it is the issuing banks that sustain most of the losses from unlawful use and for reissuing cards.[72]

The Target ruling makes it clear that banks have a right to go after merchants if they can provide evidence that retailers were negligent in securing computer systems against intruders, according to The New York Times. Target has estimated that the 2013 data breach has cost it as much as $290 million, with insurers only reimbursing about $90 million.[73]

Board Involvement in Cybersecurity

During the last two years, corporate boards of directors have become increasingly involved in cybersecurity, particularly as regulators get more aggressive and class-action suits in the wake of breaches become more plentiful.

"What you're starting to see is a person who is a cybersecurity expert joining boards to provide some leadership that might have been missing until now on the issue," Brill says.

In a 2014 survey of audit committee members conducted by Ernst and Young, only 21 percent of directors said they believed their company has cybersecurity risk well under control. Most report only occasional contact with senior IT executives.[74]

Executive search firm Spencer Stuart argued in an August 2015 report that the board members can actually "mitigate risk and damages by staying informed and ensuring that, in the event of a breach, their company is prepared to respond."[75]

The Ponemon Institute agrees that board involvement can actually lower the cost of breaches, even more than cyber insurance. "The key here is tone at the top," says institute CEO Ponemon. "If everyone knows at a company that the board thinks cybersecurity is important, then it becomes important to everyone at the company. And without that cultural commitment, it's really hard to be effective in combatting hackers."

LOOKING AHEAD

The Internet of Things

As scary as the cybersecurity scene seems today, it's about to get worse. In the summer of 2015, a pair of cybersecurity experts hacked into a car moving down a highway at 70 mph, with a technology reporter at the wheel. They turned on the air conditioning, played a radio station full volume and switched on the windshield wipers. Eventually, they turned the car engine off while the vehicle was still in motion—a move that threw the driver into a panic, despite his awareness of what was happening. They had developed a new hacking technique—the industry calls it a zero-day exploit—that gave them wireless control of the vehicle through its entertainment system.[76] Zero-day vulnerability refers to inadvertent holes in software as yet unknown to the vendor. Hackers take advantage of these until vendors issue fixes.

While Fiat Chrysler, the manufacturer of the Jeep Cherokee being driven, issued a software patch for the most dire of the vulnerabilities the hackers had revealed, the demonstration left the cybersecurity industry wondering what other holes designers left in the growing Internet of Things.

The Internet of Things—a world of objects connected to the Internet by systems and sensors—opens up a new playground for hackers. Experts see the threats escalating as network connectivity becomes a standard element in the operation of everything from a person's car or home, to the utilities in office buildings, to critical infrastructure industrial controls.

"Today, there are multiple devices for each member of our family and each employee in our organization," says Kelley at IBM Security. "We'll soon be living in a world in which close to everything is connected. That opens up a lot of opportunities for cybercrime and a lot of risk for people and organizations. If a hacker gets into the systems running your car, for instance, we could be looking at a potential loss of life."

By 2020, the outlook is for a significant increase in the number of devices connected to the Internet—either 26 billion if Swedish telecom Ericsson is to be believed or a stunning 50 billion, according to U.S. tech-services company Cisco Systems and German logistics giant DHL. Either vision would represent a substantial expansion, given the current total of 15 billion.[77]

The real change the Internet of Things portends, however, relates to how human communication will become even more indirect, with people increasingly talking "through" machines, according to a 2015 report by professional services firm Ernst and Young.[78] This triggers some "deeply rooted" security issues, elevating the potential for impersonation, identity theft, hacking and cyberthreats, the report said.

"In today's world of 'always on' technology and not enough security awareness on the part of users, cyber attacks are no longer a matter of 'if' but 'when,'" the report stated, noting that 70 percent of the most commonly used devices in the Internet of Things contain vulnerabilities that could be leveraged by hackers.

Kelley stresses the need to think about security in the design stage of products. Developers must begin asking themselves not just whether a product is useful but also what risks it poses, especially if attacked, she says. IBM has created a Secure Engineering Framework that helps companies anticipate the security risks of new products in the design stage when there is still an opportunity to include safeguards to ensure that software is secure when it is widely used.[79]

"That's a much safer approach than sending out patches after the product has been deployed and hackers have had a chance to analyze its vulnerabilities," she says.

An October 2015 survey of 500 automotive software developers, engineers and executives found that a majority do not believe automakers are taking security seriously enough, or empowering them to make software more secure. Additionally, they didn't think they had the training or the technology necessary to build security into their processes. The Ponemon Institute conducted the survey on behalf of two software security companies.[80]

As the attacks of cyber criminals become more sophisticated and harder to defeat and technology more complex, it becomes increasingly difficult to predict the nature of the threats that will emerge five and 10 years from now, the Ernst and Young report concluded. "We can only say that these threats will be even more dangerous than those of today. . . . As old sources of [risk] fade, new sources will rise to take their place."[81]

Chronology

1970s–1980s	**Young computer whizzes begin developing hacking techniques.**
1971	A lab working on ARPANET, the precursor to the Internet developed by the U.S. Defense Department's Advanced Research Projects Agency, creates the first self-replicating computer virus, called Creeper.
1974	David Dennis, a 13-year-old student in Illinois, carries out what may have been the first denial of service (DoS) attack.
1975	John Walker, who would go on to found Autodesk and computer-aided design, creates ANIMAL software, which self-replicates on UNIVACs, the first commercial computers produced in the United States. It is the first computer virus developed "in the wild"—that is, outside of a lab.
1982	Pennsylvania native Rich Skrenta, 15, infects Apple II computers with the Elk Cloner virus, which is spread via floppy disks.
1983	A group of teenage hackers, known as the 414s, breaks into a series of government computers, including one at the Los Alamos National Laboratory in New Mexico. . . . The term "computer virus" is coined after California graduate student Fred Cohen demonstrates how one works.
1986	Congress passes the Electronic Communications Privacy Act, which extends guarantees to cellular phone and email communications, and the Computer Fraud and Abuse Act, which gives the FBI jurisdiction over computer crimes and prohibits intentionally accessing computers without permission.
1987	High school dropout Herbert Zinn, 17, is caught after bragging on online message boards about breaking into computers at the Department of Defense, NATO and AT&T through a computer in his bedroom. He is sent to prison for nine months and fined $10,000.
1988	Robert Morris, a graduate student at Cornell University and son of a government computer expert, unintentionally lets loose the first "worm"—which immobilizes 6,000 computers, about one-tenth of those on the Internet at the time.
1989	Tim Berners-Lee invents the World Wide Web.
1990s	**Economically motivated "black hat" hackers begin to take over.**
1990	The infamous hacking group Masters of Deception, out of New York City, and hackers in St. Louis and Austin, Texas, shut down long-distance service on Martin Luther King Jr.'s birthday. . . . The federal government charges members of rival hackers Legion of Doom with breaking into BellSouth's network and stealing technical specifications for the 911 emergency telephone system.

(Continued)

	(Continued)
1993	Members of the Masters of Deception plead guilty to computer crimes and conspiracy.
1994	Russian hacker and mathematician Vladimir Levin and team siphon $10.7 million from Citibank and deposit it in accounts in Finland, Germany, the Netherlands, the United States and Israel.
1995	Kevin Mitnick, once called "America's most wanted computer outlaw," is arrested for his role in numerous hacks of computer systems and for copying valuable proprietary software from some of the country's largest cellular telephone and computer companies.
1998	Hackers take control of more than 500 U.S. Defense Department, military and private-sector computer networks in a spree dubbed Solar Sunrise. Although investigators initially blamed Iraqi operatives, it turned out to be two teenagers in California and another in Israel.
2000s	**Hacking gets political, organized and even darker.**
2003	The international hacktivist group Anonymous, represented by its signature Guy Fawkes mask, begins to take shape with the creation of the discussion board 4chan. . . . A software engineer at AOL steals 92 million screen names and email addresses and sells them to spammers.
2004	North Korea says it has trained close to 600 hackers and claims to have successfully infiltrated computer networks in South Korea and Japan.
2005	The SANS Institute, a top-level security research center in the United States, attributes a three-year-long series of coordinated attacks against U.S. government agencies and defense contractors to Chinese military hackers.
2007	Estonia's computer networks—from the president's office to the biggest banks, to newspapers and broadcasters—shut down in a large-scale cyberattack believed to have originated in Russia and be government-sanctioned. . . . A data breach at retailer TJX exposes as many as 94 million credit cards in 13 countries to fraud.
2008	Hackers steal 130 million customer accounts from Heartland Payment Systems.
2010– Present	**Hacking moves from random acts to coordinated assaults.**
2010	Google says it's the victim of cyberattacks "originating from China" that resulted in the theft of intellectual property.
2011	The black-hat hacker group LulzSec, an offshoot of Anonymous, stages several high-profile cyberattacks, including a DDoS attack that shuts down the Sony PlayStation Network for almost a month.
2013	Edward Snowden blows the lid off U.S. and U.K. government snooping and hacking. . . . The year sees a rise in data breaches, with Adobe losing 152 million user names and poorly encrypted passwords in the largest data breach to date and Target losing 40 million credit card numbers and 70 million names, addresses, telephone numbers and other personal information.
2014	Multinational e-commerce giant eBay tells 145 million customers to change their passwords after a data breach. . . . Sony Pictures pulls "The Interview," a comedy about a plot to assassinate Kim Jong Un, after hackers release embarrassing executive emails and threaten violence at movie theaters.
2015	In another year of brazen cybercrime, health care companies are prime targets, with Anthem losing 78.8 million records to a breach. . . . Chinese hackers, possibly government sanctioned, make off with data on 22 million current and former federal employees in two waves of data breaches at the U.S. Office of Personnel Management (OPM). . . . Amid threats of economic sanctions by the United States, China claims to arrest the OPM hackers and agrees to a cybersecurity pact to curb cyber-enabled theft of intellectual property.

RESOURCES

The Next Step

Company Strategy

Sposito, Sean, "PayPal, others buy stolen data from criminals to protect users," San Francisco Chronicle, Jan. 8, 2016, http://tinyurl.com/h8t3azw.

Online commerce company PayPal is among the many firms that pay middlemen or use undercover employees to purchase stolen data from cybercriminals after breaches to determine what types of data were compromised or where information is being sold.

Weinstein, Ira, and Bill Huber, "How the CFO can act as any cybersecurity team's 'quarterback,'" Baltimore Business Journal, Jan. 12, 2016, http://tinyurl.com/hf77m89.

Chief financial officers can uniquely identify and communicate about their companies' valued assets to information technology staff, allowing for more targeted security strategies, say top managers of accounting and consulting firm CohnReznick.

Cyberwarfare

Behn, Sharon, "Could IS Turn Next to Cyber War?" Voice of America, Dec. 18, 2015, http://tinyurl.com/j2uc4lt.

Islamic State hackers would likely be less interested in stealing government agency data than in attacking and disrupting U.S. industrial control systems such as energy and manufacturing structures, according to a former U.S. Defense Intelligence Agency official.

Davenport, Christian, "Raytheon wins $1 billion cybersecurity contract to battle attacks on U.S. agencies," The Washington Post, Sept. 29, 2015, http://tinyurl.com/qztxgks.

The Department of Homeland Security awarded defense contractor Raytheon a $1 billion contract to protect federal civilian agencies from cyberattacks, a growing number of which originated from outside countries in the last year.

Williams, Katie Bo, "US, China negotiating cyber warfare agreement," The Hill, Sept. 21, 2015, http://tinyurl.com/jz3tz2s.

The United States and China are negotiating a code of conduct that would prohibit either nation from launching a cyberattack against the other's critical infrastructures and would generally apply basic international law to cyberwarfare.

Information Sharing

Brandom, Russell, "Congress passes controversial cybersecurity bill attached to omnibus budget," The Verge, Dec. 18, 2015, http://tinyurl.com/z57dwbf.

As part of a larger budget bill, Congress passed cybersecurity legislation that will allow corporations and agencies to more easily share information without being encumbered by privacy laws.

Gregg, Aaron, "Venture capitalists flock to cybersecurity information-sharing platforms," The Washington Post, Dec. 2, 2015, http://tinyurl.com/zltam2f.

Investors are pouring more money into start-ups that develop information-sharing platforms to improve companies' cybersecurity in hopes that they will profit from funding the next popular cybersecurity service.

Smith, Mat, "The FDA wants improved cybersecurity for medical devices," Engadget, Jan. 19, 2016, http://tinyurl.com/zdtrkqg.

The Food and Drug Administration released draft guidelines encouraging medical device manufacturers to coordinate and share data to reduce cybersecurity vulnerabilities.

Risk Management

Boyd, Aaron, "IG: Energy Department missing mark on risk management," Federal Times, Nov. 12, 2015, http://tinyurl.com/hbrm9kb.

The Department of Energy has been slow to identify which of its information systems should be included in a new risk-management framework and has not effectively classified some of its websites by risk priority, according to a department inspector general's report.

Joyce, Stephen, "Cybersecurity Insurance Explosion Poses Challenges," Bloomberg BNA, Dec. 22, 2015, http://tinyurl.com/gs3htcc.

The cybersecurity insurance industry has seen rapid revenue growth from insurance premiums since 2012 as more companies purchase policies to manage risks, but specialists say the industry still lacks standards for pricing, terms and policy language.

King, Rachael, "Cybersecurity Startup QuadMetrics Calculates Odds a Company Will be Breached," The Wall Street Journal, Jan. 12, 2016, http://tinyurl.com/zelssua.

An analytics company that collects clients' data to help them manage cybersecurity risks says it can forecast the likelihood of a data breach for the ensuing three to 12 months with at least 90-percent accuracy.

Organizations

Center for Applied Cybersecurity Research at Indiana University
2719 E. 10th St., Suite 231, Bloomington, IN 47408
812-856-8080
http://cacr.iu.edu/

Founded in 2003 to help the United States balance public needs, homeland security concerns and individual privacy rights when seeking cybersecurity solutions and setting policy; organizes the annual National Science Foundation Cybersecurity Summit for Large Facilities and Cyberinfrastructure and provides policy advice to the White House's 60-day cybersecurity review.

Center for Internet Security
31 Tech Valley Drive, Suite 2, East Greenbush, NY 12061 (Northeast Headquarters)

518-266-3460
https://www.cisecurity.org

International organization with 180 members in 17 countries that focuses on enhancing the cybersecurity readiness and response of public-and private-sector enterprises.

Center for Strategic and International Studies

1616 Rhode Island Ave., N.W., Washington, DC 20036
202-887-0200
http://csis.org/

Bipartisan policy think tank that specializes in the study of defense and security, regional stability and transnational challenges, including cybersecurity.

CERT

4500 Fifth Ave., Pittsburgh, PA 15213-2612
412-268-5800
www.cert.org/

Division of the Software Engineering Institute (SEI) at Carnegie Mellon University that coordinates responses to Internet security incidents.

Information Systems Security Association

12100 Sunset Hills Road, Suite 130, Reston, VA 20190
866-349-5818
https://www.issa.org/

International organization of information security professionals that promotes management practices that will ensure the confidentiality, integrity and availability of information resources.

National Cybersecurity Center of Excellence

9600 Gudelsky Drive, Rockville, MD 20850
240-314-6800
http://nccoe.nist.gov

Division of the National Institute of Standards and Technology that provides businesses with cybersecurity solutions, based on commercially available technologies.

National Cybersecurity and Communications Integration Center

Mailstop 0635, 245 Murray Lane, S.W., Building 410, Washington, DC 20598
888-282-0870
www.us-cert.gov/nccic

Division of the Department of Homeland Security that serves as a 24/7 cyber monitoring, incident response and management center; analyzes cybersecurity and communications information, shares timely and actionable information, and coordinates response, mitigation and recovery efforts.

Pew Research Center

1615 L St., N.W., Suite 800, Washington, DC 20036

202-419-4300

http://www.pewresearch.org/

Research organization that has conducted numerous surveys on the public's attitudes on cybercrime and the global cyberthreat.

Ponemon Institute

2308 U.S. 31 N., Traverse City, MI 49686

231-938-9900

www.ponemon.org

Research think tank dedicated to privacy, data protection and information security policy; has done extensive work documenting the cost of data breaches.

SANS Institute

8120 Woodmont Ave., Suite 310, Bethesda, MD 20814

301-654-7267

www.sans.org

Research and education organization that is the world's largest source for information security training and security certification.

Q&A: Joshua Goldfarb on Cybersecurity

"PREVENTATIVE TECHNOLOGIES . . . ARE ABSOLUTELY NECESSARY AND ESSENTIAL, BUT THEY ARE FAR FROM SUFFICIENT"

Joshua Goldfarb is chief technology officer for the Americas for network security firm FireEye. The company and its subsidiary Mandiant have been involved in some of the biggest data breach investigations of recent years; The Street.com, a financial news website, called FireEye the Navy SEALs of cybersecurity. Goldfarb talked with SAGE Business Researcher reporter Pat Wechsler about how companies should approach creating an effective cybersecurity strategy. This is an edited transcript of their conversation.

What do you consider the biggest cyberthreat facing companies?

The biggest threat is the undetected intrusion, the one that lingers for a long period of time and has the opportunity to steal much more sensitive information than is usually removed when an attacker doesn't have time to study the victim's computer system. That's something that organizations have really tried to grapple with.

How does that even happen when companies should be on the lookout?

Preventative technologies that we use in cybersecurity are absolutely necessary and essential, but they are far from sufficient. They mitigate some of the risk, but not all of it. The remainder requires a different approach—detection and response technology. That complements the preventative approach very well.

We see some mature organizations rounding out their risk mitigation strategy that way. But it's demanding, because it requires understanding how to filter through the tremendous amount of noise and activity within an organization. And then pull out from that the few—relatively small in number—but meaningful events that need to be investigated, then subsequently analyzed and perhaps responded to if they turn out to be malicious. Being able to do that in an efficient manner allows an organization to pick up on something soon after it happens and helps them mitigate that threat before a tremendous amount of information is lost.

Although it sounds completely simple, it's actually fairly difficult to implement in the real world. It requires a lot of knowledge and expertise, and a lot of hard work. So that's a place where most organizations are still maturing.

In finance there's auditing technology that pulls out the exceptions and automates the majority of perfectly normal actions that don't need human intervention. Is that what happens with cybersecurity detection software?

There are definitely technologies that identify unusual or aberrant cyber behavior. There are quite a number of different approaches, but most of them don't cut the noise down sufficiently for organizations to find and focus on what matters. So they end up chasing ghosts—that's the industry name for it—and the real intrusion is lost in the noise.

I don't have exact numbers, but it's my observation that there are a small number of organizations that are mature and understand what I am talking about. It's safe to say the vast majority of organizations are struggling with this. I've been doing this for 15 years, and in the beginning it wasn't entirely obvious how to do what was needed. It took me a few years to build up my skill set. For most organizations, they just haven't had enough experience yet to go through all the steps and end up with the result they need.

Are these needs on their radar? Has it reached the level of concern where the board of directors wants to review cybersecurity?

It's definitely something that at this point has board-level attention at most companies. They see the risk; the challenge is, how do you negate the risk or counter the threat? That's where I see a tremendous amount of differentiation. So they're aware of the problem, they just aren't sure what to do about it.

Is there enough consensus around risk mitigation to give companies at least a checklist of things they absolutely need?

It's helpful for organizations to have an internal response process and plan. They need to practice

(Continued)

(Continued)

continuous security monitoring; in other words, practice the "prevent, detect, analyze, respond" chain of events. Nothing is a silver bullet, but that's the one proven way I've seen to really take a strategic approach to mitigating risk. You need to enumerate the risks that are of the most concern to an organization and from there break those down into bite-size chunks that can be tackled one after the other as resources allow. That's the only way to get an organization to a greater level of maturity when it comes to cyber-risks.

It sounds like a big, time-consuming task. Do some organizations just throw up their hands and give up?

There is some fear. There's a lot of confusion, particularly among boards and business people, as opposed to tech people. But this is an approach that can show results. It doesn't happen overnight, and it takes some investment. But at the end of the process, your organization will be much more secure than where you are today.

TRENDS IN MANAGEMENT

8 FLAT MANAGEMENT
Can reducing hierarchy improve results?

Jane Fullerton Lemons

EXECUTIVE SUMMARY

Flat management techniques, spurred by the growth of technology companies, are becoming more popular, but it's an approach that can offer advantages to other types and sizes of businesses, too. Although it isn't applicable to all situations, flat management will likely keep gaining ground as the economy continues to evolve and businesses are forced to adapt. The increasing use of technology and social media, coupled with the need for businesses to make quick decisions to remain competitive, ensures flat structures will remain a viable option. Some companies take a dual approach by implementing a flat structure for certain elements of the business while maintaining a more traditional management hierarchy overall.

OVERVIEW

When Stephen Courtright teaches his business students at Texas A&M University about leadership styles, he cites the experience of a Fortune 500 health care company to illustrate flat management.

A former executive at Denver-based DaVita HealthCare Partners had been someone other employees expected to solve all their problems—and she did. "She was just kind of a do-it-all-er," Courtright says.

When a new executive took over and needed to revamp schedules for health care workers and for patient treatments, she could have done it herself, the way her predecessor would have.

But she chose a different path, opting to organize "a cross-functional team where they themselves came up with a proposal which they then proposed to the entire organization, got feedback on it, went and revised it, represented it to the other team, made final adjustments and then got the sign-off from the leader," says Courtright, assistant professor in the management department of Texas A&M's Mays Business School in College Station, Texas.

Even in the same "fairly hierarchical organization," he says, the executives took two very different approaches to handling a management issue. "Any leader in any

From *SAGE Business Researcher*,
February 2, 2015

Tony Hsieh is the CEO of Zappos, which is one of the largest US companies experimenting with flattened management structure.

Source: FREDERIC J. BROWN/AFP/ Getty Images

organization can empower their workers to solve problems. I don't care what organization—you can empower people to solve their own problems," he says. "That's the principle I want my students taking away from flat management."

Since the mid-20th century, with a global marketplace and a changing economic environment, more companies are adopting leaner and flatter management structures to remain innovative, reduce costs and retain employees.[1]

While the overall number of companies following flat management techniques remains relatively small, and they often are privately held, these firms are garnering attention for their nontraditional approaches. And data are beginning to indicate such methods can be effective, says Tim Kastelle, senior lecturer at the University of Queensland's business school in Brisbane, Australia.

"The level of success that these organizations are achieving is pretty high," he says, "so it adds up to a fairly suggestive set of cases."

Drawing on his own research, Kastelle says organizations that include front-line employees in decision-making are "way more innovative and their performance is better" than traditionally organized companies.

A traditional hierarchy is shaped like a pyramid, with one person, typically the CEO, perched at the top, followed by layers of managers, with front-line workers forming the base.

A flat structure can take various forms, but it essentially eliminates some, even all, of those layers between the folks at the top and the folks at the bottom. The flattest companies, such as game maker Valve of Bellevue, Wash., are horizontal and essentially have no managers. But many companies regarded as flat, including Google and online shoe and clothing retailer Zappos, retain some kind of management structure, albeit pared down significantly from the traditional hierarchical pyramid.[2]

Even with such changes taking place, there are still plenty of business observers who contend that while modern managers might need to redefine their roles, the roles themselves are still necessary.[3] And the experiences of some flat companies underscore the point. Even the flattest of companies still have a leader or group of leaders who can make final decisions, and some have reinstated layers of management after running into operational problems.[4]

That balance of leadership—as well the differing approaches of publicly and privately held companies—is a key factor in determining whether a business can implement a flatter management technique.

"Flat organization structures require leaders to give up a lot of control, and they typically involve the company taking a long-term view on its development," says Julian Birkinshaw, professor of strategy and entrepreneurship at the London Business School. "So if you are on a quarterly earnings cycle, it is much harder to justify this model. And analysts are also skeptical of these nontraditional organizing models," so leaders of publicly traded companies "tend to opt for more traditional structures."

Jim Belosic, co-founder and CEO of Pancake Laboratories, a Reno, Nev.-based software company that makes ShortStack software, realized he was practicing flat management as his company grew from an initial trio to more than a dozen employees. He believed the company and its culture are better for having taken that approach and urges other small business to consider the same course.[5]

"When I hire these days, I bring on people who have a manager's mentality but a producer's work ethic," Belosic wrote. "In other words, they think like managers and figure out what needs to be done, and then they do the work."

The goal, according to Traci Fenton, founder and CEO of WorldBlu, a firm that advocates flattening management through workplace democracy, is to encourage businesses to shift away from a command-and-control, top-down management style to keep up with the changing demands of the marketplace.

"We've moved from the industrial age to the information age, and the information age has given birth to a democratic age, which is an age of unprecedented participation and collaboration unlike anything we've ever seen before," she says. For companies to remain relevant, Fenton says, they must redesign their operations and rethink their management technique. "What more and more companies are realizing is that in order to be competitive, in order to be nimble, in order to attract great talent, in order to be an environment where millennials will thrive," she says, "it needs to be a flatter, more democratic organization."

Similarly, Morning Star Self-Management Institute, a research and consulting firm affiliated with Morning Star Co., a California tomato processor that embraces flat management, contends that empowered workers are happy and creative workers. While WorldBlu calls its system organizational democracy, Morning Star uses the term self-management; each is a means to a flatter management end. "It doesn't make a lot of sense to give the decision-making authority to the person that [is] furthest (literally) away from the actual work being done," according to the institute's website.[6]

Employee Engagement Ticks Up

Research demonstrates that groups of employees who manage themselves can be more productive. A study by Courtright and researchers from the University of Iowa and Texas A&M found that on the basis of data from 587 factory workers in 45 self-managing teams at three Iowa factories, "peer-based rational control corresponded with higher performance for both individuals and collective teams."[7]

Courtright explained how that translates into the workplace: "In high functioning teams, the group takes over most of the management function themselves. They work with each other, they encourage and support each other, and they coordinate with outside teams. They collectively perform the role of a good manager."[8]

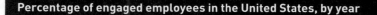

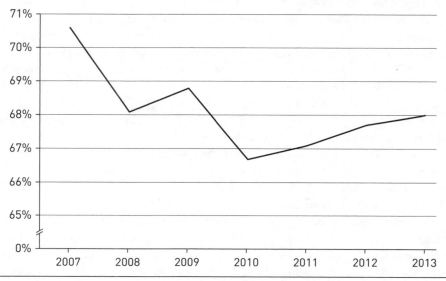

A common goal of companies with flattened management structures is to increase employee engagement by eliminating middle-management positions. According to an annual survey of nearly 5,000 organizations, the percentage of engaged employees fell to a four-year low in 2010 before rising to 68 percent in 2013.

Source: Natalie Hackbarth, David Weisser and Hilary Wright, "2014 Employee Engagement Trends Report," Quantum Workplace, July 2014, p. 11, http://tinyurl.com/klf8e2a

At Pancake Laboratories, Belosic said a flat approach allowed his company to experience advantages other businesses have reported, such as:[9]

- Making faster decisions.
- Encouraging more collaboration among employees.
- Reducing spending on unnecessary or redundant jobs.
- Spending less time on human-resource issues and more on business development.
- Freeing up management-level people to spend more time doing what they're good at and were originally hired to do.

But flat management has its drawbacks. In terms of the impact on the business as a whole, companies always take risks when they empower people, Birkinshaw says.

"Some [employees] lack the competence or the will to do a good job, and this can result in mistakes being made or people doing things that take the company in the wrong direction," he says. "The ultimate case is Enron—supremely flat, but employees were given so much freedom that they ended up creating all sorts of poorly thought-out businesses that lost the company a lot of money and contributed to its eventual demise."[10]

And when things go wrong, Birkinshaw adds, "even the really flat companies tend to become more hierarchical when a crisis or external problem hits. It is human nature to 'circle the wagons' or to go 'back to basics' when faced with a threat."

In terms of the effect on employees, critics contend such an environment can stifle career advancement for those wanting to climb the corporate ladder or can mask hidden power structures and thus could shield employees from accountability. And as flat companies hire workers who will fit in with their culture, a procedure that frequently slows the hiring process, they also may be creating a homogenous workforce. [11]

Southwest airlines encourages its employees to feel empowered and make decisions without supervisory sign-off.

Source: John Gress/Corbis via Getty Images

Despite these criticisms, the use of flat management is growing.[12] Smaller companies and the technology sector have been the most enthusiastic converts to flat management because of the collaborative nature of the business, the creative nature of the products, the need to make rapid decisions and the influx of younger workers. But larger companies and other industries are also using it, albeit with different approaches and to different degrees. And the trend is not limited to the United States, either: Companies across the globe are implementing flat management practices. Even militaries in the United States and abroad are working on ways to reduce hierarchies and empower soldiers to make rapid decisions on the battlefield.[13]

As researchers and executives assess the results of flat management techniques, these are some of the questions under debate:

Weighing the Issues

Can a flat management structure help the bottom line?

Flattening the management structure and thus empowering employees "certainly has made a big difference for companies like Google, like Southwest Airlines, 3M and many, many others," says Courtright of Texas A&M.[14]

Courtright has experienced some of the ramifications of worker empowerment during his own travels. "If you go to a Southwest baggage clerk for example, they can make a decision on the spot rather than consult with a manager above them, which is very different than say a lot of the rental car companies that you might go to," he says. "With rental car companies they have to ask their manager for anything and everything."

Clothing manufacturer W.L. Gore & Associates is "a perfect example" of nimble management, Courtright says. "They adopted this model back in the '50s, really structuring it to be more of an empowering environment, and they're one of the few privately held companies in their industry that has had as large a profit margin as they've had over the years." Gore, a Newark, Del., firm with about $3.2 billion in annual revenue and 10,000 workers—referred to as associates and sponsors, not employees and bosses—is run by the Gore family and its workers.[15] It doesn't report profit figures, but as the maker of Gore-Tex fabric, it is a leader in the outdoor gear industry.[16]

While many of the companies practicing flat management techniques began that way, some altered their structure. One example is the Brazilian conglomerate Semco Group, which grew from a family manufacturing operation. When Ricardo Semler took over the business, he restructured the company into a "radical workplace" operating with a participatory management structure.[17] The privately held firm has maintained about 20 percent growth annually for the past 30 years.[18]

Courtright and others point to research showing the correlation between employee engagement and enhanced productivity.[19]

Profits Increase at Companies With Higher Employee Engagement

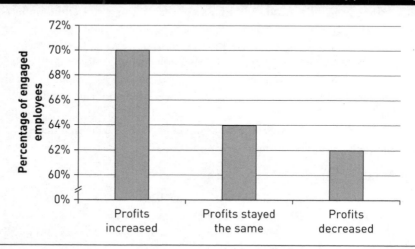

According to a survey of 5,000 organizations in 40 American cities, 70 percent of employees were "engaged"—given greater autonomy—at organizations where profits increased over the last three years, compared with 62 percent of employees who were engaged at organizations where profits decreased.

Source: Natalie Hackbarth, David Weisser and Hilary Wright, "2014 Employee Engagement Trends Report," Quantum Workplace, July 2014, p. 21, http://tinyurl.com/klf8e2a

"We've found in our study that teams who felt more empowered through a psychological perspective achieved higher performance," says Courtright, adding that other studies he has conducted confirmed those results.

"So the fact is, this model does impact the bottom line, but it does all depend on the strategy, too," he says. The key is for a company to align its organizational design and its business strategy. If the strategy requires constant innovation, such as a software company, then a flat approach could complement that. But if the strategy depends on product consistency, for instance, such as a fast-food company, then it might be more suited to a more traditional hierarchy.

Research by organizations such as Omaha, Neb.-based Quantum Workplace, which consults with companies about how to increase business by improving their employees' engagement, has found a correlation between productivity, profitability and employee engagement. An engaged workforce—meaning workers who are involved and enthusiastic about their jobs—can create a competitive advantage.

According to Quantum's studies, organizations with the highest level of engagement showed:[20]

- An 87 percent increase in revenue the following three years.

- An 86 percent increase in market share.

- A 57 percent lower employee turnover rate.

That link between employee engagement and company results illustrates the theory behind the service-profit chain, according to Greg Harris, Quantum's president and CEO. The service-profit chain, as first outlined in the Harvard Business Review in 1994, establishes relationships between profitability, customer loyalty, and employee satisfaction, loyalty and productivity.[21]

All of this relates to flat management because companies using flatter systems tend to possess more of the factors that lead to higher levels of employee engagement. So it follows that if flat management can increase employee engagement, it also can increase profitability.

"From a financial perspective that might make sense," Harris says, explaining that the flatter the organization, the more people there are who "actually touch customers and can impact the customer experience, [and] the more opportunity they have to drive client loyalty"—the elements of the service-profit chain. At the same time, he says, "the less hierarchical management you have, the fewer the layers of overhead expense."

Those factors together make the case that flat management structures can boost the bottom line, Harris says. "It's definitely a worthwhile hypothesis."

Can a flat management style work for any type of business?

Kastelle argued in "Hierarchy Is Overrated" that a flat organizational structure can work anywhere.[22] Flat management, he wrote, thrives under certain conditions, including a rapidly changing environment, the need for innovation and a shared purpose within an organization. Generally speaking, flat management works best in small and medium-sized businesses that are privately held, but Kastelle and others contend many of its principles can be applied in other scenarios.

The number and type of employees both affect a company's ability to flatten its management structure. Companies using flat structures range from small tech start-ups with a handful of employees, to the Brazilian company Semco with more than 3,000 workers, to manufacturer W.L. Gore with more than 10,000 employees.

Size becomes a factor in establishing a management structure at some point between about 80 and 150 employees, says Birkinshaw.

"I don't believe it's possible to completely get rid of hierarchy," he says. "I think hierarchy has lots of negative connotations but, actually, some level of hierarchy is necessary to make an organization of more than about 100 people work."

So the question becomes how much structure to impose, how flat a company can go. Even the flattest of organizations ultimately have a leader or management team who can make final decisions. Google, for instance, attempted to rid itself of so many managers at one point that business was disrupted and some layers were added back into the structure.[23] With about 50,000 employees, Google still remains much less hierarchical than other companies of its size, Birkinshaw says.

"Flatter is easier in small and medium-sized companies," he says. "Big companies will always have some sort of hierarchy—it is just a necessary element of being big. So the question is, can a large company be relatively flat compared to its peers?"

Flat companies also need employees who thrive in such an environment—individuals who are independent and creative. That's one reason businesses with flat management can have a longer hiring process, or even a process where fellow employees do the hiring.

Courtright discusses these considerations with his students as they contemplate their own job options. For a flat organization to work well, he says, "you have to get people whose primary motivation for going into that organization is to work on creative and challenging projects. The corporate ladder isn't all that important to them. It's the notion of continually working on new and challenging tasks. If that's what their motivation is, they'll succeed in one of these organizations."

On the flip side, "if their motivation is to climb up the corporate ladder," Courtright says, "then they'd be much better suited for a hierarchical organization where that's more possible."

Another factor affecting a company's ability to flatten its management structure is its business strategy, for instance, whether it revolves around the need for constant innovation or a consistent product. "The design of your organization has to fit its strategy," Courtright says.

On the one hand, Courtright cites the Google example. "Their strategy is to continually come up with innovative apps or products, and they're all about innovation," he says. "That's ultimately their bread and butter." Because of that mission, he continues, "they have to structure the organization in a way that fosters innovation. So they configured a very flat structure. They give workers a lot of autonomy and freedom."

On the other hand, Courtright pointed to a company like McDonald's, whose business model centers on being consistent and familiar. Because they need to remain predictable to their customers, he says, "they structure their organization to be far more hierarchical."

Flat Management vs. Corporate Hierarchy

Flat management means different things at different companies, some of which have followed the model for decades.

Morning Star, the tomato processor, has adhered to a self-management philosophy since its founding in 1970. According to the company's website, "We envision an organization of self-managing professionals who initiate communication and coordination of their activities with fellow colleagues, customers, suppliers and fellow industry participants, absent directives from others."[24]

At Morningstar, no one has a boss, employees negotiate their responsibilities with their peers, and workers have to get the tools they need to do their jobs—meaning if you need an $8,000 welding machine, you order it. The company's business units negotiate customer-supplier agreements, employees initiate the hiring process when they need help, and disagreements are resolved through a mediation process that can, but rarely does, end up on the president's desk for a final decision. [25]

Nick Kastle, a business development specialist, explained how his working for Morning Star differed from his previous employer: "I used to work in a company where I reported to a VP, who reported to a senior VP, who reported to an executive VP. Here, you have to drive the bus. You can't tell someone, 'Get this done.' You have to do whatever needs to be done."[26]

Valve, the software maker and game developer, has been bossless since it began in 1996.[27] The company's handbook—with the subtitle "A fearless adventure in knowing what to do when no one's there telling you what to do"—is available online.[28]

"It's a classic example of one of the most extreme forms of flat management," says Cliff Oswick, professor of organization theory at City University London's Cass Business School. The company has no job titles, and the desks have wheels so employees can move around the office.[29]

"Your challenge is to add value where you can," he says. "So you decide which project you want to work on; you decide when you want to enter or leave a project, and the whole process of evaluating your performance is done by your peers, including the level for remuneration."

Since its founding in 1958, "Gore has been a team-based, flat lattice organization that fosters personal initiative," according to the company's website. "There are no traditional organizational charts, no chains of command, nor predetermined channels of communication."[30]

The company's president and CEO, Terri Kelly, said it's not realistic to expect a single leader to have all the answers. "It's far better to rely upon a broad base of individuals and leaders who share a common set of values and feel personal ownership for the overall success of the organization. These responsible and empowered individuals will serve as much better watchdogs than any single, dominant leader or bureaucratic structure."[31]

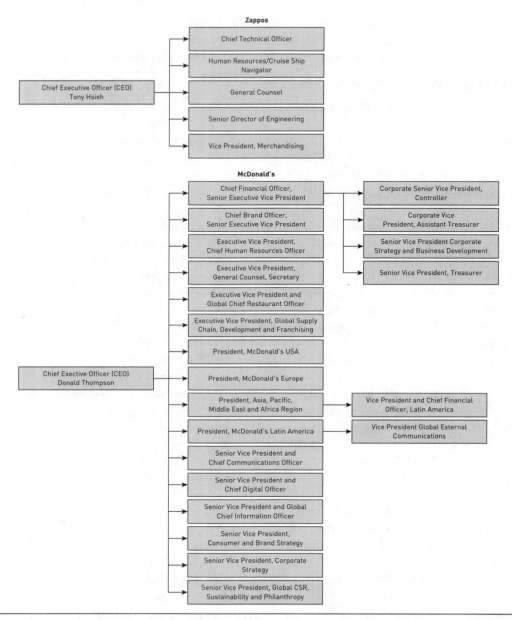

Online shoe retailer Zappos adopted a flattened approach to executive management in December 2013 and has six executives over two levels of its corporate hierarchy. McDonald's, by contrast, has a top-down hierarchical corporate structure with 16 different executive positions in just the second level of its hierarchy.

Source: Zappos organizational structure from "Zappos," The Official Board, updated June 20, 2014, http://tinyurl.com/okd8n4u; McDonald's organizational structure from "McDonald's," The Official Board, updated Sept. 9, 2014, http://tinyurl.com/d3er25l, and Our Company/Leadership, McDonald's, accessed Nov. 19, 2014, http://tinyurl.com/7r6nenm

Zappos, the online retailer, recently adopted a management style known as holacracy, which seeks to integrate the advantages of top-down and bottom-up structures.[32] As the company's CEO Tony Hsieh told employees in announcing the plan, "Darwin said that it's not the fastest or strongest that survive. It's the ones most adaptive to change."[33]

"We're classically trained to think of 'work' in the traditional paradigm," John Bunch, a Zappos employee who is helping lead the transition to holacracy, told the online business news site Quartz.[34] "One of the core principles is people taking personal accountability for their work. It's not leaderless. There are certainly people who hold a bigger scope of purpose for the organization than others. What it does do is distribute leadership into each role. Everybody is expected to lead and be an entrepreneur in their own roles, and holacracy empowers them to do so."

For Zappos workers on a day-to-day basis, that translates to more clarity about who owns what, says Alexis Gonzales-Black, who also is helping lead the change to holacracy. "If you need to get something done, rather than emailing a bunch of people, you can look up exactly who is in charge of something," she says. "For many people, it's also meant expanding the scope of their work. In the old system, you might have been siloed into one kind of role, but now that it's more open, people are reaching across circles and taking on work outside of their main area."

Semco, the Brazilian portfolio manager that grew from a manufacturing company, has long practiced "what has variously been called participative management, corporate democracy, and 'the company as village.'"[35]

The military in the United States and elsewhere—long characterized by a hierarchical chain of command—also is working to adopt flatter management techniques to improve its ability to respond quickly to new forms of warfare.[36] That was underscored by comments about the military's future from retired U.S. Army Gen. Stanley A. McChrystal and Gen. Martin E. Dempsey, chairman of the Joint Chiefs of Staff, in which each acknowledged the need to streamline the management structure to allow for swifter decisions.[37]

Navy SEALS, for instance, must rely on distributed decision-making in the field.[38] The Israeli military also uses flatter management techniques to increase flexibility and efficiency.[39]

Military leaders "have been putting a huge amount of effort into figuring out how to make distributed decision-making more effective," says Oswick. "Because what they've discovered is that, in a battle, if you're relying on chain of command, you're not fast enough, and you will lose."

Can a company have a strong leader and a flat management structure?

The role of the CEO is changing along with the social and business climate that is fostering the move toward flatter management.

David Stein, the co-chief executive of software company Rypple, has a message fellow CEOs may find hard to hear: "They're just not that into you."[40]

"My job is important," Stein wrote in 2011, "but I don't flatter myself that I'm the most important person around in the eyes of my customers or most of our team. I certainly am not from my customers' perspective—or even from the perspectives of most employees."

But as many researchers have noted, flat structures still need managers.

"One of the things that is a little bit deceptive in all of this is that when people talk about flat, it's very rare that people are actually advocating we'll have a group of 2,000 people that are all exactly equal," says Kastelle of the University of Queensland. "What people are arguing for when they say flat is, 'Let's go from seven layers for 1,000 people down to three.' So if you do that you still end up with some leadership that is giving us some guidance and setting the course."

In a recent essay for MIT Sloan Management Review, professor of strategy and organization Nicolai J. Foss and economist Peter G. Klein made the case for why business managers still matter.[41]

"The new environment suggests the need for a redefinition of the traditional managerial role," Foss and Klein wrote. "Despite all the changes that have occurred, there is a strong need for someone to define the organizational framework within which a business operates. We argue that, in the knowledge economy, the main task for top management is to define and implement these organizational rules of the game."

That view is not so different from what proponents of flat management advocate. "They argue that you still need some source of entrepreneurial vision, strategy and guidance in your organization," says Kastelle, "which I think is, for the most part, true."

To reconcile the argument that managers still matter with the move toward flatter structures, the outsize roles that some CEOs have played may come under scrutiny, according to Oswick of City University London. "One of the things that's happened is the rock star CEO—the idea that in order to be successful you need a highly charismatic individual to lead—is becoming more difficult to sustain," he says.

Flat organizations don't buy into the concept that one individual knows best, Oswick says. Rather, it's a collective process.

"The successful, highly effective CEO of the future will be less concerned about what they think and more concerned with what the collective thinks and will involve a number of stakeholders in the decision making process," Oswick says. "It will be less about them as key individuals and will be more about them managing, coordinating, and engaging the efforts of others."

Courtright agrees. "In flat organizations, or these self-managing teams, it doesn't mean the leadership goes away." Rather, "it's just different. So instead of the top leader calling the shots, they provide information and resources so that the team can effectively self-manage."

BACKGROUND

Assembly Lines and Managers

Management principles have evolved significantly since Adam Smith put quill to paper in 1776 to write "The Wealth of Nations," which outlined a new understanding of economics and the role of individuals in the economy.[42] As the manufacture of goods moved from the home and the guild to factories and mills, the Industrial Revolution in the 19th century changed thinking about how to manage business and labor.

Workers were brought together under one roof to manufacture products, increasingly using machines. As technology improved and markets expanded, entrepreneurs began experimenting with assembly lines and mass production. Elihu Root developed an assembly system for gunmaker Samuel Colt by dividing the manufacturing process to simplify it. Then, in 1913, Henry Ford perfected the assembly line so his motor company could churn out Model Ts cheaply and efficiently.[43]

The assembly line and other innovations required a new kind of business model, leading to modern management theories that developed around three broad concepts:[44]

- Scientific management was developed by Frederick Winslow Taylor, an American engineer, in the late 19th and early 20th centuries. He was the first to apply scientific methods to workplace issues, with a specific focus on improving economic efficiency and worker productivity.[45]

- Bureaucratic management was developed in the early 20th century by Max Weber, a German sociologist and political economist, who expanded on the principles of scientific management. He advocated dividing organizations into hierarchies and establishing strong lines of control and authority.[46]

- The human relations movement in management, fostered by behavioral sciences, began in the mid-20th century, to counter the dehumanizing elements of earlier management theories and to emphasize that companies prospered when their workers prospered.[47]

Fast-forward another century: As society moved from the industrial era into one based on technology and information, many business observers argued management must change yet again to remain competitive.[48]

As Foss and Klein recapped in their essay for MIT Sloan Management Review, the Industrial Revolution brought the decline of small-scale, cottage production and the rise of large, integrated businesses. "Adam Smith's invisible hand was replaced with what business historian Alfred D. Chandler Jr. famously described as the 'visible hand' of management," they wrote. "But now that pendulum appears to be swinging in another direction."[49]

What Taylor saw as rigidly organized factories of docile and obedient workers, they continued, "has been eclipsed by loosely structured teams of highly trained and empowered knowledge workers. Indeed, the 'visible hand' of management has morphed into a system of loose networks, virtual businesses and peer-to-peer interactions."

'Seismic' Changes

Hierarchical management styles trace their roots to the likes of Taylor, Weber and Ford, all of whom were born before the end of the American Civil War in 1865.[50] The change that's needed in an era of advancing technology, generational shifts and globalized workforces and marketplaces, says Oswick of the City University London, is of the same magnitude as the move away from scientific and bureaucratic theories that occurred in the mid-20th century.

"On an organizational level, I think this is as significant as the shift from bureaucracy to flexible forms of organizing," he says.

In 2009, business consultant Gary Hamel published a landmark essay, "Moon Shots for Management," in which he argued that management styles dating to the late 19th century had "reached the limits of improvement."[51]

Business executives and experts "must face the fact that tomorrow's business imperatives lie outside the performance envelope of today's bureaucracy-infused management practices," Hamel wrote in the Harvard Business Review.

In 2008, Hamel convened a group of leading business scholars, executives and observers to outline a "roadmap for reinventing management." The consensus, Hamel said, was that "equipping organizations to tackle the future would require a management revolution no less momentous than the one that spawned modern industry."[52]

One of the scholars who attended that 2008 meeting with Hamel was Birkinshaw of the London Business School. The hierarchical management model, he says, "is coming under pressure because companies have to adapt more quickly to the rapid changes going on in the business markets." Hierarchy may be useful in stable times, he adds, but in a fast-paced, customer-oriented business environment, the old model has been found "wanting, it's been found to be deficient."

Others who study business trends share the view that management must change to succeed. "In this new world, 20th century management involving tight control of workers and measurement of outputs is no longer appropriate or effective," wrote business consultant Steve Denning.[53]

Japanese Assembly Lines

The roots of today's flat management structures date to the auto industry of the 1970s and 1980s, when American automakers realized they needed to learn from the Japanese approach.[54] Toyota gained notice when "they gave every employee on the assembly line the power to stop the entire line if there was something wrong," says Kastelle of the University of Queensland.

In the 1980s and 1990s, General Motors tried to emulate that approach with its Saturn line, following the Japanese automakers' flat management philosophy. And, for a while, Saturn proved to be a management success.

"The whole point of that was they had set up Saturn as an independent so that they could learn how to manufacture in a different way," Kastelle says. "The Saturn division did, in fact, do that incredibly successfully and then came back into the core business. The idea was, those ideas were going to flow through the rest of GM when, in fact, what happened was that the machine of General Motors just crushed all of that independent bit of Saturn so at that point the whole experiment fell over."

Honda and Toyota remain fairly hierarchical, Birkenshaw says, "but have figured out how to balance the need for top-down control with the opportunity for bottom-up input."

In contrast, General Motors seemed to tire of the Saturn effort after just a few years, according to John Paul MacDuffie, a Wharton management professor and co-director of what's now known as the Program on Vehicle and Mobility Innovation, a research consortium. "The story of Saturn is not so much the boldness of the ideas, but that GM was unable to follow through," he said. "It just never figured out how to take the lessons that could be learned at Saturn and apply them elsewhere."[55]

The management challenges in other industries were equally daunting. "Back when this was starting to come in the '80s, when the [flat] practice was starting to be talked about more and more, it really was the manufacturing organizations that were [experimenting], and it was a complete shift in mindset for them," Courtright of Texas A&M says. "In some cases they were successful, and in some they weren't."

'Engaged, Not Led'

In the 1990s and 2000s, technological change accelerated, and the Internet and social media became integral to business. This propelled the move toward flatter management techniques, in part because information no longer flowed down from the top of a management pyramid, but instead spread horizontally.

Oswick points to three social and technological changes that have allowed flat management to gain favor:

- The ability to communicate and disseminate information in real time through technology and with social media. Informal channels can challenge information disseminated through formal channels. "If a message comes down formally from the top downwards," Oswick says, "already people who are stakeholders for the organizations are contacting people they know to come in to tweet on it in real time."

- A shift in social attitudes that has occurred gradually over the last 20 to 30 years. Younger workers are more likely to "want to be engaged, not led," he says. "So that creates a very different dynamic."

- The slow reaction time of traditional hierarchical organizations because they're very structured and rules-governed. "In an increasingly turbulent world," Oswick says, "organizations need to be flatter so they can be more responsive and dynamic in the way that they treat challenges within their environment, but also the way to drive innovation."

CURRENT SITUATION

Flat as Philosophy

Companies increasingly are moving away from traditional hierarchies, incorporating techniques aimed at reducing bureaucracy and distributing decision-making.

Turning to a flatter structure requires a two-tiered approach, says Courtright, involving not only a company's organizational flow chart but also the mindset of its employees. "When you think about flat management, what's really at the heart of it is to do away with layers of management and allow people to have more freedom and control of work," he says. "There's sort of this structural perspective to it, and then there's the psychological perspective to it."

Oswick agrees: "I think flat management has taken that one step further, insofar as it's not really about structure anymore. I think flat management is more about philosophy, a way of doing things that moves away from hierarchy more towards networks."

These networks encompass groups of employees, working together and managing themselves, and spread out horizontally; they sometimes represent the business form of societal phenomena, such as crowdsourcing, due to technology that allows for real-time communications. People want to be part of the process, Oswick says.

"We increasingly see the organizational equivalent of flash mobs and groups of employees self-organizing and instigating change," Oswick says, meaning "collective groups of employees coalescing around a common interest with mutual gain."

Generational changes appear to be a factor as well. When Courtright discusses flat management with his students at Texas A&M, "to them it's almost a given. They're not surprised that this is what should be done. I don't think that was the case 30 years ago when we were teaching business. It would've been a far more rogue practice than it is now. Now it just makes sense. And students of mine look for that when they go and get a job."

Although some researchers hesitate to put too much emphasis on the generational element, Harris of Quantum Workplace has seen similar indicators. Research by Quantum has found that flatter organizations draw younger job applicants because they offer more autonomy.[56]

"They want to have more impact quicker," Harris says. "They don't want to be a small cog in the wheel, and we're seeing that in recruitment. Today, talent is more likely to get excited about a role than they are a company name."

Different Approaches to Flatness

While the flat management concept covers many different approaches, there are companies that offer specific methods to help businesses streamline. Each aims to improve efficiency, speed communications and empower workers with more decision-making authority, but each takes a different approach. Among them:

- "Holacracy" gained attention after Zappos announced it would implement this method, which is offered by its founding company, HolacracyOne.[57] The online retailer's move generated widespread interest and scrutiny about how holacracy works and whether it will be successful.[58] Another business using holacracy is Medium, a publishing website from the founders of Twitter.[59]

- WorldBlu advocates a slightly different management approach based on what it calls "organizational democracy."[60] The underlying philosophy, according to founder Fenton, is that organizational design leads to organizational culture. "I believe in giving power to people; I believe in eliminating hierarchy as much as possible, but you still have to have some level of hierarchy," she says. "Hierarchy isn't necessarily bad. It's the bureaucracy and the mindless hierarchy that you want to get rid of."

- The Morning Star Self-Management Institute espouses yet another model based on the principles developed at the Morning Star Co., "a fundamental mind-shift in the way we view human organizations, management and organizational strategy": Empowered workers, it has argued, are creative workers.[61] This approach has gained attention in business circles since the 2011 publication of the essay, "First, Let's Fire All the Managers."[62] In that article, business consultant Gary Hamel asserted that "with a bit of imagination, it's possible to transcend the seemingly intractable trade-offs, such as freedom versus control, that have long bedeviled organizations" and that "we don't have to be starry-eyed romantics to dream of organizations where managing is no longer the right of a vaunted few but the responsibility of all."[63]

Not Without Downsides

As companies grow, flat management structures can present problems, and some have dealt with issues concerning career development, employee grievances, office politics and even the lack of social diversity among employees with such similar workplace styles.[64] Two of the leading flat software companies—GitHub and Valve—have addressed problems, often in a public manner fueled by social media.

After leaving the company, former Valve employee Jeri Ellsworth characterized the experience as "a lot like high school."[65] "The one thing I found out the hard way is that there is actually a hidden layer of powerful management structure in the company and it felt a lot like high school. There are popular kids that have acquired power in the company, and then there's the troublemakers, and everyone in between," she said on the Grey Area, a podcast about game development.[66]

GitHub, another tech company with a flat management structure, also faced personnel issues, following public accusations of sexism and intimidation that played out on social media after a former employee left the company. That situation led the company to strengthen human-resource procedures and establish leadership-training programs as well as create distinct managerial positions.[67]

Jason Fried, founder and CEO of the Chicago-based software company Basecamp, formerly known as 37Signals, recounted his company's experience when a successful employee wanted to be rewarded with managerial duties and a new title. "The really strange thing was the reason this employee and I decided it was time to part ways," he wrote in a column for Inc. magazine. "The issue was ambition—not a lack of it, but more of it than we could use."[68]

None of this surprises researchers who study management techniques. They acknowledge that leaders—whether based on expertise, personality, initiative or other traits—will inevitably emerge. The question then becomes, according to Courtright, whether it is better to have formal leadership imposed on employees or informal leadership that arises naturally.

"That's how it's supposed to work," says Courtright, who explains, "With natural leadership emerging, that means there has to be consensus among the organization that this person is worthy of following, basically, versus in a hierarchical organization where you really have no choice."

These researchers also acknowledge what the companies on the leading edge have found: There's a risk in being among the first to make such changes. But, the other side of that coin is that if companies wait for such changes to become established knowledge, they will fall behind.

LOOKING AHEAD

'The Trend Is Inescapable'

With societal factors propelling a move toward flatter management techniques, flat management observers say the approach will gain popularity.

"The trend is inescapable, just as the trend away from bureaucracy occurred from the 1920s to the 1950s," says Oswick of the City University London. Flat management "will be the dominant form of organization 15 to 20 years from now."

Karl Moore, an associate professor of strategy and organization at McGill University's Desautels Faculty of Management in Montreal, wrote about the situation from a generational perspective with business student co-author Kyle Hill.[69] "From business to the public service to the military, the conclusion is profound: hierarchy is not collapsing, but it is declining," they wrote. "All sectors need to rethink their organizational structure and work environment. The public service needs to shed its layers of hierarchy. The military needs to move from command-and-control practices to consultative leadership. And to remain competitive postmodern businesses need to reduce bureaucracy and facilitate engagement."

The military is working to do that. In discussing his vision for 2020, Gen. Dempsey used the language of business to outline the need for military change: the impact of "viral effects," the "rapidity of change" and the "cascading and merging of technology" are compelling the move.[70]

"We have to be agile enough to see ourselves and to adapt on a far tighter cycle than ever before in our history, and I think we can do that," he said in a 2011 speech. Dempsey, chairman of the Joint Chiefs of Staff, was then Army chief of staff.

To accomplish that, Dempsey said, the Army plans to empower its forces from the "bottom up." That was the theme of a 2012 "Mission Command" white paper that advocated allowing smaller groups to operate in a "decentralized" manner that would allow forces to adapt and respond more quickly.[71]

For Kastelle, that such changes are taking place in the military as well as the business community underscores the lasting nature of the transformation.

"I view that as a pretty important lead indicator in all of this," he says, "that the militaries of the world are trying to figure out, 'How do we give our lowest-ranking members more decision-making authority so that they can use it effectively.'"

Ultimately, Oswick says, "it's here to stay." The need for businesses to flatten organizations and move away from traditional hierarchies is more than a management fad. "This is something which is far more enduring, because it is a slow shift in social attitudes changing," he says, "and it's a slow but gradual shift in technological change."

He says, "This is enduring and significant, and I can't see how—short of us going back to not using technology, to using carrier pigeons rather than email—short of doing that, I can't really see how this trend would be reversed."

Chronology

1770–1900	**Business complexity leads to development of new management techniques.**
1776	Adam Smith writes "The Wealth of Nations," outlining a new understanding of economics.
1800s	Industrial Revolution brings the rise of mills and factories, where workers are under one roof to manufacture products, increasingly using machines.
1880s	Frederick Winslow Taylor introduces the concept of scientific management, designed to improve economic efficiency; he later publishes his "Principles of Scientific Management."
1901–1960s	**Management techniques advance.**
1913	Henry Ford perfects the assembly line.
1920s	Max Weber introduces the concept of bureaucratic management, focusing on standardized procedures and a clear chain of command.
1940s	Drawing on behavioral sciences, human relations management begins to develop, emphasizing that companies prosper when their workers prosper.
1954	Abraham Maslow publishes his hierarchy-of-needs theory of what motives people, paving the way for his later work on what he called enlightened management.
1954	In his book "The Practice of Management," Peter Drucker introduces the five basic roles of managers, which are to set objectives, organize tasks, motivate and communicate, measure performance, and develop people.
1958	Clothing manufacturer W.L. Gore & Associates is founded and becomes a pioneer of flat management techniques.
1970s–1990s	**Flat management gains a following.**
1970	Tomato processor Morning Star Co. is founded, employing self-management techniques.
1986	Six Sigma, a set of techniques and tools to improve business efficiency and production quality, is developed at Motorola. Although it began as a quality-control concept in the manufacturing sector, it has evolved into a widely used management philosophy focused on customer service and product improvement.

(Continued)

	(Continued)
1988	General Motors prepares to open its first Saturn plant, where it attempts to emulate Japanese automakers' management and production techniques by giving its workers more authority. Production ends in 2009.
1990s–2010s	**Rise of the Internet and the spread of social media accelerate management changes.**
1996	Valve Software is founded with no formal management structure.
2001	A group of 17 software developers publishes the "Agile Manifesto," which proposes alternatives to traditional project management through collaboration among self-organizing, cross-functional teams.
2009	Management consultant Gary Hamel publishes a landmark essay in the Harvard Business Review, "Moon Shots for Management," in which he argues that management styles dating to the late 19th century have "reached the limits of improvement."
2010s	Business and military leaders implement flatter management strategies.
2012	Joint Chiefs of Staff Chairman Martin E. Dempsey issues white paper detailing the need for greater "mission command"—decentralized decision-making in the field—as a key element of military preparedness.
2013	Online shoe and clothing retailer Zappos becomes the largest company to adopt the holacracy management technique.

RESOURCES

The Next Step

Leadership

Hu, Elise, "Inside The 'Bossless' Office, Where The Team Takes Charge," National Public Radio, Aug. 26, 2013, http://tinyurl.com/ocyeqah.

More companies, such as software company Menlo Innovations in Ann Arbor, Mich., are adopting "bossless" office environments to more quickly serve customers and compete for the best employees.

Vasagar, Jeevan, "Experiment with a bit of anarchy," The Financial Times, Jan. 28, 2014, http://tinyurl.com/pwkyzsu.

Berlin-based technology start-up 6Wunderkinder eliminated middle-management positions after beginning to grow; it then introduced "ground rules" for self-managed project teams to follow that align with the company's business goals.

Military Hierarchies

Boss, Jeff, "Why Hierarchy Is Outdated: The (Long Overdue) Need For Organizational Adaptability," Forbes, June 6, 2014, http://tinyurl.com/ozvgloc.

A former U.S. Navy SEAL says businesses should apply combat mission lessons such as removing deference to "rank" and changing decision-making routines to become more adaptable.

McCauley, James, "Quality Over Quantity: A New PLA Modernization Methodology?" The Jamestown Foundation, July 17, 2014, http://tinyurl.com/pvsa8qq.

A Chinese People's Liberation Army's colonel argued in a paper published in November 2013 that one of the military branch's top priorities should be flattening command structures to better integrate joint operations.

Sanborn, James, "Cyber steps up its role on the battlefield," Air Force Times, Aug. 25, 2014, http://tinyurl.com/nks56hn.

The U.S. Marine Corps gave cyberspace advisers more authority over tactical operations, rather than requiring them to gain approval from commanders.

Profitability

Brown, Jonathan, "Workers' co-operatives: One for all, all for one," The Independent (U.K.), Jan. 9, 2014, http://tinyurl.com/q7gxl2z.

The co-op food distributor Suma Wholefoods in West Yorkshire, United Kingdom, generates millions in profit and provides employees bonuses thanks to its flat structure and employee-based decision-making process.

Long, Yun, "Reno's Saint Mary's hospital in the black one year after turning for-profit," Reno (Nev.) Gazette-Journal, June 30, 2013, http://tinyurl.com/q4wq28o.

St. Mary's Regional Medical Center in Reno, Nev., became profitable immediately after being acquired in July 2012 by hospital chain Prime Healthcare Services, which introduced a flat structure that requires approval only from the CEO to implement decisions.

Sangani, Priyanka, "Harvard legend John Kotter advocates 'dual operating system' for winning in a turbulent world," The Economic Times (India), May 16, 2014, http://tinyurl.com/qx239d5.

Harvard professor and management consultant John Kotter believes large companies need to introduce flatter, more parallel management structures within existing hierarchies to remain efficient and successful.

Restructuring

Groth, Aimee, "Zappos is going holacratic: no job titles, no managers, no hierarchy," Quartz, Dec. 30, 2013, http://tinyurl.com/ppxhwc5.

Zappos CEO Tony Hsieh restructured the online shoe and clothing retailer by replacing top-down hierarchy with "holacracy," which distributes power among circles of employees with changing roles.

Hutson, Matthew, "Espousing Equality, but Embracing a Hierarchy," The New York Times, June 21, 2014, http://tinyurl.com/pbqyqu3.

Companies such as Internet search firm Google and design firm IDEO have retained some degree of structural hierarchy while adopting flatter management structures.

Jargon, Julie, "McDonald's Plans to Change U.S. Structure," The Wall Street Journal, Oct. 30, 2014, http://tinyurl.com/q4f3gm4.

Fast-food giant McDonald's plans to eliminate layers of management and create more autonomous consumer "zones" to adapt to local tastes after reporting declining quarterly profits.

Organizations

HolacracyOne
1741 Hilltop Rd., Suite 200, Spring City, PA 19475
484-359-8922
holacracy.org

The company that developed the management theory of holacracy.

Morning Star Self-Management Institute
500 Capitol Mall, Suite 2050, Sacramento, CA 95816
916-925-6500
self-managementinstitute.org

Research and education company that advocates a management model based on the principles developed at the Morning Star Co.

WorldBlu
316 E. Court St., Iowa City, IA 52240
202-251-8099
worldblu.com

A company that advocates the management theory of organizational democracy.

Q&A: Zappos and Holacracy

'WE'RE THE LARGEST COMPANY TO EVER DO THIS'

Alexis Gonzales-Black works at online shoe and clothing retailer Zappos, where she is leading the organizational change to holacracy, a management philosophy that seeks to replace the top-down approach with a managerial operating system that distributes power across all levels of an organization. She spoke with SAGE Business Researcher reporter Jane Fullerton Lemons about the shift. This is an edited transcript of the conversation.

Why did Zappos decide in 2013 to change its management structure?

The best way to describe the "why" behind holacracy is with an anecdote from a book called "Triumph of the City" by Ed Glaeser. [Zappos CEO] Tony [Hsieh] read the book and something really resonated with him, which is that as a city doubles in size, the productivity per resident typically increases. So as cities become more dense, they actually get smarter and more effective. The opposite tendency is true for organizations. As organizations get larger, they become less efficient, less productive. There is less flexibility and agility. The thinking behind [the change] was, "How can we make Zappos function more like a large city and less like a large business?" That's the "why" behind it, and when we looked around at different models of self-organization, holacracy emerged as the most comprehensive model.

How is the implementation going?

It's going well. One of the design challenges of holacracy is how complicated and nuanced it is. It's not easily implemented, particularly when you're challenging notions of rigid management hierarchy that have been around for as long as we all have been in the professional world. It is really difficult. We've begun to see some bright spots, and some case studies emerge, as to how people are using holacracy. There are no road maps for where we are, because we're the largest company to ever do this. It's a lot of unknowns. The story is still unfolding.

What has been the most challenging aspect of implementing this new design?

What's challenging is that it is incredibly detailed, and it's not a bullet-pointed list. It's something that you really have to take the time to read and understand. Probably the most persistent challenge to change is the behavior and mind-set challenges that come with a new organizing system that really distributes authority and gives people the power and the responsibility to step up and own their roles in ways they haven't before.

What has been the most surprising element you've seen?

We really had our expectations set high, and we had a lot of ideas about what this could do for the company, so I wouldn't say surprising, but I would say inspiring. The most inspiring things that have happened is, it has really given a platform for folks in the company who are eager to find new ways to add value to the company and eager to maximize their value across functional areas to really address problems that haven't been addressed by the company for a while.

What advice do you have for other companies?

One of the lessons we've learned is the importance of addressing the behavior and mind-set shifts that are required early on. It's one thing to give people the technical tools, but it is quite another to begin the shift in thinking that's required. Another thing is that you learn through experience. So as much as you can teach people about self-organization, until they get really great models and stories for themselves—until they have that light-bulb moment when they're like, "Wow, the way I do my work is truly different now"—then it doesn't really take hold.

Will Zappos stay with holacracy? Is there any chance you would switch to something different or return to the old ways of managing?

Tony always is the authority. As the person who signs and ratifies the holacracy constitution for the company, he retains the authority to take that back at any moment that he wants to. Eighty percent of the company's work is captured in holacracy, and we're beginning to see these stories emerge about how this is working for folks. But part of self-organizing is that you get real data about how things are operating, evolving the structure and working

(Continued)

(Continued)

with that data. We really want that evolution. Tony always uses the Darwin quote: "It's not always the strongest or most intelligent of the species that survives; it's the most adaptable to change." Part of moving toward a self-organizing system is that evolution, and if at some point we get data that that's not actually serving the overall mission and purpose of our company—which is to deliver happiness to our shareholders, our customers, our employees—then we'll use that data to make whatever decision we need to. There are never any promises; changes are built into the DNA of what we do, but there's a lot of energy and excitement around this.

Looking down the road, how is this new management structure going to affect the company?

If we get this right, what you'll see over the next year, the next part of our story, is a lot more rapid evolution. You'll see more advancement and innovations, and at a pace that maybe you haven't seen before, which is exciting and also scary because as humans we naturally crave stability, we crave predictability. If we do this right, then our company will be smarter, more organized and more courageous—not just the company, but each person. The mission is that people leave Zappos better than when they got here, as both professionals and as humans. That's the larger vision that I would share.

WORK-LIFE BALANCE
Can flexibility help both workers and employers?
Vickie Elmer

EXECUTIVE SUMMARY

Policies that help employees balance the demands of work and life, once viewed as benefits bestowed largely on women by benevolent bosses, have evolved into strategies to achieve corporate goals. Studies show such policies increase both productivity and profitability and help companies hire and retain talented professionals. They are especially popular with millennials, who are pushing for greater flexibility in the workplace. While work-life programs traditionally have benefited working mothers, they also help fathers and other caregivers. Globalization and technological advances have spurred more companies to broaden their work-life policies, but putting such programs into practice can be complicated. Managers must measure work based on results or other markers instead of hours worked. And as established companies and start-ups increasingly operate via distributed or remote teams, where team members may be scattered around the world, managers must rethink how to oversee and motivate employees. Moreover, if not carefully implemented, work-life policies can lead to unequal treatment of staff or circumstances in which employees put in too many hours working from home.

OVERVIEW

Indra K. Nooyi spoke with unusual frankness during the 2014 Aspen Ideas Festival about the difficulty of balancing her family life and her job as CEO of PepsiCo.[1] She mentioned guilt, coping mechanisms, missed "class coffees" at her child's school and her secretary's role in deciding whether her daughter could play Nintendo.

"I don't think women can have it all. . . . We pretend we have it all," said Nooyi, who has led one of the world's biggest food and beverage companies since 2006. "Every day you have to make a decision about whether you are going to be a wife or a mother. In fact, many times during the day you have to make those decisions."[2]

Men, too, struggle to balance work and the rest of life. In August 2014, the CEO of a fast-growing U.S. database company decided to give up his job to spend more time with

From *SAGE Business Researcher*,
January 12, 2015

Vice President of Solutions (on video screen) telecommutes from Boston during a Solutions meeting. Telecommuting is one of the most popular ways to allow employees to balance work with the rest of their lives.

Source: Anne Cusack/Los Angeles Times via Getty Images

his family. Max Schireson, head of MongoDB, wrote in his blog, "The only way to balance was by stepping back" from his demanding job in favor of time with his "wonderful kids," then 14, 12 and 9.[3]

Commentators praised his decision as a milestone in the ongoing work-life debate about time, energy and priorities.[4]

Even for employees far below the executive ranks of Nooyi and Schireson, work often consumes personal life. Forget the 9-to-5 or even 8-to-7 day; many people work 7 to 11—answering emails just before bed or contacting colleagues in India and China at midnight.[5] Workers who frequently check emails outside of work are more likely to experience "a lot of stress" than those who rarely or never look at messages outside their offices, Gallup surveys found. [6]

Separately, Gallup researchers analyzed the results of 263 research studies of 192 organizations worldwide and concluded that companies with high employee engagement—a measure of satisfaction and connection to the job and employer—reported 22 percent higher profit and 37 percent lower absenteeism than companies with lower engagement scores.[7]

Yet in some jobs and corporate cultures, heavy workloads or stress remain serious issues even though companies have offered new benefits or flexible arrangements. Some companies use the "work-family narrative" to discuss a problem working mothers and fathers experience, when the underlying issue is a corporate culture demanding long work hours, according to research by Irene Padavic, a sociology professor at Florida State University, and Robin Ely, a Harvard professor of business. Managers assume women are more likely to quit their jobs because of work-life demands, they said, although in reality turnover was identical for men and women.[8]

Corporations have responded by offering programs that give employees more control over when and where they work. While some companies offer such programs to make employees' lives easier, many use them strategically to meet corporate goals. For example, work-life programs can be highly effective in recruiting and retaining talented young mothers or singles in their 20s, as well as in engaging workers who might otherwise decline promotions or jump ship to "get a life."

Yeo & Yeo, an accounting and computer consulting firm with nine offices in Michigan, competes with larger and better-known accounting firms for new graduates and experienced CPAs by offering a 40-hour week much of the year, while staffers at many other firms routinely work 50 or more hours. Yeo workers also may receive an "overtime bonus"—in money or time off—for extra hours they put in during tax season or other busy periods, says Kym Hess, the company's human resources director. "We're trying to sway them," and

Salaried Employees Work Longer Hours

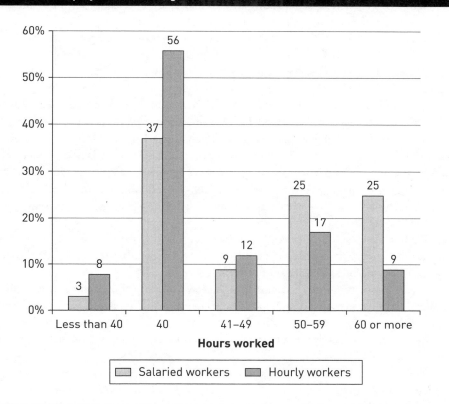

Full-time U.S. workers who are paid by the hour tend to report working shorter weeks than those who are salaried. Half of salaried employees say they work 50 hours or more a week, compared with 26 percent of those who are paid hourly. On average, salaried full-time employees in the United States work an average of five hours more per week (49 hours) than hourly full-time employees (44 hours).

Note: Percentages do not add to 100 due to rounding.

Source: Lydia Saad, "The '40-Hour' Workweek Is Actually Longer—by Seven Hours," Gallup, Aug. 29, 2014, http://tinyurl.com/jwlzo3l.

soon-to-graduate college students get excited when they realize "we're not burning them out," she says.

Even in a tight market for accountants, where multiple job offers are common, most candidates accept Yeo's offer, Hess says. And thanks to the 40-hour week and a customized flexibility plan for workers, the firm's annual turnover rate has remained at about 7 percent of staff annually, compared with around 25 percent for the accounting field overall, she says.

Work-life flexibility programs provide opportunities for managers to improve results and enhance shareholder value—but they also may lead to problems, including unequal treatment of staff and the difficulty of getting away from work.

Globalization and technological advances are key reasons companies are adopting work-life programs. As both established companies and start-ups increasingly operate via distributed or remote teams, where team members may be scattered around the world, managers must rethink how to oversee and motivate employees.

"The business necessity, that's where it's evolved," says Ellen Ernst Kossek, a Purdue University management professor who has written dozens of reports on work-life issues.

Many smaller companies and start-ups are committed to flexibility and distributed teams as a way to hire talented engineers, sales professionals and others to expand their business or move into new markets faster. Smaller companies are now leaders in flexible practices, says Ellen Galinsky, president of the Families and Work Institute, noting interest among executives in well-being and in creating a collaborative culture even when employees work physically apart.

High real estate costs, the need for business continuity in extreme weather, rapidly rising health care costs, corporate cutbacks and demand for specialized professionals also have driven adoption of flexible work arrangements, experts say.

In companies where workers have a strong sense of well-being, staff turnover is drastically lower—on average 10 to 29 percentage points below companies with poorer well-being scores, Gallup's research shows.[9] More than two-thirds of managers told Boston College researchers that flexible programs have a "positive or very positive effect on productivity" and quality of work.[10]

Companies that have strong cultures and work-life arrangements are more successful than their peers, advocates argue.[11] "The basic premise is that employees are more committed to their work when the company acknowledges their needs and gives them the tools and the ability to produce results," says Fran Rodgers, a pioneer in advising companies on work-family issues who co-founded Work/Family Directions in 1983, now Boston-based WFD Consulting. "This has been studied over and over. Removing barriers to producing work in and of itself produces results, but the morale and commitment boost are the real payoffs."

Workers around the globe say they want such programs. In 20 countries, at least 70 percent of the people responding to a recent survey say work-life balance is more important than a successful career. In most of these countries, half or more of the people have not accepted the notion that fulfillment stems from a prominent professional position.[12]

A growing population of elderly people and more singles and single parents could drive demand for even more flexibility. Singles are more willing to try entrepreneurship or to switch jobs—but they often have no partner to help when their pooch, child or grandma gets sick.[13]

Yet some companies pulled back on work-life adaptations in the wake of the 2007–09 recession, saying they needed their teams together during trying times. In 2013, Yahoo told all home-based workers to return to company offices. With the company facing shaky business prospects, Yahoo CEO Marissa Mayer wanted all hands on deck to collaborate on new ideas—"and that starts with physically being together," an in-house memo said.[14] Others followed suit, including Bank of America, which scaled back telecommuting in late 2014.[15]

Elsewhere, many executives pay lip service to flexible arrangements or establish benefits such as free meals, kegs of beer and the like that sound fun but also encourage workers to spend more hours at the office. Others seek to cultivate their "employer brand" with flexible policies, even though many workers find them hard or impossible to enjoy.

"It's one thing to have a policy out there. It's another thing to make a commitment to it," says Carol Sladek, a partner at human resources consulting firm Aon Hewitt who has specialized in work-life flexibility for more than 25 years.

Headquarters of Yahoo in Sunnydale, Calif.; the company in 2013 told all of its home-based workers that they had to work from company offices to make collaboration easier.

Source: Justin Sullivan/Getty Images

In fact, managers who take leave, whether for family or personal illness, receive fewer promotions and salary increases than those who do not, even controlling for performance ratings, some researchers have found.[16]

Flexible programs often are not available to most of the workforce, a Boston College study found.[17] Blue-collar, retail and service workers are among those left out, partly because their jobs require them to be physically present on factory floors or behind fast-food or store registers.

Some companies' practices, such as last-minute shift scheduling, make it difficult for working parents or others who juggle multiple roles or jobs. Laws giving workers the right to predictable hours, making it easier to care for family or to go to school, have passed in San Francisco and Vermont.[18] Experts expect other places to follow suit, and for more business leaders to buy into varied working hours and approaches.

"Progress is going to come from a new generation of leaders," says Rodgers. Millennials—that is, the youngest generation of workers, many now in their 20s or still in their teens—are expected to demand flexibility and create new approaches that contribute to their life satisfaction and company profit.

Already, the work-life field has evolved from a focus on family, mothers and young children to a broader mandate to appeal to singles, young people and almost-retired workers. Even the terminology has changed, from work-family to work-life balance to work-life integration—and now many simply call it flexibility.

As the workplace continues to evolve, here are some of the major questions that managers and researchers are debating:

Weighing the Issues

Do work-life initiatives pay off for employers?

Ryan LLC, a Dallas-based tax services firm with 1,600 employees, once had a reputation as a "highly skilled, albeit well-paid, sweatshop."[19] Fifty-hour workweeks were required, and workers were ranked by hours logged. Staff turnover was high—more than one-fourth of the firm's staff departed one year.

However, in 2008, "we did a 180," says Delta Emerson, Ryan's chief of staff, who for years had urged top executives to adopt greater work-life accommodations. Within months, Ryan started a "work anywhere, anytime, as long as the job gets done" approach.

Now hourly staff may use a "remote time clock," Emerson says, to check in when they are working away from the office. "Turnover went down and client satisfaction went up," she says—turnover, at 18.5 percent in 2007, fell to around 10.4 percent by 2014. And that's a big savings: Each worker who departs Ryan costs about $150,000 in lost expertise, productivity, training and more, Emerson estimates.

The initial investments—money spent on training managers, buying laptops and changing policies and health plans—showed a positive return. "Revenue went way up. Employee engagement went way up," she says.

Emerson offers this advice to companies seeking to establish a flexible culture: "Connect the dots to ROI [return on investment]. Figure out the business case; it's there."

Flexibility advocates cite numerous studies that say such programs can be a smart business strategy. "We have tons of research—even 10 years ago, we had super confirming clear research: Allowing workers to work flexibly benefits both the organization and the employee," says Judi Casey, founding director of the Work and Family Researchers Network, an organization of scholars and others who focus on flexibility. After years of studying working mothers, child care and the effects of two-earner couples on families, "cutting-edge researchers" have moved onto analyzing flexibility's role in engaging workers and older workers, according to Casey. Some are researching fathers or the impact of sleep on worker productivity.

Companies offering flexibility find it easier to recruit and retain talented workers, with turnover often half the level of others in the industry, according to research by Great Place to Work Institute, which studies and measures business environments and produces the annual Fortune list of best employers.[20] Such workers are more likely to be strong promoters of their employer—which is useful in hiring and in landing new clients, according to a report from management consulting firm Bain & Co.[21]

Employers add employee and family flexibility programs largely because it's in their best interest to do so, according to researchers. In a survey of 1,051 for-profit and nonprofit employers, the Families and Work Institute found that three of the five main stated reasons for adopting flexible programs and benefits gave business a boost: retaining employees, recruiting employees and increasing productivity. (The other two reasons were helping employees manage work and family life, and to comply with the law.)[22]

Workplace flexibility does add costs, especially when the programs are new. Development and execution can eat up hundreds of staff hours, as can management training. And work-life arrangements may not pay off if they are poorly executed or don't match employees' needs and expectations, experts say.

"Flexibility needs to be in the interest of employees as well as employers or it's not flexibility at all," says Ellen Bravo, executive director of Family Values @ Work, a network of coalitions working to win paid leave through laws like those endorsed by voters in Massachusetts and three cities in November 2014. [23]

Poor oversight also can be costly. U.S. Patent and Trademark Office workers, based in their homes, repeatedly lied about their hours, and many received bonuses for work they didn't do, The Washington Post reported. Managers had few tools to monitor the patent examiners.[24] Quality issues surfaced too, in part because staffers did not work for "long periods, then rushed to get their reviews done at the end of each quarter," The Post said, citing information provided to an oversight agency.

Some executives say telecommuting won't work in their company because they believe being at the office pays off. Google—which repeatedly tops surveys of best places to work—strongly discourages the practice. Executive Chairman Eric Schmidt explained, "Part of that is a teamwork thing. . . . A lot of conversations are informal; the entity moves forward when people are around." [25]

Nonetheless, experts say offering flexibility to workers provides payoffs for companies:

- Flexibility may build shareholder value. Companies that made Fortune magazine's best-places-to-work list outperformed the Russell 3000 and the S&P 500 stock indices by a wide margin—gaining two to three times as much in value.[26]

- Company overhead expenses decline when workers no longer have set space in corporate offices. Corporate real estate and utility bills fall; other expenses may decline too. Through teleworking programs that started 20 years ago, IBM estimates that it saves $200 million a year in U.S. and European office and real estate costs—on top of $1.9 billion the company made from selling property.[27]

- Flexible work schedules may reduce absenteeism and staff departures or turnover. Research shows turnover is lower when workers' lives are considered—and that working mothers are much more likely to leave 50-hour-a-week jobs in male-dominated occupations.[28]

- Individuals who work from home may be more productive and often put in longer hours, either because of shorter commutes, because they take fewer breaks or sick days or because they're grateful for the accommodation. [29] Telecommuters log five to seven more hours a week than those who do not work from home part of the time. [30]

- Workers dealing with exhaustion or family stress may help erode customer satisfaction and hurt customer service through negative job attitudes or fake smiles, researchers have found. [31]

Realizing gains can require patience, however. "Not every change leads to an improvement in productivity the next month," Kossek says. Instead, worker well-being is a long-term investment, she says, that improves the corporate culture and brand over time, the same way a major league team may lift a city's reputation.

Will companies provide work-life flexibility to all employees?

Millennials, who make up an ever-increasing share of the workforce, have become the "it" focus of employers with jobs to fill.[32] Yet with all the emphasis on recruiting young professionals, experts say flexibility programs for blue-collar workers and baby boomers are lagging.

To attract and retain young workers, some companies are adjusting work hours, offering flexibility and quickening the pace of promotion. For instance, Ocean Spray Cranberries created a "Culture Club" of employees in their 20s and 30s to hear their perspectives on work.

"We know we're going to have to think differently if we want to keep young people here," said Jane Borkowski, Ocean Spray's vice president of human resources. [33]

Some companies focus on a child-friendly atmosphere—which may draw more workers with kids. At Palo Alto Software in Eugene, Ore., the staff's children are welcome to come in as necessary. "We have never grown faster, nor been more financially successful," CEO Sabrina Parsons wrote. "Oh, and we also had an office baby boom—there have been 10 babies born in the past year."[34]

Says Cali Williams Yost, chief executive of Flex + Strategy Group consulting in Madison, N.J., and an author of books on flexible work, "The smart ones, the companies that really rely on young talent—for example, accounting firms—have been forced to truly figure this out, to offer some degree of flexibility. They're just not going to get people to work for them if they don't."

Two-thirds of human resources managers say flexible work benefits will be increasingly important to retain highly skilled workers, and almost half have already used them to keep a staffer, according to a 2013 Society for Human Resource Management (SHRM) report. [35] Almost one-third of employers said participation rates are rising and SHRM indicated that "cultural barriers to such benefits are starting to erode."[36]

Yet many companies offered flexible arrangements to less than half of their staff, and employers were most likely to say that only 1 percent to 25 percent of their eligible workers used each flexible work arrangement, SHRM found in a 2014 survey.[37]

Many companies adopt flexible programs after they hit a crucial pain point—a big problem that cannot easily be lived with or solved. Three "particular pain points" motivate employers: high real estate costs, trouble attracting or retaining female staff and difficulty recruiting millennials, says Williams Yost, who works with employers on flexible arrangements. "A number of challenges and goals can be achieved with the same flexibility," she says. "It's truly driven by a real market need."

The market need applies to engineers, senior managers and electricians, who are in high demand, but not to waiters or cleaning crews who are easier to find. [38] The increases in flexibility intended to entice millennials also appeal to baby boomers who care for aging parents or visit grown children at faraway universities or towns.

"Flexibility has got to be practiced flexibly," says Lisa Horn, director of the Workplace Flexibility Initiative at SHRM. Some jobs require a physical presence: treating dental patients, packing pet costumes for shipment or running machinery on a factory floor. When

More Employers Offer Flexible Shifts, Phased Retirement

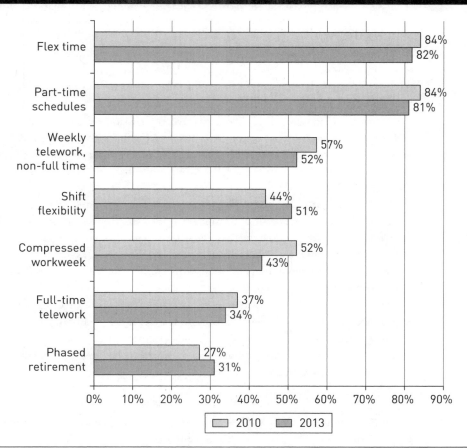

Among employers surveyed in 2010 and 2013, the share of those offering weekly part-time telework schedules fell by 5 percentage points, and the share offering compressed workweeks fell by 9 points. Additionally, fewer employers offered flex time, full-time telework and part-time schedules. However, the share of employers offering shift flexibility jumped 7 percentage points, and the share of employers providing phased retirement rose by 4 percentage points.

Note: Based on respondents to WorldatWork's Survey on Workplace Flexibility; 2010 = 537 employers; 2013 = 566 employers

Source: "Figure 2: Prevalence of Workplace Flexibility Programs, 2010 Comparison," WorldatWork, October 2013, p. 12, http://tinyurl.com/m74zhxm

such a job is tied to set hours or a specific location, the employer is likely to limit flexibility. This fuels debate about the class divide: While software developers can work from a favorite café as they please, baristas cannot get a reliable work schedule that allows them to attend classes or arrange a babysitter.[39]

Labor Secretary Thomas Perez noted that those who work "in retail or in hospitality or at a call center," or those who hold two jobs, don't have the option of taking time off to celebrate children's birthdays or go to pick up a sick relative in the middle of a work day.[40]

When workers perceive that employers aren't granting work-life benefits fairly and equitably, they might retaliate by coming to work late, taking longer breaks or even "creating their own flexibility in order to restore equity and repair the situation," T. Alexandra Beauregard of the London School of Economics wrote.[41]

At many companies, flexibility is granted on a case-by-case basis, and managers' mindsets or backgrounds can affect their decisions. Purdue's Kossek calls this "individual deal-making" or a "micro-climate" of flexibility. When workers cut secret deals with a boss, she says, "then workers overwork, or are really constantly available as a way to keep the flexibility."

Employers need to be careful that in recruiting one group and offering extra benefits and flexibility they aren't setting themselves up for a discrimination lawsuit. Title VII of the Civil Rights Act of 1964 requires equal treatment in offering benefits and applying company policies. A woman, minority or anyone in a protected class could claim "disparate treatment," a key legal requirement to show discrimination, if he or she is denied a work-from-home arrangement that others have.[42]

Employers need to offer clear policies and guidelines on flexible work, stressing the results they expect and how they will measure success, says Kate Lister, president of Global Workplace Analytics, a California research and consulting firm specializing in telework and flexible work. Then the worker and manager may personalize the arrangement to fit the job and the individual's work styles, she says.

Can a flexible culture thrive if the CEO is a workaholic?

Before Ernst & Young CEO Mark Weinberger took the top job at the accounting firm, he sought permission and buy-in from his four children.

They placed a condition on him moving up: maintain family commitments.[43] Weinberger's first test came when he gave his first speech as CEO in China. Afterward, he was asked if he would take selfies at the Great Wall with his team.

No, he said: He had to hurry home to be at his daughter's driver's test the next day—a promise he had made a year earlier. "Not a single person remembered the terrific speech I gave, but everybody remembered I went home for my daughter," Weinberger told Time. "It brought home to me how powerful leading by example is."

For every Weinberger who is promoting flexibility and modeling commitment to family, there are other bosses who demand long hours and complete focus on business. Work-life practices come as much from cultural presumptions and a boss's expectations as they do from policies and proclamations, experts say.

"Senior leaders are always, always critical—not just what they say but what they do, and who gets rewarded and who doesn't," says Galinsky, president of the Families and Work Institute.

To change a culture, it's important that senior leaders believe in the value of change, a survey of influential work-life experts found.[44] Otherwise, leaders pose a real barrier to change. Four in 10 human resources managers told WorldatWork, a nonprofit association for HR management professionals, that resistance by top managers explains why they do not allow telecommuting.[45]

Former General Electric CEO Jack Welch, for instance, made it clear that he thinks women who want to reach the top of a corporation cannot telecommute or take parental leave for a year. "There's no such thing as work-life balance" for female leaders, he told an SHRM conference in 2009. "They've got to make the tough choices and know the consequences of each one."[46]

Some derided Welch's comments as out of touch, outdated and insensitive to the complexities working mothers face.[47] Yet his views represent a traditional mindset that has not disappeared.

At the accounting firm Ryan, it took Emerson almost three years to persuade the CEO to change the long-hours culture. "He was the toughest sell," she says. He relented when a valued employee told him she was going to quit to start a family, even though she loved her job. Then he shocked Emerson, saying: "People can work anywhere, anytime, as long as they get their jobs done."[48]

In many cases, however, flexible work arrangements show up first with a sympathetic or open-minded lower-level manager, then spread gradually. A manager makes an exception to keep a talented analyst or to land a promising millennial. "Flexibility comes from the bottom up and from the middle up," says Sladek of Aon Hewitt. "It's not necessarily endorsed by business leaders."

She has gone into companies and found "all kinds of stuff going on that no one admitted to." Recently, a human resources manager told Sladek that at least one-third of new hires received an extra week of vacation because they demanded it.

"Research shows that an organization's work-life culture—all the unwritten yet well understood norms and expectations about how people are supposed to work, and what it means to be a good employee—has enormous power over behavior," according to Monique Valcour, a professor of management at the EDHEC Business School in France.[49]

A new CEO could bring changes, as could a merger or acquisition, but they may not take root for years if a culture is entrenched, says Mark Graham Brown, a performance consultant and author. For example, he says Nestle Purina PetCare's work-hard-then-leave-at-5:30 culture has not changed since a 2001 buyout—and the company has won regional and national work-life accolades since then.

Not all workaholic bosses expect workers to put in the same long hours they do. "The Happy Workaholic," a study by management professors Stewart Friedman of the Wharton School at the University of Pennsylvania and Sharon Lobel of Seattle University, found that some leaders respected employees who wanted shorter hours or more family time.[50]

Says Friedman: "As an executive, as a supervisor, it pays for you to take account of the whole person. . . . Understand the whole person standing in front of you; there are clear benefits."

BACKGROUND

Women at Work

Work-life boundaries or work-life conflict are relatively recent notions, with roots in the mid-20th century. They're closely tied to the history of women in the workplace.

For much of history, work and family took place together, often on a farm. As with home-based entrepreneurs today, work and family, chores and life were jumbled in one big pot and one place. Men, women and children worked closely together to grow crops, tend livestock, and produce butter and other dairy products.[51]

Of course, some women have always worked outside the home, including as servants. In the 1800s, women increasingly were also business owners, teachers and more. The first American female doctor began practicing in 1850.[52]

The Industrial Revolution led women to factory work, where they were paid less than men. Some textile mills, despite harsh conditions, were all-female workplaces, where workers lived together in boarding houses and, in some instances, walked off the job together to protest low wages and poor working conditions.[53]

In the early 1900s, demand for clerical workers grew, and so more young women were recruited into the workforce.[54]

Few companies offered workers paid vacations or other benefits. Pay was low: In 1909, the average factory worker earned $3.80 an hour (in 1999 dollars) compared with $13.90 in 1999. The average workweek in manufacturing was 53 hours in 1900, and many people worked six days a week, compared with about 40 hours and five days in recent years in the goods-producing sector.[55]

Few laws protected workers. Children ages 10 to 15 made up 6 percent of the labor force in 1900, usually because families needed their wages. Workers often were assigned to 12-hour factory shifts.[56]

The Progressive Era reformers of the 1890s to 1920s started campaigns that led to new child labor laws in numerous states. A few states established workers' compensation laws, though many were quite limited or did not stand up to legal challenges.[57]

In 1911, a fire broke out at the Triangle Waist Factory, a clothing sweatshop in New York City. Within minutes, 146 workers were killed, mostly women, some as young as 14. The tragedy led to new state laws mandating safety equipment, including automatic sprinklers, which two decades later were incorporated into New Deal federal laws.[58]

The 40-Hour Week

The Fair Labor Standards Act, which took effect in 1938, established the 40-hour workweek, as well as set a minimum wage.[59] It was among the New Deal measures enacted in response to the Great Depression, when President Franklin Delano Roosevelt was eager to get more money in circulation and to add jobs.[60] Other worker protections on safety and security followed.

During World War II, women built airplanes and guns.[61] After the war, though, returning soldiers took back those jobs. They also got married and started the baby boom. By then, the "little woman belongs at home" view was entrenched in middle-class attitudes and popular culture. Still, many lower-and working-class women needed jobs.

One in three women were in the civilian labor force in 1950; by 1970, the figure was 43.3 percent.[62] Prosperity increased demand for workers.[63] Starting in the 1960s, two trends changed perspectives and conversations: the women's liberation movement, and the civil rights laws and their broad interpretation.

The women's liberation movement, with its demands for equal pay for equal work, brought change in some fields. Help-wanted ads, long segregated into men's and women's jobs, dropped that approach as women sued for equal treatment.

Female workers also gained legal protections. The Equal Pay Act of 1963 required employers to pay men and women the same wages for the same work.[64] In 1965, shortly after the Equal Employment Opportunity Commission (EEOC) was established, the commissioners ruled that Title VII outlawed corporate policies that required managers to fire female workers when they married.[65] (Title VII is a section of the Civil Rights Act of 1964 that prohibits employment discrimination based on race, sex, national origin and religion.) It wasn't until the Pregnancy Discrimination Act of 1978 that companies had to stop firing women when they were visibly expecting.

Early work-family research in the 1960s looked at women's careers and the relationship between work and family, especially the effect of working mothers on children's education and self-worth.

Women increasingly joined the labor force as inflation and several recessions (1973–75, then 1980 and 1981–82) prompted families to seek two incomes.

In the 1970s, many companies introduced Employee Assistance Programs (EAPs), which provide workers with confidential resources and counselors to deal with stress, alcohol and family problems; firms began to consider their workers' child care needs, with some opening on-site day care centers.

Increasing numbers of work-family programs began in the early 1980s, bolstered by working mothers and feminists. Among the standard-bearers were Deloitte, DuPont, Hewlett-Packard, IBM and Xerox, Rodgers says.

Although there was some discussion of fathers' roles, for the most part, work-family issues were seen as women's issues. That reality was driven home in media reports about women's juggling acts and the growing interest in Working Mother magazine's list of best places to work. Companies began to see the value in a "family friendly" reputation for recruiting and retaining female staff, according to a study of the evolution of work-life issues led by Brad Harrington, a Boston College management professor who is executive director of the school's Center for Work & Family.[66]

"Organizations that evolved from a work/family perspective began with a focus on working mothers and the need for quality childcare. Organizations that evolved from an EAP perspective identified the early links between employee stress, depression and illness, and decreased productivity," Harrington wrote.[67]

Accounting firms such as Ernst & Young and Deloitte took the lead in part because they needed more workers, and women were taking accounting jobs, then quitting.

Looking for ways to retain women after they had children, the accounting firms introduced part-time and non-partner tracks and created women's networks and councils.[68] "They were driven to flexibility for women because the number of graduates of accounting programs were not enough to replace the accountants [who were] going to retire in the next 10 years," says Williams Yost of the Flex + Strategy Group.

For example, the 1997 Ernst & Young survey of employees contained 3,071 written comments regarding work-life balance and stresses, even though two years earlier, CEO Phil Laskawy had created and led a task force to help women with career development and advancement.[69] In 1997, offices in San Jose and Palo Alto, Calif., were chosen for prototype work/life balance programs to reduce turnover and reshape the culture. A telecommuting pilot and new policies on checking voicemail on weekends were among the changes, according to a paper on Ernst & Young written by Wharton professor Friedman.[70]

Some companies developed on-site child care centers or agreed to offer compressed workweeks or unconventional start times outside the normal 8 a.m. or 9 a.m. for working mothers. "It felt like a tremendous amount of progress because a lot of things were being added," says Rodgers, founder of WFD Consulting.

Mostly, though, benefits and programs were "grafted onto the existing basic corporate systems," so most improvements were superficial, Rodgers says. Part-time schedules and child care subsidies sounded nice but didn't change corporate mindsets or cultures.

Yet companies started to jockey for the recognition they received from the media best-of lists. Executives encouraged their human resources departments to offer benefits, often with minimal guidance on how those benefits could be implemented, and no training of managers, says Fred Van Deusen, a Boston College work-life researcher who worked for Hewlett-Packard for 20 years.

For some employees, however, work hours rose. "The sense that there was no such thing as a 40-hour workweek became pervasive, especially for professionals," Rodgers says.

This attitude came as a number of jobs were ruled exempt, or sometimes exempt, from U.S. overtime rules in the 1980s and 1990s, from reporters to insurance claims adjusters to assistant managers. More recently, the number of class-action lawsuits over the possible denial of overtime pay has increased for seven years, and the U.S. Labor Department has actively prosecuted companies that "misclassify" workers as exempt from overtime or as independent contractors instead of employees.[71] The department has collected millions of dollars in back pay for workers at a bank, oil and gas companies and clothing maker Levi Strauss, which required assistant managers to attend off-the-clock meetings and fill in during staff shortages.[72]

Mommy Track Debates

Over time, women also became worried that they would end up on the "mommy track," a term that grew out of a 1989 Harvard Business Review piece that proposed two career paths: "career primary" and "career and family."[73] In debates in public forums and across kitchen tables, some wondered if working mothers were placed on that slower track without their consent; others asked whether women could "have it all."

The Family and Medical Leave Act, signed into law in 1993, gave workers at many companies the right to 12 weeks of unpaid leave to care for themselves, a new baby or a close relative who was ill. It was considered a major advancement, even as some questioned how low-income workers could afford to take time off without pay. Almost two-thirds of those who needed family leave but did not take it were women.[74]

In the 1990s, laptop computers—then mobile phones, Palms and BlackBerrys—made it easier to bring work to play dates and swim meets. A fad for fun workplaces—plenty of foosball and food in offices—characterized the dot-com boom of the late 1990s, but with few exceptions, flexibility was not served as regularly.

"These benefits are not being offered out of largesse. It's done because organizations want employees to work 24/7," Gerald Ledford, a senior research scientist at the University of Southern California's Marshall School of Business, told The New York Times. "If you never have to leave to get your dry cleaning, to go to the gym, to eat or even go to bed, you can work all the time."[75]

At many companies, work-life balance remained a woman's issue, often relegated to the human resources department, which was run by women. (Recently, nearly three-quarters of human resources managers were women; by contrast, women hold 41 percent of all management jobs.[76]) Rodgers says she became disillusioned that more changes and improvements were not taking root. Women wanted improvements, but "I was always amazed how timid they were," she says.

In the last 10 years, though, Sladek at Aon Hewitt says she has seen a big change at large and midsize companies that value flexible work. "Workplace flexibility has become more of a reality of the day-to-day culture and not offered by exception," she says.

Some changes occurred after the Sept. 11, 2001, terrorist attacks, as companies wanted to protect themselves from business interruptions or the loss of key workers. Thousands died that day, and others opted to change careers so they could do something that offered more purpose or connection. Business continuity and protection from earthquakes, floods, hurricanes and more motivated some companies to move more workers to home offices, says Jim Ware, a futurist and the founder of The Future of Work, a California research and advisory firm.

Rising health care costs and obesity rates contributed to the growth of wellness programs and company-sponsored gyms and kickball leagues. Sixty-four percent of employers offered wellness programs in 2013, up from 59 percent in 2009. The growth was faster for health screenings and bonuses or other rewards for completing some health programs.[77] One-third of employers offer an on-site lactation/mother's room, up from 25 percent in 2009, SHRM found.

But the wellness campaigns don't always work, and some have faced legal challenges. The EEOC has sued a few employers under the Americans with Disabilities Act for requiring health tests.[78]

Over the last decade or so, freelancing and self-employment have become bigger pieces of the economy in the United States, United Kingdom and many parts of Europe. Self-employment in Britain is at its highest levels in almost 40 years, with 15 percent of the workforce working for themselves, more than double the rate in 1975.[79] Taxi driving, construction and carpentry are among the most common jobs.

CURRENT SITUATION

Flexible Work Gains Acceptance

Today's work world has become more eclectic, fragmented and contradictory.

Virtual teams, with members living and working around the globe, are increasingly common, even as workers seek connections with colleagues. "People value those same interactions" whether they sit 10 feet or 1,010 miles apart, says Sara Sutton Fell, president of FlexJobs, which researches and advertises virtual and telework openings.

Companies from ADP to Xerox are creating thousands of telecommuting jobs.[80] Yet many of the fastest-growing fields require presence: home health aides and brick mason assistants, occupational therapy assistants and skin care specialists.[81]

Diverse work teams, with people from many cultures, eras and ethnicities and more openly gay, lesbian or transgendered individuals, require thoughtful and respectful management. Otherwise, managers risk lawsuits for transgender discrimination—the federal government filed the first two in September 2014.[82] Managers must lead five generations and bridge the differences in style and substance.[83]

Worker shortages are increasing in the United States, Argentina, India and elsewhere.[84] At the same time, high unemployment among youth remains a serious issue in countries including Spain and Greece. Mothers still are left out of the job market in some countries.[85]

Flexible work is gaining acceptance in the United States, experts say. Although fewer employers allow summer or six-month sabbaticals, more of them offered occasional flexible work locations and control over overtime hours in 2014 compared with 2008.[86] Fewer companies say personnel policies get in the way of providing flexibility.

"People are more productive and content and willing to go the extra mile when they're seen as a whole person and their life matters—and they can take responsibility to organize their work time," says Bravo of Family Values @ Work, citing research from the National Association of Working Women, which she led, and also the Carnegie Foundation.

While some employers embrace flexibility, "we're still working with companies that basically haven't put anything in place," says Van Deusen, senior researcher at Boston College's Center for Work & Family. Change is "very evolutionary," he says, because corporate cultures evolve more slowly than worker expectations.

One change that has spread quickly is the move toward freelance and independent contractor jobs. An estimated 34 percent of the U.S. workforce, including those who moonlight or have "side gigs," now is doing some form of freelancing, and the number of "non-employer businesses"—generally self-employed individuals—rose 29 percent from 2002 to 2012.[87]

Companies see the advantages: lower payrolls, no paid vacation or pension to fund and no requirement to follow many U.S. labor laws. Yet many workers like it, too: Some 58 percent of women who work as independent contractors choose to do so for the flexible schedules, compared with 43 percent of men, and women also were more likely to see working independently as a way to have more time for family or personal pursuits, according to data provided by the Freelancers Union.[88]

Some workers who still clock in find their days extended by before-hours meetings or after-hours security clearance. Amazon workers at the online retailer's Nevada warehouse say security screening takes as long as 25 minutes, uncompensated. "If people are stuck in your building and they're not allowed to leave, why don't you go ahead and pay them?" Amazon staffer Jesse Busk told Bloomberg News.[89] About 12 lawsuits against Amazon and its temporary-employment firms raise questions about what hours must be compensated under the Fair Labor Standards Act. The company argued the screenings are not directly part of workers' jobs; in December 2014, the Supreme Court ruled that Amazon does not have to pay them for that time. The security lines do not meet the court's 1956 standard of being "integral and indispensable" activities, Justice Clarence Thomas wrote.[90]

Wellness and Worker Advocacy

Wage theft cases also have been brought against McDonald's, FedEx, hotel chains and other companies, where workers charge they failed to receive overtime or tip income.[91] In one case, a McDonald's franchisee settled and paid $500,000 to 1,600 workers who allegedly were shorted on pay.[92] Yet lawyers representing employers say companies have become more careful about complying with wage laws after much-publicized lawsuits were filed against Wal-Mart and others a decade ago.

New organizations, often paired with labor unions or women's or progressive business groups, are advocating for legislation to provide paid sick time, paid family leave and changes in corporate practices around schedules, minimum wage and more, Bravo says. Voters passed paid sick leave initiatives in November 2014 in Massachusetts and three cities, and advocates see momentum in some locales.[93] In January 2015, President Obama backed programs for paid leave for federal workers and for paid sick days for all.[94]

The advocacy groups work on behalf of low-skilled, low-paid staff whose work lives have improved little: fast-food workers, retail workers and domestic workers, says Bravo, an advocate for female workers for 40 years. "People see the connection between minimum wage and sick days and pregnancy discrimination" and workplace flexibility, she says.

The EEOC still receives about 3,500 charges of pregnancy discrimination a year, down from 4,000 in 2010.[95] Companies that settled pregnancy suits in 2014 include J.C. Penney, a Holiday Inn franchisee and Weight Watchers.

One case that has reached the Supreme Court involves a UPS delivery driver who said she was placed on unpaid maternity leave instead of going to a less strenuous job, as her doctor advised.[96] The case is important to women in blue-collar jobs "with a physical component," lawyer Samuel Bagenstos told The Washington Post. "Employers have to provide workers who are pregnant the same accommodations that they would provide other workers" whether they are covered by the Americans with Disabilities Act or the Pregnancy Discrimination Act. The delivery company's main argument is that the workers' union contract does not require or authorize UPS to "disrupt the seniority system by giving temporary, alternative positions to employees unable to perform their normal work assign-ments." Lower courts backed UPS, but a host of women's and antiabortion groups are siding with the mother.[97] The Supreme Court heard arguments in December 2014.

While the Supreme Court and the EEOC in Washington define federal treatment of worker rights and discrimination, California has become a trendsetter in state workplace legislation, providing paid family leave and mandatory paid sick leave. The state recently gave new rights to temporary workers, including holding a "client employer" equally as responsible for paying wages as the contract labor company.[98]

An emerging area involves worker schedules and ensuring that flexibility does not harm workers or deprive them of pay. San Francisco and Vermont have mandated that employers consider worker requests for flextime without retaliation; such "right to request" laws are being considered elsewhere.[99]

Half of Parents Find Work-Family Balance Difficult

"Work scheduling is becoming more and more important," Purdue's Kossek says. She says she is starting to see innovation at some industrial manufacturers, service firms and union-ized employers. For example, a major retailer allows staff to work fewer hours in the sum-mer, when children are off school, and more during the holiday season, when business is busiest, and average hours the rest of the year.

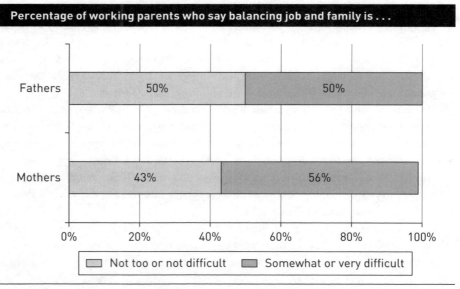

A slightly higher share of working mothers than working fathers agree that balancing work and family responsibilities is "somewhat" or "very" difficult.

Note: Parents with children under 18; responses for "don't know/refused" not shown.

Source: Kim Parker and Wendy Wang, "Modern Parenthood," Pew Research Center, March 14, 2013, http://tinyurl.com/d4rnkxg

Although some employers aim for win-win approaches, company needs—required by the global business climate and a desire for extended customer service hours—drive many of these schedule changes. The bottom-line focus on flexibility has drawbacks, including the idea that every arrangement must pay off within one or two quarters, Kossek says.

Yet millennials are eager to find jobs where flexibility is the norm and where paternity leaves are paid. "Work-life balance and flexibility isn't just a woman's issue. It's a human issue," says David Ballard, who heads the American Psychological Association's Center for Organizational Excellence.

Time for Caregiving

Many baby boomers are postponing retirement, either because they lost so much ground during the 2007-09 recession or because about one-third have not started saving for their post-career lives.[100] In many countries, the official retirement age is rising and could reach 69, notably in Denmark and Italy, where the pensionable age is linked to life expectancy.[101]

Care for elderly relatives will be an issue for workers, managers and employers, experts say. The share of caregivers in the U.S. tripled from 1994 to 2008, with 57 percent of caregivers who are 50 or older working and two-thirds of them female, a MetLife report found.[102] An estimated 39.7 million Americans had elder-care responsibilities in 2013, half of them while working. Nearly half were 45 to 64 years old.[103] Yet younger workers are not exempt: Two in 10 Generation Xers, who are in their 30s and 40s, help parents or other older relatives an average of 11 hours a week.[104]

Workers increasingly must manage blended families, or are single parents, a trend that Galinsky sees affecting work-life flexibility and career plans. Staff may have multiple roles as caregivers: their grandchildren living with them, aging parents needing assistance, children or close friends with health problems or a partner with cancer. Little wonder then that workers, especially younger ones, say they are willing to give up a portion of their pay for more personal time, perhaps to allow for caregiving responsibilities.[105]

Not every sector has bought into flexibility. Fields such as law and management consulting may require 60-to 80-hour weeks. The number of people working more than 49 hours a week saw a huge increase in the 1980s and 1990s, government data show.[106]

Yet over the longer term, Americans' workweeks have declined considerably. In 1900, workers in manufacturing clocked 53 to 59 hours on average and by 1964 that had fallen to 38.7 hours; recently it has been around 34.5 hours, according to the Bureau of Labor Statistics.[107] (When they self-report their hours, Americans often overestimate them by 5 to 10 percent.)[108]

Vacation time has gone from the standard two weeks to a strategic selling point. Some employers offer summer hours, workout or ski breaks or Friday afternoon bike rides.[109] Others compete for talent by offering extra vacation time to experienced accounting professionals, among others.[110] "People are valuing their time away" from work and demanding vacation time upfront, says executive recruiter Jennifer Killingback, who works at d. Diversified Services in suburban Detroit.

A few companies even offer unlimited vacation days.[111] Virgin Group's announcement that U.K. and U.S. salaried workers may take as much time off as they like, whether a few hours or a month away, sounds enticing. The catch, of course, may be getting staffers to take that time. At some companies, staffing cuts make it difficult to take advantage of generous leave policies. Or, "people take less time off because they feel they're not sure if this is really a commitment to them or that this is more a PR thing," MIT Sloan School of Management professor emeritus Lotte Bailyn told The Huffington Post.[112]

At a few leading companies, including some accounting firms, the trend is toward "forced down time" and requiring workers to take a certain number of vacation days, says Lister of Global Workplace Analytics. "They're starting to learn this" after lean years where staff has been stretched and pushed to produce, she says.

LOOKING AHEAD

The future could bring more video cameras into home offices to give continuous connection with colleagues– or a commute by driverless car that provides more time to finish paperwork.

As technology advances and makes remote work easier, the biggest changes in the next 10 years may be in corporate and managerial perspectives. Flexible work arrangements could become so ingrained and expected that they no longer will be considered benefits or accommodations, some work-life experts say, but rather will be part of the way work happens.

HR Employees Predict Flex Benefit Growth

"If things continue to go in the way they're going, someday flexibility will be the way that we work," says Galinsky, president of the Families & Work Institute.

A few leading researchers are starting to look at work-life topics through that prism. "They look at flexibility as business strategy for engagement, for retention," says Casey, the founding director of the Work and Family Researchers Network, who left the organization in October 2014.

Remote work and virtual teams could be more commonplace. "People will get used to people who are somewhere else" and yet on their team on a company project, says Ware, head of the consulting firm The Future of Work. They will co-create the same data sets or marketing presentations from three locations, because the collaboration tools will be "better, faster, cheaper," he says.

Labor shortages, especially in science and technical fields and among skilled labor such as electricians, could give workers more power to negotiate arrangements that work for them.[113] In those conditions, "employees will exercise more control over work selection, workload, and salary," Intel predicted in a paper examining the future of work.[114]

Such shortages will be most severe in Germany, Japan, Austria and Poland, while the United States will face moderate shortages, a Conference Board report forecasts.[115]

Percentage Saying Flex Work Arrangements to Become More Common in 5 Years

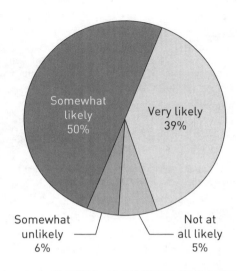

Nine out of 10 human resources professionals responding to a survey said it is "somewhat likely" or "very likely" flexible work arrangements will be more common in five years.

Source: "SHRM Research Spotlight: Overview of Flexible Work Arrangements (FWAs)," Society for Human Resource Management, October 2014, http://tinyurl.com/kru677p

More than two-thirds of employers say they believe flexible work will be increasingly important as a way to retain talented individuals, while half said family-friendly benefits will grow more crucial within five years, an SHRM survey found.[116] Health care plans and retirement savings have been the most-used tools to help persuade staff to stay—and those will continue to grow.

Depending on the economy and the political climate, paid family leave could become the law in the United States in the next several years, Purdue's Kossek and a few other experts say, as more cities and states adopt paid sick time and other advances.

Ballard at the American Psychological Association sees a "convergence" of worker and business interests. "It's the realization that the well-being of the workforce and the performance of the organization are inexorably linked," he says. So more decentralized workplaces will mean shorter commutes, more flexible places—and lower costs.

Joyce Gioia, a futurist and the president of the Herman Group, says she's hopeful that automation and advanced technologies could "inform the opportunity for work-life balance moving forward. If we have the right software, eventually we may be able to get a full day's work done in four hours"—and that would leave more time for other pursuits.

Chronology

1910s–1930s	**Rise of industry leads to often-difficult working conditions.**
1906	Doubleday publishes Upton Sinclair's "The Jungle" about the harsh treatment and terrible conditions in the meatpacking business; the book originally had appeared as a Socialist newspaper serial.
1912	Bread and roses strike in Lawrence, Mass., started by immigrant women, grows to include 23,000 men, women and children seeking better working conditions and adjusted wages after legislature cuts workweek from 56 hours to 54.
1920	U.S. Department of Labor creates a Women's Bureau to address effective employment of female staff.
1936	Government requires federal contractors to adopt eight-hour workday, with safe working conditions.
1938	Fair Labor Standards Act lays out standard hours for workweek, sets 25-cent-per-hour minimum wage and abolishes child labor in many industries.
1960s–1970s	**Awareness of women in the workplace grows.**
1961	President John F. Kennedy establishes the President's Commission on the Status of Women at the urging of former first lady Eleanor Roosevelt.
1962	"The Other America: Poverty in the United States," by Michael Harrington, acts as catalyst for expanded U.S. federal benefits.
1963	Equal Pay Act prohibits wage discrimination on account of sex.
1964	Women who work in companies with 15 or more employees cannot be discriminated against on the basis of sex, according to Title VII of the Civil Rights Act of 1964.
1971	Shoemaker Stride Rite opens what's generally regarded as the first U.S. on-site corporate child care center.
1974	Employee Retirement Income Security Act (ERISA) sets standards for retirement, health coverage and other benefits employers offer.
1978	Pregnancy Discrimination Act requires employers to treat pregnant employees as they would other temporarily disabled workers.
1980s–1990s	**Work-life flexibility goes mainstream.**
1986	First Working Mother magazine list of Best Companies for Mothers highlights good employers; list ends up on front page of Wall Street Journal, raising visibility. It has been published annually since.
1989	Harvard Business Review publishes the early "mommy track" piece, "Management Women and the New Facts of Life," in which Felice N. Schwartz, a longtime advocate for women in the workplace, suggests women with children belong on a slower career track than others, drawing backlash and debate.
1990	Americans with Disabilities Act gives employees "reasonable accommodations" at work for chronic and serious health conditions.
1993	Family and Medical Leave Act provides for many employees to receive 12 weeks of unpaid time off, with continued health benefits, for a new baby, illness or family health problems.
1994	Wharton School holds first roundtable to teach business leaders about work-life integration; it's one of the first schools to incorporate work-family issues into its MBA curriculum.
1996	Scott Adams publishes "The Dilbert Principle," a collection of cartoons poking fun at management and work culture.

1998–2000	Dot-com boom creates wave of quirky benefits and emboldens some workers to demand stock options or sleep-late schedules.
2000s–Present	**Recession changes the job market.**
2003	The New York Times publishes "The Opt-Out Revolution," documenting highly educated professional women bowing out of workforce after hitting "the maternal wall."
2004	California becomes first U.S. state to mandate paid family leave, effective in 2004, paid for by an insurance fund. An estimated 13.1 million workers are covered.
2007–09	Deepest recession since the Great Depression wipes out millions of jobs in the United States, especially in construction and manufacturing; jobless rate peaks at 10 percent. Global financial crisis felt around the world.
2010	Affordable Care Act overhauls health insurance, establishes marketplace effective 2013 for those without employer-paid insurance, including many freelancers and independent contractors, to obtain medical insurance.
2013	Yahoo ends work-from-home option, bringing all employees back to office to encourage more innovation and collaboration. . . . "Lean In: Women, Work, and the Will to Lead," by Facebook executive Sheryl Sandberg, launches debate about women in management.
2014	Supreme Court rules against Amazon workers being paid for time spent awaiting security checks, considers UPS pregnancy accommodation case.

RESOURCES

The Next Step

Flexible Benefits

"How Many People Telecommute?" Global Workplace Analytics, undated, http://tinyurl.com/kl9ul3s.

Workplace consulting firm discusses the many data sets available to measure the work-at-home population.

McGregor, Jena, "More proof that flexibility programs work," The Washington Post, May 9, 2014, http://tinyurl.com/mksq9st.

A National Institutes of Health-funded study found workers with flex time were more likely than those without such benefits to feel they had control over their schedules and enough time to spend with family.

Sveen, Lauren, "Working it out: Companies can benefit from unconventional hiring," The Denver Post, Oct. 5, 2014, http://tinyurl.com/o6lvguq.

The president of a Denver employee recruitment firm writes that businesses that hire more part-time and contract workers save money and can offer employees more flexible work schedules.

Wiltz, Teresa, "Can Flextime Help Working Families Have It All?" Stateline (Pew Charitable Trusts), Sept. 30, 2014, http://tinyurl.com/nqdp5ak.

Some states and cities are adopting laws directing employers to consider employee requests for flexible work schedules without a worker being punished or fired.

Paternity Leave

Guilford, Gwynn, "The economic case for paternity leave," Quartz, Sept. 24. 2014, http://tinyurl.com/m399s8b.

The experience of countries, including Sweden and Iceland, shows that paternity leave helps economies by reducing the pay gap between men and women.

Krawczynski, Jon, "Pro sports becoming more open to paternity leave," The Associated Press, April 14, 2014, http://tinyurl.com/nlgnx7x.

American professional sports leagues are offering more benefits to athletes who are new fathers, such as three days of paid paternity leave for Major League Baseball players.

Lewis, Katherine Reynolds, "New dads confront uphill battle for paternity leave," Fortune, June 10, 2014, http://tinyurl.com/kfhxb2p.

Employers in 70 countries are required to provide paid paternity leave, compared with just 12 percent of U.S. employers who provide that benefit, according to a Society for Human Resource Management survey.

Ludden, Jennifer, "More Dads Want Paternity Leave. Getting It Is A Different Matter," National Public Radio, Aug. 13, 2014, http://tinyurl.com/owypbgt.

More men in the United States are requesting paternity leave, but only 10 to 15 percent of employers provide it, according to a University of Oregon sociologist.

Wellness Programs

Powell, Robert, "More companies offer financial wellness programs," USA Today, Sept. 27, 2014, http://tinyurl.com/p53t6wm.

Programs that assist employees with managing their finances could reduce absenteeism and save companies $3 for every $1 they spend, according to a Consumer Financial Protection Bureau report.

Sanger-Katz, Margot, "Latest Good News in Health Spending: Employer Premiums," The New York Times, Sept. 10, 2014, http://tinyurl.com/o7v4ogs.

An annual survey published by the Kaiser Family Foundation found that health insurance premiums increased by 3 percent between 2013 and 2014.

Weber, Lauren, "Wellness Programs Get a Health Check," The Wall Street Journal, Oct. 10, 2014, http://tinyurl.com/kfpj2jm.

Employee wellness programs that reward workers for healthy behaviors and punish them for unhealthy ones struggle to balance concern for employee health with the potential for invading privacy and inviting lawsuits.

Workplace Attitudes

Edwards, Verity, "A Hudson survey shows social skills help drive workplace productivity," The Australian, Sept. 19, 2014, http://tinyurl.com/q94csay.

An international survey by a recruitment group found younger employees value independence more than social interaction, while older workers value work friendships and collaboration.

Ho, Catherine, "Rise in retaliation claims reflect changing laws, attitudes about workplace bias," The Washington Post, Nov. 2, 2014, http://tinyurl.com/ohucvrp.

Eight years of growing retaliation claims reported to the Equal Employment Opportunity Commission, including 38,539 charges reported in 2013, indicate attitudes and laws regarding workplace discrimination are shifting.

Kratz, Greg, "Balancing act: Survey—Workers choose telecommuting to avoid office politics, interruptions," Deseret News, Oct. 7, 2014, http://tinyurl.com/orhs47f.

A 1,500-person survey found more than half of job seekers say they prefer working from home rather than their offices for important assignments, with 61 percent of respondents listing "avoiding office politics" as their main reason.

Organizations

American Psychological Association Center for Organizational Excellence
760 First St., N.E., Washington, DC 20002
202-336-5900
www.apaexcellence.org

Advocates for "psychologically healthy workplaces" by providing resources and giving annual awards.

Engage for Success
IPA Somerset House, West Wing 2nd Floor, Strand, London WC2R 1LA, United Kingdom
info@engageforsuccess.org
Twitter @Engage4Success
www.engageforsuccess.org

British organization that promotes the benefits of employee engagement; provides case studies and other research.

Families and Work Institute
267 Fifth Ave., 2nd Floor, New York, NY 10016,
212-465-2044
Twitter @FWINews
www.familiesandwork.org

Nonprofit research center that specializes in changing workplace and family needs; administers When Work Works Award.

Gallup Inc.
901 F St., N.W., #400, Washington, DC 20004
202-715-3030
www.gallup.com

Long-established research firm that conducts surveys on well-being, work hours, worker views.

Glassdoor
Building A, 100 Shoreline Highway, Mill Valley, CA 94941
415-339-9105
Twitter @Glassdoor
www.glassdoor.com

Website where employees anonymously share view of bosses, hiring and more; also compiles lists of top 25 companies for work-life balance and for culture and values.

Human Resource Executive Online
747 Dresher Rd., Suite 500, Horsham, PA 19044-0980
215-784-0910
Twitter @HRExecMag
www.hreonline.com

Website that focuses on talent management, benefits, employee engagement.

National Alliance for Caregiving
4720 Montgomery Lane, Suite 205, Bethesda, MD 20814
301-718-8444
Twitter @NAA4Caregiving
www.caregiving.org

Coalition of organizations focused on issues and research related to family caregivers, elder care and more.

National Partnership for Women & Families
1875 Connecticut Ave., N.W., Suite 650, Washington, DC 20009
202-986-2600
Twitter @NPWF
www.nationalpartnership.org

Nonprofit that conducts research, advocacy on paid sick days, flexibility and other topics.

New Ways of Working
P.O. Box 1030, Los Gatos, CA, 05031
408-354-8001
Twitter @NewWOWNetwork
www.newwow.net

Business organization that shares best practices and information on workplace changes.

Society for Human Resource Management
1800 Duke St., Alexandria, VA 22314
800-283-7476
Twitter @SHRM
www.shrm.org

Largest professional association for human resources; provides information, research, policy and more on talent management.

World at Work and Alliance for Work-Life Progress
14040 N. Northsight Blvd., Scottsdale, AZ 85260
877-951-9191
Twitter: @WorldatWork
www.awlp.org/awlp/home/html/homepage.jsp

Human resources organization that focuses on pay, rewards, engagement. Gives awards to innovators, highlights studies and more. Also read Newsline for surveys, news and other information: http://tinyurl.com/nfuxkge.

Work and Family Researchers Network
c/o Patricia Miller, Department of Sociology, University of Pennsylvania, 3718 Locust Walk, Philadelphia, PA 19104-6299
215-898-1569
Twitter @WFRN
https://workfamily.sas.upenn.edu

Member organization for academics and others who study flexibility, work-family and related topics.

Q&A: Stew Friedman: Allow Employees Flexibility and They Make It Work

"IT'S POSSIBLE TO FIND MORE FREEDOM THAN YOU CURRENTLY THINK YOU HAVE"

Stew Friedman believes in harmony and integration for work and life—plus a healthy dose of experimentation and innovation in work practices. He's not some New Age guru; he's a professor at the University of Pennsylvania's Wharton School and former head of leadership development at Ford Motor Co. who focuses on management and has written books on leadership and consulted with major corporations. Friedman, author of "Total Leadership" (Harvard Business Review Press, 2008) and "Leading the Life You Want: Skills for Integrating Work and Life" (HBR Press, 2014) spoke with SAGE Business Researcher reporter Vickie Elmer about work-life flexibility. This is an edited transcript of the conversation.

Can work-life flexibility thrive when top executives don't practice it? How does having a workaholic boss affect the culture and hours?

Over a decade ago, Sharon Lobel [a Seattle University management professor] and I published a paper titled "The Happy Workaholic: a Role Model for Employees" in which we explained that as long as the boss truly understands, accepts, and embraces the fact that not everyone is like him or her—that everyone brings different assets to the organization and has unique responsibilities, commitments and passions outside of work—then he or she is able to support his or her team members so that they can live and work as they choose.

Seems like that kind of boss must be rather rare. For those who don't get this exceptional enlightened workaholic boss, how does a 70-hour-a-week boss affect things?

Life is much easier, of course, if you've got a boss who gets it. But even under the most draconian circumstances, it's possible to find more freedom than you currently think you have, if you're smart about it. That means experimenting with small changes that you are confident will bring demonstrable value to your boss—as he or she sees it—and to the rest of your life.

The key: Be relentless in pursuing new ways of getting things done that bring mutual value. This increases your chances of getting others on your side. "I'd like to try working at home on Wednesdays for the next month, because I think that will make me more efficient and productive," you might say. "Can we try this and, if at the end of the month my performance doesn't improve, from your point of view, we can go back to the way things were, or try something different, OK?"

You've been brought in as a consultant to sell management on cultural changes and greater flexibility. What compelling, robust argument and research will you use?

It's quite straightforward: Research shows that when you give people the freedom to experiment with how they get things done in order to improve performance and satisfaction in all parts of their lives, then they are indeed able to do so. They pursue what I call "four-way wins": better results at work, at home, in the community and in the private realm of mind, body and spirit.

The key is to encourage experimentation and continual innovation with a persistent focus on results that matter, in all domains of life.

Tell us about some of the work-life adjustments and accommodations you've made—either for yourself or for someone who works with you.

When my children were younger, I arranged my schedule so I could have breakfast with them and walk them to the school bus. But I was up well before anyone else in the house, working in my home office, and I worked again in my home office after my children went to bed.

Now one of my small company's primary employees resides in California; all our work is virtual and revolves around her schedule, as she's been home-schooling her daughter.

And the payoff?

The payoff has been that I have a first-rate employee who is loyal, committed to our work, and gives 100 percent of her effort to bring her considerable talents to bear on our goals.

How much of the flexibility needs to be open to all workers, of all ages, stages and situations, versus targeted programs for important-worker demographics?

Fair and equitable does not mean the same, it does not mean equal. As long as everyone has the same opportunity to request the type of unique flexibility their life requires, that's fair. Young parents might need flexibility to pick up children from child care or attend school functions. Middle-aged folks might need flexibility to deal with aging parents. Younger folks might need flexibility to engage in activities uniquely meaningful to them, like training for a marathon, and that will energize them at work and increase their loyalty to the company. What's important is explicitly recognizing how this flexibility benefits the collective interests of the team or organization. Without that focus, resentment is sure to follow.

Sounds like a laudable but complex approach. Any great examples of employers that have mastered this fair but different approach?

I did this myself when I was a senior executive at Ford Motor some years ago, during a two-and-a-half-year period when I was on leave from my academic position at Wharton, running the Ford Leadership Development Center. I asked each member of my team to identify one goal in life beyond work that was very important and how, by pursuing that goal and getting my support and the support of our team, they would be creating value for us and for Ford. Everyone's needs were different; one man wanted to read to his children before bed and making this possible for him changed his view of our company for the better, not to mention having a positive impact for his family. This increased commitment to our collective goals and our performance.

Q&A: Sara Sutton Fell: Communication Is Key for Managers

"MEASURE PROGRESS ALONG THE WAY, TWEAK AS NECESSARY"

When any of the 40 workers and independent contractors at FlexJobs wants to chat with CEO Sara Sutton Fell, they don't stop in to see her. Instead, they knock on her virtual door or send her an email or text. FlexJobs is a virtual company that helps clients land flexible and telecommuting jobs. In 2014, the company won the When Work Works award from the Society for Human Resource Management and the Families and Work Institute.

Sutton Fell spoke with SAGE Business Researcher reporter Vickie Elmer about what it takes to manage remote workers. This is an edited transcript of the conversation.

What are the top three (or so) skills that managers need to develop if they're going to be effective at managing remote and freelance workers?

Communication is really key. You need to be able to communicate REALLY well verbally and in writing. In a remote environment, you can't rely at all on body language, gestures, facial expressions.

Asking a lot of questions is critical, too. It's the only way you're going to get a good sense of what's going on in your remote team. And provide guidance and a "home base" for people so they don't feel isolated.

How do you effectively supervise remote employees without being Big Brother?

The key is active management. In an office, you can rely a lot on passive management techniques like walking past someone's cubicle or bumping into them in the hallway. In a virtual environment, you have to actively engage with your employees. Check in on chat and email throughout the day.

It's a lot of basic management—make sure people are clear on the tasks. You have deadlines, you have goals, you have check-in points, where you can discuss if there are problems or needs.

(Continued)

(Continued)

How do you set up clear measures of their results?

This really depends on the particular role. Our management team has started keeping a record of all the projects they're working on, and keeping monthly statistics on the things that we can count. Numbers really do help to show how things are moving along. For each role, determine what the goals are, then figure out ways to track these on a regular basis and in a way that makes it easy to compare results.

What are the specific concerns with a multinational (or even multi-time-zone) workforce? How do you deal with varying laws governing work?

It requires attention, but it can be done. Companies like Xerox, PwC, American Express, K12, SAP, UnitedHealth Group, Aetna, Kaplan, ADP, Sodexo, Humana and Hilton all have success with remote workforces while operating as multinationals.

Businesses need to be cognizant of different tax and employment laws wherever they hire people. I'd recommend a company to work with an individual or a team who are very well-versed in employment law and tax law to make sure you're operating properly, and treating your employees and contractors correctly.

Automattic [a blogging services company] has a large distributed workforce and crosses countries and time zones. They're a really interesting case study in being creative and forward-thinking on remote workforces. At our last check, they have 235 "Automatticians" working in 29 countries, 174 cities and 36 U.S. states—all working from home.

When people are splitting their time between office and home or home and client offices, what works in sharing space, schedule, etc.? Is any company the trendsetter in this?

A variety of options could keep your workplace in line with everyone's movements. Virtual office environments like Sococo offer a way to "see" a remote team at work. Co-working spaces are growing in popularity and provide a "real" professional office space on the fly, when they really need it. It's a great option for meeting clients when you otherwise work from home.

What are some easy measures that a manager could gather to show the economic value/payoff to the employer of flexible work and telework?

This is where those clear measures come in. Track the progress your team makes month over month to show the increase in productivity. Track things like sick days taken, which usually reduce with remote work; hours worked, which typically increases; and the operating costs in your office, which should decrease when people work from home—utilities, office supplies and so on.

Look at other measures too, like the hours your customer service remains open with people working in different time zones. Get creative and determine which measurements work best for you.

What advice do you have for those stuck in traditional thinking about work, or how to get started?

I'd recommend starting a trial or test remote work program with a very small group of outstanding employees.

Start with people working home for one day each week, or something small like that. Then build up to people working 100 percent remotely. Measure progress along the way, tweak as necessary. Telecommuting isn't all-or-nothing. There are many shades to remote work, and starting small can help prove its worth to skeptical managers.

How can you tell if a worker is ready (responsible, dedicated, professional, engaged enough) to become a remote worker? Any good online assessment tool for this yet?

While there isn't a specific assessment for remote workers, a personality assessment might be a good start—though it shouldn't be used in and of itself. The traits you're looking for in a good remote worker include self-management, independence, initiative, communication skills. You want someone who asks a lot of GOOD questions and speaks up when they need assistance.

10 PAID LEAVE
Should companies offer better policies?
Sharon O'Malley

EXECUTIVE SUMMARY

The United States is the only industrialized nation that does not require companies to offer paid leave to its workers to care for a baby, a sick relative or themselves. That is changing slowly, economists say, as more companies recognize that it makes business sense to provide paid leave to their employers. Silicon Valley, which is in a recruiting war with its tech rivals for the best talent, has taken the lead in offering more-generous time-off policies. But outside of the technology sector, many businesses—especially small ones—find it impractical or too expensive to offer paid leave. As few as 6 percent of low-wage earners can take paid maternity leave, and more than 40 percent of U.S. employees have no paid sick days.

Among the key takeaways:

- In the absence of federal guidance on the issue, talent-hungry corporations are writing their own rules in an effort to recruit and retain skilled young employees.

- President Trump during the 2016 campaign became the first Republican nominee to endorse paid maternity leave, but he has not pushed to enact such a policy.

- One survey found that 45 percent of firms with fewer than 100 employees would support a mandatory leave policy funded through employer and employee payroll contributions.

OVERVIEW

When Facebook Chief Operating Officer Sheryl Sandberg announced an upgrade to the tech giant's package of paid leave policies in February, she framed the issue in vividly personal terms, recalling how much her children needed her when her husband died unexpectedly in 2015.

And then Sandberg issued a stark challenge to other businesses to "step-up and lead" by adopting similar policies facilitating family leave.

From *SAGE Business Researcher*,
May 8, 2017

"Making it easier for more Americans to be the workers and family members they want to be will make our economy and country stronger," Sandberg wrote in a Facebook post announcing the new policy. "Companies that stand by the people who work for them do the right thing and the smart thing—it helps them serve their mission, live their values, and improve their bottom line by increasing the loyalty and performance of their workforce."[1]

Facebook is offering its 17,000 employees up to 20 paid days off to grieve the death of an immediate family member and 10 days for the loss of an extended family member; it already offers four months of paid parental leave to new mothers and fathers. Employees of the social media company also have a newly minted six weeks of paid time to care for a seriously ill relative and three days to spend with a family member suffering from a short-term illness.[2]

Few corporations outside of Silicon Valley have adopted such robust paid leave policies; in fact, just 12 percent of U.S. private-sector workers have access to paid family leave through their employers, according to the Department of Labor.[3] As few as 6 percent of low-wage earners may take paid maternity leave.[4] More than 40 percent of U.S. employees have no paid sick days.[5]

But Facebook is just the latest in a string of high-profile technology businesses to up their game when it comes to paying employees for the time they take off to care for a baby, a sick relative or themselves. Adobe in 2015 expanded its paid parental leave program to 26 weeks for new moms; Amazon excuses pregnant employees, with pay, for four weeks before they give birth and 10 weeks after.

Similarly, Apple lets expectant mothers take off four weeks before a birth and 14 weeks after, and fathers and adoptive or foster parents get six weeks of paid family leave.[6] Birth mothers who work for Google and Squarespace can take 18 weeks of fully paid leave.[7] And Netflix outdid all of its competitors with a 2015 parental leave policy that pays new mothers and fathers their regular salaries for up to a year after childbirth or an adoption.[8]

In addition, a handful of companies, including General Electric, Grubhub, Netflix and LinkedIn, offer some employees unlimited time off for illness, vacations and family matters.

Employees Average 10 Paid Vacation Days

Outside of the tech industry, a few financial and personal services firms like Deloitte; hospitality chains like Hilton; retailers like Starbucks; and energy companies like Duke Energy in North Carolina have improved their paid parental leave policies over the past few years.

Many smaller businesses, on the other hand, work informally with their employees to accommodate family and medical absences on a case-by-case basis rather than writing formal policies, says Aparna Mathur, resident scholar in economic policy studies for the conservative think tank American Enterprise Institute in Washington, D.C. "Small businesses can work something out with employees if they take leave," she says. "They feel much more responsibility in some ways toward their employees because there are so few of them."

"The big picture is that companies are recognizing that it makes business sense to provide paid . . . leave," says Sarah Fleisch Fink, director of workplace policy and senior counsel

About two-thirds receive between 5 and 14 days

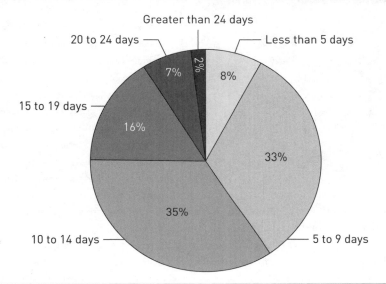

The majority of private industry workers receive between five and 14 paid vacation days after one year of employment with their company. The average number of paid days was 10 among private-sector employees; only 2 percent received more than 24 days of paid vacation.

Notes: Employees either are granted a specific number of days after completion of the indicated length of service or accrue days during the next 12-month period. Employees eligible for paid vacations but who have not fulfilled the minimum service requirement are listed as receiving 0 days.

Source: "Table 38. Paid vacations: Number of annual days by service requirement, private industry workers, March 2016," Bureau of Labor Statistics, U.S. Department of Labor, March 2016, http://tinyurl.com/lz2pxuv

for the nonprofit National Partnership for Women & Families, an advocacy organization focusing on work and family, workplace fairness and women's health. "They recognize it because it improves employee morale; it can increase productivity and reduce turnover; it can help them compete for talent. Otherwise, we wouldn't see—almost weekly— companies coming out with these policies."

Although the 24-year-old federal Family and Medical Leave Act requires companies with more than 50 employees to allow staff members to miss up to 12 weeks of work for childbirth, a long sickness or a loved one's serious illness—and to guarantee that their jobs or something comparable will be waiting for them when they get back—the United States is the only industrialized nation without a policy to pay them for it.[9]

In the absence of federal guidance on the issue, talent-hungry corporations and state governments are writing their own rules in an effort to recruit and retain skilled young employees.

Amazon is rethinking its parental leave policies in an effort to attract Millennials. Pregnant employees can take four weeks off with pay before they give birth and 10 weeks after.

Source: Carsten Koall/Getty Images

"They're going above and beyond the law," says Corinne Jones, president of consulting firm CJC Human Resource Services in New York. "As their HR advisers, we're saying, 'Here's what you need to do to retain the best employees.'"

From California to Boston, competition for qualified employees, especially in technical and other high-skill fields, has become fierce as the U.S. economy continues to improve and the labor market tightens.[10] Millennials, many of whom have delayed marriage and children, are slowly beginning to start their families and are shopping for employers offering family-friendly benefits.[11]

"Millennial employees like tech," says Kenneth Matos, vice president of research for the Park Ridge, Ill., consulting firm Life Meets Work. "So Amazon, Netflix, American Express, they're rethinking their parental leave policies to try to expand them to deal with the attractive people. Their jobs used to be their priority. But now they want to become parents."

As early as 2015, the professional services firm Ernst & Young found in a study that 74 percent of Millennials consider paid parental leave "important."[12]

So, apparently, does President Trump, who, during his 2016 campaign, became the first Republican presidential nominee to endorse paid maternity leave.[13] During his January address to Congress, the president proposed that mothers get six weeks of paid, post-childbirth leave. The plan has come under fire by advocates of paternity leave, who cite the importance of fathers in shaping the culture of a new family.

An April Gallup Poll showed that 81 percent of Americans—both Republicans and Democrats—support federal legislation for paid maternity leave.[14]

But Trump has not made the effort a major policy emphasis. Part of the holdup, says Fink, is the difficulty in finding a way to pay for the benefit.

In most countries with mandates for paid parental leave and sick days, the national government foots the bill. Federal lawmakers, especially Republicans, are not keen on doing that in the United States.

"We've realized that parental leave has tentacles," says Rose Stanley, a senior practice leader at human resources trade association WorldatWork, "which is probably why organizations and even the government are going, 'What do we do with this?' . . . How are organizations paying? Should they have to pay? How are they able to pay? . . . We want to know."

For small businesses, Stanley says, "it's obviously financially going to be an issue."

In a memo to state legislators before they adopted New York's paid family leave law, which will take effect next January, said Frank Kerbein of the. Center for Human Resources of the Business Council of New York State. The law, he wrote, will burden small businesses with the cost of replacing employees while they are on extended leaves. Plus, he said business owners—not the government—should determine employment policies for their companies.[15]

In fact, the 1993 federal Family and Medical Leave Act exempts businesses with fewer than 50 employees from having to allow even unpaid leave for extended absences. But most state proposals would apply to all companies, regardless of the size of their workforces.

Still, a survey by the advocacy group Small Business Majority found that 45 percent of firms with fewer than 100 employees would support a mandatory leave policy that is paid for through employer and employee payroll contributions.[16]

Mathur confirms that most businesses, even small ones, agree that employees are entitled to paid time off to care for family. "Neither employers nor employees are opposing the policies," she says. "They know the larger problem is not having access to paid leave when you need it."

Studies by economists and family advocates generally have reached the same conclusion: Offering paid time off for childbirth, family medical emergencies, annual vacations and even the sniffles retains female employees, makes working parents more productive on the job, improves families' financial security and lowers young mothers' dependence on government assistance. Plus, it boosts a business's bottom line because it saves employers from having to recruit, hire and train replacements for moms who decide not to return to work after childbirth.[17]

"Organizations as a whole want to give, and they want to get back," says Stanley. "They know that the way they get back productivity, innovation and creativity is by treating their employees in a way that works well for both of them. But a lot of organizations don't have that mindset.

"They are beginning to."

As businesses, legislators, family advocates and employees weigh in on the pros and cons of employer-and government-paid leave, here are some of the issues being debated:

Weighing the Issues

Is paying for leave good for businesses?

When Google increased its paid maternity leave from 12 to 18 weeks in 2007, it cut the number of new mothers who quit their jobs in half.[18]

"It may sound counterintuitive, but the research—and Google's own experience—shows a generous paid maternity leave actually increases retention," Susan Wojcicki, CEO of Google subsidiary YouTube, wrote in the The Huffington Post. "When women are given a short leave, or they're pressured to be on call, some decide it's just not worth it to return."[19]

Wojcicki's point: Technology firms, which spend enormous time and money recruiting and training female employees, can stop the ones they already have from leaving when they want to spend more time bonding with their babies.

Companies that offer substantial paid family leave to employees agree.

"Paid parental leave will help us recruit and retain the next generation of highly skilled workers," Melissa Anderson, chief human resources officer for Charlotte, N.C.-based Duke Energy, said of the firm's decision to offer the benefit for the first time this year.[20]

The electric utility had little choice, as it recruits from the same talent pool as a handful of other large, Charlotte-based companies that already offer paid family leave.

The same is true for any company in a competitive field. A year ago, Ernst & Young boasted that its new policy to provide 16 weeks of parental leave at full pay for new mothers and fathers in its U.S. offices "blows our competitors' benefits out of the water." EY also added policies to offer up to $25,000 for fertility, surrogacy, adoption and egg-freezing services.[21]

Five months later, competitor Deloitte splashed back, with an announcement the firm called "a first of its kind for professional services," matching EY's 16 weeks of paid leave, but offering it to any caregiver-employee, including those with sick relatives and elderly parents.[22]

Those generous benefits are aimed at potential employees, who apparently are taking notice. In a November-December 2016 survey of 5,934 adults who took or wanted to take paid family or medical leave, that benefit was cited more than any other as the most helpful, according to the nonpartisan Pew Research Center.[23]

The employer also benefits, according to various studies: New mothers who take paid leave typically return to work within nine to 12 months of childbirth, and first-time moms who use the benefit are more likely to return to the same employer than those who do not take it, according to the National Partnership for Women & Families.[24] In addition, Congress' Joint Economic Committee has found that businesses gain from retaining workers—especially those who are highly skilled—that they might lose without a paid leave benefit. And they save on the "sizable costs" of recruiting, hiring and training replacement employees.[25]

Evidence of that can be found in California, the first of four states to enact paid maternity leave laws for all businesses. The state, which passed its milestone program in 2002, uses employee and employer payroll taxes to pay new mothers and fathers 55 percent of their salaries, up to $1,173 per week, for six weeks to bond with a new child.[26] Employees who care for seriously ill family members may also use the benefit.

Similarly, many of the private-sector companies that offer paid maternity leave funnel the benefit through their group disability plans, according to Derek Winn, lead consultant with Business Benefits Group, a Fairfax, Va.-based benefits broker. New fathers, however, do not qualify for disability benefits, he says.

A Labor Department study found in 2014 that adding the California benefit increased the amount of time new mothers are absent from work by about two-and-a-half weeks. But researchers concluded that the cost to cover their duties during their leaves might be offset by mothers who take the leave rather than quitting their jobs. A separate study found that California's law "had either a positive effect or no effect on productivity, profit, morale and costs." In that study, California businesses owners said the paid leave policy did not affect their firms' performance or profit margins.[27]

While businesses reap best-in-class recruitment and retention status from a paid parental leave benefit, so does the economy, the Labor Department said. New mothers who are earning while on leave are less likely to tap public assistance benefits, the department said. The department has found that because paid maternity leave makes it easier for women to continue working after they have children, it contributes to female labor force participation.[28]

Some small-business owners, however, say these results don't apply to them. Jeb Breithaupt, owner of an 11-employee remodeling firm in Shreveport, La., says each member of his small staff has a skills-specific job. Anyone's extended absence, he says, would substantially slow business down.

Like others, Breithaupt says a government-enforced paid leave benefit would burden his company more than it would a corporation.

Like-minded business owners pushed hard—unsuccessfully—against a District of Columbia proposal to create a fund to pay private-sector employees up to 90 percent of their wages for a family or medical leave of eight weeks.

"You can't treat a mom-and-pop operation the same as a national chain; [they] operate on a much smaller profit margin," D.C. council member Nathan Ackerman explained. He called for an exception for businesses with fewer than 50 employees.[29]

Should the federal government mandate paid time off for public-and private-sector employees?

Whether Congress will enact a national law requiring paid leave for new parents after the birth of a child has—fairly suddenly—become a conversation about "when" rather than "if."

During the 2016 presidential campaign, Trump endorsed such a law, reportedly at the urging of his daughter, Ivanka, the mother of two sons and a daughter.[30] The break with conservative tradition has given hope to advocates of a federal family and medical leave law that provides for at least some wage replacement for new parents and for other employees who may miss work to care for a seriously ill loved one.

Still, neither Trump nor the Republican-controlled Congress has made paid leave a priority, at least for this year, says attorney Joan C. Williams, chair and director of the Center for WorkLife Law at the University of California's Hastings College of Law. "The good news is that Ivanka Trump is interested in paid leave," she says. "The bad news continues to be that the House is not, and now the Senate presumably isn't, either."

Trump's support came at a time when a fair number of conservatives, including those at the American Action Forum, a center-right think tank, and the American Enterprise Institute, were already tossing around ideas for establishing a federal paid-leave benefit.

A pre-election proposal from the American Action Forum promoted a paid leave benefit for employees with incomes lower than $28,000. The proposal called for low-income workers to take home up to $3,500 over 12 weeks.[31] And Republican Sen. Deb Fisher of Nebraska reintroduced her Strong Families Act, which would create a tax incentive for businesses to offer two weeks of paid family leave a year. Fisher introduced the bill in 2014 and 2015 without success.[32]

Advocates from both political parties have suggested that this might be a better year for such proposals, thanks partly to Trump's embrace of a paid leave law, coupled with a renewed attention to women's issues brought about, in part, by half a million participants in a women's march on Washington and around the country the day after the president's inauguration.[33]

Trump has not offered many details of what he might propose, only that he would like to offer new mothers six weeks of paid leave after childbirth. After criticism from advocates of paternity leave, he indicated he might be willing to allow paid leave for new fathers as well.[34]

Mathur of the American Enterprise Institute says a reluctance to pass a federal paid leave law remains among members of Congress—and it is driven by politics.

"We traditionally have few policies that are considered anti-business," she says. "Some people phrase it as a mandate on businesses to provide this leave, and businesses have to figure out how to pay for it. . . . [They believe] this is not something the government needs to do. Businesses need to do it on their own at whatever cost is comfortable to them. It's more the politics of it that has prevented the U.S. from passing this legislation."

WorldatWork's Stanley agrees.

"I don't know if America wants to run that way," she says. "What's unique in the U.S. is that companies take it upon themselves to figure out how we become more competitive, how that competitiveness helps build up our brand, our profitability, our shareholder value. It is sort of what America is known for."

As is true with so many legislative efforts, competing proposals are making their way through Congress.

Trump's original plan, which has not yet been introduced in Congress, would reserve wage replacement to working birth mothers. Most advocates support a broader law that covers adoptive and foster parents as well as any employee who misses work to care for a seriously ill relative.[35]

Matos of Life Meets Work is one of them. Limiting paid leave to birth mothers, he says, could "re-create the gender divide that creates the same problems for women in terms of career advancement and opportunity. . . . Even if we supported getting this maternity leave through, it would make any [proposals] in the future even harder for a broader, less gender approach to parental leave."

Still, Matos says, "The current political climate is very volatile. It could really go in more directions than I can understand."

Most Small Businesses Support Paid Family Leave

Congressional Democrats have issued their own version of paid leave in the Family and Medical Insurance Leave (FAMILY) Act, which would pay for wage reimbursement with a 0.2 percent surtax on wages paid by both employers and employees.[36] The proposal calls for 12 weeks of paid leave at 66 percent of monthly wages for employees who give birth or adopt a new child, fall seriously ill or need to care for an immediate family member with a long-term health condition.[37]

Democrats offered up this bill, without success, in 2013 and 2015. Sen. Kirsten Gillibrand, D-N.Y., and Rep. Rosa DeLauro, D-Conn., modeled it on statewide paid leave laws in California, New Jersey, Rhode Island and New York, which pay employees on leave from self-sustaining funds dispersed by the state governments.[38]

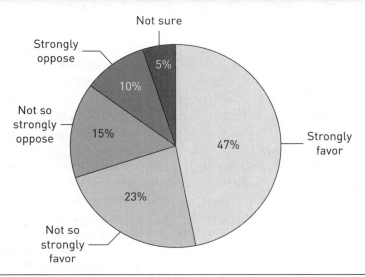

Almost 50 percent strongly favor establishment of a national paid leave program

- Not sure — 5%
- Strongly oppose — 10%
- Not so strongly oppose — 15%
- Not so strongly favor — 23%
- Strongly favor — 47%

Seventy percent of small businesses showed some level of support for creating a national paid leave program, the Family and Medical Insurance Leave (FAMILY) Act. While 47 percent said they strongly favored the newly introduced legislation, which would be funded through employee and employer contributions and ensure up to 12 weeks of partial income, a quarter of respondents opposed the measure.

Source: "Small Businesses Support Paid Family Leave Programs," Small Business Majority, Center for American Progress, March 30, 2017, http://tinyurl.com/k9bstug

It failed, in part, because critics—including many Republicans and some businesses—objected to imposing additional government regulations on companies, despite evidence that the California law on which it was modeled has reported a neutral effect on the state's businesses.[39]

Its fate this year is anyone's guess, says Fink of the National Partnership for Women & Families. "There appears to be a recognition that there is a problem with not having paid family leave, on both sides of the aisle. . . . It's progress."

Can employees take paid leave without damaging their careers?

In Singapore, a universal Employment Act guarantees employees with six or more months on the job 14 paid sick days each year and 60 days of paid hospital leave. But Singapore Airlines employees have accused their company of retaliating against those who take advantage of that legal right by denying them promotions.

The airline has a more generous leave policy than the national law requires: It offers 28 days of paid medical leave and six months off, with pay, for a hospital stay brought on by a chronic or prolonged illness. It bases promotions, in part, on points that employees earn each year for their service. Workers have claimed that the firm deducts points for each medical absence.

The airline has denied those claims.[40]

In the United States, no federal mandate requires employers to pay workers for sick days, parental leave or vacations. Yet studies show that employees who work for firms that voluntarily offer them often are reluctant to use the benefits for fear of derailing their careers.

The travel company Expedia's 2016 Vacation Deprivation report, for instance, revealed that Americans left an average of three paid vacation days apiece unclaimed last year.[41] That added up to 375 million unused paid days off.

In the survey of 9,424 working adults in 28 countries, 9 percent of Americans said they worried that their absence from work would "be perceived negatively," according to Expedia. About 14 percent reported feeling guilty for taking time off, the survey found. In fact, 6 percent said they felt so guilty that they did not take any time off in 2016.[42]

Yet 21 percent of Americans in the survey ranked additional vacation as their "second most-prized work incentive," trailing flexible work hours by just 1 percent.[43]

That practice isn't new. Project: Time Off, an advocacy group that promotes a cultural shift toward embracing time off from work as essential to success and good health, found that Americans' use of vacation days has dipped during most years since 2000.[44]

And the practice is not limited to vacations. Although the number of employers offering paid family leave policies is expanding, their use by new mothers is not, according to research by Ohio State University economist Jay Zagorsky.[45]

In an interview, Zagorsky said some women blame their choice to eschew paid leave on a perception that they will stall their career progress. But more likely, he says, the women cannot afford to take the leave because the income replacement their employers offer is rarely 100 percent.

For example, in California—the first state to adopt a policy for paid maternity leave, and later, for paternity leave for all public-and private-sector employees—those taking paid family leave qualify for reimbursement of 55 percent of their weekly wages for up to six weeks.[46] "Not everyone can afford to take half pay or no pay," Zagorsky says. "If you live paycheck to paycheck and you have the possibility of taking off two months, but of taking off those two months without any [or full] pay, it might not be financially feasible."

The result: The number of women taking maternity leave in 2015 was about the same as it was in 1994, an average of 273,000 per month, Zagorsky's research showed. The use of an extended leave after childbirth is static, he says, even though four states and the District of Columbia have added paid leave policies since 1994 and the economy has grown by 66 percent.[47]

Zagorsky calls the statistics "surprising and troubling."

The American Enterprise Institute's Mathur says the think tank's studies have shown that California mothers would have taken longer maternity leaves if their wage replacement were greater than 55 percent. "Paid leave is definitely an improvement over unpaid leave," Mathur says, "but how you design the paid leave policy is important."

Mathur points to the latest National Compensation Survey from the Bureau of Labor Statistics (BLS), which reports that 13 percent of private-sector workers in the United States have access to paid family leave.[48] But the 2012 BLS American Time Use Survey shows that fewer than 10 percent of employees who took paid or unpaid leave for any reason used it to care for children or sick family members.[49]

The use of paid leave by new fathers across the United States, on the other hand, increased from 5,800 men a month in 1994 to 22,000 a month in 2015, Zagorsky's research revealed.[50]

And while 47.5 percent of women who took maternity leave in 2015 were paid something during their absence from work, 70.7 percent of men on leave were, according to Zagorsky's report.[51]

Matos observes that men who take time off to bond with a newborn or care for a sick family member are more likely than women to be embraced when they return to the office.

"People will say, 'He's a father now; he needs this job,'" says Matos. But for women who take extended leaves, he says, "people will not be giving her her assignments back."

Matos says many women and men "feel afraid to offer information to their bosses about taking time off for maternity and family." He says he looks forward to the day when executives and managers will say, "I know this is a tumultuous time. Let's figure something out that works for both of us."

Until then, Matos says, new mothers who would like to work while raising their families will quit their jobs in larger numbers than necessary. And bosses, he says, "will wish they would have told them [what they needed] before they quit."

BACKGROUND

European Head Start

America has no national law guaranteeing working mothers will continue to earn all or part of their salaries while they are on maternity leave. Four states—California, New Jersey, New York and Rhode Island, plus the District of Columbia—have statewide laws that provide pay to new parents on leave.

California's landmark 2002 law came 119 years after the world's first paid leave law, which Germany enacted countrywide in 1883.[52]

The Europeans pioneered both unpaid and paid maternity leaves. Switzerland was the first country in the world to offer working mothers time off to give birth, when it adopted a law in 1877 providing for eight weeks of upaid leave for use before and after childbirth. That law forbade factory workers from returning to work for six weeks after delivery.

A year later, Germany enacted a three-week leave law, also unpaid. In 1883, Germany amended its policy to legislate paid leave for three weeks after a birth for women who had insurance. Austria-Hungary did the same; both laws left the amount of the payment up to the women's insurance companies.[53]

Over the next 30 years, Great Britain, Portugal, Norway, Sweden, Holland and Belgium passed national laws providing unpaid time off from work for childbirth. In 1911, Sweden opened maternity and convalescent homes, where working women and their babies could stay as the moms recovered from childbirth. Two years later, France joined Switzerland as one of two European countries that allowed maternity leave to begin before a baby was born. And by then, Luxembourg, Switzerland and Sweden had adopted Germany and Austria-Hungary's paid maternity leave model.[54]

Today, the United States is the only developed country without a paid parental leave mandate. Of the 193 countries in the United Nations, only a handful have no national paid leave policy; besides the United States, the others are Papua New Guinea, Suriname and several South Pacific Island nations.[55]

Federal Intervention

Work and family advocates were able to garner bipartisan political support in Congress to pass the 1993 Family and Medical Leave Act (FMLA), but not until the legislation had been proposed—and failed—nine times over nine years.[56]

FMLA requires employers with 50 or more employees to allow them 12 weeks a year of unpaid leave for the following reasons:

- To deliver and care for the employee's newborn baby;

- To adopt or accept a child for foster care;

- To take care of a seriously ill spouse, child or parent;

- To take medical leave when the employee is seriously ill and unable to work;

- To deal with any urgent demands created by the status of an employee's next of kin as an active duty or reserve member of the military. The law allows 26 weeks of unpaid leave for an immediate family member to care for a seriously injured or ill military member.

Employees who use FMLA leave have jobs waiting when they return. However, the law does not require employers to offer returning workers their original jobs; they are entitled to positions with the same pay and benefits as the ones they had before they took the leave.[57]

FMLA is not intended as a stand-in for sick days, which 56 percent of small-business employees and 79 percent of employees at larger companies had access to in 2016, according to the Bureau of Labor Statistics.[58] Sick days—as opposed to family and medical leave—are for employees to use when they wake up with the flu or a migraine headache and need to miss a day or two of work, for example.

The Labor Department's Wage and Hour Division amended its interpretation of the FMLA in 2015 to update its definition of "spouse" to include eligible employees in same-sex marriages. The change brought the law into compliance with a 2013 U.S. Supreme Court decision that overturned the 1996 Defense of Marriage Act. That act held that "marriage" and "spouse" referred only to a union between a man and a woman.[59]

The FMLA applies to public- and private-sector employees in all states. It does not, however, restrict states or private businesses from voluntarily offering more generous medical and family leave benefits to their employees. It also does not prohibit companies with fewer than 50 employees—those exempt from FMLA—from offering their own family and medical leave benefit.

After California enacted its law in 2002, New Jersey followed in 2008, Rhode Island in 2013 and New York in 2016. In 2007, Washington Gov. Christine O'Grady Gregoire signed a state law for paid family leave, but it never took effect because of a lack of funding. In 2017, the District of Columbia adopted a paid family leave law, which will take effect in 2020.[60]

In 2006, San Francisco became the first city to require local businesses to offer paid sick days to all employees, including part-timers and temporary workers.

Source: DeAgostini/Getty Images

Paid Leave Policies Proliferate

Between 2015 and 2017, 71 large American companies adopted their own versions of paid family and medical leave, according to the National Partnership for Women & Families. Aside from tech companies, the list includes retailers such as Nordstrom, which offers birth mothers 12 weeks of paid leave; restaurant chains such as Starbucks, where working moms who do not work in stores get 18 weeks of paid leave for childbirth and store employees get six weeks of paid and 12 weeks of unpaid leave; and financial firms, including American Express, whose new policy allows up to 28 weeks for its working parents.[61]

Some of the companies offer a few weeks of paid leave and an optional allotment of additional unpaid weeks; others include paid time off to care for sick relatives; and many offer lengthy paid leaves to adoptive and foster parents.

Family and medical leave laws are more comprehensive than state and corporate policies for sick days. While the federal government does not require that employees receive paid sick leave, nearly 40 state and local governments do.[62]

San Francisco in 2006 became the first city to enact its own law requiring local businesses to pay employees for the days they miss due to illness. The law requires employers to pay all employees, including those who work part time or in temporary jobs, for sick days. Employees accrue their sick days at a rate of one hour for every 30 hours worked after 90 days on the job.[63]

Between 2007, when the law took effect, and 2009, the proportion of San Francisco businesses offering paid sick days increased from 73 percent to 91 percent, mostly at firms with fewer than 100 employees, indicating that many of the city's larger firms were voluntarily offering the benefit before the law required it. By 2009, 99 percent of San Francisco firms with more than 20 employees offered sick leave, according to research published in the American Journal of Public Health.[64]

Connecticut became the first state to enact a paid sick day law in 2012. Since then, California, Massachusetts, Oregon, Vermont, Arizona and Washington have adopted laws requiring employers to offer paid sick days to employees.[65] Connecticut's law is for employees who have worked at least 680 hours, and the leave is accrued.[66]

In addition, 30 cities and two counties—Montgomery County, Md., and Cook County, Ill.—have sick day laws.[67] In a handful of other states, paid sick days legislation is working its way through legislatures.

The proposed federal Healthy Families Act would require businesses with 15 or more employees to offer each employee up to seven paid sick days per year to recover from illness, visit doctors, care for ill family members or attend school meetings about a child's health condition or disability.[68]

WorldatWork has estimated that organizations offer an average of seven to 11 days of sick time off each year.[69]

For the past decade, companies have drifted away from the traditional model for sick days, which allows employees to accrue hours every pay period to be used for sick days later. In a 2016 WorldatWork survey, a growing number of human resources professionals in most industries said they prefer to offer sick and vacation days in a single bucket, called a Paid Time Off, or PTO, bank.

For example, 42 percent of HR managers in publicly traded companies said they use paid time off banks; 51 percent of privately held firms prefer PTO banks; and 44 percent of nonprofits and private-sector companies use them.[70]

CURRENT SITUATION

A Double Edge

Netflix reaped positive publicity last August when it announced that it would begin allowing new mothers and fathers to take as much leave as they wanted with full pay during the first year after a child's birth or adoption. Virgin, which owns the airline Virgin Atlantic, was likewise praised when it announced in 2015 that it would offer up to 52 weeks of leave, paid at 100 percent of the new parents' salary, to biological and adoptive parents.

In both cases, it turned out, the policies came with a catch: Netflix's paid leave offer applied only to salaried employees who work in the entertainment company's digital operations, and not to those working in DVD distribution centers. That left at least 450 of its 3,500 workers without the benefit.[71] And at Virgin, which employs more than 50,000, just 140 qualified for paid parental leave.[72]

The benefits "rang hollow," says Matos of Life Meets Work. The announcements, he says, were deliberately sketchy on details so they would reap the greatest public relations value. But they reflected a practice not uncommon among businesses vying for a limited number of highly skilled technical workers such as engineers and IT professionals: The most valued employees are offered the best benefits, he says.

Still, both companies caught flak from the media and the public. One Netflix fan collected almost 8,000 signatures urging the movie streaming and DVD distribution company to make warehouse workers, including hourly employees, eligible. "It's wrong for Netflix to create two classes of employees," the fan, Shannon Murphy, wrote in a blog on Coworker. org. "Already, there's a divide between higher income earners (especially in the tech industry) and low-wage workers in terms of access to important benefits like parental leave."[73]

In response, Netflix created a paid leave policy for hourly employees in its streaming, DVD distribution and customer service divisions, but the benefits differ. Hourly workers in the streaming operation get 16 weeks of fully paid maternity, paternity or adoption leave; customer service employees get 14 weeks; and DVD-side workers get 12 weeks.[74]

More criticism followed over the two-track policy.[75] "I hate to see a pattern where some workers have access to important benefits and others don't," Katie Bethell, a member of the Working Families Party, who helped collect 100,000 signatures on petitions her group delivered to Netflix headquarters. "Tech companies aren't considering this as a fundamental thing for the health of their employees, they're looking at [paid leave] as a way to attract employees."[76]

But a Netflix spokeswoman defended the company's decision: "Across Netflix, we compare salary and benefits to those of employees at businesses performing similar work," Anne Marie Squeo wrote in an email. "Those comparisons show we provide all of our employees with comparable or better pay and benefits than at other companies."[77]

Mattos says that practice is business as usual among companies with a workforce divided between highly prized, highly skilled workers and those whose jobs require little training and are easier to fill.

At Walmart, the largest U.S. private employer, only salaried employees are eligible for parental leave: 90 days for new mothers and 14 days for dads. More than 40 percent of its workers are paid hourly and do not qualify for the benefit.[78]

In fact, approximately 40 million American employees do not have access to paid sick days; just 20 percent of low-wage workers have that benefit, according to the White House Council of Economic Advisers.[79] The Labor Department has estimated that about four out of 10 workers do not have access to paid leave of any type.[80]

Like Netflix, however, some others are beginning to level the playing field, although Virgin has stuck to its limited benefit. The National Partnership for Women & Families counted 89 companies that expanded their paid family leave policies between 2015 and 2017 to make them at least somewhat more inclusive.[81] Late last year, for example, Hilton Hotels and Resorts began offering 10 weeks of paid parental leave to all of its 40,000 U.S. employees, from C-suite executives to housekeepers and waiters.[82]

Matt Schulyer, chief human resources officer for Hilton Worldwide, said Millennials, who make up half of the hospitality chain's workforce, spurred the decision, which was about "being able to attract and retain the workforce of today and the workforce of tomorrow."[83]

LOOKING AHEAD

Maybe Next Year

Advocates of paid leave remain dubious about the chances that the United States will enact a law to pay employees for time off from work—at least not soon.

They predict that at large companies—and not just those in technology fields—the benefits divide between the haves and have-nots will keep expanding unless Congress acts by passing a universal, national law that provides pay to all working parents with new children; to employees who are caregivers to sick children and elderly parents; and to anyone who has to miss work, even for a day, because of a personal illness.

And the advocates don't anticipate that is about to happen. Even though Trump's interest in paid leave has amplified the national conversation about the lack of such a law, the chance that Congress will adopt one is slim as long as Republicans and Democrats disagree about which employees to cover and how to pay for it.

That's the conclusion of Williams, the Center for Worklife Law attorney, who says the lack of a federal law is what has driven the decision by Netflix and others who deem employees with hard-to-recruit skills more worthy of paid leave benefits than those in unskilled, hourly positions.

Benefits Boost Employee Morale

"This is the drawback of handling parental leave at an enterprise [business] level, which, by the way, no other industrialized economy does," she told NPR. "If you handle parental leave at the enterprise level, the incentives for the enterprise are to give a rich benefits package to highly valued, high human-capital workers and not give it to hourly workers. . . . That's just a structural reality."[84]

In an interview with SBR, Williams suggested that Congress adopt an imperfect bill, just to get one on the books. "It's going to be so difficult to pass anything that they should package it any way they can pass it," she says.

Mathur of the American Enterprise Institute agrees: Lawmakers, she says, "are serious about having a policy . . . at least a minimum policy."

But even paid leave advocates don't agree what that policy should look like. Attorney Fink of the National Partnership for Women & Families says Trump's idea for a mothers-only benefit "isn't a sufficient proposal. . . . It's progress that there's a recognition that there's a public policy problem," she says, but "it would be harmful to pass a bill that only provides paid leave to mothers. . . . It could lead to sex discrimination in hiring, and in promotions."

That split could perpetuate the status quo, the advocates say. "There's no simple answer," Zagorsky, the Ohio State University researcher, says.

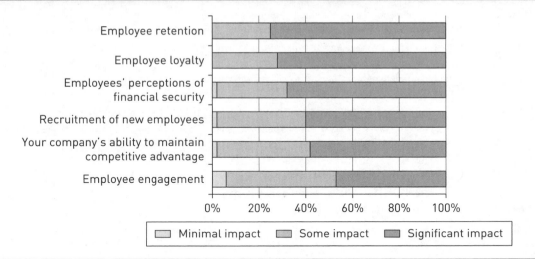

More than 70 percent of employers said retention and loyalty were significantly affected

In a 2016 survey, about three-quarters of employers said company benefits had a significant impact on employee retention and loyalty. A majority also said benefits help a company maintain its competitive advantage.

Note: The survey question asked, "To what extent have the benefits you offer had an impact on each of the following?"

Source: "Commitment to the Future: 10 Years of The Principal 10 Best Companies," Harvard Business Review Analytic Services, April 24, 2016, p. 6, http://tinyurl.com/knybwpf

Chronology

1877–1928	**Europe adopts world's first maternity leave laws.**
1877	Switzerland becomes the first country to adopt an unpaid maternity leave law; a year later, Germany becomes the second European nation to do so.
1883	Germany and Austria-Hungary adopt paid maternity leaves of three weeks after delivery for insured women.
1960s–1970s	**Temporary disability insurance laws pave way for maternity leave.**
1960s	California, Hawaii, New Jersey, New York and Rhode Island enact temporary disability insurance laws to protect employees from income loss in the case of a short-term medical disability. New mothers eventually are covered under these laws.
1978	The Pregnancy Discrimination Act requires companies that offer temporary disability programs to cover pregnancy. The act also prevented employers for firing women solely on the basis of pregnancy.
1980s–1990s	**Unpaid family leave becomes law.**
1984	Congressional Democrats introduce the Family and Medical Leave Act, which would allow employees to take up to 12 weeks of unpaid leave from work after the birth of a child or to care for a seriously ill family member. The bill is reintroduced every year until 1993, when it becomes law.

(Continued)

	(Continued)
1987	A California court rules that most employers have to allow pregnant women four months of unpaid disability leave and guarantee them their jobs when they return to work.
2000–2009	**First paid family leave and sick-days laws take effect.**
2002	California becomes the first state to create a paid family leave program to provide income replacement to new mothers and to employees with caregiving duties for seriously ill family members.
2006	The city of San Francisco becomes the first U.S. jurisdiction to enact a paid sick-day law.
2007	Washington state's governor signs a paid family leave law; however, the law never takes effect because of a lack of funding.
2008	New Jersey enacts the country's second state paid family leave law. . . . Washington becomes the second U.S. city to adopt a paid sick-day law.
2010–2017	**Cities and local jurisdictions pass paid sick-day laws.**
2011	Seattle enacts a paid sick-day law.
2012	Connecticut becomes the first state to require employers to offer paid sick days. The law covers only nonexempt, hourly workers in service-sector firms of more than 50 employees.
2013	The Rhode Island Legislature passes the country's third state paid family leave law. . . . New York City enacts a paid sick-day law and expands it in 2014. . . . Eight municipal governments in New Jersey pass sick-day laws.
2014	California expands the definition of "family member" in its paid family leave program to include seriously ill siblings, grandparents, grandchildren and parents-in-law. The original program covered only parents, children, spouses and registered domestic partners.
2015	The U.S. Department of Labor's Wage and Hour Division amends the definition of "spouse" in the 1993 Family and Medical Leave Act to include eligible employees in legal, same-sex marriages.
2016	New York passes a statewide paid family leave law, the fourth such law in America. . . . Presidential candidates Hillary Clinton, a Democrat, and Donald Trump, a Republican, publicly support paid family leave. . . . Paid sick-day statutes pass in nine jurisdictions, from Spokane, Wash., to Elizabeth, N.J.
2017	The District of Columbia enacts a paid family leave law, which will take effect in July 2020.

RESOURCES

The Next Step

Company Policies

Bort, Julie, "Sheryl Sandberg on tragically losing her husband: 'I'm a different person now,'" Business Insider, April 24, 2017, https://tinyurl.com/mldxk9a.

Facebook COO Sheryl Sandberg, whose husband died unexpectedly two years ago, announced in February that Facebook employees will receive up to 20 days paid annual leave to mourn an immediate family member's death, and 10 days to mourn for an extended family member.

Kharpal, Arjun, "Tech firms are giving staff paid leave for political engagements amid fear of immigration crackdown," CNBC, April 18, 2017, https://tinyurl.com/kj36kfs.

A technology startup company, reacting in part to President Trump's anti-immigration rhetoric, adopted a policy on April 18 that gives employees paid leave for political engagements, including protests.

Lewis, Cora, "Women Ironworkers Will Get Six Months Of Paid Maternity Leave," BuzzFeed News, April 17, 2017, https://tinyurl.com/k3kbs2b.

Following the lead of tech companies such as Adobe, Netflix and Spotify, the male-dominated ironworkers union now offers female employees up to six months maternity leave.

International Standards

Bruner, Raisa, "Chinese Workers at Factory for Ivanka Trump's Clothing Maker Earn About $62 a Week: Report," Time, April 25, 2017, https://tinyurl.com/mheo5uf.

The Fair Labor Association watchdog group found that Chinese factory workers who make clothing for Ivanka Trump's brand worked excessive hours for below minimum wage last year and received only five paid leave days per year.

Millington, Alison, "Italy could soon offer women three days of paid menstrual leave each month," Business Insider, March 29, 2017, https://tinyurl.com/kq3wgr3.

The lower house of Italy's parliament is considering a proposal that would allow women to take three paid leave days each month for any "painful periods" they experience.

Singhi, Namrata, "Microsoft India employees to get family caregiver leave," The Times of India, April 24, 2017, https://tinyurl.com/n3dfr68.

Microsoft India announced that employees who need to care for an immediate family member with a serious health condition will receive four weeks annual paid leave; workers who adopt a child or have a child via surrogacy will receive 26 calendar weeks of paid leave; and paternity leave will increase to six weeks.

Lawsuits

Blau, Reuven, "JetBlue hit with suit for violating New York paid sick leave law," New York Daily News, April 1, 2017, https://tinyurl.com/lxtbtot.

New York City's Consumer Affairs Department accuses JetBlue in a lawsuit of using progressive punishments—including possible termination—to discipline employees who called in sick.

Hopkins, Kathleen, "Ocean County judge sues, claims discrimination," Asbury Park Press, April 25, 2017, https://tinyurl.com/kfkep2v.

A New Jersey Superior Court judge sued his two bosses, saying they tried to force him to resign because he has a 19-year-old son with multiple disabilities.

Salazar, Martin, "Lawsuit targets proposed sick leave ordinance," Albuquerque Journal, April 3, 2017, https://tinyurl.com/k8s6ggy.

Businesses and trade associations in Albuquerque, N.M., sued city officials, arguing a proposed sick leave ordinance is unconstitutional and would hurt businesses and the city's economy.

State Legislation

Booker, Christopher, and Connie Kargbo, "Can Rhode Island's paid family leave be a national model?" PBS NewsHour, April 16, 2017, https://tinyurl.com/l2nqme3.

Rhode Island taxes private-sector employees to finance a program that provides paid leave for part-time and full-time workers, a policy that smaller companies say may hurt productivity.

Dawson, James, "State lawmakers considering family leave bills," Delaware Public Media, April 23, 2017, http://tinyurl.com/m2f8mo2.

Delaware lawmakers are studying proposals that would give three months of paid leave to state employees who have worked full time for at least a year, and an additional six weeks of unpaid leave to mothers who are expecting twins and require hospitalization during pregnancy.

Sagarin, Susan, "D.C. Enacts Paid Family Leave But Lacks Funding For Implementation," Bloomberg BNA, April 17, 2017, http://tinyurl.com/ldekpgz.

The District of Columbia's Universal Paid Leave Act, which entitles employees to 90 percent of their salary while on leave, won approval from a congressional review board in April, but the city may not be able to afford it.

Organizations

The American Action Forum

1747 Pennsylvania Ave., N.W., 5th Floor, Washington, DC 20006
1-202-559-6420
www.americanactionforum.org/

A self-described center-right nonprofit that focuses on domestic policy challenges such as paid leave, health care and tax reform.

Center for American Progress

1333 H St., N.W., Washington, DC 20005
1-202-682-1611
www.americanprogress.org/

An independent, nonpartisan policy institute dedicated to developing new policy ideas in areas such as criminal justice, disability, the economy, education and women.

Center for Economic and Policy Research

1611 Connecticut Ave., N.W., Suite 400, Washington, DC 20009
http://cepr.net/
1-202-293-5380

An organization of economists who promote democratic debate on economic and social issues through professional research and public education.

Center for WorkLife Law

200 McAllister St., San Francisco, CA 94102

1-415-565-4640

http://worklifelaw.org/

Women's leadership organization at the University of California's Hastings College of Law that focuses on jumpstarting "the stalled gender revolution."

Families & Work Institute

245 5th Ave., #1002, New York, NY 10016

1-212-465-2044

A nonpartisan research organization that studies the changing workforce and workplace, as well as the changing family.

National Partnership for Women and Families

1875 Connecticut Ave., N.W., Suite 650, Washington, DC 20009

1-202-986-2600

www.nationalpartnership.org/

Formerly known as the Women's Legal Defense Fund, this nonpartisan organization promotes fairness in the workplace, reproductive health and rights, access to affordable health care and work-family policies for working parents.

Pew Research Center

1615 L St., N.W., Suite 800, Washington, DC 20036

1-202-419-4300

www.pewresearch.org/

A nonpartisan "fact tank" that conducts public opinion polls and demographic research, and informs the public about issues involving politics, media, technology, religion, global attitudes and demographic trends.

PL+US (Paid Leave For the United States)

2973 16th St., San Francisco, CA 94110

1-415-799-9789

http://paidleave.us/#issue

A new advocacy organization whose mission is to win paid family leave by engaging Americans at the grass-roots level.

Work and Family Researchers Network

c/o the Wharton School, University of Pennsylvania, 3620 Locust Walk, Philadelphia, PA 19104-6302

1-215-898-5605

https://workfamily.sas.upenn.edu/

A membership association of interdisciplinary work and family scholars that oversees an open-access work and family subject matter repository.

WorldatWork

14040 N. Northsight Blvd., Scottsdale, AZ 85260

1-877-951-9191

www.worldatwork.org

A membership organization for human resources professionals that bills itself as "the total rewards association." Its focus is compensation, benefits and work/life effectiveness.

PERSPECTIVE

Q&A: Jeb Breithaupt on Paid Leave

"IF SOMEBODY'S NOT HERE, THERE'S A HOLE; YOU'VE GOT A FUNCTION THAT'S NOT BEING DONE"

Jeb Breithaupt is the owner of JEB Design/Build, a remodeling firm in Shreveport, La., with 11 employees. In an interview with SAGE Business Researcher freelance correspondent Sharon O'Malley, he explains why he opposes any government requirement that would allow small-business employees to take extended leaves, even if insurance or taxes cover their salaries. His objection: He says he can't afford to hire temporary workers to cover for employees who are absent.

How do you feel about the possibility that federal law could require you to offer your employees paid parental leave?

I'm not a big, fat corporation. If someone is out for six weeks, I would lose thousands of dollars.

Some advocates of paid parental leave say small businesses can cross-train employees to cover for each other during extended leaves.

In a big corporation, some people could probably cover for others, but small business doesn't work that way. I've got people in super-specific positions. If somebody's not here, there's a hole; you've got a function that's not being done. We can't start a remodeling job if our only drafter is out for six weeks. We're not going to get jobs drawn, so we won't sell any jobs. I can't outsource that. If my production manager was out for six weeks, I'd be able to cover to a certain extent, but I'm the owner. I'm out selling.

Do you offer any paid leave?

Full-time employees have six paid holidays per year, and we have a vacation policy: one week after the first year, and two weeks after the second. [His company offers five paid sick days a year. Employees who use them, though, have to produce a doctor's note.]

What happens when someone has a baby?

That hasn't come up. We did have a salesperson who took maternity leave, but she was paid solely on commission, so she doesn't get paid when she doesn't sell anything.

Does your limited paid leave policy hurt you when it comes to recruiting employees?

I had an opening for a bookkeeper, and I got 773 résumés.

What happens if an employee needs to take time off beyond the vacation and sick days that you offer?

We try to be flexible about stuff. I have nine full-time employees and two hourly employees. Some of them have to be here from 8 a.m. to 6 p.m., Monday through Friday. But for others, like my bookkeeper, how much we need them is job-driven. In construction, you have light weeks and heavy weeks. If we're in between jobs or if it's a light week and someone wants to work four days instead of five, that's allowed—but they forfeit their pay for the day they take off. I think that flexibility is a draw. But my drafter, I need you here Monday through Friday.

What advice would you give to legislators considering a mandate to require all businesses, including small ones, to allow employees to take extended leave for childbirth and personal or family illnesses?

Government is like a big business. They have a big-government mindset. They think there's this big pot of money and you just turn on the faucet, and there's more money. Small businesses are not like that.

How will small businesses react if Congress passes a law requiring paid parental leave?

The market will adjust. Duh: They won't hire young women. The government thinks people aren't going to change when they pass these laws. It's frustrating.

11 SUSTAINABILITY
Are businesses looking beyond profit?
Pamela J. Black

EXECUTIVE SUMMARY

Many companies, mostly large multinationals, are adopting sustainability programs and delivering annual reports on their progress toward creating a new kind of business. Within this burgeoning movement, sustainable companies give the environment and human rights the same priority as profits. Their goals include protecting the Earth to reduce the effects of climate change while innovating new products. Some of the biggest companies have succeeded in integrating sustainable principals into their corporate DNA and say that it gives them a competitive edge. Is sustainability really making a difference? Can a company go "green" and remain profitable? Will the movement spread or fade away? Many of these companies have been accused in the past of degrading the environment and depleting natural resources, and critics say they are only changing their ways because of pressure from regulators, investors, activists, communities and consumers. Others, often with the help of nonprofits, have voluntarily instituted change across their business model. But so far progress is slow.

OVERVIEW

In 2001, when Jack Welch stepped down as CEO of General Electric, the company was under attack for releasing some 1.3 million pounds of polychlorinated biphenyls (PCBs) from two plants into the Hudson River between the mid-1940s and 1977. PCBs, which are hazardous to all life forms, have invaded the food chain along miles of the Hudson and other waterways. Welch and GE denied for years that PCBs were harmful and said the river would clean itself.[1]

Welch's successor at GE, Jeff Immelt, has taken a different tack. In 2005, Immelt began "Ecomagination," which he describes as "GE's commitment to imagine and build innovative solutions to today's environmental challenges while driving economic growth."[2]

From *SAGE Business Researcher*,
February 23, 2015

Residents of Nairobi, Kenya, transfer money using the M-PESA banking by phone system, a success in places where people have access to mobile phones but not to banks. M-PESA is a joint venture between international telecom giant Vodaphone and local mobile communications firm Safaricom.

Source: Thomas Imo/Photothek via Getty Images

GE's $12 billion investment in Ecomagination generated $160 billion since 2005 in revenue. At the same time, GE reduced greenhouse gas emissions by 32 percent from 2004 levels and fresh water use by 45 percent from 2006 levels, according to GE's 2013 Global Impact Report, the latest available.[3]

In the impact report, Immelt offers a concise definition of a sustainable business: "To succeed as a global business, we need to help build the communities where we operate. We know this goes hand in hand with our ability to grow. At GE, we call this sustainability: aligning our business strategy to meet societal needs, while minimizing environmental impact and advancing social development."[4]

Sustainability has become a buzzword in boardrooms around the world. In general, the movement strives to give the environment and human rights the same priority as profit. But sustainability remains amorphous and complex and is hard to measure. Libertarians and conservatives see it as a threat to individual freedom and private property. Advocates, including some nonprofit groups and many academics, hail it as a revolution in corporate management—and even call it the "new capitalism." Statistics and anecdotal evidence vary on whether it's a growing movement or appropriate only for some giant multinational corporations. Becoming sustainable requires a significant investment of time and money. That might be why only 10 percent of companies, mostly big multinationals, have fully embraced it.[5]

Corporations such as Alcoa, GE, General Motors, 3M, Procter & Gamble, Hewlett-Packard, Intel, Nike and Unilever, to name a few, may be more motivated to become sustainable because their international reach makes them more vulnerable to the effects of climate change and social unrest in various parts of the world.[6] In addition, sustainable practices give them access to the fastest-growing markets in developing countries.[7]

Multinationals with long histories tend to plan 50 to 100 years in advance. That means anticipating possible risks from climate change. They are also vulnerable to reputational risk in developing countries. "In the Internet age, information travels much quicker," says Alexandra Cichon, senior vice president of business development at RepRisk, a global database of corporate sustainability risks.

Smaller companies may lack the means to make big investments, although a majority would like to reap the cost savings from sustainability, according to a survey by Cox Enterprises, the Atlanta-based cable television and Internet company.[8] "The reality is, they have a hard time justifying it without being able to see an impact right upfront," says Cox spokeswoman Elizabeth Olmstead. "Large business can make bigger investments with a longer time to make a return on their investment."

Nonetheless, more companies, big and small, are trying out sustainable practices, says John Weiss, a senior manager in the corporate program at the Coalition for Environmentally Responsible Economies in Boston, known as Ceres. "You would be hard-pressed to find some companies that aren't doing anything."

"The whole corporate responsibility movement has become irreversibly mainstream," says Bennett Freeman, senior vice president for sustainability research and policy at asset manager Calvert Investments, a sustainable and responsible investing (SRI) company based in Bethesda, Md. Although he says that the number of sustainable businesses he covers hasn't grown significantly, more and bigger asset managers are pursuing it.[9]

Whether it is growing or not, sustainability is gaining attention because of two worsening problems: climate change and population growth. Carbon dioxide emissions from fossil fuels and agriculture are raising global surface temperatures, leading to severe weather and more widespread and costly destruction of natural resources, according to scientists.[10]

Moreover, the planet's population of 7 billion is growing at the rate of 200,000 people a day. These newcomers will need food, water and shelter in a world where arable land and fresh water are disappearing. Already humans consume 50 percent more natural resources than the Earth is producing.[11]

The Triple Bottom Line

To make sustainability more graspable, John Elkington, the founder of British consultancy SustainAbility, devised the triple bottom line (TBL) in 1994.[12]

TBL consists of three concentric circles representing the three P's: planet, people and profit. The confluence of these defines sustainability, although, as an Economist blog noted, these categories can't readily be measured. "One problem with the triple bottom line is that . . . It is difficult to measure the planet and people accounts in the same terms as profits—that is, in terms of cash. The full cost of an oil-tanker spillage, for example, is probably immeasurable in monetary terms, as is the cost of displacing whole communities to clear forests, or the cost of depriving children of their freedom to learn in order to make them work at a young age."[13]

Planet

The environment includes energy, water, soil, air and biodiversity of plants and animals. Each of these could be assigned a cost as "natural capital," and all are threatened by climate change and consumption. Fossil fuels are woven through almost all aspects of modern life, and coal, oil and gas are the biggest producers of atmospheric carbon.[14] Sustainable companies try to reduce their carbon footprint by using renewable energy from solar cells and wind turbines. Renewable-energy markets have been growing with the help of government incentives. Apple, for one, gets 92 percent of its energy from renewable sources.[15]

However, it's becoming clear that multinationals can inadvertently encourage problems such as deforestation. Rainforests absorb carbon from the air and protect biodiversity. But producers in developing countries who supply multinationals with raw materials, such as coffee and palm oil, clear rain forests for farmland.

The amount of fresh water is limited and in some areas it's drying up because of overuse or climate change.[16] The supply is expected to shrink more within the next three years due to population growth and pollution. "No business can expand without water," says Lance Pierce, president of CDP North America (formerly the Carbon Disclosure Project, an international nonprofit headquartered in London). "Food and beverage companies are at the vanguard of that. It's central to their products. All over the world, watersheds are under pressure, so beverage companies are developing the capacity to understand community expectations around water."

People

The social aspect of the triple bottom line refers to human capital. At the most basic level investing in people means providing a safe and healthy work environment, and many sustainable companies stop there. But the most valuable and loyal employees work for companies that are transparent about corporate operations and value employee contributions, according to China Gorman, CEO of Great Place to Work, a global human resources consulting and research company that provides the data for Fortune magazine's "100 Best Places To Work" issue.[17]

They need to trust their leaders to be fair and honest; they want to be proud of their work and to have strong bonds with colleagues, Gorman said. "They need the organization [that] believes in them, invests in their careers, in their skills."[18]

Profit

Sustainable initiatives need to be profitable so the company itself can be sustainable, experts say. Sustainability makes economic sense across the triple bottom line because companies require educated and motivated employees, electricity, water and air. "A lot of sustainability will make you more efficient, which will lower costs," says Jason Jay, director of the Sustainable Initiative at MIT's Sloan School of Management. "A more efficient refrigerator or solar panels entail some upfront costs, but you get a benefit over time."

Measuring Sustainability

An ongoing challenge has been proving that sustainability goals contribute to the financial bottom line. As the business cliché goes, what gets measured gets managed. Many corporations still grapple with the best way to measure the value of water use, carbon emissions and employee satisfaction. "It's critical that you have metrics. You have to measure to know how you're doing and set targets," says Weiss at Ceres. "It's one thing to quantify, but it's even more important to set a time-bound target to mark progress against—where we want to go versus the previous year. We push companies to set aggressive targets."

The murkiness of gauging sustainability opens some companies to charges of "greenwashing," or misleading people about their products and processes. For example, Walmart, which announced a big sustainability campaign in 2005, is still accused by employees, unions and environmental groups of increasing its carbon footprint and underpaying

Most Companies Lack Formal Sustainability Targets

Companies with sustainable products/services, by offering

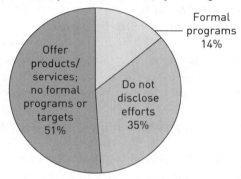

Companies with sustainable supply-chain management measures, by offering

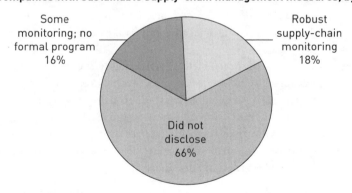

Sustainability remains elusive for most companies: Slightly more than half of the businesses surveyed by Ceres, a nonprofit that advocates for sustainability leadership, provide sustainable products or services without setting formal performance targets. The task is even tougher for those companies that try to monitor the sustainability of their supply chain: About two-thirds do not disclose how they measure their suppliers' sustainability performance. Among those that monitor their supply chains, 18 percent say they have robust monitoring systems to measure and respond to their suppliers' performance.

Source: "Gaining Ground: Corporate Progress on the Ceres Roadmap," Ceres, pp. 58, 65, from http://tinyurl.com/o2xg2pt.

workers. Walmart officials reject the charges. In February, the company announced that it will increase wages for its lowest-paid U.S. workers, who now receive the $7.25 per hour federal minimum, to $9 per hour in April and $10 per hour next year.[19]

"Most fields don't have independent standards or boards regulating whether you're sustainable or not," says Janis Balda, associate professor of sustainable enterprise at Unity College's Center for Sustainability and Global Change in Maine. "So it's very hard to know where company values are across people—planet—profits. On the whole, some greenwashing is unintentional."

How do you know if a company is really sustainable or just saying it is? Balda says that corporate websites offer a clue. Numerous awards and certifications are another. "B corporation," a designation that applies mostly to smaller companies and start-ups that often begin sustainably and are certified as environmentally sound, is yet another.[20]

There is also a big difference between companies that have incorporated sustainability into their DNA and those that are making incremental changes, says Weiss.[21] Companies that are remaking their operations to be sustainable or have started out sustainably are focused on innovating whole new products, systems and strategies in which sustainability is a given.

Some proponents of sustainability go further than examining corporate strategies, calling for a new kind of capitalism. They see technology as the means to create a more equitable society. Unilever CEO Paul Polman has pushed for a sustainable and equitable capitalism that is based on long-term planning and inclusivity. "Capitalism has served us enormously well," he said. "Yet while it has helped to reduce global poverty and expand access to health care and education, it has come at an enormous cost: unsustainable levels of public and private debt, excessive consumerism, and, frankly, too many people who are left behind."[22]

Although more companies seem interested in sustainability, actual change is glacial, Weiss says. Corporate sustainability efforts are falling way behind the pace of climate change. "It's disappointing. Companies have not gone as far as we hoped they would," he says. "We're looking out to 2020. But most companies aren't halfway toward meeting their goals."

Debate over corporate sustainability remains intense. Many of these issues will be resolved only in time—if at all. As companies struggle to define and adopt sustainable practices, they're wrestling with some of these key questions:

Weighing the Issues

Is there a business case for sustainability?

The quest to find a link between sustainability and corporate value is ongoing. If such a link exists, stock prices don't always reflect it. Nevertheless, multinationals and other companies that have adopted sustainability believe their decision has led to higher profit because of savings from efficiency, innovative products and new markets.

A lot of the research on the financial value of sustainability is positive. In a study by asset manager Sustainable Insight Capital Management, fossil-fuel-free funds outperformed the S&P 500 in one-, three-and five-year periods ending on Dec. 31, 2013.[23] A Harvard

Business School study showed that every dollar invested in a portfolio of sustainable companies in 1993 would have grown to $22.60 by 2011, versus $15.40 for a portfolio of companies less focused on sustainability.[24] CDP's 2014 study, "Climate action and profitability," concludes that companies in its Leaders Index generated an 18 percent higher return on equity and 21 percent higher dividends than their less sustainable peers.[25] "The most recent look at the climate performance leadership index shows that it outperforms the Bloomberg world index by 9.6 percent," says CDP's Pierce.

However, other studies find no added value in sustainability: A 2014 report by asset manager TIAA-CREF found no advantage over the long term, but no disadvantage either.[26]

The discrepancy between findings may have to do with varying definitions of sustainability among asset managers and corporations. A recent McKinsey study argued that the link between stock price and sustainability was weak because successful companies were failing to communicate their progress clearly. Instead, the companies were busy figuring out their own internal measures, which were often too voluminous and confusing for investors to evaluate.[27]

"Some people will tell you there's an outperformance and others will tell you SRI is a drag," says Freeman at Calvert Investments. "Like any other asset class, SRI funds go in and out of favor."

More Companies Say Sustainability Is Good Business

Anecdotal evidence is more emphatic. "We really do believe that good business and sustainability go hand in hand," says Todd Brady, global environmental manager at Intel, a leading semiconductor chip maker. "It doesn't cost money if you see where it aligns with business." Several years ago, Intel established a conservation fund, where engineers would contribute ideas for saving on energy costs—anything from replacing light bulbs to recapturing heat. "We thought we would get a return on investment in five years," Brady says. "But the first year we made $1 million to $2 million. Today, we have $30 million in the fund, and a savings to the company of over $65 million."

Focusing on sustainability takes significant risk out of portfolios, says Calvert's Freeman. Companies that are prepared for rising commodity prices or diminishing water supplies can prepare in advance to obtain commodities at reliable costs or to install water treatment and recycling systems.

Ideally, other stakeholders, including investors, benefit from sustainability, too. Customers buy a product that doesn't harm the environment, employees have a more satisfying experience and the community benefits from investments in its welfare and the environment. Sanya Carley, an associate professor of environmental affairs at Indiana University, surveyed leaders of 12 sustainable companies. Although the switch was difficult for many companies, she said, "not a single respondent claimed sustainability didn't contribute to the bottom line."[28]

Some nonprofits are trying to establish a link between corporate value and sustainability for investors. The Sustainability Accounting Standards Board (SASB) would do

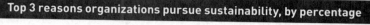

Top 3 reasons organizations pursue sustainability, by percentage

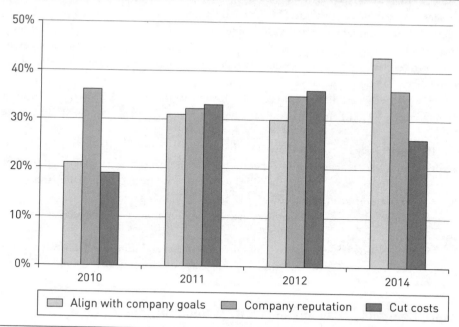

Sustainability is becoming more popular because more businesses believe it helps the bottom line: 43 percent of executives in a 2014 survey said their companies adopted sustainable practices to align with their business goals in 2014, more than double the share citing that reason in 2010. Building company reputation (36 percent) and cutting costs (26 percent) were the second- and third-most commonly cited reasons.

Note: Number of survey respondents for each year: 1,749 in 2010, 2,956 in 2011, 3,847 in 2012; and 2,904 in 2014.

Source: "Sustainability's strategic worth: McKinsey Global Survey results," McKinsey & Company, July 2014, http://tinyurl.com/nsd52el

so by setting industry standards that would be combined with Securities and Exchange Commission (SEC) financial data.[29]

Establishing that missing link could help proponents persuade more companies to come on board. "There is a lot of willingness to support sustainability efforts, but a total lack of clarity on what business should do and why," said an unidentified CEO in a U.N.-Accenture report. "We need a plan that is progressive enough, and rigorous enough, to set real priorities for action."[30]

Can companies that adopt sustainable methods compete globally?

Competitiveness is the most significant economic concern of sustainable companies, followed by market pressure and revenue growth, according to "Sustainability's Next Frontier," a study by the Sloan Management School and the Boston Consulting Group. "There is little disagreement that sustainability is necessary to be competitive—86% of respondents say it is or will be."[31]

Even those CEOs who buy in to sustainability are having trouble scaling it up from individual projects to companywide strategy. They see improving the environment and people's lives as a cost rather than a strategy; they also view sustainability as a risk they can't afford to take. "People don't understand the positive gains from this type of enterprise, and some people are too scared to try," says Balda at Unity College. "Sometimes climate change is so huge, you need to break it down for companies, and they need to hear more stories of how [sustainable practices] can succeed for them."

CEOs Increasingly See Sustainability as a Priority

Sustainability leaders, however, don't see improving the environment or society as a cost but as an opportunity to pursue innovative products, processes and markets. They have turned the double threat of dwindling resources and growing need into motivation for new business models with clearer values and purpose. This helps businesses differentiate themselves with consumers, attract top talent, protect their suppliers and compete globally. "We've set out to double the size of our business while reducing our environmental footprint and increasing positive social impact," says Jessica Sobel, manager of sustainable living and strategic initiatives at Unilever North America.

Electronics giant Siemens has sold offshore wind turbines that have saved 4 million metric tons of carbon dioxide a year, compared with traditional sources of power generation. Sales of turbines and smart electric grid meters have provided 42 percent of the company's business. The carbon savings was worldwide, and not just the company's own footprint.[32]

Vodaphone entered a joint venture to produce M-PESA, with Safaricom, the leading mobile communications company in Kenya. M-PESA allows people to bypass banks by storing and transferring money with their mobile phones.[33] A new Safaricom product, M-KOPA, is a solar lighting and charger system that people can buy with small payments over the course of year.[34]

In 10 years, 70 percent of global growth could occur in developing countries. To appeal to the new rising middle class, companies will have to build trust, listen to consumers, and quickly innovate new solutions, according to McKinsey & Company.[35]

Companies, in other words, will need to create products that have resonance for local populations. They will need a "deep understanding" of local culture and customer segmentation, according to the Boston Consulting Group.[36]

"We source locally, market and produce locally, and hire and distribute locally, and that gives us a tremendous insight into the markets we serve and an edge in actually operating sustainably," said Coca-Cola CEO Muhtar Kent.[37]

Unilever's Sustainable Living Plan merges health and education with business: It teaches children in developing countries how to wash with soap and to brush their teeth. According to the company's website, these things improve oral health and raise self-esteem.[38] They also

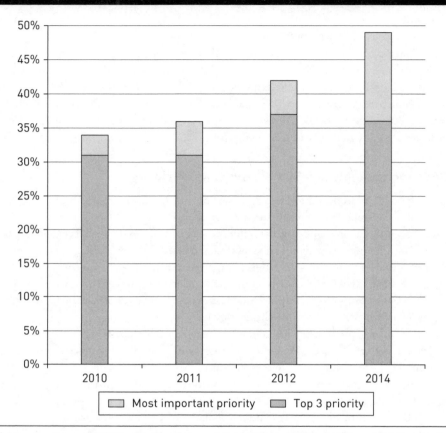

☐ Most important priority   ☐ Top 3 priority

The percentage of CEOs who viewed sustainability as either an "important" priority or a top three priority rose from 34 percent in 2010 to 49 percent in 2014. While 36 percent said it was a top three priority in 2014, down 1 point from 2012, the share who said it was important jumped from 5 percent to 13 percent.

Note: Number of survey respondents for each year: 175 in 2010, 265 in 2011, 364 in 2012; and 281 in 2014.

Source: "Sustainability's strategic worth: McKinsey Global Survey results," McKinsey & Company, July 2014, http://tinyurl.com/nsd52el

familiarize an up-and-coming market with Unilever's brand and products—and put the company in a favorable light.[39]

Some congressional Republicans and business leaders see a downside to sustainability: Efforts to go green can increase the cost of doing business and make American firms less competitive overseas, they say. They especially deride many environmental regulations as anti-business; as the 2012 GOP platform put it, new greenhouse gas regulations "will harm the nation's economy and threaten millions of jobs over the next quarter century."[40]

Do sustainable business practices help society?

Unilever's Polman, who is seen as the leader of the sustainable business movement, says that the role of business is to serve society. In a commentary, he wrote: "In the next ten years, I think you are going to see many more initiatives undertaken by groups of businesses to protect their long-term interests and the long-term interests of society."[41]

Business and society cannot exist without each other, according to Michael Porter, a professor at the Harvard Business School and a leading authority on competitiveness. Business needs a healthy society to create evolving demand, and society needs businesses for jobs, wealth creation and innovation, he wrote in an article titled "Strategy and Society." He went on to say, "Any business that pursues its ends at the expense of the society in which it operates will find its success to be illusory and ultimately temporary."[42]

Porter cited how Nestle helped a dirt-poor town in northern India become prosperous. Farmers barely scratched out a living from their cow's milk. They were unable to travel to market without risking the milk going sour. Cows' yields were low and newborn calves kept dying. Nestle, which wanted to expand into India, aided the farmers by sending veterinarians and refrigerated trucks to transport their milk to a central processing center. The town flourished as a result. [43]

Ending poverty is one of the goals of sustainability, and helping people is one of the three bottom lines. Stories of creating better working conditions, sending kids to school instead of to a factory or farm and elevating the lot of women in villages are more and more common for companies. At the same time, the reverse outcome—stories about abusive working conditions at home and abroad—can badly harm a corporation's brand.

Big corporations have always had philanthropic arms. And this continues, but increasingly they have a sustainable bent. Some corporations contribute directly to communities through grants and gifts. Dow Chemical gives $25 million to science and technology education to "build the workforce of tomorrow."[44] Target awards grants to Feed America, Unicef and school reading programs.[45] Ford Motor regularly buys supplies from minority- and female-owned businesses.[46] Hewlett-Packard works with Conservation International, using its technology to help scientists measure species' decline in 16 tropical rainforests in 14 countries, according to Nate Hurst, HP's global director of environmental progress.

Rather than making random donations to worthy charities, a recent Harvard Business Review article about Corporate Social Responsibility (CSR) suggested that the most productive social initiatives should be coordinated across the entire enterprise. The authors cited PNC, which consolidated its fragmented CSR budget behind a Grow Up Great program that helps underserved populations in its neighborhoods. This "correlates better with its employees' motivations and is likely to yield significant benefits to the communities the bank serves and relies on."[47]

Socially responsible programs can also generate value for the company. A cement company in India created a program to restore groundwater to arid areas around its mines. The land became farmable, and the company was able to bargain for more mining property.[48]

Sustainable companies in about 25 states in the United States have the option to become benefit corporations (similar to, but not the same as, B corporations like Ben and Jerry's), a status that commits them to meeting certain social and environmental goals of their choosing. This frees them to pursue social goals without being liable for suits claiming they're not putting shareholder value first. They could now, however, be sued by other constituents for not meeting their social and environmental goals.[49]

BACKGROUND

'Silent Spring'

Concern about sustainability originated with the modern environmental movement, which began in the years after World War II. The massive war effort spawned new technologies, materials and chemicals. As factories proliferated, U.S. manufacturers snapped up natural resources from around the world and freely spewed effluents, emissions and toxins from their operations into the environment.

Such pollutants, if noticed, were considered signs of prosperity until the marine biologist and nature writer Rachel Carson published her ground-breaking 1962 book "Silent Spring," about the insecticide DDT. DDT was used during the war to delouse soldiers and clear South Pacific islands of mosquitos. After the war it was widely sprayed in the United States. In "Silent Spring," Carson showed how DDT was killing insects, birds, fish and small animals, and was lodging in human tissue, where it causes genetic mutations and cancer.[50]

"Silent Spring" raised public awareness of environmental problems. People started to worry about what other invisible chemicals might be affecting them.[51]

Paul Ehrlich's 1968 book, "The Population Bomb," raised the specter of unchecked population growth and consequent consumption degrading the environment. This was apparent as postwar urban sprawl and the rise of the car reconfigured much of the country. The resulting smog in the biggest cities, Los Angeles and New York, caused stinging eyes, asthma, bronchitis and cardiac problems, much as it does in Beijing today.[52] Other causal links were established. Nitrogen oxides and sulfur dioxide from industrial smokestacks were combining with hydrogen and oxygen to form acid rain, which was killing plant and animal life in and around lakes and rivers.[53]

EPA Versus Business

Growing awareness of the destructive effects of oil spills, raw sewage, toxic dumps and overbuilding led to public pressure to clean up the environment.[54] A 1969 New York Times editorial called the environmental cause "more permanent, more far-reaching, than any issue of the era."[55] In 1970, President Richard M. Nixon established the Environmental Protection Agency (EPA) to direct the war on pollution. The new agency consolidated the duties of various governmental departments that had had jurisdiction over water, soil waste and air. A few months later, 20 million people turned out for the first Earth Day.

EPA's first administrator put business on notice when he announced that the agency had "no obligation to promote commerce or agriculture."[56] Congress then passed the Endangered Species, Clean Air and Safe Drinking Water acts.

EPA began slapping businesses with fines and lawsuits for pollution damage. As a result, manufacturers came to see the agency and the environment as the enemy, and pollution cleanup as an onerous cost and impediment to business. Where companies did comply with regulations, their solution, dubbed "end of pipe," was to spend money for costly cleanups of damage already done.[57]

In the 1980s, globalization, deregulation and growing friction between the developed and developing worlds fueled awareness of unrestrained corporate growth and degradation of natural and human resources. The United Nations responded by forming the U.N. World Commission on Environment and Development (WCED), which defined sustainability for the first time in its 1987 report, "Our Common Future." Sustainability was described as "development that meets the needs of the present without compromising the ability of future generations to meet their own needs."[58]

Also called the Brundtland report for its chair, Norwegian Prime Minister Gro Harlem Brundtland, the report reframed the world as a global system where universal issues were inextricably linked: "The environment is where we all live," development is how we get ahead and society is who we are.[59] These became the three pillars of sustainability: environmental protection, social advancement and economic development.

Besides environmental issues, competitive pressures were pushing businesses to look at sustainability. In the late 1970s and early 1980s, Japan outstripped the United States in the production and sale of all kinds of goods. By comparison, American conglomerates seemed bloated, unwieldy and unfocused.[60] Japan's secret was a highly systematic management method that originated in America in the 1920s and was taught to the Japanese in the 1950s by engineer W. Edwards Deming.[61]

The method, Total Quality Management (TQM), stressed continuously analyzing production processes to eliminate unnecessary steps, make operations more efficient, improve product quality and empower and educate employees. Above all, TQM demanded the elimination of waste. To compete, some U.S. executives also adopted these principles, trimming corporate fat.[62]

Participants in the first Earth Day on April 20, 1970, chalk their messages on a New York City street. That same year, the federal Environmental Protection Agency was established. Many businesses quickly came to see the EPA as the enemy.

Source: Santi Visalli/Getty Images

Moving Toward Metrics

In 1984, a toxic chemical leak at a Union Carbide pesticide plant in India killed and maimed thousands of people.[63] In the United States, EPA responded by requiring companies handling certain amounts of chemicals to fill out a Toxics Release Inventory (TRI) of some 650 chemicals. This information was made public so communities surrounding these companies could be prepared for potential leaks.[64]

"We could argue that the TRI was one of the most important and effective pieces of social legislation ever passed," wrote Stuart L. Hart in his seminal book on sustainability, "Capitalism at the Crossroads: Next Generation Business Strategies for a Post-Crisis World."[65]

Although the inventory didn't require companies to do anything about these chemicals except report them, the TRI let companies, analysts and the public compare users, Hart said. As a result, many companies started reducing or eliminating their waste to improve their reputations. These published results were one of the first environmental metrics.[66]

Inspired by TQM and the push for greater efficiency, some companies began to reduce their toxic waste upfront, in the design and production process rather than at the end of the pipe. By planning ahead, assessing and analyzing operations and products, corporations found they not only increased their brand value but also could save millions of dollars.[67] "If you're producing something in a really dirty way and have to invest to clean it up after the fact, it's not only expensive, but a pretty poor way to run your business," says Mark Milstein, director of the Center for Sustainable Global Enterprise at Cornell's Johnson Graduate School of Management.

One way to reduce waste upfront was to substitute toxic ingredients with harmless agents that would do the same thing or to innovate new processes that recycle manufacturing materials.[68] Nike is a good example, according to MIT's Jay. Its original Nike Air shoe had a bladder under the heel that contained a potent greenhouse gas, sulfur hexafluoride. The company replaced it with nitrogen, but being a smaller molecule, the nitrogen started leaking out. "So they stumbled on a new material that could hold nitrogen and allow them to extend the bladder under the whole shoe," says Jay. Still Nike's process left waste around cutouts of shoe tops. Its designers tried different ways to improve the process, ultimately inventing the Flyknit, in which the tops are all one thread interlocking with itself, says Jay.

In 1992, government and industry members attending the first worldwide economic development conference in Rio de Janeiro called for a standardized system of corporate practices to ensure the quality of products and to facilitate international trade. The International Standards Organization (ISO) had developed a series of standards for the Total Quality Management process called the ISO 9000 series. Now it developed a new series based on environmental improvements so companies could compare their processes. The ISO 14001 followed TQM principles of planning ahead, setting and implementing goals, measuring progress and starting over. This became the base line certification for sustainability.

Around the same time, Ceres began the Global Reporting Initiative (GRI), which became its own nongovernmental organization (NGO). This initiative expanded the reporting criteria beyond the environment, social and financial goals to include governance, which required companies to report on involvement by corporate boards and behavior toward employees.[69]

The next step was eliminating waste altogether by reusing the components of a product through remanufacturing new or different products from waste in a closed cycle. The concept, called Cradle-to-Cradle (C2C), was introduced in 2002 by architect William McDonough and chemist Michael Braungart of McDonough Braungart Design Chemistry. The goal was to go beyond incremental improvements such as cutting a firm's carbon footprint by, say, 20 percent over the previous year. McDonough argued for creating a zero or positive footprint. Many companies now strive to achieve this.[70]

Shaw Floors, a leading carpet and tile maker based in Dalton, Ga.,, was an early C2C manufacturer. It built a machine that could chew up old carpet and spew out the basic nylon fiber it was made from. Shaw spins this fiber into fresh carpet, which it can do indefinitely without degrading the product. The company has collection centers around the country for its used carpet. By reclaiming and remanufacturing its basic raw material, it kept most of the finished product out of landfills.[71]

Supply Chains

U.S. companies in the late 20th century began outsourcing their manufacturing to take advantage of cheap labor in developing countries. Starting in 1991, the press and activists denounced Nike for employing mostly women and children in Southeast Asian factories in abusive conditions where they were exposed to dangerous equipment and toxins, as well as subjected to emotional abuse. These laborers were paid little, and 70-hour workweeks were common.[72] The company at first blamed these problems on its subcontractors, but public protests and falling stock values forced Nike to take responsibility. "The Nike product has become synonymous with slave wages, forced overtime and arbitrary abuse," then-CEO Philip Knight said. "I truly believe the American consumer doesn't want to buy products made under abusive conditions." Nike started auditing the factories and publishing detailed reports on conditions there.[73]

The company went on to become a top sustainability leader, but the scandal became a warning to other executives about what attacks on their reputations could do.

U.N. guiding principles said businesses' corporate social responsibility extended to their "business relationships." Companies began looking into their supply chains and found plenty to worry about. They started urging their suppliers to abide by their sustainability goals and to follow environmentally sensitive practices. Yet only 54 percent of corporate leaders who thought they should be integrating sustainability throughout their supply chains believed this had been achieved within their company, according to management consultant Accenture.[74]

CURRENT SITUATION

Integrated Reporting

Sustainability may be coming into sharper focus with the efforts to create a standard that would combine nonfinancial information with a company's hard numbers. This is called integrated reporting, which many in this field have been anticipating for a long time.

Three documents determine a company's health in the eyes of the financial market: a balance sheet, a profit and loss statement, and a cash flow statement. "But these are three documents which don't tell you very much about the overall impact of that business. So, we desperately need to develop a system to try and measure and quantify and communicate the wider stakeholder engagement," said Badr Jafar, managing director of the Crescent Group, an oil conglomerate in the UAE.[75]

Sustainability reports have long served as adjuncts to corporate financial reports. Companies often disclose their numerical progress on carbon reduction or savings from a cleaner process, but this information is easy to dismiss as window dressing.[76] Integrated reporting would combine nonfinancial data with the hard financial data investors look at to assess the value of a company. An integrated report would link environmental stewardship, treatment of stakeholders and governance decisions with the financial value of the company now and in the future.[77]

"To many people, environment, society and governance sound like tree-hugging, or a good-versus-evil thing," says RepRisk's Cichon. "Not so; it's just common sense about how to do good business."

The oldest of the three nonprofits offering integrated reporting is the Global Reporting Initiative (GRI): Its format presents side-by-side reporting of financial and sustainability information. Many companies use it for organizing their sustainability information, so it's already familiar.[78]

In the past three years the International Integrated Reporting Council (IIRC) and the Sustainability Accounting Standards Board (SASB) have developed different frameworks for integrated reporting. IIRC calls for reporting six different capital flows: financial, manufactured, human, intellectual, social and natural. These are at once both broader and simpler than the GRI's latest iteration.[79]

SASB is modeled on the Financial Accounting Standards Board (FASB), a private-sector nonprofit group that works with the SEC and businesses to set and improve officially recognized corporate accounting standards.[80] SASB is creating detailed standards for 89 industries in 10 sectors across categories that include innovation, governance and human, social and environmental capital.[81] It is hoping the SEC will adopt its standards. "These are all mission-driven organizations trying to get sustainability taken as seriously as financial information," says Cichon.

But she adds that SASB, if adopted by the SEC, would make the most difference because companies could be held liable if they run afoul of the guidelines. "Volunteer reporting is not working as well," Cichon says. It's not clear what will happen with these three different plans. And some experts are getting frustrated by the choices. "Some of us would want to see them work together more," Cichon says.

Collaborations

More companies are teaming up to address challenges, such as air pollution, that are too big for any one entity to resolve alone. Supply chain sourcing has brought companies in the same industry together in roundtables on palm oil, cotton and beef, to ensure the sustainability of these ingredients from suppliers.

Once opposed to government, which regulated them, and "tree-hugging" nonprofits, which harassed them, sustainable corporations now regularly work with both of them. In fact, many companies are crying out for government policies that will define the terrain so they can know how to proceed. Until then, these companies are stuck in limbo, not sure how to plan for the future.[82]

In the meantime, they work with nonprofits, stakeholders and competitors. "The challenge is likely to encourage a much more collaborative form of capitalism," said Unilever's Polman. "Companies will have to work with each other, not just with governments, non-governmental organizations (NGOs), and civil society. Issues like deforestation and species extinction cannot be tackled by just one company acting alone; they will require collaboration within, and across, industry sectors."[83]

GM and Honda have partnered to develop fuel cells for electric cars. Developing a battery to store significant amounts of electricity would be a huge breakthrough. Electric cars could drive much longer without recharging, and renewable energy could be stored for use when the sun isn't shining, or the wind blowing. "For almost a century, we've been searching for batteries that are cheap enough to use in cars," says Julie Gorte, senior vice president for sustainable investing at Pax World Management, an investment company. "Now they cost $38,000 per kilowatt."

Honda and GM have filed the most patents in battery development, and Honda intends to introduce its offering in 2015. Fuel cell batteries enable electric cars to drive farther than existing electric vehicles before recharging (in minutes) and electric vehicles can accelerate quickly, according to the Greencar Congress, a website devoted to news about sustainable mobility.[84]

Ocean Spray and Tropicana teamed up to save on transportation costs. Tropicana was shipping its products to a distribution center in New Jersey in refrigerated trains, which returned empty. Ocean Spray was trucking its products to Florida because the train line didn't go close enough to its warehouses. But Tropicana trains did. Reluctant to share with a rival at first, Ocean Spray was able to save considerable money and emissions by shipping its products south on Tropicana's empty train.[85]

Regulations

EPA is set to go ahead with President Obama's clean-power plan announced in June 2014, which calls for a 30 percent reduction of carbon emissions from power plants over 2005 levels by 2030. These proposed rules are supposed to go into effect in June 2015.[86] More recently, the president announced a goal to cut methane gas emissions from oil and natural gas by 40 percent to 45 percent from 2012 levels by 2025. Methane is a more potent greenhouse gas than carbon.

EPA will work with industry and the states to achieve these goals while still allowing the fossil fuel industry to grow, the White House says. The plan would give money to the Department of Energy to develop ways to help natural gas companies seal leaks during transmission, for example.[87]

Congressional Republicans and fossil fuel industry leaders object to both plans. "The Obama administration's latest attack on American energy reaffirms that their agenda is not about the climate at all," said Thomas Pyle, president of the Institute for Energy Research. "It's about driving up the cost of producing and using natural gas, oil, and coal in America."[88] The National Association of Manufacturers has long lobbied for giving equal opportunity to all energy sources. The fossil fuel industry, led by logging, mining and oil conglomerate Koch Industries, has helped fill Congress and most state governorships with sympathetic Republicans via a PAC that allows unlimited giving.[89] Whether the clean power plan and other environmental regulations take effect may depend on who becomes the next president.[90]

LOOKING AHEAD

Optimistic Predictions

Experts say the sustainable business movement is gaining momentum.[91] It may grow in fits and starts, but it will no doubt spread among more companies as it continues to be defined and to evolve, they argue. The growing threat of climate change, a new tech-savvy workforce, greater regulation and better understanding of how to profit from sustainability could mean that sustainability is here to stay. "Even if we ignore it, it doesn't cease to be real," says Christopher Cooke, manager of the measurement science working group at The Sustainability Consortium. "There is a groundswell of companies that realize if they want longevity and consumer respect and loyalty that sustainability really helps."

"We will see increased awareness of sustainability issues in business and investing, often prompted by some disaster or series of disasters," says Pax World's Gorte. "I think the perception of how to manage and measure corporate vulnerabilities to the physical risks of climate is a good bet to become more popular in investment and business over the next half-decade."

The need for skilled labor will be another incentive driving sustainable development. As more baby boomers retire, millennials will take over the workforce. These valuable "knowledge workers" are tech savvy and innovation minded. They want meaningful work and won't hesitate to leave if they don't get it, according to several experts.[92] Surveys show they are a good fit for sustainable values. They want corporate transparency and believe that success should be measured by more than profits.[93]

According to studies, millennials want training, career goals, feedback, competitive wages, work/life balance and other perks. They want to feel they are serving the greater good. Sustainable companies are more likely to attract and retain them, and millennials may reshape companies in sustainable ways.[94]

Some millennials, called "social entrepreneurs," are starting innovative programs to solve the pressing social needs of poor communities around the world. Others are founding companies based on new sustainable technology. For example, two college students worked for 10 years to find a cost-effective way to make plastic out of methane. Using a biological catalyst, AirCarbon, they developed a product that not only creates petroleum-free plastics but also removes a dangerous greenhouse gas from the atmosphere. The AirMaster carpet by Desso cleans the air in a room by attracting particulates and allergens. EcoATM by

Outerwall is an ATM that takes recycled products in exchange for cash and sells them through a network of buyers. BioTrans collects and grinds up leftovers at restaurants into a biomass that it stores until it can be hauled to plants to be used as biogas.[95]

Technology, too, can further the cause of sustainability. Big data and the ability to analyze it will illuminate new sustainable business models and manufacturing operations. Most companies will need more and more powerful software to create smart products and run the Internet of Things. Accenture reports that "we may begin to achieve speed and scale in transformation only when business is able to capture the potential from digital infrastructure solutions and digitization." As Praveer Sinha, CEO of Tata Power Delhi Distribution, put it: "The technology transformation has to come; technology is the game-changer."[96] For example, GE, which manufactures a variety of smart products, from toasters to jet planes, is increasingly run by smart technology.[97] The company uses a combination of sensors, software and nanotechnology to design planes and trains that can report in advance when the machinery needs maintenance, and jet planes with turbines that can adjust to save fuel.

"If you went to bed last night as an industrial company, you're going to wake up this morning as a software and analytics company," said GE's Immelt.[98]

Chronology

1960s–1970s	**Environmentalism takes hold, setting the stage for the rise of the sustainability movement.**
1962	Rachel Carson's "Silent Spring" describes the link between chemicals and human health. Her trail-blazing book leads to greater environmental awareness.
1968	Paul Ehrlich's "The Population Bomb" warns of environmental degradation from population growth and overconsumption.
1970	The U.S. Environmental Protection Agency (EPA) is established with independent powers to regulate the environment. …Millions turn out to attend the first Earth Day to celebrate the importance of the environment.
1971	The cause of acid rain—industrial pollutants—is discovered.
1973	OPEC cuts oil supplies to the United States, leading to gasoline shortages and long lines at the pump.
Mid-1970s	Leaks are found at a chemical dump at Love Canal in upstate New York; the government is forced to buy nearby poisoned homes.
1980s–1990s	**The sustainability movement emerges.**
1980s	Total Quality Management, a system for eliminating waste from the production process, is adopted by some leading companies.
1984	A leak at a Union Carbide chemical plant kills thousands of people in Bhopal, India.
1985	Chlorofluorocarbons (CFCs) used in refrigerants, cleaning fluids and aerosol cans are found to cause holes in the Earth's ozone layer.
1986	EPA establishes the Toxics Release Inventory, where companies list their toxic chemicals.
1987	The World Commission on Environment and Development, also known as the Brundtland Commission, defines "sustainability" in a report called "Our Common Future."

(Continued)

	(Continued)
1989	Exxon Valdez spills some 11 million gallons of oil into Prince William Sound off Alaska. . . . Nonprofit Ceres is founded in the wake of the Exxon Valdez spill to bring together environmentalists and capitalists to form a sustainable business model.
1994	John Elkington introduces the triple bottom line as a way for companies to organize economic, social and environmental costs and achievements.
1996	The International Standards Organization publishes the first sustainability standards.
1997	The Global Reporting Initiative issues guidelines for reporting on sustainable issues. About 100 companies sign on.
2000s–Present	**Sustainability goes mainstream.**
2002	Architect William McDonough and chemist Michael Braungart publish "Cradle to Cradle: Remaking the Way We Make Things," proposing a closed system for remanufacturing used products to eliminate waste.
2004	In "The Fortune at the Bottom of the Pyramid—Eradicating Poverty Through Profits," management guru C.K. Prahalad writes about the huge potential market for companies able to sell to people making less than $1.25 a day.
2006	"An Inconvenient Truth," the Academy Award-winning documentary by former Vice President Al Gore, publicizes the evidence for global climate change.
2010	BP's Deep Water Horizon rig explodes, spilling 210 million gallons of oil in the Gulf of Mexico. . . . International Integrated Reporting Council, an attempt to integrate sustainability and financial reporting, is founded.
2012	Sustainability Accounting Standards Board starts writing sustainability accounting standards that include environmental risks and social factors. These would be integrated with financial annual reports.
2013	Oil companies start putting a dollar value on carbon in anticipation of a possible carbon tax.
2014	President Obama announces a clean power plan, which would cut carbon pollution from existing power plants.

RESOURCES

The Next Step

Accountability

Conti, David, "Center for Sustainable Shale Development aims to raise standards," Pittsburgh Tribune-Review, Jan. 11, 2015, http://tinyurl.com/o32g39t.

The Pittsburgh-based Center for Sustainable Shale Development, created in 2013 to certify natural gas companies for sustainable standards, aims to broaden its regulation of Pennsylvania's energy industry in 2015.

Leinaweaver, Jeff, "Might new financial tools translate ESG data into real-world loss and profit?" The Guardian (U.K.), Nov. 25, 2013, http://tinyurl.com/o2osvoh.

Bloomberg and Thomson Reuters have created databases containing economic, social and governance data from thousands of businesses to enable reporters and organizations to hold companies accountable for sustainability initiatives.

Roston, Eric, "Sustainable Companies Want to Be Transparent—But Not Too Transparent," Bloomberg, Feb. 11, 2014, http://tinyurl.com/p6b95tn.

Corporate counsel are wary of sharing too much information, as companies make environmental impact, social issue and corporate governance data more publicly accessible, according to the director of a sustainability consulting firm.

Environmentalism

Doyle, Alister, "IKEA may tighten carbon rules to protect environment," Reuters, Oct. 13, 2014, http://tinyurl.com/l32rtbt.

Swedish furniture retailer Ikea will shift energy investments away from fossil fuels and toward solar and wind power in 2015, while also purchasing more wood and cotton from sustainable sources.

Elgin, Ben, "No More Faking It: Companies Ditch Green Credits, Clean Up Instead," Bloomberg Businessweek, Dec. 17, 2014, http://tinyurl.com/n9h2zu3.

More companies are dismissing the positive effects of purchasing renewable-energy credits, each equating to one hour of renewable-energy supply, in favor of pursuing their own renewable energy.

Strom, Stephanie, "Walmart Aims to Go Greener on Food," The New York Times, Oct. 6, 2014, http://tinyurl.com/mzb97jx.

Walmart plans to collaborate with food suppliers to reduce its environmental footprint resulting from food production, to improve access to healthy foods and to reward farmers for sustainable practices.

Philanthropy

Kozlov, Klara, "New survey shows FTSE 100 companies have increased charitable giving," The Guardian (U.K.), Aug. 14, 2014, http://tinyurl.com/nfwqyvm.

Research by the U.K.-based Charities Aid Foundation shows charitable donations by companies in London's FTSE 100 stock exchange nearly doubled between 2007 and 2012.

Seervai, Shanoor, "Indian Companies and Charities Aren't Ready for New Giving Law," The Wall Street Journal, April 11, 2014, http://tinyurl.com/pq864ju.

India's nonprofits must learn to manage more philanthropic donations after a new law took effect requiring companies to give 2 percent of their profits to causes such as hunger, gender equality and environmental sustainability.

Shwab, Klaus, "Business in a Changing World," Foreign Affairs, Jan. 6, 2015, http://tinyurl.com/ol6l4dt.

Global business will benefit long-term if companies innovate in corporate governance, philanthropy, social entrepreneurship, citizenship and accountability, according to the executive chairman of the World Economic Forum.

Profitability

Grene, Sophia, The bottom line is a sustainability one," Financial Times (U.K), Sept. 21, 2014, http://tinyurl .com/ps4vq22.

A study by researchers from the University of Oxford's Smith School of Enterprise and the Environment indicates that practicing sustainability directly correlates to improved stock price performance for companies.

Kukil, Bora, "New Report On Global Corporate Sustainability Practices Shows Talkers Outnumber The Doers," International Business Times, Dec. 18, 2013, http://tinyurl.com/p3cw572.

According to research by the MIT Sloan Management Review and The Boston Consulting Group, there are more companies claiming to pursue sustainability for increased profits and reputational gains than companies that actually pursue those actions.

Miller, Joe, "War on waste makes sustainable business more profitable," BBC, May 19, 2014, http://tinyurl .com/pevv485.

International waste management companies and sustainability nonprofits working with major corporations advise their clients that sustainable disposal makes most busi- nesses more competitive.

Organizations

American Sustainable Business Council
401 New York Ave., N.W., Suite 1225, Washington, D.C. 20005
202-595-9302
http://asbcouncil.org

A national advocacy group that works for a sustainable economy.

CDP (formerly the Carbon Discovery Project)
132 Crosby St., 8th Floor, New York, NY 10012
212-378-2086
www.cdp.net

Major nonprofit that works with companies and other stakeholders to transform business to prevent climate change.

Ceres (the Coalition for Environmentally Responsible Economies)
99 Chauncy St., 6th Floor, Boston, MA 02111
617-247-0700
www.ceres.org

Nonprofit for investors and businesses in sustainability that has numerous studies about industries, company rankings, and sustainability advice.

GreenBiz Group
350 Frank H. Ogawa Plaza, Oakland, CA 94612

510-550-8285

www.greenbiz.com

A varied and thorough source of news, reports and events.

International Institute for Sustainable Development

61 Portage Ave. E., 6th Floor, Winnipeg, Manitoba, Canada R3BOY4

204-958-7700

www.iisd.org.

International public policy research and lobbying institute for sustainable development.

Sustainability Consortium

Arizona State University Global Institute of Sustainability, P.O. Box 873511,

Tempe, AZ 85287-3511

480-965-1770

www.sustainabilityconsortium.org

Trade association seeking a scientific foundation for innovation to improve consumer product sustainability.

Sustainable Manufacturer Network

833 Featherstone Rd., Rockford, IL 61107

815-399-8700

http://sustainablemfr.com

Industry association that promotes "cost-effective, environmentally and socially responsible manufacturing."

U.S. Forum for Sustainable and Responsible Investment

1660 L St., N.W., Suite 306, Washington, DC 20036

202-872 5361

www.ussif.org

Association for professionals, firms, institutions and organizations engaged in sustainable, responsible and impact investing.

PERSPECTIVE

Pro/Con: Campher on Selling Green

YES

DO CONSUMERS BUY SUSTAINABLE PRODUCTS?

*Senior Vice President for Business and Social Purpose/Managing Director, Sustainability
Edelman*

Written for SAGE Business Researcher, February 2015

We somehow cling to the belief that consumers don't care about sustainability and that price and quality are the main reasons why people buy things—that social and environmental issues just don't matter. But that's simply not true. The challenge is rather that the consumer world changes in an evolutionary—not revolutionary—way.

Imagine a world without Tom's of Maine or Ben & Jerry's, Tesla, Levi's, Starbucks, Stonyfield Farms, Timberland, Seventh Generation or Chipotle. Or organic food or fair trade products. All of these have become mainstream products. And they are growing fast. Who is growing rapidly at the moment—Chipotle or McDonalds? Where do you think the biggest growth in sales lie—hybrid cars or traditional? The list goes on. Imagine how few of those products were on that same shelf 20 years ago. Many of these products have become mainstream. They are so much a part of our lives today that we forget that they are still new when considering the life of a consumer product.

Sales continue to grow each year, some faster than others. That is simply the nature of evolution.

Not every product is an iPhone—some take time to grow, and they grow by fits and starts. Companies aren't shrugging and turning their backs on consumers. They're using this evolution to transform their products and brands to drive new growth in sales and consumer support. We need to realize that sustainable products have grown up faster than we did—and so have consumers.

We are wrong when we think consumers aren't buying into sustainability and aren't buying products and brands they believe add to a more sustainable lifestyle and world. They are, but not the way we want it. That's our problem, not theirs. This is a business problem to solve, not a consumer's. We know they want to buy sustainable products (or products with sustainability as part of the brand value proposition), and we know they want to buy more. The problem is to find better ways to bring sustainability to life for consumers in ways that will resonate with them, and foster even faster growth. We know they will buy it—just don't try to sell them snake oil.

Pro/Con: Friedlander on Selling Green

NO

DO CONSUMERS BUY SUSTAINABLE PRODUCTS?

Chair, Green and Socially Responsible Business
College of the Atlantic

Written for SAGE Business Researcher, February 2015

Reflecting on a decade of green consumerism, the executive editor of GreenBiz.com, Joel Makower, wrote, "Consumers, for all their good intentions, don't really want to change. They want what they want—and what they feel they need and deserve."

Survey after survey confirms that even if consumers say they want and care about sustainable products, they're not willing to pay extra for them. Faced with the realities of the register, most consumers would rather have the money for their own bills versus paying extra to "save the planet."

The payment barrier is exacerbated by an atmosphere of confusion created by proliferating claims about the eco-friendliness of products. U.S. consumers are overwhelmed by the amount of environmental messaging they receive. In addition, limited distribution and concerns about product efficacy further inhibit sales.

Given these findings, it is hardly surprising that the Greendex 2014 Report on Consumer Choice and the Environment by National Geographic and GlobeScan concluded: "It is clear that increased environmental concern is not manifesting in substantive behavior change" on the part of consumers.

Since consumers have not changed their buying habits because of sustainable claims alone, companies launching sustainable products need to put the desires of their customers at the forefront in order to succeed.

The story of Deja Shoe embodies these lessons. It began in the 1990s as an environmental footwear company, and groups as diverse as the American Marketing Association and the United Nations lauded Deja's recycled footwear. Given the high profile of climate change and .the Rio Earth Summit in 1992, national retailers were eager to stock the shoes. Consumers, however, were another story. Sales were lackluster because shoes didn't meet customers' expectations on style, performance or price. Predictably, despite its environmental story and credentials, Deja went out of business a few years later.

Sustainably minded companies beat the competition by addressing a need that's less abstract than climate change. The sustainably focused car-sharing service Zipcar created a viable alternative to car ownership by providing the benefits of owning a car, such as convenience, along with access to multiple brands. Customers saved money and avoided hassles like parking, insurance and maintenance. In 14 years, Zipcar grew from a start-up with a few VW Beetles to being acquired by Avis for $500 million.

In a world where consumers are not motivated by sustainability alone, companies must merge their sustainability focus with customer expectations.

12

FAILURE
What can businesses learn when things go wrong?
Vickie Elmer

EXECUTIVE SUMMARY

Failure has long carried costs and stigma, both personal and professional. In some business sectors, though, notably the technology industry, failure has become acceptable, even fashionable. It's inevitable that people who try new things will not always succeed. Fear of failure stifles creativity and innovation, advocates say. Bankruptcy has become a business decision, rather than a cause for personal shame, and it can allow firms to become stronger and more nimble. Nonetheless, critical oversights and bad financial moves still hurt entrepreneurs, shareholders, workers and communities. Among the questions under debate: Is failure good for the economy? Is failure necessary for long-term success? Are there cultural and regional differences in how people react to failure?

OVERVIEW

When three friends from Grand Rapids, Mich., started a storytelling event focused on failure, they met people over coffee to discuss such questions as, "What is an impactful failure that changed the trajectory of your life?"

Their project, Failure: Lab, debuted in early 2012, when the unemployment rate in Michigan still hovered around 9 percent and its largest city, Detroit, unsuccessfully debated budget cuts and alternatives to bankruptcy.[1] People shared stories of divorce and of bad career choices, of uprooting family to move to New York and of rock CDs that cost $1 million to produce and sold only 7,000 copies. For Brian Vander Ark and his Verve Pipe band, that album resembled a "400 pound bowling ball covered in grease."[2]

Their stories, told in seven to 10 minutes, are shared on YouTube. Storytellers are asked to "dig deep for that intimate personal story of failure. It's . . . a public confession with no lessons," no uplifting comeback, said co-founder Jordan O'Neil.[3]

Humans have long feared failure. When people make mistakes, they can hurt themselves and others, their reputations and their futures. When managers and companies fail,

From *SAGE Business Researcher,*
January 4, 2016

customers, creditors, communities and employers can suffer. But public sharing of failure at venues such as Failure: Lab has become fashionable in some sectors, especially technology, where failure has lost much of its stigma. CEOs, experts and consultants share failure lessons at conferences, interviews for major media and in LinkedIn posts. The result: a business culture that increasingly celebrates what used to be shunned.

"In an age of constant change, the only real failure is the failure to try, improve and evolve. . . . These days, start-up flameouts are increasingly serving as badges of honor and—especially in Silicon Valley—failure has become a bragging right," Sheryl Connelly, Ford Motor Co.'s trend spotter and futurist, wrote in Ford's 2015 Trends report.[4]

For instance, LinkedIn co-founder Reid Hoffman has shared big lessons from his failed first venture—including the importance of finding customers from the start.[5] Start-up founders swap stories about "fail fast" and ideas that went south at F—-up Nights, another global storytelling gathering, which sometimes goes by its acronym FUN. Writers and business leaders have poured out their perspective in a growing number of failure books, such as "The Up Side of Down" by Megan McArdle and "Rising Strong" by Brené Brown.

A handful of companies even give failure awards to encourage staff to dare something different and new. Among them is a "Heroic Failure" trophy that Grey, a large New York-based advertising agency, presents for the most creative mistake. An early winner: One staffer used kitty poo buried in cat litter under a conference room table to pitch a possible cat litter client.[6] At Google X, the search company's laboratory working on shoot-for-the-moon projects, Astro Teller leads the teams of engineers and creators. He rewards failure, because it gives people courage to take risks.[7]

"The most successful people tend to be those with the most failures," Dean Keith Simonton, a University of California, Davis, psychology professor, told The Wall Street Journal.[8]

Australian futurist Wendy Elford sees value in failure and the trade-offs businesses make to manage risk while seeking innovation. "Preventing failure is enormously expensive. . . . We can't plan to succeed if everything we do is preventing losing," says Elford, who focuses on the changing nature of work.

Management guru Peter Drucker said he mistrusted any man who "never commits a blunder, never fails in what he tries to do. He is either a phony, or he stays with the safe, the tried and the trivial."[9]

Yet some companies or sectors fear losing or are so risk-averse that they cannot or will not join the "cheer failure" movement. When lives are at stake—in hospitals and nursing homes—or actuarial tables clearly spell out the risks, as they do for insurers, failure is viewed with trepidation.

What failure means and looks like may vary as widely as corporate strategies or worker ethics. At one extreme are catastrophic failures such as nuclear plant accidents; in the middle may be a missed opportunity to land a plum leadership role or a worker who ignores instructions and breaks the photocopier.

Harvard Business School professor Amy C. Edmondson suggested a "spectrum of reasons for failure," from deviance to "exploratory testing." She wrote, "In organizational life, it is sometimes bad, sometimes inevitable, and sometimes even good."[10]

The same holds true in personal life and careers; acceptance of a failure may depend on mind-set, financial and emotional health, self-confidence, support and other factors, researchers have found.

With such diversity, measuring failure requires many scales and data sets. Here are a few:

- Between 50 and 80 percent of all corporate mergers fail to add value, or may even cause serious damage.[11] Various researchers say that, historically, 50 to 75 percent to as high as 80 percent of all start-up businesses fail.[12]

- The recession of 2007–09—which some argue resulted from failed banking practices and lax regulatory oversight—cost the U.S. economy $14 trillion, or up to 90 percent of U.S. output in 2007.[13]

- In the United States, young adults are not landing full-time work. Of young men in their 20s, only 65 percent hold full-time jobs, down from 80 percent in 2000.[14] Forty percent of unemployed workers are Millennials, higher than their overall share of the population.[15]

- Approximately 1 million people and businesses in the United States file for bankruptcy every year, although the number fell 11 percent to 860,182 in fiscal 2015—the lowest tally since 2007.[16]

Bankruptcies on the Decline

Such well-known companies as American Apparel, Conseco, Texaco, Pacific Gas & Electric and Washington Mutual have filed for bankruptcy court protection, and quite a few go through Chapter 11s two or more times.[17] In a Chapter 11, named for a section of the U.S. bankruptcy laws, a company or individual gets breathing space from creditors while restructuring debts. Sometimes the next step is failure, and sometimes it is a new and stronger enterprise freed from old obligations.

Billionaire Donald Trump trumpets himself as a great leader in his bid for the Republican presidential nomination, even though he has stumbled in and out of businesses selling vodka, mortgages and airline flights.[18]

Sometimes it's difficult to tell whether a company is failing or is just reinventing itself in the face of market changes. And sometimes the disruption may backfire: When banks and others started offering subprime mortgages, the loans were seen as an innovation that opened doors to low-income consumers.[19] Yet that lending sowed the seeds of the largest financial and economic meltdown since the Great Depression.

Researchers have found that bankruptcy's stigma has faded, starting in the 1970s. This occurred as media coverage suggested a bad economy, inflation or other external factors were to blame instead of an individual's mistakes or overconsumption, according to Rafael Efrat,

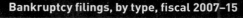

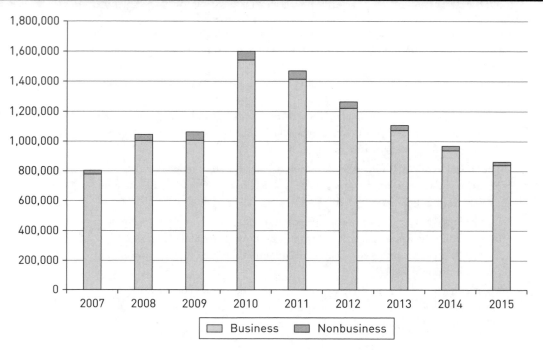

Bankruptcy filings, by type, fiscal 2007–15

Business   Nonbusiness

U.S. bankruptcy filings have declined for five years since rising to nearly 1.6 million in the aftermath of the 2007–09 recession. Nonbusiness, or consumer, bankruptcies enable individuals to sell assets or restructure payments to creditors over time to repay debts for personal expenses. Business bankruptcies provide the same options to businesses and, while less common than consumer bankruptcies, generally involve more money.

Source: "Fiscal Year Bankruptcy Filings Continue Fall," United States Courts, Oct. 28, 2015, http://tinyurl.com/py2vsc6

a California State University, Northridge, accounting professor whose team analyzed 176 articles about personal bankruptcy published by The New York Times from 1864 to 2002.[20]

"Prior to the 1960s, newspaper articles depicted debtors largely as manipulators and fraud promoters," Efrat wrote. More recently, those who were bankrupt were portrayed as "simply rash and immature" and also victims of high inflation, stock market losses or increases in society's overall personal debt.

Even if they secretly feel embarrassed by their failure or foreclosure or a screwup at their university, Americans often share those moments on social media or in support groups.

"The shame factor has really declined," says Teresa Kohl, who has worked on corporate restructurings for almost 20 years.

Yet society's acceptance of failure and bankruptcy as more common does not remove the stigma from the individual—especially if she is a business owner whose identity is closely entwined with her enterprise.[21]

Failure may still trigger shame, grief, depression and loss, experts say. When the unemployment rate rises, so do drug and alcohol abuse, as well as spousal abuse. Crime may increase if some long-term unemployed individuals see that as the way to get money, says Carl Van Horn, professor of public policy at Rutgers University and an expert in employment issues.

Sometimes fear of failure creates incentives to excel, reinvigorate the business—or offer health insurance to workers. Starbucks CEO Howard

Starbucks CEO Howard Schultz greets a barista at one of the company's stores in Charleston, S.C. His personal experience growing up is one driver of the company's policy of offering health insurance to all employees.

Source: Chip Somodevilla/Getty Images

Schultz could be Exhibit A. When he was growing up in Brooklyn, N.Y., his father held a series of jobs—truck driver, factory worker and cab driver—but then broke his ankle and couldn't work. The family had no health insurance and no income. His father's failure to provide is said to be the main driver of Starbucks offering workers, even part-time ones, health insurance coverage.[22]

Fear of failure also may have the opposite effect: It can stop women from starting businesses. It may reduce students' motivation to learn in school.[23] Executives may fear the wrath of Wall Street, which punishes stock prices if companies fail to meet profit numbers. So even those who want to experiment more or encourage risk taking must be mindful of the balancing act so they achieve profitability and other measures of success. "The pressure to perform to hit your numbers has never been greater," says Sydney Finkelstein, Dartmouth College professor of management.

People also may find it impossible to own up to an error without fear of reprisal—losing status or losing a job. "There are still plenty of cultures—which I hear discussed in executive education seminars—[where] the blaming culture exists," Finkelstein says. So managers never mention the mistakes or the misrepresented financials that could have been caught early.

Failure also may be embraced or accepted by executives "with a certain arrogance" about their decisions, Finkelstein says. They may be encouraged to experiment and undertake new products because of financial incentives that reward success with "unbelievable wealth" but carry no cost to salary if the initiative fails, he says.

Others suggest the start-up community, business professors and authors are merely branding and packaging failure. "Every age has a theory of rising and falling, of growth and decay, of bloom and wilt: a theory of nature," Jill Lepore, a professor of American history at Harvard, wrote in The New Yorker. She argued that instead of "progress" Americans now point to "innovation" to avoid questions about "whether a novelty is an improvement."[24]

As businesses and academics examine the mechanics and role of failure, these are some of the questions under debate:

Weighing the Issues

Is failure good for the economy?

Kohl, the restructuring consultant, has experienced failure and bankruptcy from almost every angle, from childhood anxieties to a career as an adviser assisting troubled companies. While she acknowledges how tough such turmoil can be, she sees real value in failure and bankruptcy—both to the U.S. economy and to individual businesses.

Her first taste of failure came as a child in rural Illinois in the late 1970s, a time of record high gas prices and interest rates. Her parents filed personal bankruptcy after running a large farm for years. "It was a horrible, horrible experience," she says.

She skipped college and went straight to work, seeking a stable employer. She chose Laventhol & Horwath, a major accounting firm founded in 1915. She worked there for almost a year. One Sunday evening, her boss called her and told her to collect her personal belongings that evening. The next day, he warned, could be too late.

The 3,500-employee firm filed for Chapter 11 bankruptcy court protection in November 1990 after losing several malpractice suits.[25] Unlike numerous companies that restructure themselves and emerge from bankruptcy, Laventhol never recovered.[26]

Two of Kohl's subsequent employers folded or went through restructurings, so she investigated a career in business overhauls.

She landed a job with a small turnaround company and learned to negotiate with banks, to evaluate the underlying problems in a business and to "fix a company," she says.

"I see companies with no other choice but to shut down unless they go through a bankruptcy," says Kohl, who has worked on corporate turnarounds and restructurings for 15 years. She's now director of SSG Capital Advisors near Philadelphia and is active in the Turnaround Management Association's New York chapter. The restructuring process "creates a renewal that can spur growth and new jobs," Kohl says.

Some economists argue it is worthwhile to redeploy assets and pull the plug on "zombie companies"—firms that are unprofitable, relying on debt or state ownership in China and elsewhere to survive.[27]

For instance, all the bankruptcies and debt restructuring in 2008–09, coming out of the financial crisis and recession, helped revive the U.S. economy and improve corporate competitiveness, according to Stuart Gilson, a professor of business administration at Harvard.[28] Businesses used Chapter 11 to auction off valuable assets or to preserve value as they reduced their debt burdens.

Tight economic times also have produced some giants. "Some of the most successful tech investments of all time—among them Google and Facebook—came about in Silicon Valley's lean times," wrote Farhad Manjoo, a New York Times technology columnist. "This is a paradox of invention, as well as of investing: Bad times feed good ideas, which in turn lead to good times, which breed complacency, waste and lots of bad business plans."[29]

Those tech companies have created thousands of jobs. Successful corporate restructurings preserved many jobs, even when they involved layoffs. All the turnaround consultants, bankruptcy lawyers and distressed-debt investors contribute to the economy, although the numbers are difficult to quantify.

Making failure easier to manage may even support new business development, researchers found in a 29-nation study. Lenient, entrepreneur-friendly bankruptcy laws correlate significantly with levels of entrepreneurship development as measured by the rate of business start-ups. "The less the downside risk involved in filing bankruptcy, the more new firms are founded," according to the business school professors who conducted the research.[30]

Bodie, Calif., an abandoned gold mining boomtown that's now a state park, is an extreme example of what can happen to a community when an important industry fails.

Source: California Department of Parks and Recreation

Clarity about the rules of bankruptcy and failure encourages risk-taking, says Thomas B. Bennett, a retired U.S. bankruptcy court judge in Alabama who is now a lawyer in Washington, D.C. "It encourages people to take risks so you're not going to be put in debtors' prison, like happened in early England [and America]. There's a way to rehabilitate yourself and move forward," he says.

Yet failure carries huge costs, to individuals and the economy. Millions of unemployed individuals and their families grapple with financial and health problems. Failed businesses and banks leave shareholders, suppliers and their communities unpaid, and in the extreme may even create ghost towns.

When businesses fail, stockholders lose—usually shares become worthless. In the case of banks, the U.S. government, which insures deposits, often arranges a marriage to a healthier bank—and gives the groom a nice check for the honeymoon. The 165 banks that failed in 2008 and 2009 during the financial crisis and recession cost the Federal Deposit Insurance Corp. (FDIC) $9 billion in incentives and loss-sharing agreements needed to entice other banks and investors to buy troubled institutions.[31]

At the individual and family level, long-term unemployment may be measured in lost confidence, repossessed cars, poor health and dunning creditor calls. In late 2015, 2.05 million workers were unemployed and looking for work for 27 weeks or longer, half the level of three years earlier but still about a quarter of all jobless individuals.[32]

When workers are unemployed or stuck in low-paying or part-time jobs, that hurts their community and the economy, says Rutgers' Van Horn. "They're not paying taxes. They're no longer consuming as much as they did before because they have no money," he says.

"It means a smaller economy, a less successful economy," Van Horn says, measured in declines to both consumer spending and GDP.

Failure can even lead to ghost towns where all the businesses have closed and all the residents departed—places such as Hashima Island, Japan, once an offshore coal-mining site where thousands lived (most recently famous as the fictional lair of a James Bond villain), or Bodie, Calif., a deserted gold rush boomtown that's now a state park.[33]

Corporate fraud, another type of failure by executives and the boards that oversee them, has been booming, with plenty of cases of accounting fraud, insider trading and kickbacks investigated by the FBI.[34] Half of senior executives worry about the effects of corruption and bribery on their business, and more than one-quarter of companies report bribery or procurement fraud.[35]

At its worst, fraud leads to a company disintegrating, as Enron did in 2001–02 after an accounting scandal by the formerly high-flying energy company led to thousands losing jobs, $2 billion in pensions disappearing and a few executives sent to prison.[36]

Even Gilson, the Harvard professor who is a big proponent of Chapter 11, acknowledged that not all firms come back strong. "Chapter 11 is likely to be prohibitively costly for a consulting firm, whose most valuable assets are intangible or capable of walking out the door; a steel manufacturer, in contrast, may suffer much less damage to its business if it files for bankruptcy," he wrote.[37]

Kohl says that while not every bankruptcy reorganization or failure ends in revitalization, turnarounds help the economy. One of her favorite cases involves Forum Health Care of Youngstown, Ohio, which owned several struggling hospitals that provided "a disproportionate amount of charity care." She represented Forum's bond insurance company, which would have to pay up if bonds defaulted; she says she still wanted to see "a win for everybody," including Forum's 4,000-plus employees. In 2010, Forum was sold out of bankruptcy to a Nashville firm that invested in new equipment but also laid off some employees.[38]

"You all have to share the pain to provide a platform for growth to the future," Kohl says. "We joke, 'Hold your nose and go forward.'"

Is failure necessary for long-term success?

Bill Gates was heading into his senior year of high school in the summer of 1972, working for a company that measured traffic patterns. The company used a machine that translated numbers into a custom paper punch tape, which then were manually repunched into computer cards.[39]

Gates' friend Paul Allen thought a machine powered by a then-novel microprocessor would work better. So they "scraped together $360" for the Intel 8008 chip and built what Gates dubbed Traf-O-Data.

"When the guy from the county that Seattle's in came to see it, it didn't work," Gates said in an interview.[40]

Traf-O-Data landed few clients, and Gates and Allen moved on. Yet their small company had served as a catalyst and a testing ground for something much bigger.

"It confirmed to me that every failure contains the seeds of your next success. It bolstered my conviction that microprocessors would soon run the same programs as larger computers, but at a much lower cost. . . . This was the essential step toward . . . the creation of Microsoft," Allen recalled.[41]

Gates and Allen, who co-founded Microsoft in 1975, are in good company in their faith that failure is a stepping stone to success, and a launching pad for innovation. Many start-up founders and business school professors—as well as super-successful author J.K. Rowling—say failure fosters better leaders and stronger companies.

For some, a stumble offers gifts: resilience, faith in the ability to come back, perhaps a new opportunity. For others, though, failure in career or business may lead to poverty and depression. How failure affects individuals and businesses has been widely researched, with myriad conclusions.

Lessons from failure last longer than those based on success, a University of Colorado, Denver, researcher found, based on his study of rockets and airlines. "Whenever you have a failure it causes a company to search for solutions, and when you search for solutions it puts you as an executive in a different mind-set, a more open mind-set," said Vinit Desai, an assistant professor of management who also has studied failure in other sectors.[42]

Not everyone learns from failure, though. Entrepreneurs need an "intuitive cognitive style" and mentoring to really extract valuable lessons from their huge mess-ups, entrepreneurship professors Brandon Mueller of Oklahoma State University and Dean A. Shepherd of Indiana University found.[43]

Many serial entrepreneurs continue to be overly optimistic and do not reflect on their missteps, so they fail a second time, according to others who have studied the process.[44] And even though the start-up community has embraced the "fail fast" mantra, it really applies to the little details of an enterprise, not the big things, wrote David Brown, co-founder of business accelerator Techstars.[45]

Yet failure leads some people to their big thing. Rowling was 28, jobless and poor, her marriage failing, when she returned to writing. The famous result: Harry Potter. She told part of her story in a 2008 Harvard commencement address: "Failure meant a stripping away of the inessential. I stopped pretending to myself that I was anything other than what I was, and began to direct all my energy into finishing the only work that mattered to me."[46]

That rebuilding grew into an empire, with seven Harry Potter books, eight movies, countless merchandising spin-offs and two Wizarding World sections at theme parks, collectively worth about $24 billion.[47] Rowling's personal net worth is estimated at $1 billion.

While the idea of failure as a necessary building block to success sounds enticing, there's plenty of contrary evidence—including people who string together success after success. Entrepreneurs with a track record of success are "much more likely to succeed than first-time entrepreneurs and those who have previously failed," a team of Harvard business professors found.[48]

Despite many powerful comebacks, not every chief executive who goes down in flames returns stronger and better. Only about 35 percent of the 450 executives studied by two management professors ended up in another top job within two years of their departure.[49] The others either took consulting or teaching posts or disappeared into obscurity or retirement.

Trendy celebrations of failure are evolving into "failure porn" that "desensitizes one to the horrors of failure," wrote venture capitalist Geoff Lewis of Founders Fund. "I recoil when the merits of failure are so vastly overstated and its agonies are so trivialized."[50] People seem to ignore the costs: psychological trauma and a feeling of worthlessness for founders, huge losses for investors and jobs that evaporate, leaving families struggling.

"When you believe your vision is important, celebrating failure of any sort would be perverse. . . . (Yet) the failure pendulum has swung too far toward celebration. I'd like to see it swing back a bit toward fear," Lewis wrote.

Fear of failure certainly grips people who are stuck in low-paying jobs or out of work for months or years. About one-third of Americans worry they may not be able to pay their rent or mortgage, and 60 percent fear they will not have enough money saved for retirement, according to a 2015 Gallup Poll. Unmarried women, African-Americans, Latinos and anyone who earns less than $30,000 a year are the most likely to express worry about six or more financial areas of life. [51]

Americans Worry About Financial Failure

Are there cultural and regional differences in how people react to failure?
Bennett, who retired from the bankruptcy bench in June 2015, presided over thousands of cases a year during 20 years in Birmingham, Ala. They ranged from poor single parents to what in 2011 was the largest municipal bankruptcy in U.S. history, that of Jefferson County, Ala., which includes Birmingham. He was known for his rule-from-the-bench and work-through-the-holidays approaches.[52]

"There is no difference based on age, gender or race on how people react to bankruptcy," Bennett says, based on his experience.

At least in Alabama, the stigma of bankruptcy persists, even though it has declined, he says. "Nobody comes in and talks about failure in the way you're talking about," Bennett says. Celebration of failure seems rooted in Silicon Valley and a few other tech centers—although there's evidence it is spreading around the world.

Only 41 percent of those polled in Japan agree with the statement, "People today brag more about failure than they did in the past." But in Brazil, 73 percent see that happening. In the United States, 57 percent report more bragging about big setbacks.[53]

"In some Asian cultures, the ideas of speaking up when something's going wrong is unbelievably difficult," says Dartmouth's Finkelstein, whose book "Why Smart Executives Fail" was a best-seller in Japan.

Fear of failure may hold back people in some cultures from starting businesses more than others. For example, 50 percent of people in Vietnam said worry about failing could halt their plans compared with about 13 percent in Botswana and Uganda and 24 percent in Argentina. The highest levels were found in Greece, at almost 62 percent.[54]

Greeks Fear Business Failure the Most

Women are more risk-averse and have less experience with failure than men, researchers have found. They are more likely to take calculated risks and develop backup plans in case problems develop, while men are more likely to rely on their self-confidence.[55] Women also fear failure more than men, and their craving for success diminishes by their 40s.[56]

Young people ages 18 to 24 with a desire to start businesses are much more likely to say they fear failure than those who are over 35, and also are less likely to claim they hold the necessary skills and resources for entrepreneurship.[57]

Poll: How worried are you about each of the following financial matters?

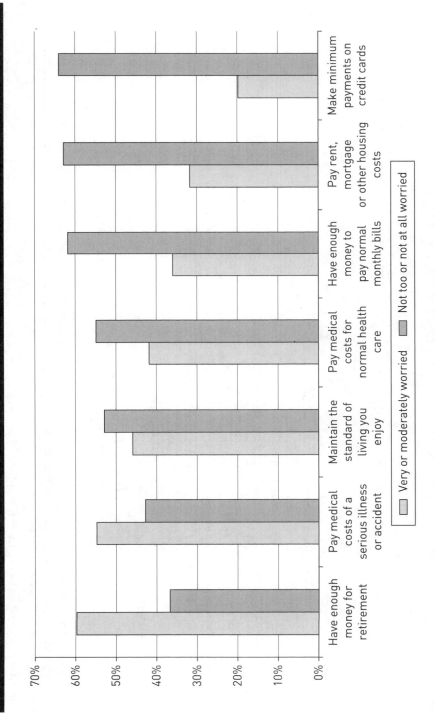

Legend: Very or moderately worried ▢ Not too or not at all worried ▢

Categories: Have enough money for retirement · Pay medical costs of a serious illness or accident · Maintain the standard of living you enjoy · Pay medical costs for normal health care · Have enough money to pay normal monthly bills · Pay rent, mortgage or other housing costs · Make minimum payments on credit cards

Y-axis: 0% – 70%

A majority of Americans said they were very or moderately worried about being able to save enough money for retirement or being able to pay medical bills after a serious health problem, according to a Gallup Poll. About one-third of respondents said they were very or moderately worried about being able to pay for normal monthly bills or housing costs.

Source: Lydia Saad, "Americans' Money Worries Unchanged From 2014," Gallup, April 20, 2015, http://tinyurl.com/lhjp9jx

Note: Results based on surveys of 1,015 U.S. adults from April 9–12, 2015.

Percentage of adults under 65 years old who say they fear failure, by country, 2014

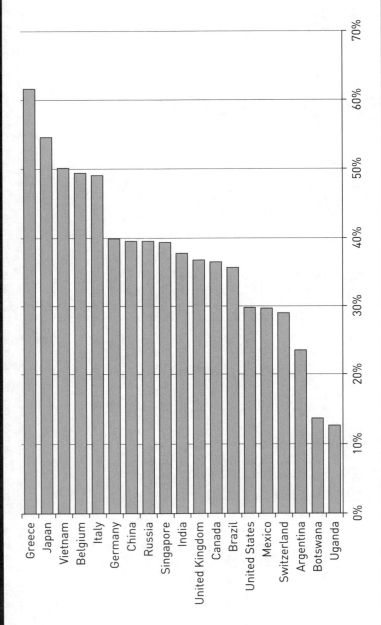

Note: Based on surveys of more than 206,000 people in 73 economies.

Sixty-two percent of adults under age 65 in Greece and 55 percent of those in Japan told researchers their fear of failure would prevent them from starting a business, well above the rate of 30 percent in the United States. Fear of entrepreneurial failure was even lower among adults in Argentina (24 percent) and African countries such as Botswana (14 percent) and Uganda (13 percent).

Source: "Global Entrepreneurship Monitor: 2014 Global Report," Global Entrepreneurship Research Association, 2015, pp. 32–33, http://tinyurl.com/j3fn7nb

Children may develop very different mind-sets about mistakes based on how they are reared. Those who are cocooned from their missteps can grow up stunted. "Out of love and a desire to protect our children's self-esteem, we have bulldozed every uncomfortable bump and obstacle out of their way, depriving our children of the most important lesson of child-hood: that setbacks, mistakes and failures are the very experiences that will teach them how to be resourceful, persistent, innovative and resilient," wrote Jessica Lahey, a journalist and the author of "The Gift of Failure."[58]

Geography, gender or parenting style do not explain all the nuances and variety of our feelings and behaviors around failure. Fons Trompenaars, a Dutch organizational theo-rist, and Peter Woolliams, a British international business culture expert, described five key dimensions that create differences around failure: [59]

- The degree over which an individual believes he controls his environment—or is controlled by it.

- Whether rules or relationships are more important.

- Whether failures are pinned to the individual or to the community or team.

- Whether the workers come from nonidentifying cultures (where failures are seen "as simply an idea that didn't work") or identifying cultures; two-thirds of American and Dutch survey respondents blame the idea, while only 12 percent of Japanese and 24 percent of Chinese respondents do.

- Whether status is granted based on performance or position.

Trompenaars and Woolliams cited an example of German and American engineers working for the same company, semiconductor maker AMD, in a joint brainstorming ses-sion in Dresden, Germany. American workers said the Germans were slow, risk-averse and lacked creativity in exploring new ideas. But the Germans felt the Americans offered unde-veloped ideas without having done their homework. AMD found a middle ground for the two, but too often such encounters end in frustration or failure.

Companies may have a variety of micro-climates for failure, suggests Paul J.H. Schoemaker, a strategic management consultant who also teaches at the University of Pennsylvania's Wharton School. For example, for a pharmaceutical company, "failure is endemic" in research and development. "They start with 9,000 drugs to get to one that is interesting."

However, once a drug has been tested and is approved for sale, manufacturing "has to be a very tight process. Mistakes are frowned upon," he says.

BACKGROUND

Debtors' Prison

In imperial Rome, debtors could be arrested; if they did not repay, they were enslaved. In ancient Ireland and India, creditors would hold vigil outside the debtor's door until paid.[60]

In other places, failing to pay debts could lead to death, sometimes brought on by long imprisonments. "Not only freedom and honor but life itself was at the mercy of the creditor," wrote Louis Edward Levinthal, author of "The Early History of Bankruptcy Law." Gradually though, creditor claims became directed at the borrower's property instead of his person, wrote Levinthal, a Philadelphia judge in the mid-20th century.[61]

An individual who went bankrupt in 16th-century England was a fraud and an "offender"; in France such people were labeled deceivers or squanderers.[62]

Debtors' prisons, imported along with bankruptcy codes from England, were common in the United States for almost 200 years, starting in the 1600s. Often overcrowded and disease-ridden, the prisons housed both criminals and debtors, who often received the only long-term sentences.[63]

The United States adopted its first bankruptcy laws in 1800, borrowed liberally from England's pro-creditor ordinances.[64] The bankruptcy codes applied only to merchants and cases initiated by creditors, and contained a five-year sunset provision. Congress repealed the laws after only three years, citing excess costs and corruption.[65]

Two more times in the 1800s, in 1841 and 1867, Congress passed federal bankruptcy legislation only to repeal it a few years later. Often the nation's leaders were pressed to act after economic crisis.

The new country's economy was turbulent, with panics and crashes interspersed with periods of growth and business development. The "Panic of 1819" was caused by loose credit, heavy debts by the U.S. government and farmers and plunging cotton prices. It was, according to one account, "America's first great economic crisis."[66]

Customers started runs on U.S. banks, withdrawing money because of fears the banks were unstable, while farmers and cotton farmers could not meet loan payments.[67] That panic was followed by the cotton market crash of 1825, which pushed the South into a depression.

Despite such setbacks, in the early 1800s, failure was mainly a business term—although preachers also would use it for "heathens" and others who fell from grace, historian Scott A. Sandage wrote in "Born Losers: A History of Failure in America."[68]

That started to shift when success and ambition became more fashionable than piety. People began to abhor failure and blame it on a lack of initiative or talent, Sandage wrote. By the 1840s, the "go-ahead principles" took root and spread beyond New York as mining and railroads and more brought thoughts of success to many.

Failure and bankruptcy became accepted as part of American enterprise. "Business failure permeated the 19th century United States," wrote Duke history professor Edward J. Balleisen, who cited estimates that 95 percent of mercantile shops failed both before and after the Civil War. "Throughout the era, farmers from every part of the country lost their land because they could not make mortgage payments, while large numbers of artisans and manufacturers found themselves unable to meet their obligations. In the biggest cities and the smallest hamlets, a host of mercantile firms experienced bankruptcy."[69]

His analysis of 503 bankruptcies in New York City and vicinity from the 1830s and 1840s shows they were mostly filed by men (only nine women), usually in the "prime of their lives," and three-quarters were married.

During this time, many men were unable to pay their bills and landed in debtors' prisons. There were campaigns to abolish these unhealthy cells, including some penned from the prisons themselves.

Kentucky became the first state to outlaw those institutions, in 1821—just two years after nature painter John James Audubon was sent to a debtors' jail after his Kentucky business failed.[70] U.S. law forbade federal debtors' prisons in 1833.[71] By 1870, the "dismal cages" had been outlawed in almost all the states and territories.[72]

Bankruptcy laws in the United States gradually grew more liberal and helpful to individuals and business owners in trouble. By the 1850s, many states had extended help to families, exempting from seizure and sale not only clothing, furniture and household goods but also a home and 40 or 50 acres, plus the debtor's tools of trade.[73]

The Civil War and trying times caused Congress to adopt new bankruptcy codes in 1867, providing protection for corporations for the first time.[74] They were repealed in 1878.

The U.S. statutes were far more lenient than elsewhere; French historian and political writer Alexis de Tocqueville commented on the "strange indulgence that is shown to bankrupts" in the United States compared with Europe's still-stern laws.[75]

Evolution of Bankruptcy

With rapid growth in commerce and movement into new territories after the Civil War, Americans embraced the "self-made man" approach. "The great American Assumption was that wealth is mainly the result of its owner's effort and that any average worker can by thrift become a capitalist," wrote W.E.B. Du Bois, co-founder of the NAACP, the nation's oldest civil rights organization.[76]

This sentiment led countless people to risk their life savings to buy farms or start businesses, only to fail. Ten years after Samuel Clemens wrote "Adventures of Huckleberry Finn" in 1884 to great acclaim, a company the man known as Mark Twain established filed for bankruptcy.[77]

A large-scale economic failure started in the South and Great Plains in the 1880s, punctuated by a deep agricultural crisis.[78] Wall Street took note in 1893, as one-fourth of U.S. railroads went bankrupt and a worldwide depression took hold.

Lawmakers debated the merits of various kinds of bankruptcy, voluntary as well as involuntary, in which creditors force a business or individual to liquidate. In 1898, Congress again passed federal bankruptcy laws that for the first time included a precursor to Chapter 13, which "really opened the doors for the modern understanding that businesses and individuals are vulnerable to shocks beyond their control," says Mary Hansen, an American University economics professor. "That thinking was the basis for the modern social safety net."

Chapter 13, then known as a "wage earners plan," enables individuals with regular income to create a repayment plan for part or all of their debts over three to five years. During this period, creditors are forbidden from continuing collection efforts.[79]

The 1898 law, though promoted by creditor interests, was "in many respects strikingly debtor-friendly," wrote David A. Skeel Jr., a professor of corporate law at the University of Pennsylvania.[80]

By 1900, as inventors were working on the first automobiles in Michigan and Indiana, bankruptcy had a solid foundation in the U.S. economy and legal code. Perfectionist Henry Ford's first company, Detroit Automobile, produced only 20 cars; the enterprise went bankrupt in 1901.[81]

Around that time, Michigan and Ohio were considered "cradles of innovation," Hansen says, with tinkerers working on horseless carriages of all sorts and the Wright brothers and others building airplanes. "Whenever you have high rates of business formation, you by definition have high rates of business failure," she says.

The Hindenburg airship that crashed in New Jersey in 1937 was not the first innovative transportation device to fail spectacularly—to "go up in flames" as some would dub a huge mistake. The Stanley Steamer, a transmission-less steam-powered car, debuted in 1897; its engines were smaller and more powerful than internal combustion gasoline engines.[82] The cars were fast, too: In 1906, steam-powered cars set a land speed record of 127 mph. Yet Ford Motor Co.'s assembly line-produced Model T cost much less, so by 1924, the last Stanleys were built.[83]

Fifty years later, Ford began a new car line called Edsel, named after the founder's only son. Because of low quality and an unusual front-end design that some said looked like a toilet seat, it never caught on. The Edsel was discontinued after three years, with only 2,846 cars sold in its final year, 1960.[84]

The panic of 1907 was a key turning point in U.S. failure history, Hansen says, because it led to the creation of the Federal Reserve system, which oversees the U.S. banking and money system. That panic was brought on by failed speculations and concerns about the safety of financial institutions and a weak U.S. economy.[85]

The other pivotal moment was the Great Depression of the 1930s, which sent families in search of new homes and lives in California and elsewhere. That 10 years of economic contraction resulted in some 7,000 bank failures and an unemployment rate of 25 percent.[86]

"The Great Depression really set the stage for the Great Society programs, which are our modern safety net," Hansen says. Social Security and many other government programs have their roots in President Franklin D. Roosevelt's Depression-fighting New Deal; other safety net programs, including Medicare and Medicaid, date to President Lyndon B. Johnson's Great Society of the 1960s.

Hansen is leading a project to digitize bankruptcy court records from the early 20th century, by taking samples from more than 2 million boxes of records in the National Archives. She has learned that many of the business bankruptcies of the Great Depression resulted not from bank failures but from trade credit evaporating. Small businesses just would not sell to other businesses on credit. Proprietors would say, "I can't extend you three months longer" on balances owed, and so the small grocer or milliner would go bankrupt, she says.

Access to Credit for Everyone

The 1940s and 1950s were prosperous times. After World War II, the Baby Boom, coupled with low unemployment and low inflation, meant Americans bought cars and stereos and invested in college educations.[87]

But credit cards and credit laws created a new avenue for failure. Introduced in 1958, Visa, then known as BankAmericard, and MasterCard, which debuted in 1966 as Master Charge, were held by 16 percent of U.S. families in 1970. By 1995, about two-thirds of all families had at least one card, and when single-store and other credit cards were added, that rose to three-quarters of all individuals and families.[88]

The seeds of overextension and rising consumer bankruptcies were sown in the 1970s, with the spread of bank credit cards and the 1974 passage of the Equal Credit Opportunity Act (ECOA), Hansen says. Before that law banned discrimination in lending based on gender, marital status, race and national origin, women found it difficult to land a mortgage or car loan.[89] Afterward, credit for women became more available, she says.

"The big story is access to credit. If you think of bankruptcy as being tied to access to credit, it no longer is a huge terrible thing. It's an obvious manifestation of risk in the modern economy," Hansen says. While consumers' debt grew from credit cards, businesses borrowed more money through private equity and junk bonds, used to create leveraged buyouts (LBOs) through the 1980s. But buyouts slowed markedly in 1989–90; by 1991, 26 of 83 big boom-time LBOs had defaulted on their debt, and 18 had filed for Chapter 11.[90]

Busts Keep Following Booms

The 21st century brought another boom and bust cycle, fueled by new financial instruments. Lenders created an array of mortgages that made borrowing to buy a home seem easy, even for people with bad credit or shaky job histories. These subprime mortgages deteriorated in quality for six years, 2001 to '06, and the companies creating and reselling mortgage-backed securities were aware of the growing risks. Foreclosures mounted, and by late 2006, "an unusually large fraction of subprime mortgages" made just months before were delinquent or facing foreclosure.[91]

The problems that started in the mortgage market erupted in the financial crisis of 2008; financial companies including investment bank Lehman Brothers died or went bankrupt, while the government bailed out others. Millions of Americans lost their homes to foreclosure. The Federal Reserve Bank failed to halt the spread of "toxic mortgages," and it and other regulators were unprepared for the panic and fallout, according to numerous analyses.[92]

Lehman Brothers Tops Largest Bankruptcies List

From its peak in 2008 to 2010, the U.S. economy lost 8.8 million jobs in a wide variety of sectors, from construction to manufacturing and professional and business services.[93] From 2008 to 2011, almost 5 million Americans filed for personal bankruptcy.[94] Some 80 percent of Americans either lost their job or knew a family member or friend who were out of work in the recession, says Van Horn of Rutgers, author of "Working Scared (Or Not at All)."

In the early 2000s, Richelle Shaw, who's now a motivational speaker and business coach, lost rental properties she owned in Las Vegas as well as her small telephone company. In her worst days, she "slept on the floor," she says. "I went without power for 18 days." She

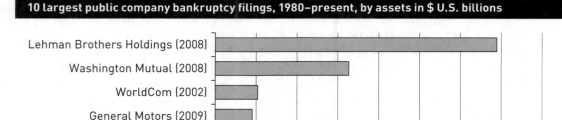

10 largest public company bankruptcy filings, 1980–present, by assets in $ U.S. billions

Investment bank Lehman Brothers filed for the largest-ever U.S. bankruptcy action in September 2008 with $691 billion in assets, more than twice that of second-ranked Washington Mutual, which filed that same month. Financial services firms filed for five of the 10 largest bankruptcies since 1980; the rest came from automotive, energy and communications companies.

Source: "20 Largest Public Company Bankruptcy Filings 1980 – Present," BankruptcyData.com, New Generation Research, undated, http://tinyurl.com/lphhuu

filed for personal bankruptcy in 2006, after her business imploded from a heavy debt load. She laid off all her workers, including her mother.

A few years ago, Shaw started talking about her failure in her speeches and writing. "Failure happens throughout your life. If you're lucky, it will happen early so you can bounce back from it," she says.

"If you have never failed before, you haven't reached your fullest and best self," says Shaw, echoing the sentiments of more famous women such as Oprah Winfrey and J.K. Rowling.

CURRENT SITUATION

"A Cultural Moment"

Duke University adjunct professor Erin Parish is surrounded by failure, some of it intentional, in the first-year class she teaches and in her family and personal life.

She teaches students about failure and risk aversion, about social movements around failure and about tackling an "impossible task."

"It's definitely a cultural moment," Parish says, with failure praised, probed and feared in America today. She traces that partly to all the tech start-ups and to the growing number of standardized tests children take. "They talk about how there are no safety nets in high school to fail," she says.

She has experienced and studied stumbles for years, with a "failed job, failed marriage," she says. "I tried a graduate program and it didn't work for me." She ended up earning her doctorate in cultural anthropology from Duke.

"These students are more anxious at an early age than I was. They have more of a view of failure as this real thing to avoid," she says. Yet what they see as their big failures—receiving an 87 on a paper or not getting into Harvard—are shared easily in class and on social media.

Such is the dichotomy of failure today, where it's seen as a fashionable performer singing about "epic fails" and "superb smash-ups" as well as a tough headmaster doling out lessons and opportunities to innovate or reinvent. Yet not everyone embraces the performer or headmaster; a backlash against elevating failure is growing, too.

Failure has turned into a cliché, with not enough context and meaning, some say. "We don't want to set ourselves up to be a failure society where it's all wonderful and everyone will now get a trophy or kudos for failing," said Rebecca "Kiki" Weingarten, a career and education coach.[95]

For example, in Detroit, some people reject what's called "ruin porn"—photos of crumbling and abandoned buildings. One critic called it the "uncritical and exploitative celebration of Detroit's postindustrial landscapes."[96] Others dismissed the photos as intrusive and one-dimensional because they ignored Detroit buildings being rehabbed or those that remain well-tended.

Detroit, of course, has experienced years of decline and failure. One-third of the homes in the city have gone through foreclosure since 2005, a trend that has reduced property values and decimated neighborhoods.[97]

Yet the city's failings, which result in homes priced at $5,000 and commercial buildings at a fraction of what they would cost in Chicago or Los Angeles, are drawing investors and new residents. In the year before and after 2013, when the city filed for the largest U.S. municipal bankruptcy, Detroit and its backers have pushed a new message of Detroit as "a comeback city" with new investment, new art galleries and new restaurants.[98]

Corporate Costs

Even though more companies see value in modest failure, big mistakes are costly to reputations and bottom lines. Some strong corporations have taken hits for major mistakes. Toyota paid a $1.2 billion settlement in 2014 to halt a criminal probe into its efforts to deceive regulators and the public about sudden acceleration problems and a sticky gas pedal that led to fatalities and accidents.[99] Volkswagen officials employed deceptive software so up to 11 million vehicles could pass emissions tests; the scandal exposed in 2015 is expected to cost the German automaker billions of dollars.[100] Also in 2015, Halliburton agreed to pay $18.3 million in back wages to more than 1,000 workers who were misclassified as salaried workers.[101]

Amid a mobile communications boom, some cellphone makers stumbled. "Motorola in the 1990s was more powerful than Apple today. It had 60 percent market share. . . . Just flying high," says Finkelstein at Dartmouth. Now Motorola's share is around 5 to 6 percent.[102]

"As powerful as the iPhone is today, it wouldn't surprise me that they would also be surpassed," Finkelstein says.

He sees the rate of failures increasing, and measures it partly by attrition of Fortune 100 firms. "The rate at which companies fall out of the top 100 has gone up by 50 percent since the ranking was first published in 1955. For example, the 10-year attrition rate from 1955 to 1965 was 20 percent; from 2005 to 2015 it was 30 percent—a 50 percent increase in attrition rate," he says.

Finkelstein's annual list of the worst CEOs shows three main storylines: CEOs who follow the wrong strategies and don't change things; corporate governance issues; and questionable, unethical or borderline illegal activity. Many of these executives lose their jobs within a year, he says.

Some of the CEOs work for companies that end up in Chapter 11, such as American Apparel's former CEO Dov Charney, who made the 2014 list.[103]

The American Bankruptcy Institute proposed changes to U.S. bankruptcy laws in December 2014, to shift power away from corporate creditors and make reorganization more affordable for small privately held companies with less than $10 million in assets. The proposal would also raise the amount an employee may collect as a priority creditor to $25,000 from the current $11,725.[104]

Bennett, the former bankruptcy judge, says Congress is unlikely to pass any significant changes to U.S. bankruptcy laws any time soon. One change that could take place could be to Chapter 9, the provision that covers municipalities such as Detroit and Jefferson County, Ala., Bennett's best-known case.

Selling Failure and Hating It

Sharing your failure has become so popular in the start-up world that the blog for venture capital database CB Insights gathered dozens of them in a 2014 post titled "51 Startup Failure Post-Mortems," updated by the end of 2015 to 146 failures.[105]

Michael Roberto, a management professor at Bryant University, said the embrace-failure movement has taken hold "because so many corporate cultures have become so intolerant of experimentation and people have become so afraid to fail that they have become reluctant to try new things." He added: "We still need to be careful about not labeling all failures as equally 'useful.'"[106]

Some experts say, though, that the "fail fast" and "fail forward" mantras are mostly just hype; leaders know a few social media posts will not erase the effects of a huge misstep. "The key, really, shouldn't be to embrace failure but to embrace resilience and the ability to bounce back," said Rob Asghar, a management consultant and the author of "Leadership Is Hell."[107]

For some, resilience is a pipe dream. In a Rutgers report, seven in 10 workers 50 and older who hold part-time jobs because they cannot land better ones say they earn less than they need to live; 35 percent have sold possessions and 25 percent borrowed from family or friends.[108] More than a third are cutting costs—including food and upkeep on their homes—because most say their financial situations are "only fair" (about 50 percent) or "poor" (one-third).

Parish plans to talk to her undergraduates about creating a safety net for failure—financial, intellectual and emotional screwups. And she will highlight the "fictions of the self-made man" and the "shallow marketing of failure as the American Dream 2.0. It drives me crazy," she says.

"We talk about paradox a lot," Parish says. "Do you want stability or transformation? There's always paradox at play."

LOOKING AHEAD

Predicting and Averting Failure

Within a few years, a computer algorithm may scan the huge array of data collected by universities or employers for signs of flameouts—or to offer a prescription for avoiding catastrophe.

Already, at the Massachusetts Institute of Technology, by tracking how long students spend on a course website compared to their peers, a computer can anticipate when someone is about to drop out of an online course.[109] With the right intervention, perhaps that alert could avert a small failure for both the student and the teacher.

Increasingly, companies may use software to predict which workers are getting antsy. Candidates flagged are six times more likely to leave their job within 120 days than their peers.[110]

In hospitals and businesses, experts already use predictive analytics to anticipate such things as heart failure and which equipment components will stop working. Edward Altman, a New York University finance professor who focuses on bankruptcy, calculates a "Z-score" that provides a measure of corporate health or default by tracking liquidity, earnings, stock market valuation and solvency. "Many companies are repeating some of the mistakes of the past" by adding too much debt, according to Altman.[111]

In the future, predictive analytics may warn of larger failures, although tracking internal data on sales, repeat customers or employee turnover may not be enough to warn of a bankruptcy. "The information most likely to influence the future comes from looking out the window, not in the mirror," wrote Accenture's Jeanne Harris and Mark McDonald, referring to global economic and marketplace changes, vs. internal metrics.[112]

Managers must evolve and master new techniques for using predictive futures, instead of basing decisions on past experiences and data, whether they want to anticipate success or failure or something else, Harris and McDonald wrote.

And they must learn to get past the "blame game" and superficial lessons and head in "novel strategic directions," wrote Harvard's Edmondson. Even in companies with systems such as Total Quality Management to find problems, many staffers are loath to share bad news with bosses and colleagues. Edmondson suggested that management adopt strategies of openness and humility and of asking and answering questions.[113]

Elford, the Australian futurist, says acceptance of failure in business and life will continue to gain momentum. She expects a move toward finding "safe to fail" and recovery-from-failure strategies.

"We need to shift to being a master of failure and honoring failure and laughing at it. I don't think we are training people well enough," she says.

Yet Elford also notes that some trends may slow acceptance of failure. Helicopter parenting is one example, where parents coddle and protect their children. Another: Leaders fear ambiguity when they consider a huge array of future outcomes. Often, they seek to narrow the scope and focus of their future view to one point or set of questions. A manager thinks: "I will succeed or fail based on your answer to my question: 'Do you like your chair?'" she says. Yet for consumers, the important topic perhaps is not the chair, but a comfortable environment on the job or something else entirely. She says successful leaders must be open to such ambiguity.

"Everything you ignore is where failure begins," Elford says.

Chronology

1800s	**Bankruptcy laws take shape.**
1800	U.S. Congress adopts first federal bankruptcy laws, modeled after a 1732 English law.
1821	Kentucky becomes the first U.S. state to outlaw debtors' prisons.
1898	Congress approves changes to bankruptcy law that give businesses more financial options.
1920s–1930s	**Great Depression brings widespread failure.**
1929	After a speculative boom, the U.S. stock market experiences a devastating crash. In the years that follow, thousands of farms and small businesses close or are seized by banks for unpaid loans.
1930s	Throughout the 1930s, the Depression ripples globally, with unemployment rates at more than 30 percent in most European countries in some years, and even higher in Germany, still struggling to recover from its defeat in World War I.
1937	The Hindenburg, an airship that was considered a marvel of the skies, crashes in New Jersey, ending the dirigible era.
1950s–1970s	**Big companies suffer setbacks.**
1958	Toyota Motor Co. sells only 288 vehicles in the United States after its debut a year earlier. The company does not succeed until it introduces the Corona in 1965.
1970	Two years after a merger creates a huge railroad giant, Penn Central Transportation goes bankrupt in what at the time is the largest U.S. bankruptcy. The company's assets are sold off over the next several years, many of them to a new company, Conrail.
1978	The Bankruptcy Reform Act establishes Chapter 11 reorganization. Bankruptcy filings rapidly increase at an average annual rate of 7.6 percent between 1980 and 2004.
1980s–1990s	**Savings and loan crisis leads to widespread collapses.**
1982	The unemployment rate soars to a post-World War II record of 10.8 percent.
1988	The savings and loan crisis peaks, with 190 thrift failures.
1994	Euro Disney, open for two years, restructures its debt in an attempt to resolve financial problems.

1996	"Debt," a game show in which winning contestants receive prize money to eliminate their debts, airs on Lifetime Television.
2000s– Present	**The dot-com bubble bursts and financial markets buckle.**
2000	The super-heated market in technology stocks plummets—what has become known as the bursting of the dot-com bubble.
2001	Energy giant Enron, which had been hailed for its innovation, files for Chapter 11 and lays off 4,000 employees.
2005	Congress passes the Bankruptcy Abuse Prevention and Consumer Protection Act, making it harder for individuals and families to file for Chapter 7 protection. . . . An early version of YouTube fails as a dating site, leading the founders to switch to video sharing.
2006	Bankruptcy filings plummet 70 percent to 618,000, down from more than 2 million the previous year.
2008	The growing subprime mortgage crisis erupts into a full-blown financial crisis, followed by the worst recession since the 1930s.
2009	FailCon, the first of a number of business conferences featuring executives who share their failure stories and lessons, launches in San Francisco.
2011	The European Commission Enterprise and Industry Group introduces "Second Chance" policy in the hopes of reducing stigmatization of failed entrepreneurs. . . . Harvard Business Review publishes a special "Failure" issue that discusses the many angles for identifying and learning from failure.
2013	With debts of $18 billion, the city of Detroit files for Chapter 9 bankruptcy, the largest municipal bankruptcy filing in U.S. history.
2014	The Science Gallery at Trinity College in Dublin, Ireland, debuts the "Fail Better" exhibition, a public display of failed ventures, to promote discussion of how failure sparks creativity.
2015	Business bankruptcies in Japan hit a 25-year low. . . . Because of low crude oil prices, dozens of U.S. oil and gas companies go bust. . . . Puerto Rico grapples with a debt crisis that could lead to default on its bond obligations.

— **By Rivan Stinson and Vickie Elmer**

RESOURCES

The Next Step

Bankruptcy

Gleason, Stephanie, and Ted Mann, "GE Says Quirky Has Hurt Its Reputation," The Wall Street Journal, Dec. 3, 2015, http://tinyurl.com/qcqjdlg.

General Electric's partnership with a bankrupt home-technology invention start-up that reportedly failed to provide adequate customer service harmed General Electric's reputation, according to bankruptcy court documents.

Martin, Peter, "Free to fail in Malcolm Turnbull's new $1.1 billion innovation plan," The Sydney Morning Herald, Dec. 7, 2015, http://tinyurl.com/j4upsha.

New Australian laws will permit directors of bankrupt firms that have restructured debts to continue operating the businesses and allow them to start others, part of a national effort to help Australian entrepreneurs.

Schram, Lauren Elkies, "To Declare, or Not to Declare Bankruptcy?" Commercial Observer, Nov. 11, 2015, http://tinyurl.com/hbbbkyu.

Chapter 11 reorganizations can help real estate developers in weak markets to refinance projects, continue operating businesses while repaying creditors and push lenders to modify their original repayment terms, according to real estate lawyers.

Cultural Differences

Duarte, Daniel, "Journalist Andrés Oppenheimer Tells Latin America to 'Create or Die,'" PanAm Post, July 15, 2015, http://tinyurl.com/zmnzls3.

Latin America has discouraged innovation by stigmatizing business failure and ostracizing entrepreneurs who do not succeed on first attempts, according to a book by an Argentinean journalist.

Nguyen, Hoang, "The entrepreneur teaching Japan how to take more risks," BBC, Sept. 14, 2015, http://tinyurl.com/pyo3vzb.

A Japanese entrepreneur who sold his first software company to Microsoft at age 33 now invests in start-ups in Japan, where he says disapproving cultural attitudes toward failure have stifled entrepreneurship.

Sheftalovich, Zoya, "EU pushes for business without borders," Politico Europe, Oct. 28, 2015, http://tinyurl.com/jd63ofl.

The European Commission has proposed regulations that aim, among other objectives, to make it easier for entrepreneurs behind bankrupt businesses to start new firms, although a Lithuanian member of the European Union Parliament says the EU could do more to improve the entrepreneurial climate.

Economic Effects

Guilford, Gwynn, "China's latest refusal to fix its state-owned companies is bad news for the global economy," Quartz, Sept. 16, 2015, http://tinyurl.com/poyjhxj.

The Chinese government props up bankrupt state-owned enterprises by continuing to lend to them, leading to overproduction and market inefficiencies.

Howitt, Peter, "Failures and job losses are integral to economic growth," The Globe and Mail, Sept. 2, 2015, http://tinyurl.com/jxn2nhh.

Company failures and job cuts lead former employees to innovate and start competitive firms that create new jobs, thereby contributing to economic growth, says a Canadian economist.

Shane, Scott, "Is Declining Business Failure Holding Back Entrepreneurship?" Entrepreneur, March 11, 2015, http://tinyurl.com/h8r7sc2.

Government aid to failing businesses may inadvertently hold back the creation of start-ups, according to a professor of entrepreneurial studies at Case Western Reserve University.

Technology Sector

Griswold, Alison, "Startups With Shorter Names Are More Likely to Succeed, Study Finds," Slate, Feb. 9, 2015, http://tinyurl.com/konkyuw.

New businesses named after their founders are 70 percent less likely to succeed than other firms, and those with names of three words or less are 50 percent more likely to succeed, according to a study by Massachusetts Institute of Technology researchers.

Maney, Kevin, "In Silicon Valley, Failing Is Succeeding," Newsweek, Aug. 31, 2015, http://tinyurl.com/jmbgmbx.

Silicon Valley's technology industry has embraced failure as acceptable for many companies, an uncommon trait that has made the region's success difficult to replicate.

Voorhis, Dan, "Can Wichita get its entrepreneurial mojo back?" The Wichita Eagle, Dec. 12, 2015, http://tinyurl.com/jpm4pdp.

A group of entrepreneurs in Wichita, Kan., is working to attract investors to fund the city's technology businesses, but the director of an entrepreneurship nonprofit says many cities are unprepared for the high failure rate of such businesses.

Organizations

American Bankruptcy Institute

66 Canal Central Plaza, Suite 600, Alexandria, VA 22314
703-739-0800
www.abi.org

Membership-based institute that connects bankruptcy professionals and provides educational and research resources.

Business Plan Archive

3318 Van Munching Hall, College Park, MD 20742
301-405-0559
www.businessplanarchive.org

Online archive at the University of Maryland's Robert H. Smith School of Business that contains business plans and other documents of failed dot-coms and technology companies from the 1990s, with access limited to research and educational purposes.

FailCon

www.thefailcon.com

Conferences for start-up founders and others to discuss and study their past business failures to prepare for later success.

Failure: Lab

Grand Rapids, MI 49504

616-292-7277
http://failure-lab.com/

Group that organizes storytelling events around personal or professional failures.

Historical Bankruptcy Cases Project
4400 Massachusetts Ave., N.W., Washington, DC 20016
202-885-1000
http://www.american.edu/cas/economics/bankrupt/

A research effort at American University that is working with the National Archives to digitize bankruptcy cases from 1898 to 1978 for scholars; also offers research projects such as the extent to which women and African-Americans were involved in early bankruptcies.

International Failure Institute
Durham, NC 27708
http://internationalfailureinstitute.org/

Group of scholars, students, activists and artists seeking to understand the productive role of failure in learning and creativity by sharing stories, conducting classes and more.

National Association of Consumer Bankruptcy Attorneys
2200 Pennsylvania Ave., N.W., 4th floor, Washington, DC 20037
800-499-9040
www.nacba.org

Membership organization of consumer bankruptcy lawyers providing education, advocacy and some consumer resources.

The Success-Failure Project
5 Linden St., Cambridge, MA 02138
617-495-7680
www.successfailureproject.bsc.harvard.edu

An effort of Harvard University's Bureau of Study Counsel to provide resources aimed at students to discuss success and failure in context and to explore their own definitions of them.

Turnaround Management Association
150 North Wacker Drive, Suite 1900, Chicago, IL 60606
312-578-6900
www.turnaround.org

Membership organization of corporate turnaround-industry professionals that provides educational resources and hosts events.

U.S. Bankruptcy Court

E. Barrett Prettyman U.S. Courthouse, 333 Constitution Ave., N.W., Washington, D.C. 20001
www.uscourts.gov

One of the 94 federal judicial districts handling approximately 1 million business, individual and other bankruptcy cases filed each year.

Q&A: Paul Schoemaker on Mistakes

"EXPERIMENTATION AND MISTAKES WILL ADD UP TO SUCCESS AND BRILLIANCE, IF YOU ARE STRATEGIC"

Paul J.H. Schoemaker knows a lot about mistakes, and believes in their power. An entrepreneur, consultant and educator who has taught at the University of Pennsylvania's Wharton School, he has researched such subjects as navigating the unknown future and how managers deal with emerging technologies. His numerous books include "Brilliant Mistakes: Finding Success on the Far Side of Failure," which explores how businesses and business leaders can accelerate learning and innovation through mistakes.

"Success is really the sum total of many mistakes," Schoemaker says. Yet many people never "construct the silver lining" or see how they learn from their mistakes. "There is a tension in organization between learning and performing. Leaders have to balance that a bit."

Schoemaker discussed mistakes with SAGE Business Researcher reporter Vickie Elmer in an interview and follow-up emails. This is a consolidated and edited version of that discussion.

Give us a couple of examples of brilliant mistakes—not penicillin, but something any person could screw up.

To test their theories, David Ogilvy, the advertising genius, ran ads that he and his team did not believe would work. They knew they would waste half their budget—but they didn't know which half. So they experimented, including with a famous Hathaway shirt advertisement. Ogilvy added a man with an eye patch at the last minute. The ad was a brilliant success, ran for a long time and received several industry prizes.

This works well in training, too. If you want your team to get better, first, teach them to frame any mistake as a learning opportunity. Second, build on principles of positive psychology to deal with setbacks and failure as something temporary, isolated and valuable. Then emphasize that learning is the goal. A British girls' school declared a Failure Week because the headmistress wanted the girls to understand it's acceptable and completely normal not to succeed at times.

Has anyone been able to measure the time it takes between a major failure and the context or resilience that turns it into something valuable?

This question is too general, for the range is wide: Penicillin took several decades to become a workable drug for humans, whereas other insights happen in a flash. One example: Physicist Michael Faraday discovered induction currents by accidentally moving some equipment sitting on his laboratory bench.

Companies in many sectors are expected to be risk averse and protect value and reputation. How could an individual or group encourage their bosses or company to open up to accepting or even embracing mistakes?

Clearly, it takes leadership to change an organizational culture to move away from only pursuing perfection, and leaving or creating some room for the kind of exploration that almost by necessity entails mistakes. To quote Einstein: If you have never made a mistake, you never tried anything new.

Tell us the story of your friend in the Netherlands whose father went bankrupt—and what ripples that caused.

In many Germanic cultures, perfection is prized and failure abhorred. I was born and raised in a small town in the Netherlands called Deventer. The father of one of my school friends had a company in the pharmaceutical business, which fell on hard times and was closed, with loss of jobs and much money. This failure was widely viewed as a very shameful event in the local community. He was no longer an accepted member of society and felt his only option to continue a seminormal family life was to emigrate to North America. All this happened before it was cool to be an entrepreneur and take risks. If you failed big, you would essentially become a persona non grata in this traditional culture.

Many countries still suffer from such low tolerance for failure, and the price they collectively pay is low innovation.

In more innovation-oriented economies, such as the USA or Israel, the market will sort out which failures were due to incompetence, negligence, fraud or bad luck—and people have a second chance if the latter. As [Microsoft co-founder] Bill Gates noted, he looks for people who took risks, have scars and want to try again. He reckons that they learned valuable lessons on someone else's dime and are the smarter for it.

If you could design a game that taught people to become comfortable with failure and mistakes in business and careers, what would it look like?

I think of business as "the game" that most of us play. And within the business world, we experience three distinct approaches to risk taking:

- For the "innovation game," film makers, scientists and others use a strategy to "try a lot of things." Only a few of them will be winners, and that's all that success requires. So top economists or journalists may write 200 articles in a career, and only 10 of them are cited in the Nobel Prize, in the case of science.

- In the "performance game," which airline or fast-food services play, you will mostly be judged by percentages or ratios—such as performance metrics about on-time arrivals. So you do not want to introduce too many variables here, and you emphasize consistency by keeping things simple and highly programmed, as McDonald's does so well.

- Brain surgeons and nuclear power plants play the "loss avoidance game." They build in redundancies or strive for perfection in technique because the aim is to avoid a catastrophe.

These different environments require different leadership styles, and they each have very different capacities to tolerate and bounce back after a big mistake. In business, as well as in life, you need to know what game you are playing.

In the preface to "Brilliant Mistakes," you observe, "For most people, the problem is not that they make too many mistakes but too few." Why is that a problem today, given that profit margins are often razor thin and change is a constant?

If that is your business environment, you should try to get out of it because it is mostly a red ocean; that is, a place where many competitors imitate each other and compete on the same basis. The promise of mistakes is that they get you out of this trap and create blue oceans, those new market spaces where there is unmet demand.

The caveat to that statement is you have to do it very strategically. Most people are risk averse, which means they don't explore as widely around their assumptions, or their mental models, as they should. Organizations exacerbate this because they reward people for results most of the time, and not so often on good intentions or good process. If your intention is to change a business model or if you're in a new environment, I think you should have more tolerance for mistakes than is typically the case in companies. Experimentation and mistakes will add up to success and brilliance, if you are strategic and willing to take some risks.

How can I start using my mistakes better to head toward success?

Think about which mistakes have taught you the most and least in your life. Assess the cost-benefit ratio of each and then try to make more of the favorable ones. These are the ones where the cost of experimentation is low and the rewards potentially enormous.

Once you start to test and challenge commonly held assumptions, take time to make midstream adjustments based on feedback, and try to turn early mistakes into stepping stones toward eventual success. In business, create an ecosystem of customers, employees, peers and friends who help manage the winding road of innovation through mistakes.

It is unfortunate that the terms "mistake" or "failure" have such negative connotations in common parlance. Better terms would include tests, experiments, or pilots. Or as a comedian once suggested, why don't we call failure "time released success"? They key is to make hay when things go haywire, while realizing that discovery can only occur when mistakes are allowed to happen. And to see setbacks and silver linings as an essential part of the journey.

NOTES

CHAPTER 1

1. Simon Sinek, "Millennials in the Workplace," interview with Tom Bilyeu, Dec. 28, 2016, http://tinyurl.com/jpxlyw5.

2. Ibid.; Philip Bump, "Here Is Where Each Generation Begins and Ends, According to Facts," The Atlantic, March 25, 2014, http://tinyurl.com/jhvnkpg.

3. Leila Abboud, "Uber's $69 Billion Dilemma," Bloomberg, March 16, 2017, http://tinyurl.com/yd3pbke9; Lauren Thomas, "Airbnb just closed a $1 billion round and became profitable in 2016," CNBC, March 9, 2017, http://tinyurl.com/j9qtlsb.

4. Leslie Hook, "Year in a word: Gig economy," Financial Times, Dec. 29, 2015, http://tinyurl.com/yaswd5u9.

5. Ian Hathaway and Mark Muro, "Tracking the gig economy: New numbers," Brookings Institution, Oct. 13, 2016, http://tinyurl.com/yap56sj2.

6. "The 2017 Deloitte Millennial Survey – Apprehensive millennials: seeking stability and opportunities in an uncertain world," Deloitte, 2017, http://tinyurl.com/h4arf2c.

7. Sinek, op. cit.

8. Jonathan Berr, "For entrepreneurs, odds of success are low," CBS Moneywatch, May 12, 2014, http://tinyurl.com/ycwaqb4x.

9. Timothy Ferriss, "The 4-Hour Workweek: Escape 9-5, Live Anywhere, and Join the New Rich," Crown Publishing Group, 2007.

10. Penelope Trunk, "5 Time management tricks I learned from years of hating Tim Ferriss," blog post, Jan. 8, 2009, http://tinyurl.com/93q2go.

11. Jia Tolentino, "The Gig Economy Celebrates Working Yourself to Death," The New Yorker, March 22, 2017, http://tinyurl.com/m8nouaq.

12. Ibid.

13. Ibid; Bryan Menegus, "Lyft Thinks It's 'Exciting' That a Driver Was Working While Giving Birth," Gizmodo, Sept. 22, 2016, http://tinyurl.com/j35a6q6.

14. Noam Scheiber, "How Uber Uses Psychological Tricks to Push Its Drivers' Buttons," The New York Times, April 2, 2017, http://tinyurl.com/m8tts6l; Eric Newcomer, "Uber Plans Millions in Back Pay After Shorting NYC Drivers," Bloomberg, May 23, 2017, http://tinyurl.com/mw7jena.

15. Mike Isaac, "Uber Embraces Major Reforms as Travis Kalanick, the C.E.O., Steps Away," The New York Times, June 13, 2017, http://tinyurl.com/y9qjroz4.

16. Mike Isaac, "Uber Founder Travis Kalanick Resigns as C.E.O.," The New York Times, June 21, 2017, http://tinyurl.com/ybfvccb3.

CHAPTER 2

1. "Every day in the sharing economy, there are . . . ," Peers, undated, accessed July 15, 2015, http://tinyurl.com/q2czmqn; Ellen Huet, "Uber Says It's Doing 1 Million Rides Per Day, 140 Million In Last Year," Forbes, Dec. 17, 2014, http://tinyurl.com/pjyhavq.

2. Scott Austin, Chris Canipe and Sarah Slobin, "The Billion Dollar Startup Club," The Wall Street Journal, updated July 2015, http://tinyurl.com/pbfqsfk.

3. "FTC To Examine Competition, Consumer Protection, and Economic Issues Raised by the Sharing Economy at June Workshop," press release, Federal Trade Commission, April 17, 2015, http://tinyurl.com/ombw5u5.

4. "The sharing economy – sizing the revenue opportunity," PricewaterhouseCoopers, undated, accessed July 1, 2015, http://tinyurl.com/oxrhsbm.

5. "Written Testimony of Philip Auerswald," House Committee on Small Business, Jan. 15, 2014, http://tinyurl.com/nhu3o2u.

6. Colleen Walsh, "The big share: HBS historian examines a new kind of connectivity," Harvard Gazette, Aug. 5, 2014, http://tinyurl.com/pwon95b.

7. Boyd Cohen and Jan Kietzmann, "Ride On! Mobility Business Models for the Sharing Economy," Organization & Environment, Aug. 13, 2014, http://tinyurl.com/psqaqlp.

8. Walsh, op. cit.

9. Liz Krueger, "Letter to FTC Regarding the 'Sharing Economy,'" May 28, 2015, http://tinyurl.com/pzrn57o.

10. Brian Chesky, "Who We Are, What We Stand For," Airbnb blog, Oct. 3, 2013, http://tinyurl.com/o8sdzx6.

11. Mark John, "UberPOP halts service in France after clampdown, protests," Reuters, July 3, 2015, http://tinyurl.com/p6j4aje.

12. Walsh, op. cit.

13. Eric T. Schneiderman, "Airbnb in the City," New York State Office of the Attorney General, Oct. 14, 2014, http://tinyurl.com/m8pqffb.

14. Annie Karni, "De Blasio administration files first lawsuit against apartments operating as illegal hotels through sites like Airbnb," New York Daily News, Oct. 17, 2014, http://tinyurl.com/qguha7n.

15. Mike Isaac and Natasha Singer, "California Says Uber Driver Is Employee, Not a Contractor," The New York Times, June 17, 2015, http://tinyurl.com/qzmxqgl.

16. Frank Shafroth, "The Unforeseen Fiscal Challenges of Uber-Like Services," Government Technology, March 20, 2015, http://tinyurl.com/pmh3mlj.

17. Benjamin Davis, Tony Dutzik and Phineas Baxandall, "Transportation and the New Generation," U.S. PIRG Education Fund and the Frontier Group, April 2012, http://tinyurl.com/764qecl.

18. Shafroth, op. cit.

19. "Staff memo to the House Committee on Small Business," House of Representatives Committee on Small Business, Jan. 10, 2014, http://tinyurl.com/ovysxfu.

20. Jonathan V. Hall and Alan B. Krueger, "An Analysis of the Labor Market for Uber's Driver-Partners in the United States," Working Paper #587, Princeton University, Jan. 22, 2015, http://tinyurl.com/n5norw8.

21. Sarah Cannon and Lawrence H. Summers, "How Uber and the Sharing Economy Can Win Over Regulators," Harvard Business Review, Oct. 13, 2014, http://tinyurl.com/ntpcweq.

22. Cohen, op. cit.

23. Rachel Botsman and Roo Rogers, "What's Mine is Yours: The Rise of Collaborative Consumption," 2010, p. 114.

24. Maya Kosoff, "Uber Drivers Across The Country Are Protesting Today—Here's Why," Business Insider, Oct. 22, 2014, http://tinyurl.com/ojcwaxx.

25. Ibid.

26. Matthew Feeney, "Level the Playing Field—by Deregulating," Cato Unbound, Feb. 10, 2015, http://tinyurl.com/onphurf.

27. Arun Sundararajan, "Peer-to-Peer Businesses and the Sharing (Collaborative) Economy: Overview, Economic Effects and Regulatory Issues," House Committee on Small Business, Jan. 14, 2014, http://tinyurl.com/pm3r3c5.

28. Feeney, op. cit.

29. James Niccolai, "Uber and Lyft fail to convince judges their drivers are merely 'contractors,'" Computerworld, March 12, 2015, http://tinyurl.com/ocwr69j.

30. Isaac and Singer, op. cit.

31. "Topic 762—Independent Contractor vs. Employee," Internal Revenue Service, updated May 27, 2015, http://tinyurl.com/yonzjs.

32. Arun Sundararajan, "A Safety Net Fit for the Sharing Economy," Financial Times, June 22, 2015, http://tinyurl.com/q8w6ude.

33. Yochai Benkler, "Sharing Nicely: On Shareable Goods and the Emergence of Sharing as a Modality of Economic Production," The Yale Law Journal, 2004, Vol. 114, pp. 273–358.

34. Kevin Kelly, "We Are the Web," Wired, August 2005, http://tinyurl.com/p2zdsbw.

35. Ibid.

36. Dustin S. Klein, "Visionary in obscurity," Smart Business, July 22, 2002, http://tinyurl.com/o42v34t.

37. Nicole Achs Freeling, "The Nerd's Revenge," California CEO, February 2001, http://tinyurl.com/ojfvam8.

38. Zigmund, "Step Back in Time with Pierre Omidyar and Jeff Skoll," The Chatter Newsletter, eBay, 2005, http://tinyurl.com/qaqx4la.

39. Alex Stephany, "The Business of Sharing," New York, 2015, p. 71.

40. Ibid., p. 87.

41. Mimi Whitefield, "Airbnb Cracking the Cuban Market," The Miami Herald, July 5, 2015, http://tinyurl.com/noq6f5u.

42. Stephany, op. cit., p. 73.

43. Chase, op. cit., p. 8.

44. Ibid., p. 9.

45. Ibid., p. 13.

46. "History & Background Information," Freecycle, undated, accessed July 17, 2015, http://tinyurl.com/qjzml3k.

47. "About Zopa," Zopa, undated, accessed July 17, 2015, http://tinyurl.com/25g8bo.

48. "Alternative Financial Services: A Primer," FDIC Quarterly, April 27, 2009, http://tinyurl.com/p643omd.

49. For background, see Robin D. Schatz, "Crowdfunding," SAGE Business Researcher, Feb. 9, 2015, http://tinyurl.com/pk4alyg.

50. Patrick Hoge, "Colorado becomes the first state to pass law embracing Uber, Lyft et al.," San Francisco Business Times, June 5, 2014, http://tinyurl.com/pee39hf.

51. Alicia Freese, "Fair Share? Officials Struggle to Regulate Vermont's 'Sharing Economy,'" Seven Days, April 8, 2015, http://tinyurl.com/padu6gt.

52. Joseph Rose, "Portland Makes Uber and Lyft Legal – For Now," The Oregonian/OregonLive, April 22, 2015, http://tinyurl.com/ofp2fgx.

53. Brian Heaton, "California Bill Takes Aim at Home-Sharing Websites," Government Technology, May 4, 2015, http://tinyurl.com/ozytgds.

54. John Ribeiro, "Uber stops operations in Kansas over new legislation," PC World, May 6, 2015, http://tinyurl.com/nbkqqup.

55. Sam Sanders, "Santa Monica Cracks Down On Airbnb, Bans 'Vacation Rentals' Under A Month," NPR, May 13, 2015, http://tinyurl.com/oqgozky.

56. Joe Fitzgerald Rodriguez, "SFO, SFMTA ask state for stricter regulations of Uber and Lyft," The San Francisco Examiner, May 27, 2015, http://tinyurl.com/od9rnu3.

57. "Governor signs bills giving green light to rideshare services Uber and Lyft," The Associated Press, The Las Vegas Sun, May 29, 2015, http://tinyurl.com/nheq467.

58. Martyn Williams, "Lyft to pay $300K, make insurance changes in settlement with N.Y.," Computerworld, June 18, 2015, http://tinyurl.com/nlxcr68.

59. "The Road Ahead," Uber document submitted to the Portland, Ore., Bureau of Transportation, undated, accessed July 17, 2015, http://tinyurl.com/omrzatv.

60. Don Jergler, "Uber Announces New Policy to Cover Gap," Insurance Journal, March 14, 2014, http://tinyurl.com/pbq2w4t.

61. Brian R. Fitzgerald, "Airbnb: Accidents Can Happen, So Here's $1 Million in Liability Insurance," Digits, The Wall Street Journal, Nov. 20, 2014, http://tinyurl.com/np4t583.

62. Emily Badger, "Airbnb is about to start collecting hotel taxes in more major cities, including Washington," The Washington Post, Jan. 29, 2015, http://tinyurl.com/nac6kdd.

63. Elaine S. Povich, "How Governments Are Trying to Tax the Sharing Economy," Governing, June 18, 2014, http://tinyurl.com/o6kgtao.

64. Robert Reich, "The Share-the-Scraps Economy," Feb. 2, 2015, http://tinyurl.com/mjyjwyg.

CHAPTER 3

1. Danielle Ivory and Keith Bradsher, "Regulators Investigating 2nd VW Computer Program on Emissions," The New York Times, Oct. 8, 2015, http://tinyurl.com/oqbl2ab.

2. Jack Ewing, "Volkswagen, Hit by Emissions Scandal, Posts Its First Loss in Years," The New York Times, Oct. 28, 2015, http://tinyurl.com/ptqgr2c.

3. Karl Russell et al., "How Volkswagen Got Away With Diesel Deception," The New York Times, Jan. 5, 2016, http://tinyurl.com/h697u97.

4. James Temperton, "AVG can sell your browsing and search history to advertisers," Wired UK, Sept. 18, 2015, http://tinyurl.com/oat9j68.

5. Corey Ciocchetti, "The Eavesdropping Employer: A Twenty-First Century Framework for Employee Monitoring," May 29, 2010, available at SSRN, http://tinyurl.com/jfy8enl.

6. "The Latest on Workplace Monitoring and Surveillance," American Management Association, Nov. 17, 2014, http://tinyurl.com/yjb4q4a.

7. Marc Rotenberg, "Comments of the Electronic Privacy Information Center to the Office of Science and Technology Policy Request for Information: Big Data and the Future of Privacy," Electronic Privacy Information Center, April 4, 2014, http://tinyurl.com/hbo2xvx.

8. Kashmir Hill, "How Target Figured Out A Teen Girl Was Pregnant Before Her Father Did," Forbes, Feb. 16, 2012, http://tinyurl.com/hp97tbj.

9. "Big Data in Private Sector and Public Sector Surveillance," Electronic Frontier Foundation, 2014, http://tinyurl.com/hm2j37f.

10. "Gartner Says, By 2018, Half of Business Ethics Violations Will Occur Through Improper Use of Big Data Analytics," news release, Gartner Inc., Oct. 7, 2015, http://tinyurl.com/hyxkypl.

11. "2012 Institute Initiatives," Business Roundtable Institute for Corporate Ethics, undated, accessed Jan. 20, 2016, http://tinyurl.com/hdvrj73.

12. George W. Reynolds, "Ethics in Information Technology," 2015, p. 12.

13. For background, see Chuck McCutcheon, "Whistleblowers," CQ Researcher, Jan. 31, 2014, http://tinyurl.com/hno4xsl.

14. "Big Data & Analytics," IDC, undated, accessed Jan. 20, 2016, http://tinyurl.com/z8o2fa8.

15. "Data Brokers: A Call for Transparency and Accountability," Federal Trade Commission, May 2014, http://tinyurl.com/mwury6w.

16. Neil M. Richards and Jonathan H. King, "Big Data Ethics," Wake Forest Law Review, May 19, 2014, p. 393, http://tinyurl.com/hz33hlm.

17. "A Review of the Data Broker Industry: Collection, Use, and Sale of Consumer Data for Marketing Purposes," Committee on Commerce, Science and Transportation staff report, Dec. 18, 2013, http://tinyurl.com/zdqh2lk.

18. Rotenberg, op. cit.

19. Kate Tummarello, "Rockefeller: 'Data brokers' worse than NSA spying," The Hill, Dec. 18, 2013, http://tinyurl.com/ltry4zu.

20. "A Review of the Data Broker Industry," op. cit.

21. Testimony of Tony Hadley before the Senate Committee on Commerce, Science and Transportation, Dec. 18, 2013, http://tinyurl.com/jyz9deb.

22. Testimony of Jerry Cerasale before the Senate Committee on Commerce, Science and Transportation, Dec. 18, 2013, http://tinyurl.com/glgg6se.

23. Steve Lohr, "Unblinking Eyes Track Employees," The New York Times, June 21, 2014, http://tinyurl.com/n5zpsjs.

24. "The Latest on Workplace Monitoring and Surveillance," op. cit.

25. Andrew McAfee, "In Praise of Electronically Monitoring Employees," Harvard Business Review, Oct. 24, 2013, http://tinyurl.com/hbzwux9.

26. Ciocchetti, op. cit.

27. Ibid.

28. Bruce Schneier, "Data and Goliath: The Hidden Battles to Collect Your Data and Control Your World," 2015, p. 109.

29. "Lawsuit accuses Wells Fargo of using Net to discriminate," The Associated Press, CNET, Sept. 6, 2002, http://tinyurl.com/zgljzk5.

30. Written testimony of Jim Allchin, State of New York v. Microsoft Corp., U.S. District Court, May 3, 2002, http://tinyurl.com/j7f6c7j.

31. Stephen Shankland, "Governments to see Windows code," CNET, Jan. 30, 2003, http://tinyurl.com/zo53s8v.

32. John Carroll, "Proprietary software: A defence," ZDNet, Dec. 16, 2003, http://tinyurl.com/hhkpbl6.

33. Comments of General Motors LLC before the U.S. Copyright Office, March 27, 2015, http://tinyurl.com/hntwwzu.

34. "Big Data and Privacy: A Technological Perspective," President's Council of Advisers on Science and Technology, May 2014, p. 3, http://tinyurl.com/p92vpo5.

35. Ibid.

36. Samuel D. Warren and Louis D. Brandeis, "The Right to Privacy," Harvard Law Review, Dec. 15, 1890, http://tinyurl.com/nzkpn8t.

37. Reynolds, op. cit., p. 156.

38. Mark J. Furletti, "An Overview and History of Credit Reporting," discussion paper, Federal Reserve Bank of Philadelphia, June 2002, http://tinyurl.com/gnnlr7g.

39. Ibid.

40. "Data Brokers: A Call for Transparency and Accountability," op. cit.

41. "Federal Trade Commission 2014 Privacy and Data Security Update," Federal Trade Commission, 2014, http://tinyurl.com/h32cyxz.

42. "Privacy in Cyberspace, Module 3; Introduction: Privacy in the Workplace," Berkman Center for Internet and Society, Harvard Law School, undated, accessed Jan. 21, 2016, http://tinyurl.com/7jvco6f.

43. Ibid.

44. Ciocchetti, op. cit.

45. Ibid.

46. Ibid.

47. Robert M. Hunt, "You Can Patent That? Are Patents on Computer Programs and Business Methods Good for the New Economy?" Business Review, 2001, p. 7, http://tinyurl.com/h3bpyk8.

48. In re Alappat, 33 F.3d 1526 (Fed.Cir. 1994), http://tinyurl.com/h5mxlwk.

49. "Big Data: Seizing Opportunities, Preserving Values," the White House, February 2015, http://tinyurl.com/gqzaa5w.

50. "S. 668—Data Broker Accountability and Transparency Act of 2015," March 4, 2015, http://tinyurl.com/jouorxp.

51. Susan Taplinger, "DMA Expresses Disappointment with New 'Data Broker' Bill," Direct Marketing Association, Feb. 13, 2014, http://tinyurl.com/nlote3q.

52. "S. 668: Data Broker Accountability and Transparency Act of 2015," GovTrack, undated, accessed Jan. 21, 2016, http://tinyurl.com/zzd9tzc.

53. "Administration Discussion Draft: Consumer Privacy Bill of Rights Act of 2015," the White House, undated, accessed Jan. 21, 2015, http://tinyurl.com/oydmctk.

54. "Analysis of the Consumer Privacy Bill of Rights Act," Center for Democracy & Technology, March 2, 2015, http://tinyurl.com/h6be4wy.

55. "CEA: Government Must Not Stifle Innovation While Protecting Privacy," news release, Consumer Technology Association, Feb. 27, 2015, http://tinyurl.com/zs7gxtj.

56. "Statement on the Commerce Department's Consumer Privacy Legislative Discussion Draft," news release, The Internet Association, Feb. 27, 2015, http://tinyurl.com/jgntyaj.

57. Richards and King, op. cit., p. 395.

CHAPTER 4

1. Frank Kalman, "MetLife's Global Mobility Surge," Talent Management, May 1, 2015, http://tinyurl.com/hozwqnn.

2. Ibid.

3. "Culture at Work. The value of intercultural skills in the workplace," British Council, undated, accessed March 8, 2016, http://tinyurl.com/gktl7pd.

4. Janina Conboye, "How valuable is international work experience?" Financial Times, Nov. 6, 2013, http://tinyurl.com/gu7rsbc.

5. "World Investment Report 2011," United Nations Conference on Trade and Development, 2011, http://tinyurl.com/z5r3cld; Eric Kolodner, "Transnational corporations: Impediments or catalysts of social developments?" United Nations Research Institute for Social Development, undated, accessed March 9, 2010, http://tinyurl.com/j9tqw5b.

6. "The World's Top 100 Non-Financial TNCs Ranked by Foreign Assets," Topforeignstocks.com, Sept. 16, 2014, http://tinyurl.com/zuq5ehl.]

7. "Talent mobility: 2020 and beyond," PwC, undated, accessed March 8, 2016, http://tinyurl.com/z29cshd.

8. Shirley J. Daniel, Fujiao Xie and Ben L. Kedia, "2014 U.S. Business Needs for Employees with International Expertise," Internationalization of U.S. Education in the 21st Century conference, April 2014, http://tinyurl.com/hftpezd.

9. "World Investment Report 2011," op. cit.

10. "Talent mobility: 2020 and beyond," op. cit.

11. Paula Caligiuri, David Lepak and Jaime Bonache, "Managing the Global Workforce," 2010, p. 105.

12. Erin Griffith, "Vente-Privée USA to shut down," Fortune, Oct. 27, 2014, http://tinyurl.com/z3n8a5x.

13. Robert Salomon, "Global Vision: How Companies Can Overcome the Pitfalls of Globalization," 2016, p. 12.

14. Ibid., p. 5.

15. Ibid., p. 7.

16. "World Investment Report 2011," op. cit.

17. "Talent mobility: 2020 and beyond," op. cit.

18. Ibid.

19. Ibid.

20. Ibid.

21. Paula Caligiuri, David Lepak and Jaime Bonache, "Managing the Global Workforce," 2010, p. 87.

22. Jay A. Gonger and Ronald E. Riggio, "The Practice of Leadership: Developing the Next Generation of Leaders," 2012, Jossey Bass.

23. "Ready-Now Leaders: 25 Findings to Meet Tomorrow's Business Challenges: Global Leadership Forecast 2014-2015," The Conference Board and Development Dimensions International, undated, accessed March 8, 2016, http://tinyurl.com/zrvk5yt.

24. Dyan Machan, "Cultural Ambassador," Barron's, March 9, 2013, http://tinyurl.com/zgf43te.

25. Lillian Cunningham, "Novartis CEO talks about drug costs, paying doctors and 'doing the right thing,'" The Washington Post, Sept. 24, 2015, http://tinyurl.com/zfr7psb.

26. Shirley J. Daniel, Fujiao Xie and Ben L. Kedia, "2014 U.S. Business Needs for Employees with International Expertise," for the Internationalization of U.S. Education in the 21st Century conference, April 2014, http://tinyurl.com/hftpezd.

27. "Open Doors Data," Institute of International Education, undated, accessed March 8, 2016, http://tinyurl.com/jdqboqc.

28. "Globalization of Management Education: Changing International Structures, Adaptive Strategies, and the Impact on Institutions," Association to Advance Collegiate Schools of Business (AACSB) International, 2011, http://tinyurl.com/jb4enfn.

29. Ibid.

30. Daniel et al., op. cit.

31. Kellye Whitney, "Special Edition: Executive Education," Chief Learning Officer, Feb. 22, 2016, http://tinyurl.com/j523mxg.

32. Ibid.

33. "Social Media: Enabling HR Service Delivery," Deloitte, undated, accessed March 9, 2016, http://tinyurl.com/zkgvvql.

34. Jack Simpson, "How L'Oréal uses social media to increase employee engagement," Oct. 22, 2015, http://tinyurl.com/hczyhoa.

35. Shareen Pathak, "Lenovo created an internal social network to improve employee engagement," July 28, 2015, http://tinyurl.com/jsxsbuf.

36. Mike Swift, "At Google, groups are key to company's culture," The San Jose Mercury News, June 22, 2011, http://tinyurl.com/6z422zf.

37. "Foster a Fair and Inclusive Google," Google Diversity, undated, accessed May 27, 2016, http://tinyurl.com/omdxqmq.

38. Kristin Burnham, "Social Business: Slow And Steady Worked for Philips," Information Week, May 20, 2014, http://tinyurl.com/j5zff9z.

39. Ibid.

40. Charlene Li, "Why No One Uses the Corporate Social Network," Harvard Business Review, April 7, 2015, http://tinyurl.com/pkhx32b.

41. Jed Greer and Kavaljit Singh, "A Brief History of Transnational Corporations," Global Policy Forum, 2000, http://tinyurl.com/jnm5twy.

42. Ibid.

43. "Multinational Corporation," Encyclopaedia Britannica, undated, accessed March 9, 2016, http://tinyurl.com/gl7lbda.

44. Ralph Ossa, "Multinational Firms and Foreign Direct Investment," undated, accessed March 9, 2016, http://tinyurl.com/zjakhlq.

45. "Our History," Ford Motor Co., undated, accessed March 9, 2016, http://tinyurl.com/l2c3fwp.

46. "Our Company: History," Colgate-Palmolive Co., undated, accessed March 9, 2016, http://tinyurl.com/768ysam.

47. Alan M. Rugman, ed., "The Oxford Handbook of International Business," 2009, p. 48, http://tinyurl.com/j94vb5k.

48. Ibid, p. 49.

49. "Understanding the WTO: Basics," World Trade Organization, undated, accessed March 9, 2016, http://tinyurl.com/z46yskm.

50. "Understanding the WTO," World Trade Organization, undated, accessed March 9, 2016, http://tinyurl.com/zwmreku.

51. "Treaty Establishing the European Coal and Steel Community, ECSC Treaty," European Union, undated, accessed March 9, 2016, http://tinyurl.com/hjz8kpo.

52. "The history of the European Union," European Union, undated, accessed March 9, 2016, http://tinyurl.com/hw6joxy.

53. "NAFTA: History," GlobalEdge, undated, accessed March 9, 2016, http://tinyurl.com/gtvx8a5.

54. "CFR Backgrounders," Council on Foreign Relations, undated, accessed March 9, 2016, http://tinyurl.com/h655huj.

55. "TPP: What is it and why does it matter?" BBC News, Feb. 3, 2016, http://tinyurl.com/psjahsa.

56. Eric Kolodner, "Transnational corporations: Impediments or catalysts of social developments?" United Nations Research Institute for Social Development, November 1994, http://tinyurl.com/j9tqw5b; "World Investment Report 2011," op. cit.

57. "General Electric Company," Reference for Business, undated, accessed March 9, 2016, http://tinyurl.com/zxnpjex.

58. "World Investment Report 2013," United Nations Conference on Trade and Development, 2013, http://tinyurl.com/px9xegg.

59. "Our Beginnings," Shell Global, undated, accessed March 9, 2016, http://tinyurl.com/gsgw6te.

60. "World Investment Report 2013," op. cit.

61. Ibid. For other years, see http://tinyurl.com/z8ew6un.

62. Ibid.

63. Ibid.

64. "What's Next: Future Global Trends Affecting Your Organization," The Economist Intelligence Unit, undated, accessed March 9, 2016, http://tinyurl.com/jtafcmo.

65. "Talent mobility: 2020 and beyond," op. cit.

66. Ibid.

67. Ibid.

68. "Global Employee Mobility – Increased Diversification Across Types of International Assignments Used," Mercer, Dec. 1, 2015, http://tinyurl.com/hn7zgrn.

69. MetLife Global Leadership Development Program, undated, accessed March 9, 2016, http://tinyurl.com/jc8mfov.

70. "Labor force, female (% of total labor force)," the World Bank, undated, accessed March 9, 2016, http://tinyurl.com/zhuqofy.

71. "Talent mobility: 2020 and beyond," op. cit.

72. Mark McGraw, "The Expat Gender Gap," Human Resource Executive Online, Aug. 22, 2013, http://tinyurl.com/hyuksfk.

73. "Talent mobility: 2020 and beyond," op. cit.

74. "2015 Global Mobility Trends Survey Report," Brookfield Global Relocation Services, 2015, p. 14, downloaded from http://tinyurl.com/jb76hep.

75. "2015 Global Mobility Trends Survey Report," op. cit., p. 15.

76. "Globalization of Management Education: Changing International Structures, Adaptive Strategies, and the Impact on Institutions," op. cit.; "Global 500 2015," Fortune, http://tinyurl.com/lx78j4f.

77. "What's Next: Future Global Trends Affecting Your Organization," op. cit.

78. "Social Media: Enabling HR Service Delivery," op. cit.

79. "What's Next: Future Global Trends Affecting Your Organization," op. cit.

80. "Global Employee Mobility," op. cit.

81. Ibid.

82. Ibid.

83. Elaine Pofeldt, "Shocker: 40% of Workers Now Have 'Contingent' Jobs, Says U.S. Government," Forbes, May 25, 2015, http://tinyurl.com/h32wfcz.

84. "The World in 2050: Will the shift in global economic power continue?" PwC, February 2015, http://tinyurl.com/ojomu5d.

85. "2015 World Population Data Sheet," Population Reference Bureau, undated, accessed March 9, 2016, http://tinyurl.com/oxnmhbg.

86. "Engaging and Integrating a Global Workforce," SHRM Foundation, February 2015, http://tinyurl.com/j4l7rz3.

87. "Talent mobility: 2020 and beyond," op. cit.

CHAPTER 5

1. "Raise," Secret Deodorant, http://tinyurl.com/z3dsatu.

2. Carrie Lukas, "Sorry Secret: Women Shouldn't Sweat The Wage Gap," The Federalist, May 6, 2016, http://tinyurl.com/hz5onlf; Lelia Gowland, "Secret Deodorant Tried (And Failed) To Explain The Wage Gap," ThinkProgress, May 6, 2016, http://tinyurl.com/hvaon2g.

3. "The Council on Women and Girls: Economic Empowerment Accomplishments," The White House Summit, June 2016, http://tinyurl.com/z39f5av; "Gender Pay Inequality," Joint Economic Committee, U.S. Congress, April 2016, http://tinyurl.com/z669qj9.

4. Cassie Werber, "Yet more research proves it: Companies with women in senior roles are more profitable," Quartz, March 8, 2016, http://tinyurl.com/gwupjd6.

5. Lauren Weber and Rachel Louise Ensign, "Promoting Women Is Crucial," The Wall Street Journal, Sept. 27, 2016, http://tinyurl.com/hs6eblq.

6. Marcus Noland, Tyler Moran and Barbara Kotschwar, "Is Gender Diversity Profitable? Evidence from a Global Survey," Peterson Institute for International Economics, February 2016, p. 8, http://tinyurl.com/j8l82xp.

7. "Breaking away: The path forward for women in alternatives," KPMG, September 2015, p. 10, http://tinyurl.com/zfvmee9.

8. "Women in S&P 500 Companies," Catalyst, Sept. 19, 2016, http://tinyurl.com/qcnwko5; "Women CEOs Of The S&P 500," Catalyst, Sept. 30, 2016, http://tinyurl.com/oxc43te.

9. "A Deeper Dive Into the Composition of Fortune 1000 Executive Teams," DiscoverOrg, http://tinyurl.com/zb6oa9d.

10. Deborah Gillis, "How women can fast-track success and get top jobs," CNBC, March 3, 2015, http://tinyurl.com/glj5exg.

11. "The real reasons fewer women make it to the C-suite," Advisory Board, Oct. 1, 2015, http://tinyurl.com/z9nt75w.

12. Ibid., p. 5.

13. Ibid., p. 11.

14. Ibid.

15. Larry Kim, "After Shattering Glass Ceiling, Women CEOs Fall Off the Glass Cliff," Inc., Oct. 28, 2014, http://tinyurl.com/gmtkpgr; Susanne Bruckmuller and Nyla R. Branscombe, "How Women End Up on the 'Glass Cliff'," Harvard Business Review, January-February 2011, http://tinyurl.com/jht9xhw.

16. Rachel Feintzeig and Joann S. Lublin, "Female CEOs, Still a Rarity, Face Extra Pressures," The Wall Street Journal, Aug. 9, 2016, http://tinyurl.com/gt55z8a.

17. Jennifer Reingold, "Why Top Women Are Disappearing From Corporate America," Fortune, Sept. 9, 2016, http://tinyurl.com/hafp9fx.

18. Tanya Basu, "Timeline: A History of GM's Ignition Switch Defect," NPR, March 31, 2014, http://tinyurl.com/zuyky4h.

19. Manuel Roig-Franzia et al., "The fall of Roger Ailes: He made Fox News his 'locker room' – and now women are telling their stories," The Washington Post, July 22, 2016, http://tinyurl.com/jsfebo4; Gabriel Sherman, "The Revenge of Roger's Angels," New York magazine, Sept. 2, 2016, http://tinyurl.com/hrjtdjf.

20. John Koblin, "Roger Ailes Stands Defiant as Fox Settles Lawsuits," The New York Times, Sept. 6, 2016, http://tinyurl.com/gluy7kc.

21. "2015 Working Mother 100 Best Companies," Working Mother, http://tinyurl.com/zoj5gw9;

Michael Cohn, "KPMG Gender Discrimination Lawsuit Expands," Accounting Today, May 13, 2016, http://tinyurl.com/zmk94o2; Jeffrey Tobias Halter, "Gender discrimination in organizations is still a real issue in 2016," New York Daily News, Aug. 10, 2016, http://tinyurl.com/zzxhses.

22. Valentina Zarya, "Female CEOs Have a 1 in 4 Chance of Being Targeted by Activist Investors," Fortune, Aug. 16, 2016, http://tinyurl.com/hpwneqz.

23. Molly Gamble, "Women Make Up 73% of Health-care Managers But Only 18% of Hospital CEOs," Becker's Hospital Review, July 27, 2012, http://tinyurl.com/zyhyj3x; Sydney Ember, "For Women in Advertising, It's Still a 'Mad Men' World," The New York Times, May 1, 2016, http://tinyurl.com/hqcyxen; Barri M. Blauvelt, "Breaking Barriers: Lessons from the Top Women in Pharma and Healthcare," PM360, Jan. 16, 2014, http://tinyurl.com/gvbddx7; Quoctrung Bui, "Who Studies What? Men, Women And College Majors," NPR, Oct. 28, 2014, http://tinyurl.com/j6zp8d4.

24. "The Rockefeller Foundation launches '100x25' campaign to reach 100 women CEOs of the Fortune 500 companies by 2025," press release, the Rockefeller Foundation, May 12, 2016, http://tinyurl.com/hhywwvp.

25. Tanaya Macheel, "Women in Banking: Tackling the Gender Gap, Inside and Out," Sept. 1, 2016, http://tinyurl.com/zeq5bwh; "Accounting MOVE Project," 2016, Accounting & Financial Women's Alliance, http://tinyurl.com/hfs6wcd.

26. Nancy Altobello, "Why Building A Pipeline Of Female Leaders Is In Your Company's Best Interest," Forbes, March 7, 2016, http://tinyurl.com/hz3fv8v.

27. Brent Lang, "Patricia Arquette's Comments Draw Praise, Unleash Controversy," Variety, Feb. 23, 2015, http://tinyurl.com/mbve5cn.

28. "Written Testimony of Lisa M. Maatz," U.S. Equal Employment Opportunity Commission, March 16, 2016, http://tinyurl.com/j9cst2o.

29. Linda Babcock and Sara Laschever, "Women Don't Ask: Negotiation and the Gender Divide," Princeton University Press, 2003.

30. Linda Babcock and Sara Laschever, "Negotiation and the Gender Divide," Women Don't Ask, undated, http://tinyurl.com/2esecup.

31. Danielle Douglas-Gabriel, "Study finds prolonged gender wage gap among college graduates," Chicago Tribune, Sept. 13, 2016, http://tinyurl.com/jdbgvzf.

32. "Written Testimony of Lisa M. Maatz," op. cit.

33. Alicia Adamczyk, "6 Excuses for the Gender Pay Gap You Can Stop Using," Money, April 12, 2016, http://tinyurl.com/hq42hxp.

34. Lydia Dishman, "A Detailed Look At How Complex Equal Pay Day Really Is," Fast Company, April 12, 2016, http://tinyurl.com/h34akpe.

35. Dr. Andrew Chamberlain, "Demystifying the Gender Pay Gap: Evidence from Glassdoor Salary Data," Glassdoor.com, March 23, 2016, http://tinyurl.com/znxed63.

36. Ibid., p. 23.

37. Elizabeth Olson, "Female Lawyer's Gender-Bias Suit Challenges Law Firm Pay Practices," The New York Times, Aug. 31, 2016, http://tinyurl.com/zjvunb7.

38. Kristina Launey and Annette Tyman, "High Profile Pay Equity 'Champions': U.S. Women's Soccer Players File EEOC Wage Discrimination Charge," Seyfarth Shaw, March 31, 2016, http://tinyurl.com/juxuc5r.

39. "City Of Alexandria Finds Substantial Gender Equity In Employee Compensation," AlexandriaNews.org, Sept. 12, 2016, http://tinyurl.com/jcno8t8.

40. Lisa Bertagnoli, "Nonprofits hiring more female CEOs, but they make less," Crain's Chicago Business, Sept. 13, 2016, http://tinyurl.com/gotvwl2.

41. Greg Bensinger, "Amazon Survey Shows Equal Gender Pay Among Its Workforce," The Wall Street Journal, March 23, 2016, http://tinyurl.com/hgtyyha.

42. "Fact Sheet: White House Announces New Commitments to the Equal Pay Pledge," The White House, Aug. 26, 2016, http://tinyurl.com/jzmlkbs.

43. Zachary A. Goldfarb, "Male-female pay gap remains entrenched at White House," The Washington Post, July 1, 2014, http://tinyurl.com/h26rbhb.

44. Tom Starner, "Microsoft, Facebook both announce they have reached gender pay equality," HR Dive, April 12, 2016, http://tinyurl.com/zbg2gn5.

45. "Questions and Answers, Notice of Proposed Changes to the EEO-1 to Collect Pay Data fr

Certain Employers," U.S. Equal Employment Opportunity Commission, http://tinyurl.com/glwyavc.

46. Ariane Hegewisch et al., "Pathways to Equity: Narrowing the Wage Gap by Improving Women's Access to Good Middle-Skill Jobs," Institute for Women's Policy Research, March 2016, http://tinyurl.com/gmtwzoe.

47. Kerry Ann Rockquemore, "Mentors vs. Sponsors," Inside Higher Ed, June 3, 2015, http://tinyurl.com/z8obh7w.

48. "White Paper: Advocacy vs. Mentoring," Sylvia Ann Hewlett Associates, undated, http://tinyurl.com/zqdzony.

49. Ibid.

50. Ibid.

51. Ibid.

52. "Unlocking the full potential of women at work," McKinsey & Company, 2012, http://tinyurl.com/hcgqbpg.

53. Alex Molinaroli, "Closing the gender gap in senior management," World Economic Forum, Jan. 18, 2016, http://tinyurl.com/jj3v6pk.

54. "Sponsoring Women To Success," Catalyst, 2011, http://tinyurl.com/o5jze6s.

55. Katty Kay and Claire Shipman, "The Confidence Code," 2015, http://tinyurl.com/gprqj28.

56. Jessica Stillman, "Another Reason to Lean In: Other Women Will Thank You," Women 2.0, March 13, 2013, http://tinyurl.com/hj9geb5.

57. "White Paper: Advocacy vs. Mentoring," op. cit.

58. Kristen Jones and Eden King, "Stop 'Protecting' Women from Challenging Work," Harvard Business Review, Sept. 9, 2016, http://tinyurl.com/j6vaxm3.

59. Ibid.

60. "Workplace mentors benefit female employees more than men," ScienceDaily, Oct. 12, 2015, http://tinyurl.com/hztxfdv.

61. Maxwell Murphy, "Women, Minorities, Continue CFO Gains in 2015: Study," The Wall Street Journal, Feb. 2, 2016, http://tinyurl.com/hbw59wb.

62. "Arjuna Capital: Amazon Reverses Itself On Pay Equity Fight, Shareholder Resolution To Be Withdrawn," PR Newswire, March 23, 2016, http://tinyurl.com/j83amgd.

63. Clare O'Connor, "Meet The Woman Investor Pushing Amazon, Google, And More To Close Gender Pay Gap," Forbes, March 29, 2016, http://tinyurl.com/zz5f5ff; Katie Johnston, "She's pressing top companies on pay equity," Boston Globe, May 21, 2016, http://tinyurl.com/j6s6tjg.

64. Cole Stangler, "As Proxy Season Arrives, Activist Shareholders Are Challenging Corporations On A Range Of Labor Practices," International Business Times, March 24, 2016, http://tinyurl.com/jkh4p7v.

65. Elizabeth Weise, "Intel diversity stats show slow pace of progress," USA Today, Feb. 3, 2016, http://tinyurl.com/grfulbt.

66. Aarti Shahani, "Intel Discloses Diversity Data, Challenges Tech Industry To Follow Suit," NPR, Feb. 3, 2016, http://tinyurl.com/zf3b64s.

67. Steven Musil, "Microsoft's female workforce shrank 2 percent last year," CNET, Nov. 23, 2015, http://tinyurl.com/zzulohr.

68. Lauren Weber, "Why Employers Are Making Pay Equity a Reality," The Wall Street Journal, Sept. 26, 2016, http://tinyurl.com/zhl4bt7.

69. Bourree Lam, "The Two Women Who Kicked Off Salesforce's Company-Wide Salary Review," The Atlantic, April 12, 2016, http://tinyurl.com/h3gxfhp; Cindy Robbins, "Equality at Salesforce: The Equal Pay Assessment Update," March 8, 2016, http://tinyurl.com/zvq2k2o.

70. Kristin Chessman, "16 Legendary Women Entrepreneurs," Entrepreneur, Aug. 6, 2008, http://tinyurl.com/hcarokd.

71. David Holahan, "How Brownie Wise got the Tupperware party started," USA Today, July 11, 2016, http://tinyurl.com/hokmhda.

72. "Women's Roles in the 1950s," Gale, 2001, http://tinyurl.com/z9ee3yw.

73. George Guilder, "Women in the Work Force," The Atlantic, September 1986, http://tinyurl.com/on8k72m.

74. Ibid.

75. Kate Dries, "What You'll Learn From A *Woman's Dress for Success Book* from 1977," Jezebel, July 30, 2013, http://tinyurl.com/zuvm2qq.

76. Kate Stone Lombardi, "As a Magazine Folds, a New Venture Begins," The New York Times, Dec. 9, 2001, http://tinyurl.com/z98fp88.

77. U.S. Census Bureau, "Disparities in STEM Employment by Sex, Race, and Hispanic Origin," Sept. 2013, p. 5, http://tinyurl.com/z69pjyd.

78. Nicholas St. Fleur, "Many Women Leave Engineering, Blame The Work Culture," NPR, Aug. 12, 2014, http://tinyurl.com/j9mghmz.

79. "Women in Leadership," Pew Research Center, Jan.14, 2015, http://tinyurl.com/ztgfssl.

80. Louann Brizendine, "The Female Brain," Random House, 2006, http://tinyurl.com/zqauzba.

81. Dan Goleman, "Are Women More Emotionally Intelligent Than Men?" Psychology Today, April 29, 2011, http://tinyurl.com/pap39c5.

82. Marti Barletta, "Understand that Women Often Have Hidden Financial Control," blog, http://tinyurl.com/gpftxfn.

83. Marti Barletta, "Women's Spiral Buying Path," blog, http://tinyurl.com/gpftxfn.

84. Fran Durekas, "Helping Get On-Site Child Care," Working Mother, Nov. 30, 2009, http://tinyurl.com/hbr8lkj.

85. Stephen Marche, "Home Economics: The Link Between Work-Life Balance and Income Equality," The Atlantic, July/August 2013, http://tinyurl.com/h7annrg.

86. Lawrence Mishel, Elise Gould and Josh Bivens, "Wage Stagnation in Nine Charts," Economic Policy Institute, Jan. 6, 2015, http://tinyurl.com/kqhsc3c; Aaron Stern, "Day Care Now Costs More Than College Tuition in Most States," Newsmax, April 11, 2014, http://tinyurl.com/jhzxq56.

87. Wendy Wang, Kim Parker and Paul Taylor, "Breadwinner Moms," Pew Research Center, May 29, 2013, http://tinyurl.com/p78gmjv.

88. "The real reasons fewer women make it to the C-suite," Advisory Board, Oct. 1, 2015, p. 11, http://tinyurl.com/z9nt75w.

89. Damian Troise and Matt Ott, "Paid family leave benefits rising in some sectors, regions," The Associated Press, Aug. 2, 2016, http://tinyurl.com/zyhk55p.

90. Richard Pérez-Peña, "How the Trump and Clinton Child Care Plans Stack Up," The New York Times, Sept. 14, 2016, http://tinyurl.com/hn4nck8.

91. Bryce Covert, "The Fight Working Moms Won," The New York Times, Sept. 17, 2016, http://tinyurl.com/h5bo45p.

92. Susan K. Livio, "You probably don't know N.J. allows paid family leave, study says," NJ.com, March 30, 2016, http://tinyurl.com/hce55dp.

93. "U.S. Talent Shortage Survey," The Manpower-Group, 2015, http://tinyurl.com/hlv77gz.

94. "Mending the gender gap," PwC, May 2013, http://tinyurl.com/h5dgfur.

95. "Unlocking the full potential of women at work," McKinsey, 2012, http://tinyurl.com/hcgqbpg.

96. Nicole Stephens and Evan Apfelbaum, "The Real Reasons Diversity Programs Don't Work," Fortune, Aug. 16, 2016, http://tinyurl.com/gn9qwpo.

97. Ibid.

98. "iRelaunch Comprehensive List of Career Reentry Programs Worldwide," iRelaunch, http://tinyurl.com/j7yh4cv; Vivian Giang, "Why Re-Entrance Programs Aren't Working," Fast Company, June 27, 2016, http://tinyurl.com/guqnr5s; and Salvador Rodriguez, "Silicon Valley To Women Who've Left Tech: Please Come Back," International Business Times, Jan. 28, 2016, http://tinyurl.com/hyf53m4.

99. Stephens and Apfelbaum, op. cit.

100. "Women Entrepreneurs 2014: Bridging the Gender Gap in Venture Capital," Babson College, 2014, http://tinyurl.com/j55klqr.

101. Kate R. Salop, "The One Thing That Will Get More Women In the C-Suite," Fortune, March 8, 2016, http://tinyurl.com/zxb52my.

102. Nick Timiraos, "How Older Women Are Reshaping U.S. Job Market," The Wall Street Journal, Feb. 22, 2016, http://tinyurl.com/gn25fyn.

103. Robin J. Ely, Pamela Stone and Colleen Ammerman, "Rethink What You 'Know' About High-Achieving Women," Harvard Business Review, Dec. 2014, http://tinyurl.com/l4dzsoe.

104. Sava Berhané, "How To Make Gender Equality At Work Matter To Everyone," Fast Company, Oct. 23, 2015, http://tinyurl.com/h459ymy.

CHAPTER 6

1. Jeanette S. Martin and Lillian H. Chaney, "Global Business Etiquette: A Guide to International Communication," 2012.

2. "Clarizen Survey: Workers Consider Status Meetings a Productivity-Killing Waste of Time," Clarizen, Jan. 22, 2015, http://tinyurl.com/nbgpbye.

3. "American Time Use Survey," Bureau of Labor Statistics, 2014, http://tinyurl.com/yku9t89.

4. Peter M. Monge, Charles McSween and JoAnne Wyer, "A Profile of Meetings in Corporate America: Results of the 3M Meeting Effectiveness Study," Center for Effective Organizations, November 1989, p. 12, http://tinyurl.com/zb3hhwj.

5. Been Kim and Cynthia Rudin, "Learning About Meetings," Massachusetts Institute of Technology, June 8, 2013, http://tinyurl.com/zfxkzex.

6. Julian Birkinshaw and Jordan Cohen, "Make Time for the Work That Matters," Harvard Business Review, September 2013, http://tinyurl.com/jq9v9vg.

7. Sigal Barsade and Olivia A. O'Neill, "Quantifying Your Company's Emotional Culture," Harvard Business Review, Jan. 6, 2016, http://tinyurl.com/zmb6pfc.

8. Steven G. Rogelberg et al., "Lateness to meetings: Examination of an unexplored temporal phenomenon," European Journal of Work and Organizational Psychology, January 2013, http://tinyurl.com/jth9f4o.

9. Monge, McSween and Wyer, op. cit.

10. Gretchen Gavett, "What People Are Really Doing When They're on a Conference Call," Harvard Business Review, Aug. 19, 2014, http://tinyurl.com/z2fcj9a.

11. Phyllis Korkki, "Telecommuting Can Make the Office a Lonely Place a Study Says," The New York Times, Jan. 2, 2016, http://tinyurl.com/zbrrv5u.

12. Website of Edward Sturm, http://tinyurl.com/hm7xsx3.

13. Margaret Rouse, "Agile project management," TechTarget, August 2011, http://tinyurl.com/gws2ge9.

14. Bill Mears, "Justice Ginsburg ready to welcome Sotomayor," CNN.com, June 16, 2009, http://tinyurl.com/zpr5llw.

15. Ibid.

16. "When What You Know Is Not Enough: Expertise and gender dynamics in task groups," Insight/Kellogg School of Business, May 2007, http://tinyurl.com/hgnm56s.

17. Deborah Tannen's website, http://tinyurl.com/jhxftmf.

18. Gina Stepp, "Deborah Tannen: Communicating with Style," Vision, Winter 2009, http://tinyurl.com/hsv6bea.

19. Chris Bart and Gregory McQueen, "Why Women Make Better Directors," International Journal of Business Governance and Ethics, 2013, http://tinyurl.com/ztdwfkm; "Women Make Better Decisions Than Men, Study Suggests," ScienceDaily, March 26, 2013, http://tinyurl.com/zhofq2f.

20. Marti Bartletta, "Men Are So Emotional! Why Women Are Better Buyers," MartiBarletta.com, Feb. 9, 2016, http://tinyurl.com/hq9tx22.

21. Erin White, "Deloitte Tries a Different Sales Pitch for Women," The Wall Street Journal, Oct. 8, 2007, http://tinyurl.com/zfdpj8j.

22. Scott Schieman, Markus Schafer and Mitchell McIvor, "When Leaning In Doesn't Pay Off," The New York Times, Aug. 10, 2013, http://tinyurl.com/mmuzpxj.

23. Gary Richardson, "Medieval Guilds," EH.net Encyclopedia, March 16, 2008, http://tinyurl.com/zrshm23.

24. "An interview with Frank M. Bryan," University of Chicago Press, 2003, http://tinyurl.com/nzxxb.

25. "Norman Rockwell [1894–1978], Freedom of Speech, The Saturday Evening Post, 1943," Picturing America, National Endowment for the Humanities, http://tinyurl.com/jo9qtdt.

26. For a good account of the convention, see Catherine Drinker Bowen, "Miracle at Philadelphia: The Story of the Constitutional Convention, May to September 1787," 1986.

27. Helen B. Schwartzman, "The Meeting: Gatherings in Organizations and Communities," 1989.

28. Schwartzman, ibid., pp. 57–58; "Melville Dalton papers, 1941-2003," Online Archive of California, undated, accessed Feb. 2, 2016, http://tinyurl.com/zhlerf5.

29. "Short History of Robert's Rules," The Official Robert's Rules of Order website, http://tinyurl.com/ztphvhc.

30. "Constitution and Bylaws," Midwestern History Association, http://tinyurl.com/gunobjq.

31. Schwartzman, op. cit., p. 41.

32. "Chapter 17 – Strategies for Individual Motions Illustrated," Westside Toastmasters, http://tinyurl.com/jlk64xf.

33. Schwartzman, op. cit., p. 7.

34. Ibid., p. 43.

35. Peter Abrahamsson Lindeblad, "Organisational effects of virtual meetings," IIIEE Theses, September 2012, http://tinyurl.com/jxw8998.

36. Joe Mullich, "The New Face of Face-to-Face Meetings," The Wall Street Journal and Sprint, undated, http://tinyurl.com/mw9cz2.

37. "Meetings in America," Verizon, 1998, http://tinyurl.com/6kldp5c.

38. "Meetings in America V: Meeting of the Minds," MCI, 2003, http://tinyurl.com/gr8qxfp.

39. Kim and Rudin, op. cit.

40. "Anthropology in Practice" exploring the human condition," Scientific American, http://tinyurl.com/3jsdx99.

41. Rachel Emma Silverman, "Where's the Boss? Trapped in a Meeting," The Wall Street Journal, Feb. 14, 2012, http://tinyurl.com/jtkrgv7.

42. "What It Takes to Collaborate," Herman Miller, 2012, http://tinyurl.com/z4x7m4u.

43. Paul Graham, "Maker's Schedule, Manager's Schedule," PaulGraham.com, July 2009, http://tinyurl.com/nl5h5z.

44. Ibid.

45. Jill Duffy, "The Best Online Collaboration Software for 2015," PC magazine, Aug. 6, 2015, http://tinyurl.com/jgtd9la.

CHAPTER 7

1. Alan E. Brill, "From Hit and Run to Invade and Stay: How Cyberterrorists Could Be Living Inside Your Systems," Defense Against Terrorism Review, Fall 2010, pp. 23–26, http://tinyurl.com/h4ur8sj.

2. Peter Maass and Megha Rajagopalan, "Does Cybercrime Really Cost $1 Trillion?" Pro Publica, Aug. 1, 2012, http://tinyurl.com/c73fp6d.

3. "Net Losses: Estimating the Global Cost of Cybercrime," Center for Strategic and International Studies, June 2014, http://tinyurl.com/hcadx9o.

4. "Cybercrime will Cost Businesses $2 Trillion by 2019," Security, May 12, 2015, http://tinyurl.com/q4xdojo.

5. "Hackers Inc.," The Economist, July 12, 2014, http://tinyurl.com/jdwamzj.

6. "Comprehensive Study on Cybercrime," United Nations Office on Drugs and Crime, February 2013, p. 17, http://tinyurl.com/bncy969.

7. Brill, op. cit.

8. "Advanced Persistent Threats: How they Work," Symantec, undated, accessed Dec. 7, 2015, http://tinyurl.com/qzenuoq.

9. Andrea Peterson, "The Sony Pictures hack, explained," The Washington Post, Dec. 18, 2014, http://tinyurl.com/hqn9bql.

10. Brian Krebs, "Email Attack on Vendor Set Up Breach at Target," Krebs on Security, Feb. 12, 2014, http://tinyurl.com/oab53g7.

11. Ahiza Garcia, "Target settles for $39 million over data breach," CNN Money, Dec. 2, 2015, http://tinyurl.com/gome6a9; Jia Lynn Yang and Amrita Jayakumar, "Target says up to 70 million more customers were hit by December data breach," The Washington Post, Jan. 10, 2014, http://tinyurl.com/hd83vcy.

12. Ellen Nakashima, "Chinese government has arrested hackers it says breached OPM database," The Washington Post, Dec. 2, 2015, http://tinyurl.com/hjluugw.

13. "'Anonymous' hackers hit PlayStation and Sony websites in revenge for lawsuit," The Daily Mail, April 6, 2011, http://tinyurl.com/3sfydx6.

14. Chloe Albanesius, "Did Anonymous Hack Sony's PlayStation Network or Not?" PCMag, May 4, 2011, http://tinyurl.com/6c2b9pp.

15. Chloe Albanesius, "Spanish Police Arrest 'Anonymous' Members for Sony PlayStation Hack," PCMag, June 10, 2011, http://tinyurl.com/68eedzl.

16. Rob Price, "A security firm claims it was Russia that hacked Sony—and that it still has access," Business Insider, Feb. 5, 2015, http://tinyurl.com/zsnk8os.

17. "APT1: Exposing One of China's Cyber Espionage Units," Mandiant, February 2013, http://tinyurl.com/bjnsvjo; Nicole Perlroth, "Hackers in China Attacked The Times for Last 4 Months," The New

York Times, Jan. 30, 2013, http://tinyurl.com/az7s5ep.

18. Bruce Stokes, "Extremists, cyber-attacks top Americans' security threat list," Pew Research Center, Jan. 2, 2014, http://tinyurl.com/hmu8cjp.

19. Warwick Ashford, "Sony hack exposes poor security practices," Computer Weekly.com, Dec. 4, 2014, http://tinyurl.com/zw49jjx; Aaron Boyd, "OPM breach a failure on encryption, detection," Federal Times, June 22, 2015, http://tinyurl.com/zde47hs.

20. Larry Ponemon, "Cost of Data Breaches Rising Globally, Says '2015 Cost of Data Breach Study: Global Analysis,'" Ponemon Institute and IBM, May 27, 2015, http://tinyurl.com/zjozwe8.

21. "Target's data theft leaves CEOs everywhere on the hot seat," Bloomberg News, The Boston Globe, May 7, 2014, http://tinyurl.com/gwqqmcv; Evan Perez and Wesley Bruer, "OPM Director Katherine Archuleta steps down," CNN, July 11, 2015, http://tinyurl.com/gpxgrd4; and Dave McNary, "Amy Pascal Talks Getting 'Fired,' Sony Hack and Angelina Jolie Emails in Candid Interview," Variety, Feb. 11, 2015, http://tinyurl.com/okoxxlt.

22. Charles Arthur, "Sony suffers second data breach with theft of 25m more user details," The Guardian, May 3, 2011, http://tinyurl.com/osps3mq.

23. Chloe Albanesius, "Sony LulzSec Hack: What You Need to Know," PCMag, June 3, 2011, http://tinyurl.com/3r5jvaf; Peter Bright, "Sony hacked yet again, plaintext passwords, e-mails, DOB posted," Arstechnica, June 2, 2011, http://tinyurl.com/ksccn2b; and Keith Stuart and Charles Arthur, "PlayStation Network hack: why it took Sony seven days to tell the world," The Guardian, April 27, 2011, http://tinyurl.com/ozc92xb.

24. Lorenzo Franceschi-Bicchierai, "Sony Pictures leak shows employees used worst passwords ever," Mashable, Dec. 2, 2014, http://tinyurl.com/zooaa3s.

25. John Gaudiosi, "Why Sony didn't learn from its 2011 hack," Fortune, Dec. 24, 2014, http://tinyurl.com/qfdate3.

26. Robert Lemos, "Sony Pegs Initial Cyber-Attack Losses at $35 Million," eWeek, Feb. 4, 2015, http://tinyurl.com/z5mnrwm.

27. Bob Moritz and David Burg, "How corporate America can fight cybersecurity threats," Fortune, Feb. 17, 2015, http://tinyurl.com/jhfsxh5.

28. "95% of Small Businesses Lack Cyber Security Insurance: Survey," Carrier Management, May 4, 2015, http://tinyurl.com/jnsvayl.

29. Tara Seals, "Home Depot: Massive Breach Happened Via Third-Party Vendor Credentials," Infosecurity magazine, Nov. 7, 2014, http://tinyurl.com/z9222g4.

30. "FERC Eyes Development of Supply Chain Cyber Controls in New Reliability Standards," news release, Federal Energy Regulatory Commission, July 16, 2015, http://tinyurl.com/h4jj5v6.

31. "Framework for Improving Critical Infrastructure Cybersecurity," National Institute of Standards and Technology, Feb. 12, 2014, http://tinyurl.com/l9ydeyh.

32. Taylor Armerding, "NIST's finalized cybersecurity framework receives mixed reviews," CSOonline, Jan. 31, 2014, http://tinyurl.com/zt48lot.

33. Julie Brill, "Stepping into the Fray: The Role of Independent Agencies in Cybersecurity," Keynote Address Before the Center for Strategic and International Studies, Sept. 17, 2014, http://tinyurl.com/zvblepd.

34. Richard Raysman and Francesca Morris, "What CIOs Need to Know About the FTC Cybersecurity Ruling," CIO Journal, The Wall Street Journal, Aug. 31, 2015, http://tinyurl.com/plejspd.

35. "Why you should adopt the NIST Cybersecurity Framework," PricewaterhouseCoopers, May 2014, http://tinyurl.com/zcxsdzc.

36. Armerding, op. cit.

37. Alina Selyukh, "U.S. offers companies broad standards to improve cybersecurity," Reuters, Feb. 12, 2014, http://tinyurl.com/jgenx9k.

38. Matthew Pennington, "US advised to examine 'hack back' options against China," The Associated Press, Nov. 17, 2015, http://tinyurl.com/olb3h3a.

39. "The NSA files: Edward Snowden's surveillance revelations explained," The Guardian, Nov. 1, 2013, http://tinyurl.com/lfe3629.

40. Ellen Nakashima, "House set to produce first major cyber legislation in years," The Washington Post, April 22, 2015, http://tinyurl.com/j83vqgu.

41. David E. Sanger and Nicole Perlroth, "Senate Approves a Cybersecurity Bill Long in the Works and Largely Dated," The New York Times, Oct. 27, 2015, http://tinyurl.com/zn6vxk3.

42. Pennington, op. cit.

43. National Cybersecurity and Communications Integration Center website, Department of Homeland Security, Sept. 30, 2015, http://tinyurl.com/z684jdy.

44. Ellen Nakashima, "House set to produce first major cyber legislation in years," The Washington Post, April 22, 2015, http://tinyurl.com/j83vqgu; Tom Risen, "Cybersecurity Bill Passes in Senate," U.S. News & World Report, Oct. 27, 2015, http://tinyurl.com/hlkrp5z.

45. Andrew Couts,"Senate Kills Cybersecurity Act of 2012," Digital Trends, Aug. 2, 2012, http://tinyurl.com/gn8tnfj.

46. Andrea Peterson, "Senate passes cybersecurity information sharing bill despite privacy fears," The Washington Post, Oct. 27, 2015, http://tinyurl.com/qjljuj3.

47. Phil Lapsley, "The Definitive Story of Steve Wozniak, Steve Jobs, and Phone Phreaking," The Atlantic, Feb. 20, 2013, http://tinyurl.com/ay8vt48.

48. Abraham Riesman, "Twilight of the Phreaks: The Fates of the 10 Best Early Hackers," Motherboard, March 9, 2012, http://tinyurl.com/hjd9yzo.

49. Andy Greenberg, "Kevin Mitnick, Once the World's Most Wanted Hacker, Is Now Selling Zero-Day Exploits," Wired, Sept. 24, 2014, http://tinyurl.com/leapoaz; Steven Brandt, "A Review, Masters of Deception: The Gang That Ruled Cyberspace," SF Site, http://tinyurl.com/hxzbefa.

50. Susan W. Brenner, "Cybercrime: Criminal Threats From Cyberspace," 2010, p. 16, via Google Books, http://tinyurl.com/h7ztt5s.

51. "Russian Hacker Is Sentenced To 3 Years in Citibank Heist," Dow Jones Newswires, The Wall Street Journal, Feb. 24, 1998, http://tinyurl.com/zypevsx; Amy Harmon, "Hacking Theft of $10 Million From Citibank Revealed," Los Angeles Times, Aug. 19, 1995, http://tinyurl.com/jolpd4r.

52. "Comprehensive Study on Cybercrime," op. cit., p. 39.

53. "A History of Anonymous," InfoSec Institute, undated, accessed Dec. 7, 2015, http://tinyurl.com/no7gzp9.

54. Ryan Singel, "War Breaks Out Between Hackers and Scientology—There Can Be Only One," Wired, Jan. 23, 2008, http://tinyurl.com/hd66hll.

55. "Anonymous activists target Tunisian government sites," BBC, Jan. 4, 2011, http://tinyurl.com/j2lmlc4; Peter Svensson, "Anonymous Hacker Group Attacks Egyptian Government Sites," The Huffington Post, Feb. 2, 2011, http://tinyurl.com/4vkzxm9.

56. Gaudiosi, op. cit.

57. Charles Arthur, "Anonymous says Sony accusations over PlayStation Network hack are lies," The Guardian, May 5, 2011, http://tinyurl.com/jsp7499; Fahmida Y. Rashid, "Sony Data Breach Was Camouflaged by Anonymous DDoS Attack," eWeek, May 5, 2011, http://tinyurl.com/hhh3f2u.

58. Andrew Griffin, "Anonymous group takes down Isis website, replaces it with Viagra ad along with message to calm down," The Independent, Nov. 26, 2015, http://tinyurl.com/oknlugj.

59. George Gao, "What Americans think about NSA surveillance, national security and privacy," Pew Research Center, May 29, 2015, http://tinyurl.com/hgdks9u.

60. Daniel Castro, "How Much Will PRISM Cost the U.S. Cloud Computing Industry?" Information Technology & Innovation Foundation, Aug. 5, 2013, http://tinyurl.com/zzll63e.

61. Don Clark, "Cisco CEO: 'Never Seen' Such a Falloff in Orders,'" The Wall Street Journal, Nov. 14, 2013, http://tinyurl.com/z6suo3o.

62. Anna Fifield, "N Korea's computer hackers target South and US," FT.com, Oct. 4, 2004, http://tinyurl.com/hjlc6us.

63. Dave Lee and Nick Kwek, "North Korean hackers 'could kill,' warns key defector," BBC, May 29, 2015, http://tinyurl.com/jk3jmyh.

64. Tim Jordan, "Hacking: Digital Media and Technological Determinism," 2008, via Google Books, http://tinyurl.com/zfsbnhl.

65. Ibid.

66. Jonathan Krim and David A. Vise, "AOL Employee Charged in Theft of Screen Names," The Washington Post, June 24, 2004, http://tinyurl.com/jgnhbye.

67. Ross Kerber, "Banks claim credit card breach affected 94 million accounts," The New York Times, Oct. 24, 2007, http://tinyurl.com/huskzqq.

68. James Verini, "The Great Cyberheist," The New York Times Magazine, Nov. 10, 2010, http://tinyurl.com/gqfttnr; Kim Zetter, "Hacker Sentenced to 2ᶜ

Years for Breach of Credit Card Processor," Wired, March 26, 2010, http://tinyurl.com/hnkkbcu.

69. "Why you should adopt the NIST Cybersecurity Framework," PricewaterhouseCoopers, May 2014, http://tinyurl.com/zcxsdzc.

70. Cory Bennett, "State AGs clash with Congress over data breach laws," The Hill, July 7, 2015, http://tinyurl.com/hxtjvmf.

71. Jonathan Stempel, "FTC has power to police cyber security: appeals court," Reuters, Aug. 24, 2015, http://tinyurl.com/zpytv5o.

72. Jonathan Stempel and Nandita Bose, "Target in $39.4 million settlement with banks over data breach," Reuters, Dec. 2, 2015, http://tinyurl.com/za5skbp.

73. Nicole Perlroth, "Banks' Lawsuits Against Target for Losses Related to Hacking Can Continue," The New York Times, Dec. 4, 2015, http://tinyurl.com/o7ovw88.

74. Deborah Scally, "Managing Cyber Risk: Are Companies Safeguarding Their Assets?" Corporate Board Member Magazine and NYSE Governance Services, 1st Quarter 2015, http://tinyurl.com/zf768js.

75. Michael Dickstein and Jonathan R. Visbal, "Cybersecurity: The Board's Role," Spencer Stuart, August 2015, http://tinyurl.com/hqun6m9.

76. "Security experts hack into moving car and seize control," Reuters, CNBC, July 22, 2015, http://tinyurl.com/qdcfk47.

77. Phil Goldstein, "Ericsson backs away from expectation of 50B connected devices by 2020, now sees 26B," Fierce Wireless, June 3, 2015, http://tinyurl.com/hsjhupt; Barbara Vergetis Lundin, "50 billion connected IoT devices by 2020," Smart Grid News, April 21, 2015, http://tinyurl.com/psnlrf3.

78. "Cybersecurity and the Internet of Things," Ernst and Young, March 2015, p. 1, http://tinyurl.com/hfgd3ar.

79. Axel Buecker et al., "Security in Development: The IBM Secure Engineering Framework," IBM Redguide, March 18, 2010, http://tinyurl.com/hqxt4yo.

80. "Car Cybersecurity: What do the automakers really think?" The Ponemon Institute, p. 2, http://tinyurl.com/gul2sx4.

81. "Cybersecurity and the Internet of Things," op. cit.

CHAPTER 8

1. Tim Kastelle, "Hierarchy Is Overrated," Harvard Business Review, Nov. 20, 2013, http://tinyurl com/ksaur6h.

2. David A. Garvin, "How Google Sold Its Engineers on Management," Harvard Business Review, December 2013, http://tinyurl.com/oggkvhu.

3. Nicolai J. Foss and Peter G. Klein, "Why Managers Still Matter," MIT Sloan Management Review, Fall 2014, http://tinyurl.com/pzm64b4.

4. Garvin, op. cit.

5. Jim Belosic, "5 Ways A Flat Management Structure Can Empower Your Business," American Express Open Forum, Aug. 29, 2013, http://tinyurl.com/mf93gh8.

6. "What Is Self-Management?" Morning Star Self-Management Institute, http://tinyurl.com/ozkccme.

7. Stephen Courtright, G.L. Stewart and M.R. Barrick, "Peer-Based Control in Self-Managing Teams: Linking Rational and Normative Influence With Individual and Group Performance," Journal of Applied Psychology, March 2012, http://tinyurl.com/p3u5e58.

8. "Is Peer Pressure Better Employee Motivator Than Money?" Insurance Journal, Aug. 7, 2012, http://tinyurl.com/nlo24c4.

9. Colette Meehan, "Flat Vs. Hierarchical Organizational Structure," Houston Chronicle/Demand Media, http://tinyurl.com/3gdycj3.

10. For more on Enron, see Susan Boswell, "The Smartest Guys in the Room: Management Lessons from Enron's Leaders," Baltimore Post-Examiner, Dec. 22, 2012, http://tinyurl.com/kmmr6h8.

11. Klint Finley, "Why Workers Can Suffer in Bossless Companies Like GitHub," Wired, March 20, 2014, http://tinyurl.com/obu4gv6.

12. Jacob Shriar, "Can A Flat Hierarchy Really Work?" Officevibe, Jan. 8, 2014, http://tinyurl.com/kwdzj4g.

13. "Mission Command Center of Excellence," U.S. Army Combined Arms Center, updated Aug. 28, 2014, http://tinyurl.com/l6wqx32.

14. Drake Baer, "Does Google Need Managers?" Fast Company, Nov. 25, 2013, http://tinyurl.com/l97kcz3; "Strategic Alignment Business Cases," Advance! Business Consulting, 2009, http://tinyurl.com/lhvsfaw; and Marc Gunther, "3M's innovation revival," Fortune, Sept. 24, 2010, http://tinyurl.com/l6vhwye.

15. "W.L. Gore & Associates," Forbes, updated October 2014, http://tinyurl.com/nr4w5yu; "A

Team-Based, Flat Lattice Organization," W.L. Gore & Associates, undated, http://tinyurl.com/yq6aup.

16. Mike Kessler, "Insane in the Membrane," Outside, March 7, 2012, http://tinyurl.com/cgaycx8.

17. Polly LaBarre, "Forget Empowerment—Aim for Exhilaration," Management Innovation eXchange, April 25, 2012, http://tinyurl.com/bu2y3rn; Mehdi Kajbaf, "The most radical workplace in the world and 10 reasons why it's worked for 30 years," Organizational Effectiveness Solutions blog, Oct. 8, 2012, http://tinyurl.com/ledzqak.

18. Kastelle, op. cit.

19. Courtright, et al., op. cit.

20. "Employee Engagement," Quantum Workplace, undated, http://tinyurl.com/p4dnk23.

21. James L. Heskett, et al., "Putting the Service-Profit Chain to Work," Harvard Business Review, July 2008, http://tinyurl.com/n9bc6vu.

22. Kastelle, op. cit.

23. Garvin, op. cit.

24. "Self-Management," Morning Star Co. Self-Management, undated, http://tinyurl.com/mfv5qtq.

25. Gary Hamel, "First, Let's Fire All the Managers," Harvard Business Review, December 2011, http://tinyurl.com/ms4ufk3.

26. Ibid.

27. "Welcome to Valve," Valve Software, undated, http://tinyurl.com/k6qfkpa; Claire Suddath, "Why There Are No Bosses at Valve," Bloomberg Businessweek, April 27, 2012, http://tinyurl.com/kjj7kcp.

28. "Handbook for New Employees," Valve Software, March 2012, http://tinyurl.com/7a3jjyb.

29. Leo Kelion, "Valve: How going boss-free empowered the games-maker," BBC, Sept. 23, 2013, http://tinyurl.com/l3jff98.

30. "A Team-Based, Flat Lattice Organization," op. cit.

31. Terri Kelly, "No More Heroes: Distributed Leadership," Management Innovation eXchange, April 8, 2010, http://tinyurl.com/m6xqjmr.

32. "How It Works," Holacracy, undated, http://tinyurl.com/nx3rojk

33. Aimee Groth, "Zappos is going holacratic: no job titles, no managers, no hierarchy," Quartz, Dec. 30, 2013, http://tinyurl.com/ppxhwc5; Tim Kastelle, "Two Great Innovation Misquotes," the Discipline of Innovation blog, undated, http://tinyurl.com/7peof8f.

34. Groth, "Zappos is going holacratic," op. cit.

35. Lawrence M. Fisher, "Ricardo Semler Won't Take Control," strategy+business, Nov. 29, 2005, http://tinyurl.com/nkfsk6a; also see Semco Partners homepage, http://tinyurl.com/q2zdp6x.

36. "Maneuver Self Study Program," U.S. Army Maneuver Center of Excellence, updated Nov. 21, 2014, http://tinyurl.com/k26ponm.

37. "Stanley McChrystal, Military leader," TED Talks, undated, http://tinyurl.com/orscj2q; "Mission Command Concept," National Defense University Libraries, updated Oct. 7, 2014, http://tinyurl.com/mec5phr.

38. Minda Zetlin, "The Power of Flat: How organizations without managers succeed in the real world," Oracle Profit, February 2014, http://tinyurl.com/ngh2zdy.

39. Staff report, "Soldiers of Fortune," Newsweek, Nov 13, 2009, http://tinyurl.com/lrrjt7o.

40. David Stein, "Dear CEO: They're Just Not That Into You," Forbes blog, Feb. 2, 2011, http://tinyurl.com/lqyqho7.

41. Foss and Klein, op. cit.

42. Andrew Beattie, "Adam Smith and 'The Wealth Of Nations,'" Investopedia, 2014, http://tinyurl.com/k4pezer.

43. Michael T. Hannan, "The Assembly Line," Encyclopaedia Britannica, undated, http://tinyurl.com/lf3gkxf.

44. Carter McNamara, "Historical and Contemporary Theories of Management," Free Management Library, undated, http://tinyurl.com/peus5os.

45. "They Made America: Frederick Winslow Taylor," PBS, undated, http://tinyurl.com/lzd8h76.

46. Lea Terry, "The Management Theory of Max Weber," Business.com, May 20, 2011, http://tinyurl.com/oqoosp3.

47. Jeanne Dininni, "Human Relations Management Theory," Business.com, Aug. 2, 2011, http://tinyurl.com/p4wx7ly.

48. Steve Denning, "The Management Revolution That's Already Happening," Forbes blog, May 30, 2013, http://tinyurl.com/laldc4f.

49. Foss and Klein, op. cit.

50. Gary Hamel, "Moon Shots for Management," Harvard Business Review, February 2009, http://tinyurl.com/kkx6wue.

51. Ibid.

52. Ibid.

53. Steve Denning, "Leadership's #1 Challenge: Transforming Management," Forbes blog, Feb. 28, 2011, http://tinyurl.com/qcfxesr.

54. David Hanna, "How GM Destroyed Its Saturn Success, March 8, 2010, Forbes, http://tinyurl.com/yjxf934; "How GM Crushed Saturn," April 3, 2009, Newsweek, http://tinyurl.com/nn6ukdj.

55. "Saturn: A Wealth of Lessons from Failure," the Wharton School, University of Pennsylvania, Oct. 28, 2009, http://tinyurl.com/pd9zypv.

56. Natalie Hackbarth, David Weisser and Hilary Wright, "2014 Employee Engagement Trends Report," Quantum Workplace, http://tinyurl.com/molc88r.

57. "How It Works," op. cit.; Steve Denning, "Making Sense of Zappos and Holacracy," Forbes blog, Jan. 15, 2014, http://tinyurl.com/nye4tcv.

58. Nellie Bowles, "Holacracy or Hella Crazy? The Fringe Ideas Driving the Las Vegas Downtown Project," Re/Code, http://tinyurl.com/kcs53k2; "The holes in holacracy: The latest big idea in management deserves some skepticism," The Economist, July 5, 2014, http://tinyurl.com/np4vvpv.

59. "About Holacracy," Medium, http://tinyurl.com/lhjw53p.

60. "Freedom by Design," WorldBlu, undated, http://tinyurl.com/5vtupth; Glenn Llopis, "Corporations Must Bring Democracy into the Workplace: A Conversation with WorldBlu, HCL Technologies and Groupon," Forbes blog, May 16, 2011, http://tinyurl.com/lopnk54; and Laurence McCahill, "Would You Want to Work in a Fear – or Freedom-Led Workplace?" The Huffington Post, Oct. 13, 2014, http://tinyurl.com/mwtyukk.

61. "What Is Self-Management?" op. cit.

62. Josh Allan Dykstra, "Why Self-Management Will Soon Replace Management," The Huffington Post, July 16, 2014, http://tinyurl.com/q57hal4.

63. Hamel, "First, Let's Fire All the Managers," op. cit.

64. Bunkhuon Chhun, "Better Decisions Through Diversity: Heterogeneity can boost group performance," Oct. 1, 2010, Kellogg School of Management at Northwestern University, http://tinyurl.com/lmf8m4g. See also Katherine W. Phillips, Katie A. Liljenquist and Margaret A. Neale, "Is the pain worth the gain? The advantages and liabilities of agreeing with socially distinct newcomers," Personality and Social Psychology Bulletin, Dec. 19, 2008, http://tinyurl.com/lj9qxtz; and Finley, op. cit.

65. Philippa Warr, "Former Valve Employee: 'It Felt a Lot Like High School,'" Wired, July 9, 2013, http://tinyurl.com/qamqxoe; see also Twitter of former employee at http://tinyurl.com/33tfmsm.

66. Jeri Ellsworth (video), "Former valve Engineer talks about CastAR 3D glasses," Twitch (podcast), June 28, 2013, http://tinyurl.com/o7fngod; Michael French, "Valve's 'perfect hiring' hierarchy has 'hidden management' clique like high school," Develop, July 8, 2013, http://tinyurl.com/m9j3td5.

67. Evelyn Rusli, "Torment Claims Make GitHub Grow Up," The Wall Street Journal, July 17, 2014, http://tinyurl.com/p2hxfbk.

68. Jason Fried, "Why I Run a Flat Company," Inc. magazine, April 2011, http://tinyurl.com/3wmhehp.

69. Karl Moore and Kyle Hill, "The Decline but Not Fall of Hierarchy—What Young People Really Want," Forbes blog, June 14, 2011, http://tinyurl.com/6sn5qxa.

70. See Gen. Martin E. Dempsey's speech before the Royal United Services Institute for Defense and Security Studies, June 1, 2011, found in "Mission Command Concept," op. cit.

71. Gen. Martin E. Dempsey, "Mission Command White Paper," U.S. Army Chairman of the Joint Chiefs of Staff, April 3, 2012, http://tinyurl.com/n6f5wpg.

CHAPTER 9

1. Aspen Ideas Festival 2014 A Conversation with Indra Nooyi and David Bradley, June 30, 2014, http://tinyurl.com/qzw3xhq.

2. Conor Friedersdorf, "Why PepsiCo CEO Indra K. Nooyi Can't Have It All," The Atlantic, July 1, 2014, http://tinyurl.com/ms7n3p6.

3. Max Schireson, "Why I am leaving the best job I ever had," Aug. 5, 2014, http://tinyurl.com/molla8x.

4.   Jena McGregor, "The greatest memo about work-life balance ever?," The Washington Post, Aug. 6, 2014, http://tinyurl.com/mg8fqor; and Laura Lorenzetti, "When a top CEO quits to be a better dad it's a giant leap forward for women execs," Fortune, Aug. 6, 2014, http://tinyurl.com/nppew5e.

5.   Brad Stone, "Work-Life Balance and the New Night Shift," Bloomberg Businessweek, Aug. 7, 2014, http://tinyurl.com/ofap7zn.

6.   Dan Witters and Diana Liu, "Using Mobile Technology for Work Linked to Higher Stress," Gallup Well-Being, May 2, 2014, http://tinyurl.com/ocgl3ac.

7.   James K. Harter, Frank L. Schmidt, et al., "The Relationship Between Engagement at Work and Organizational Outcomes," Gallup, Feb. 2013, http://tinyurl.com/pgb7ubm.

8.   Irene Padavic and Robin J. Ely, "The Work-Family Narrative as a Social Defense," Harvard Business School, March 1, 2013, http://tinyurl.com/pfdwpou.

9.   James K. Harter, Frank L. Schmidt and Corey L.M. Keyes, "Well-being in the workplace and its relationship to business outcomes: A review of the Gallup studies," American Psychological Association, November 2003, http://tinyurl.com/ow4jhj7.

10. Fred Van Deusen, et al., "Overcoming the Implementation Gap: How 20 Leading Companies are Making Flexibility Work," Boston College Center for Work & Family, 2007, http://tinyurl.com/qeq9348.

11. "What Are the Benefits?" Great Place to Work Institute, undated, http://tinyurl.com/cl7whj5.

12. "Ipsos Global Trends 2014: Navigating the new," Ipsos MORI, 2014, http://tinyurl.com/mfcb55k.

13. Allison Schrager, "Most Americans are Single, and They're Changing the Economy," Bloomberg Businessweek, Sept. 12, 2014, http://tinyurl.com/lgqbjxt.

14. Kara Swisher, "'Physically Together': Here's the Internal Yahoo No-Work-From-Home Memo for Remote Workers and Maybe More," All Things D, Feb. 22, 2013, http://tinyurl.com/a5xxnlx.

15. Deon Roberts, "Bank of America tells more workers to come into the office," Charlotte Observer / Herald Online, Oct. 11, 2014, http://tinyurl.com/k4auwmw.

16. T. Alexandra Beauregard and Lesley C. Henry, "Making the link between work-life balance practices and organizational performance," Human Resources Management Review 19, 2009, http://tinyurl.com/n9ec3m7.

17. "Workplace flexibility still a myth to most," Sloan Center on Aging & Work at Boston College, March 17, 2014, http://tinyurl.com/p37sq5s.

18. Steven Greenhouse, "A Push to Give Steadier Shifts to Part-Timers," The New York Times, July 15, 2014, http://tinyurl.com/nlk3usd.

19. Brenda Kowske, "The Flexible Workplace Delivers Results," Bersin by Deloitte, August 2013, http://tinyurl.com/oxjlfud.

20. "What Are the Benefits?" op. cit.

21. Julie Coffman and Russ Hagey, "Flexible work models: How to bring sustainability to a 24/7 world," Bain & Co., Oct. 18, 2010, http://tinyurl.com/nnn2row.

22. Kenneth Matos and Ellen Galinsky, "2014 National Study of Employers," Families and Work Institute, 2014, http://tinyurl.com/kvz2mwt.

23. KJ Dell'Antonia, "Paid Sick Leave: On Four Ballots, and Undefeated," Motherlode, The New York Times, Nov. 5, 2014, http://tinyurl.com/mrdyw3k.

24. Lisa Rein, "Patent office filters out worst telework abuses in report to its watchdog," The Washington Post, Aug. 10, 2014, http://tinyurl.com/oldg7j6.

25. Brian Bergstein, "Google Execs Have Ideas on How to Run Your Business," MIT Technology Review, Sept. 29, 2014, http://tinyurl.com/qy4mrgq.

26. "What Are the Benefits?" op. cit.

27. Janet Caldow, "Working Outside the Box: A Study of the Growing Momentum in Telework," Institute for Electronic Government, IBM Corp., Jan. 21, 2009, http://tinyurl.com/naw36tj.

28. Youngjoo Cha, "Overwork and the Persistence of Gender Segregation in Occupations," Gender & Society, April 2013, http://tinyurl.com/q95ukfh.

29. Nicholas Bloom, et al., "Does Working from Home Work? Evidence from a Chinese Experiment," Stanford University, Aug. 18, 2014, http://tinyurl.com/o5lnsqr.

30. Mary C. Noonan and Jennifer L. Glass, "The hard truth about telecommuting," Bureau of Labor Statistics Monthly Labor Review, June 2012, http://tinyurl.com/azwgmoy.

31. Xinyuan "Roy" Zhao, et al., "The Impact of Frontline Employees' Work-Family Conflict on Customer Satisfaction," Cornell Hospitality Quarterly Jan. 9, 2014, http://tinyurl.com/pkdhbnd.

32. Alastair Mitchell, "The Rise of the Millennial Workforce," Wired, Aug. 15, 2013, http://tinyurl.com/on6jvro.

33. Leslie Kwoh, "More Firms Bow to Generation Y's Demands," The Wall Street Journal, Aug. 22, 2012, http://tinyurl.com/nalyftn.

34. Sabrina Parsons, "Why I Tell My Employees to Bring Their Kids to Work," HBR Blog Network, April 22, 2014, http://tinyurl.com/mpmmtaw.

35. "State of Employee Benefits in the Workplace – Leveraging Benefits to Retain Workers," Society for Human Resource Management, Dec. 18, 2013, http://tinyurl.com/p8znjtx.

36. Roy Maurer, "Flexwork Policies on the Rise; Participation Lagging," Jan. 30, 2015, Society for Human Resource Management, http://tinyurl.com/mg8f4sp.

37. "2014 Workplace Flexibility Survey – Overview of Flexible Work Arrangement," Society for Human Resource Management, Oct. 15, 2014, http://tinyurl.com/o625h8s.

38. Vickie Elmer, "Actually, electricians are more in demand than engineers," Quartz, June 1, 2014, http://tinyurl.com/obok9p9.

39. Jodi Kantor, "Working Anything but 9 to 5," The New York Times, Aug. 13, 2014, http://tinyurl.com/morpl8b.

40. "Remarks by Labor Secretary Thomas E. Perez, White House Summit on Working Families," U.S. Department of Labor, June 9, 2014, http://tinyurl.com/pqlr9jj.

41. T. Alexandra Beauregard, "Fairness Perceptions of Work-Life Balance Initiatives: Effects on Counterproductive Work Behavior," British Journal of Management, 2014, http://tinyurl.com/l42emut.

42. Weldon Latham, "Workplace Diversity: 5 Legal Challenges to Work/Life Programs," Diversity Inc., undated, http://tinyurl.com/lled4wh.

43. Laura Stampler, "CEO Dads Open Up About Balancing Fatherhood and Work," Time, Sept. 15, 2014, http://tinyurl.com/phe3pfn.

44. Brad Harrington, "The Work-Life Evolution Study," Boston College Center for Work & Family, 2007, http://tinyurl.com/pustv56.

45. "Survey on Workplace Flexibility 2013," Worldat-Work, Oct. 2013, http://tinyurl.com/m74zhxm.

46. Cari Tuna and Joann S. Lublin, "Welch: 'No Such Thing as Work-Life Balance,'" The Wall Street Journal, July 14, 2009, http://tinyurl.com/kuyqxev.

47. Margaret Heffernan, "Female Execs Horrified by Former GE CEO's Comments," AOL Jobs, May 7, 2012, http://tinyurl.com/kktrmy3.

48. "Micro Success Story: Ryan LLC," Corporate Voices for Working Families, undated, http://tinyurl.com/mroyv2f; "District of Columbia Workplace Winners," When Work Works press release, Jan. 24, 2014, http://tinyurl.com/lfuny6q.

49. Monique Valcour, "Give Your Organization a Work-Life Vision," HBR Blog Network, Sept. 1, 2014, http://tinyurl.com/kv3nz6l.

50. Stewart D. Friedman and Sharon Lobel, "The Happy Workaholic: A role model for employees," Academy of Management Executive, August 2003, http://tinyurl.com/m6ftlfe.

51. Kevin Wheeler, "Is There a Future for Work/Life Balance?" ERE, Aug. 9, 2009, http://tinyurl.com/m9opcq4.

52. Howard Markel, "How Elizabeth Blackwell became the first female doctor in the U.S.," PBS Newshour, Jan. 23, 2014, http://tinyurl.com/kpjzrwd.

53. "A History of Women in Industry, 1800-1880," National Women's History Museum, 2007, http://tinyurl.com/lq83ktf.

54. Leslie Foster Stebbins, "Work and Family in America: A Reference Handbook," ABC-CLIO, 2001.

55. Donald M. Fisk, "American Labor in the 20th Century," Bureau of Labor Statistics, Jan. 30, 2003, http://tinyurl.com/ko9md7d.

56. Ibid.

57. "History: Progressive Ideas," U.S. Department of Labor, http://tinyurl.com/psvqgyr.

58. "The 1911 Triangle Factory Fire," Cornell University, 2011, http://tinyurl.com/4vobubt.

59. Judson MacLaury, "A Brief History: The U.S. Department of Labor," U.S. Department of Labor, undated, http://tinyurl.com/pdbb9ot.

60. "The Great Depression," Franklin D. Roosevelt Presidential Library and Museum, http://tinyurl.com/k7mxk25.

61. "Rare color photos: 1940s working women," CBS News (from Library of Congress), various dates, http://tinyurl.com/p5bs6js.

62. "Changes in men's and women's labor force participation rates," Bureau of Labor Statistics, Jan. 10, 2007, http://tinyurl.com/7wk28o9.

63. Mitra Toosi, "A century of change: the U.S. labor force, 1950-2050," Bureau of Labor Statistics Monthly Labor Review, May 2002, http://tinyurl.com/3bwbpa.

64. "The Equal Pay Act: Equal Pay for Women," NOLO, undated, http://tinyurl.com/7mjc3c7.

65. "Milestones: 1965," Equal Employment Opportunity Commission, undated, http://tinyurl.com/m4smcco.

66. Harrington, op. cit.

67. Ibid.

68. Louise E. Single and Elizabeth Dreike Almer, "Research on Women's Advancement in Accounting," American Institute of Certified Public Accountants, April 4, 2011, http://tinyurl.com/mx5mssh.

69. Stewart Friedman, "Proving Leo Durocher Wrong: Driving Work Life Change at Ernst & Young," The Wharton Work/Life Integration Project, http://tinyurl.com/oerwblp.

70. Ibid.

71. Alfred, Richard, "The Wage and Hour Litigation Epidemic Continues," Seyfarth Shaw, May 16, 2014, http://tinyurl.com/l7aeuv9.

72. "Levi Strauss agrees to pay more than $1 million in overtime back wages to nearly 600 employees following US Labor Department investigation," U.S. Department of Labor, March 29, 2011, http://tinyurl.com/48mo3wv.

73. Meredith Chen, "Viewpoints: Women at Work: A New Debate is Born; The 'Mommy Track' Has Authorities Arguing About Women's Roles at Work," Los Angeles Times, March 19, 1989, http://tinyurl.com/m5bb8lc.

74. "Bridging the Gap: Bringing the Benefits of Paid Family Leave to American Workers," Institute for Women's Policy Research, Dec. 12, 2013, http://tinyurl.com/pz8c6f6.

75. Alina Tugend, "The Downsides of Generous Workplace Perks," The New York Times, Oct. 17, 2014, http://tinyurl.com/n3xgw6a.

76. "Highlights of Women's Earnings in 2013," December 2014, Bureau of Labor Statistics, table 2, http://tinyurl.com/oyy7v5y.

77. "2013 Employee Benefits," Society for Human Resource Management, undated, http://tinyurl.com/p59dvmh.

78. "EEOC Lawsuit Challenges Flambeau Over Wellness Program," U.S. Equal Employment Opportunity Commission, Oct. 1, 2014, http://tinyurl.com/oyj2sgx.

79. Angela Monaghan, Self-employment in UK at highest level since records began," The Guardian, Aug. 20, 2014, http://tinyurl.com/n89q9kb.

80. Vickie Elmer, "The 10 big companies with the most telecommuting options," Quartz, Jan, 9, 2014, http://tinyurl.com/kbjcl6y.

81. "Fastest Growing Occupations 2012–2022," Occupational Outlook Handbook, Bureau of Labor Statistics, January 2014, http://tinyurl.com/bpesmdc.

82. Mica Rosenberg, "U.S. government lawsuits target transgender discrimination in workplace," Reuters, Sept. 29, 2014, http://tinyurl.com/orouuvk.

83. Rebecca Knight, "Managing People from Five Generations," HBR Blog Network, Sept. 25, 2014, http://tinyurl.com/mnqy2a6.

84. "The Talent Shortage Continues," Manpower Group 2014 Talent Shortage Survey, http://tinyurl.com/odccxch.

85. Szu Ping Chan, "World trapped in 'painful jobs crisis', warns Lagarde," The Telegraph, Oct. 10, 2014, http://tinyurl.com/o4vutpb.

86. Lauren Weber, "Employers Are Getting More Flexible – Up to a Point," The Wall Street Journal, April 29, 2014.

87. Justin Fox, "Breaking Down the Freelance Economy," HBR Blog Network, Sept. 4, 2014, http://tinyurl.com/l6udzfj.

88. Data provided to Vickie Elmer and SAGE Business Researcher, Freelancers Union, November 2014; related report at http://tinyurl.com/pjxbdlt.

89. Spencer Soper, Sophia Pearson and Greg Stohr, "Amazon Workers Take Security Line Woes to Supreme Court," Bloomberg News, Oct. 6, 2014, http://tinyurl.com/lqrb8aj.

90. Adam Liptak, "Supreme Court Rules Against Worker Pay for Screenings in Amazon Warehouse Case," The New York Times, Dec. 9, 2014, http://tinyurl.com/pnetmw5.

91. Steven Greenhouse, "More Workers are Claiming 'Wage Theft,'" The New York Times, Sept. 1, 2014, http://tinyurl.com/nja6g5r.

92. Dave Jamieson, "New York Settles with McDonald's in Wage Theft Investigation," March 17, 2014, The Huffington Post, http://tinyurl.com/qgjp92r.

93. Jennifer Liberto, Sick leave policies pick up steam," CNNMoney, July 29, 2014, http://tinyurl.com/n56zwt9.

94. Julie Hirschfeld Davis, "Obama Plans to Push Paid Family and Sick Leave for Workers," The New York Times, Jan. 14, 2015, http://tinyurl.com/l46agtw.

95. "Pregnancy Discrimination Charges FY 2010 – FY 2013," U.S. Equal Employment Opportunity Commission, undated, http://tinyurl.com/lsg5l4b.

96. Nia-Malika Henderson, "Up next for the Supreme Court: Pregnant workers' rights," The Washington Post, July 3, 2014, http://tinyurl.com/obkwxha.

97. "Special Delivery," The Economist, Sept. 18, 2014, http://tinyurl.com/ln9ldw3.

98. Claire Zillman, "Wage watch: California enacts law to protect temp workers," Fortune, Oct. 3, 2014, http://tinyurl.com/mz56nsk.

99. Teresa Wiltz, "Flextime Wars Get New Fuel from States and Cities," Fiscal Times (originally Stateline), Sept. 30, 2014, http://tinyurl.com/mv5uadb.

100. Steve Vernon, "Retirement savings $14 trillion below threshold," CBS MoneyWatch, June 26. 2013, http://tinyurl.com/n8zweo3.

101. "Evolution of Work and the Worker," The Economist Intelligence Unit and SHRM Foundation, February 2014, http://tinyurl.com/kqp92hn.

102. "The MetLife Study of Caregiving: Costs to Caregivers," MetLife Mature Market Institute, June 2011, http://tinyurl.com/n37fosm.

103. "American Time Use Survey: Eldercare," Bureau of Labor Statistics, Sept. 30, 2014, http://tinyurl.com/qyapeug.

104. "The MetLife Study of Gen X: The MTV Generation Moves into Midlife," MetLife Mature Market Institute, April 2013, http://tinyurl.com/cpqfrfn.

105. "Millennial Women in the Workplace Success Index: Striving for Balance," Accenture, January 2010, http://tinyurl.com/p3wsp36.

106. Philip L. Rones, Randy E. Ilg and Jennifer M. Gardner, "Trends in hours of work since the mid-1970s," Bureau of Labor Statistics Monthly Labor Review, April 1997, http://tinyurl.com/n8s55ky.

107. Katie Kirkland, "On the decline in average weekly hours worked," Bureau of Labor Statistics Monthly Labor Review, July 2000, http://tinyurl.com/kyopjwy; Table B-2 Average weekly hours, Bureau of Labor Statistics, Oct. 3, 2014, http://tinyurl.com/y8oov3c.

108. John P. Robinson, et al., "The overestimated workweek revisited," Bureau of Labor Statistics Monthly Labor Review, June 2011, http://tinyurl.com/cyye7uk.

109. "The Best Places to Work 2013," Outside, undated, http://tinyurl.com/lzjcx7d.

110. Vickie Elmer, "Demand for accountants brings rising salaries, signing bonuses," Crain's Detroit Business, July 20, 2014, http://tinyurl.com/kolov3v.

111. Kathryn Vasel, "Very few companies offer unlimited vacation days, but these few do," CNNMoney, Sept. 24, 2014, http://tinyurl.com/l2jglya.

112. Alexander C. Kaufman, "Virgin's Unlimited Vacation Plan for Workers May Not be as Good as It Seems," The Huffington Post, Sept. 23, 2014, http://tinyurl.com/p7xptgk.

113. Elmer, "Electricians are in more demand," op. cit.

114. Tim Hansen, "The Future of Knowledge Work," Intel Labs, Oct. 2012, http://tinyurl.com/qaec64c.

115. "Growing Labor Shortages on the Horizon in Mature Economies," Conference Board, Sept. 2, 2014, http://tinyurl.com/m66axnn.

116. "State of Employee Benefits in the Workplace: Leveraging Benefits to Recruit Employees," Society for Human Resource Management, Jan. 10, 2013, http://tinyurl.com/jvuga5b.

CHAPTER 10

1. Sheryl Sandberg, Facebook post, Feb. 7, 2017, http://tinyurl.com/mntk8z7.

2. Ibid.

3. "DOL Factsheet: Paid Family and Medical Leave," U.S. Department of Labor, June 2015, http://tinyurl.com/md5vm7r.

4. "Forging Ahead or Falling Behind: Paid Family Leave at America's Top Companies," PL+US, Nov. 16, 2016, http://tinyurl.com/mkvcbbk.

5. Danielle Paquette, "When workers don't get paid sick days, everyone else is more likely to get sick," Chicago Tribune, Aug. 26, 2016, http://tinyurl.com/kaf2fu3.

6. Alicia Adamczyk, "These Are the Companies With the Best Parental Leave Policies," Money, Nov. 4, 2015, http://tinyurl.com/jbf8v27.

7. Ibid.; "Join Our Team," Squarespace, undated, http://tinyurl.com/mc5qg86.

8. Jena McGregor, "An 'unlimited parental leave policy sounds great, but will it work?" Los Angeles Times, Aug. 16, 2015, http://tinyurl.com/m5nnz7t.

9. "Key characteristics of parental leave systems," OECD Family Database, Directorate of Employment, Labour and Social Affairs, March 15, 2017, http://tinyurl.com/mclgdbw.

10. John Dodge, "The War for Tech Talent Escalates," Boston Globe, Feb. 19, 2016, http://tinyurl.com/zog2col.

11. "83% of Millennials—Now Largest Group of New Parents—Would Leave Their Job for One With Better Family/Lifestyle Benefits," Care.com, Aug. 10, 2015, http://tinyurl.com/ljep5xb.

12. "Global generations: A global study on work-life challenges across generations," Ernst & Young, 2015, http://tinyurl.com/mm8uc5s.

13. Brigit Katz, "Trump administration may amend maternity leave plan to include men," The New York Times, Feb. 7, 2017, http://tinyurl.com/l6avedx.

14. Frank Newport, "Trump Family Leave, Infrastructure Proposals Widely Popular," Gallup, April 7, 2017, http://tinyurl.com/k47mxwa.

15. Frank Kerbein, "Legislative Memo," Business Council, Feb. 4, 2016, http://tinyurl.com/l2xjop4.

16. "Health Policy Brief: Paid Family and Medical Leave," Health Affairs, Robert Wood Johnson Foundation, Nov. 21, 2016, http://tinyurl.com/n6gb9ff.

17. "The Economic Benefits of Paid Leave: Fact Sheet," Joint Economic Committee, U.S. Congress, Jan. 20, 2015, http://tinyurl.com/nylay7w.

18. Susan Wojcicki, "Paid Maternity Leave is Good for Business," The Wall Street Journal, Dec. 16, 2014, http://tinyurl.com/k3tdubl.

19. Susan Wojcicki, "Closing the Tech Industry Gender Gap," The Huffington Post, Jan. 27, 2017, http://tinyurl.com/m8jq3tk.

20. Celeste Smith, "Duke Energy to provide paid parental leave," The Charlotte Observer, Jan. 26, 2017, http://tinyurl.com/kam3wua.

21. Kristen Bellstrom, "EY Comes Out Swinging at Other Consulting Firms With New Parental Leave Policy," Fortune, April 13, 2016, http://tinyurl.com/zrn6v3h.

22. "Deloitte announces 16 weeks of fully paid family leave time for caregiving," Deloitte, Sept. 8, 2016, http://tinyurl.com/zvway5m.

23. Juliana Menasce Horowitz et al., "Americans Widely Support Paid Family and Medical Leave, but Differ Over Specific Policies," Pew Research Center, March 23, 2017, http://tinyurl.com/m7v6tfy.

24. "Paid Family and Medical Leave: Good for Business," National Partnership for Women & Families, March 2015, http://tinyurl.com/qzhnmxw.

25. "The Economic Benefits of Paid Leave: Fact Sheet," op. cit.

26. "Disability Insurance (DI) and Paid Family Leave (PFL) Weekly Benefit Amounts in Dollar Increments," California Employment Development Department, Jan. 1, 2017, http://tinyurl.com/ktkch8l.

27. Ibid.

28. "DOL Factsheet: Paid Family and Medical Leave," op. cit.

29. Alexia Fernández Campbell, "D.C.'s Battle for Paid Family Leave," The Atlantic, Dec. 19, 2016, http://tinyurl.com/mow4kpx.

30. Sean Sullivan and Robert Costa, "Donald Trump unveils child-care policy influenced by Ivanka Trump," The Washington Post, Sept. 13, 2016, http://tinyurl.com/l8qlmgd; "Inside the candidates' plans for paid leave and child care," PBS NewsHour, Sept. 14, 2016, http://tinyurl.com/znprv78.

31. Russell Berman, "A Conservative Push for Paid Family Leave," The Atlantic, Aug. 15, 2016, http://tinyurl.com/kc2x6bc.

32. Bourree Lam, "There's Superficial Agreement in Congress on Paid Family Leave," The Atlantic, Feb. 11, 2017, http://tinyurl.com/lfdk3bc.

33. Tim Wallace and Alicia Parlapiano, "Crowd Scientists Say Women's March in Washington H-

3 Times as Many People as Trump's Inauguration," The New York Times, Jan. 22, 2017, http://tinyurl.com/h9ggezt.

34. Heather Long, "Wait, did Trump endorse paid FAMILY leave?" CNN Money, March 6, 2017, http://tinyurl.com/ld7pcc5.

35. Ibid.

36. David Weigel, "Democrats get ahead of Trump with family leave plan," The Washington Post, March 14, 2017, http://tinyurl.com/n2m5xfs.

37. Jane Farrell and Sarah Jane Glynn, "The FAMILY Act: Facts and Frequently Asked Questions," Center for American Progress, Dec. 12, 2013, http://tinyurl.com/mgofkvv.

38. Claire Zillman, "Kirsten Gillibrand Is Giving Her Paid Family Leave Proposal Its First Trump-Era Test," Fortune, Feb. 7, 2017, http://tinyurl.com/z7xrxfk.

39. "Economic Effects of the Family and Medical Leave Insurance Act," Wharton School, University of Pennsylvania, Sept. 1, 2015, http://tinyurl.com/klbqezh.

40. Neyla Zannia, "SIA refutes claims that employees are penalized for taking sick leave," The Online Citizen, Feb. 9, 2017, http://tinyurl.com/m4gd6v3.

41. "Work-Life Imbalance: Expedia's 2016 Vacation Deprivation Study Shows Americans Leave Hundreds of Millions of Paid Vacation Days Unused," Expedia, Nov. 15, 2016, http://tinyurl.com/l38zw76.

42. Ibid.

43. Ibid.

44. "The State of American Vacation: How Vacation Became a Casualty of Our Work Culture," Project: Time Off, 2016, http://tinyurl.com/kqf5tze.

45. Jay L. Zagorsky, "Divergent Trends in US Maternity and Paternity Leave, 1994–2015," American Journal of Public Health, March 2017, http://tinyurl.com/l29spvb.

46. "What Is Paid Family Leave?" Paid Family Leave California, undated, http://tinyurl.com/kkbjecv.

47. Zagorsky, op. cit.

48. "TED: The Economics Daily," Bureau of Labor Statistics, U.S. Department of Labor, Nov. 4, 2016, http://tinyurl.com/l8kqcbt.

49. "Access to and Use of Leave—2011 Data from the American Time Use Survey Summary," Bureau of Labor Statistics, U.S. Department of Labor, Aug. 15, 2012, http://tinyurl.com/mwbxgpl.

50. Zagorsky, op. cit.

51. Ibid.

52. David I. Kertzer and Marzio Barbagli, eds., "Family Life in the Long Nineteenth Century, 1789–1913," Yale University Press, 2002, p. 149.

53. Ibid.

54. Ibid.

55. Jessica Deahl, "Countries Around the World Beat The U.S. On Paid Parental Leave," NPR, Oct. 6, 2016, http://tinyurl.com/ztdxu4p.

56. "History of the FMLA," National Partnership for Women & Families," undated, http://tinyurl.com/lgf4srg.

57. "Family and Medical Leave Act (FMLA) of 1993," Society for Human Resource Management, http://tinyurl.com/m35xrdp.

58. "Employee Benefits in the United States—March 2016," Bureau of Labor Statistics, U.S. Department of Labor, July 22, 2016, http://tinyurl.com/l9sdon9.

59. "Family and Medical Leave Act," Wage and Hour Division, U.S. Department of Labor, undated, http://tinyurl.com/mu524ez.

60. "State Paid Family Leave Insurance Laws," National Partnership for Women & Families, February 2017, http://tinyurl.com/l7crnbf.

61. "New and Expanded Employer Paid Family and Medical Leave Policies (2015–2017)," National Partnership for Women & Families, 2017, http://tinyurl.com/jnljruc.

62. Christine Sloane, "Maryland Senate Makes History," National Paid Sick Days Coalition, undated, http://tinyurl.com/l5bfjk4.

63. Carrie H. Colla et al., "Early Effects of the San Francisco Paid Sick Leave Policy," American Journal of Public Health, December 2014, http://tinyurl.com/lp4x2rg.

64. Ibid.

65. "Current Paid Sick Days Laws," National Partnership for Women & Families, Nov. 9, 2016, http://tinyurl.com/mt424nb.

66. "A history of paid sick leave legislation," TimeForce, undated, http://tinyurl.com/m8eyx4e.

67. "Current Paid Sick Days Laws," op. cit.

68. "H.R. 1516—Healthy Families Act," U.S. Congress, March 13, 2017, http://tinyurl.com/mb9l28m.

69. "Paid Time Off Programs and Practices," Worldat-Work, June 2016, http://tinyurl.com/zu8en2c.

70. Ibid.

71. Sam Sanders, "Netflix's New, Generous Parental Leave Policy Leaves Some Employees Out," NPR, Aug. 6, 2015, http://tinyurl.com/msf5web.

72. Susan Adams, "Virgin's New Paternity Leave Policy: It's Not Quite As Great As The Hype," Forbes, June 12, 2015, http://tinyurl.com/ko9gbfw.

73. Shannon Murphy, "Netflix: Extend paid parental leave policy to ALL employees," Coworker.org, August 2015, http://tinyurl.com/lzsp94m.

74. Shane Ferro, "Netflix Just Made Another Huge Stride On Parental Leave," The Huffington Post, Jan. 16, 2017, http://tinyurl.com/mwbrde8.

75. Gina Hall, "Activists petition Netflix to include hourly workers in parental leave policy," Silicon Valley Business Journal, Sept. 2, 2015, http://tinyurl.com/mwfn2yx.

76. Emily Peck, "Under Fire, Netflix Defends Lopsided Parental Leave Policy," The Huffington Post, Sept. 2, 2015, http://tinyurl.com/lh9unah.

77. Ibid.

78. Maggie Mertens, "Tech Companies Offer Great Perks, Just Not For Everyone," Refinery29, Aug. 10, 2015, http://tinyurl.com/lozhwno.

79. Anne D'Innocenzio, "Movement grows to require employers to offer paid sick leave for workers," U.S. News & World Report, May 19, 2015, http://tinyurl.com/ld2m4p8; Christopher Ingraham, "More than a third of American workers don't get sick leave, and they're making the rest of us ill," The Washington Post, Jan. 15, 2015, http://tinyurl.com/lawn84t.

80. "The Cost of Doing Nothing," U.S. Department of Labor, Sept. 4, 2015, http://tinyurl.com/mh68u57.

81. "New and Expanded Paid Family and Medical Leave Policies (2015–2017)," National Partnership for Women & Families, 2017, http://tinyurl.com/jnljruc.

82. Jennifer Ludden, "From Cooks To Accountants: Hilton Extends Paid Parental Leave To All," NPR, Oct. 11, 2016, http://tinyurl.com/ltdtydl.

83. Ibid.

84. Sanders, op. cit.

CHAPTER 11

1. Brendan Lyons, "Dredging up the truth: The GE PCB files," [Albany, N.Y.] Times-Union, March 8, 2014, http://tinyurl.com/lxv3kha; "Hudson River PCBs Superfund Site," U.S. Environmental Protection Agency, Oct. 30, 2014, http://tinyurl.com/yttb3r.

2. "Fact Sheet," General Electric (GE), http://tinyurl.com/mm5fvat.

3. "Ecomagination," GE, http://tinyurl.com/l45l9lv; also see http://tinyurl.com/lfxhf2w.

4. Jeffrey R. Immelt, "A Letter from the CEO," GE, undated, accessed Jan. 22, 2015, http://tinyurl.com/knmmmaf.

5. David Kiron, et al., "Sustainability's Next Frontier," MIT Sloan Management Review, Dec. 16, 2013, http://tinyurl.com/lxxtfro.

6. Jo Confino, "Best practices in sustainability, Ford, Starbucks and more," The Guardian (U.K.), April 30, 2014, http://tinyurl.com/kjewham.

7. "Emerge, splurge, purge," The Economist, March 8, 2014, http://tinyurl.com/kzh8a6d.

8. "Cox Conserves Survey – A Study of Sustainable Solutions for SMB's [Infographic]," BLUE, Oct. 7, 2014, http://tinyurl.com/oozn5y7

9. "US Sustainable, Responsible and Impact: Investing Assets Grow 76 Percent In Two Years," U.S. Social Investment Forum, Nov. 20, 2014,, Nov. 20, 2014, http://tinyurl.com/mj9p7rp.

10. "Climate Change 2014, Fifth Assessment Report," Intergovernmental Panel on Climate Change, 2014, http://tinyurl.com/3e3zv.

11. "World Footprint: Do we fit the planet?" Global Footprint Network, accessed on Feb. 4, 2015, http://tinyurl.com/c8ga5p.

12. Stuart L. Hart, "Capitalism at the Crossroads: Next Generation Business Strategies for a Post-Crisis World," 3rd ed., 2010; Timothy F. Slaper and Tanya Hall, "The Triple Bottom Line: What Is It and How Does It Work?" Indiana Business Review, 2011, http://tinyurl.com/7xt958c.

13. "The Triple Bottom Line," The Economist, Nov. 17, 2009, http://tinyurl.com/3h7jbmx.

14. "Climate Change, Overview of Greenhouse Gases," U.S. Environmental Protection Agency, updated July 2, 2014, http://tinyurl.com/cwneb4

15. "Fortune 500 Partners List," U.S. Environmental Protection Agency, Jan. 26, 2015, http://tinyurl.com/dbrmv2.

16. "Questions and answers about The WaterSense Program," U.S. Environmental Protection Agency, December 2014, http://tinyurl.com/m7ljak3.

17. "Fox Business Interviews China Gorman," Great Place to Work/Fox Business, undated, http://tinyurl.com/kk3wavz.

18. Ibid.

19. Steven Greenhouse, "On Black Friday, Walmart Is Pressed for Wage Increases," The New York Times, Nov. 28, 2014, http://tinyurl.com/mhl5gxl; Nilima Choudhury, "Walmart accused of 'greenwashing' over clean energy claims," RTCC, Nov. 18, 2013, http://tinyurl.com/ntjavhl; and Hiroko Tabuchi, "Walmart Raising Wage to at Least $9," The New York Times, Feb. 19, 2015, http://tinyurl.com/kmc87rm.

20. "What are B Corps?" B Corps, undated, http://tinyurl.com/kfjdtc8.

21. Also see Robert Eccles, et al., "How to Become a Sustainable Company," MIT Sloan Management Review, Summer 2012, http://tinyurl.com/mknrw64; Jessica Cheam, "Sustainability needs to be in a company's DNA: interview with Martin Blake," Eco-Business, Aug. 28, 2013, http://tinyurl.com/qyrt7a2.

22. Paul Polman, "Business, society, and the future of capitalism," Insights & Publications, McKinsey Quarterly, May 2014, http://tinyurl.com/nwm8eye.

23. John Willis and Paul Spence, "The Risks and Returns of Fossil Fuel Free Investing," undated, Sustainable Insight Capital Management, http://tinyurl.com/jwtl3ge.

24. Tom Randall, "Saints Beat Sinners for Sustainable Investing: Stock Chart," Bloomberg, Feb. 17, 2012, http://tinyurl.com/7nmmxa8.

25. "Climate action and profitability," CDP, 2014, http://tinyurl.com/mqhkzul.

26. Lei Liao and Jim Campagna, "Socially Responsible Investing: Delivering Competitive Performance," TIAA-CREF, September 2014, http://tinyurl.com/oshb8b3.

27. Joel Makower, "Why sustainability leaders don't impress Wall Street," Greenbiz.com, Aug. 4, 2014, http://tinyurl.com/pvtsxpx; Sheila Bonini and Steven Schwartz, "Profits with Purpose: How organizing for sustainability can benefit the bottom line," McKinsey, 2014, http://tinyurl.com/lnkfl3v.

28. Sanya Carley, et al., "Success Paths to Sustainable Manufacturing," October 2014, School of Public and Environmental Affairs, Indiana University, http://tinyurl.com/oeotxet.

29. Doug Park, "Securities Law, Not Semantics," Sustainability Accounting Standards Board (blog), Nov. 17, 2014, http://tinyurl.com/mf8yczq.

30. "The UN Global Compact-Accenture CEO Study on Sustainability 2013," September 2013, Accenture, 2013, http://tinyurl.com/nvnte9p.

31. Kiron, et al., op. cit.

32. "The UN Global Compact-Accenture CEO Study on Sustainability 2013," op. cit.

33. David Herbling, "Safaricom opens talks with Vodafone on M-Pesa license fees," Business Daily, Aug. 18, 2014, http://tinyurl.com/qdpbdp5.

34. "The UN Global Compact-Accenture CEO Study on Sustainability 2013," op. cit

35. "Winning the $30 Trillion Decathalon: How to Succeed in Emerging Markets," McKinsey & Company, October 2012, http://tinyurl.com/oqhfr2n.

36. Arindam Bhattacharya, et al., "Competing for Advantage: How to Succeed in the New Global Reality," Boston Consulting Group, January 2010, http://tinyurl.com/msox9pq.

37. "Fit for the future: Capitalising on global trends," PricewaterhouseCoopers, 2014, http://tinyurl.com/mzg6mlj.

38. "Health & Hygiene," Unilever, undated, http://tinyurl.com/kjmd7nu.

39. John Maxwell, "Beyond the BRICS: How to succeed in emerging markets (by really trying)," PricewaterhouseCoopers, http://tinyurl.com/omx9x4b.

40. "Republican Platform," GOP.com, undated, http://tinyurl.com/lltq2l2.

41. Polman, op. cit.

42. Michael E. Porter, et al., "Strategy & Society: The Link between Competitive Advantage and Corporate Social Responsibility," Harvard Business Review, December 2006, http://tinyurl.com/pe5ha5q.

43. Ibid.

44. "Dow Chemical Company Foundation: Grants for Science Education," Inside Philanthropy, accessed Feb. 4, 2015, http://tinyurl.com/myem67e.

45. "Our Community Impact," Target Corporate Responsibility, accessed Feb. 4, 2015, http://tinyurl.com/mb36358.

46. Dave Sorter, "Ford's supplier diversity development program celebrates 35th anniversary," Minority Business News, MBN USA, vol. 3, 2013, http://tinyurl.com/m8ujhmx.

47. Kasturi Rangan, Lisa Chase and Sohel Karim, "The Truth About CSR," Harvard Business Review, January 2015, http://tinyurl.com/nw4m9nl.

48. Ibid.

49. James Surowiecki, "Companies With Benefits," The New Yorker, Aug. 4, 2014, http://tinyurl.com/pst6txl; Melanie Colburn, "Making 'benefit corporations' more than just academic," Greenbiz.com, May 2, 2012, http://tinyurl.com/qx2leta.

50. Eliza Griswold, "How Silent Spring Ignited the Environmental Movement," The New York Times, Sept. 21, 2012, http://tinyurl.com/pay87b8.

51. Jack Lewis, "The Birth of the EPA," U.S. Environmental Protection Agency Journal, November 1985, http://tinyurl.com/p3lqqwy. Ibid.

52. Larry Cao, "The Price of Growth: Toxic Smog in China and Elsewhere," CFA Institute, April 7, 2014, http://tinyurl.com/pusuzy2.

53. "What Causes Acid Rain?" U.S. Environment Protection Agency, http://tinyurl.com/ybhh27l.

54. "The Birth of the EPA," op. cit.

55. Ibid.

56. Ibid.; Stuart L. Hart, "Capitalism at the Crossroads: The Unlimited Business Opportunities in Solving the World's Most Difficult Problems," 2005.

57. Hart, "Capitalism at the Crossroads: Next Generation Business Strategies," op. cit.; Timothy F. Slaper and Tanya Hall, "The Triple Bottom Line: What Is It and How Does It Work?" Indiana Business Review, 2011, http://tinyurl.com/7xt958c.

58. "Report of the World Commission on Environment and Development: Our Common Future," United Nations, March 20, 1987, http://tinyurl.com/mtpt4pu.

59. Ibid.

60. Hart, "Capitalism at the Crossroads: Next Generation Business Strategies," op. cit., p. 27.

61. "History of Quality," Business Performance Improvement Resource, http://tinyurl.com/d8tdsxr; "Total Quality Management," Inc., http://tinyurl.com/mmtoazp; and "History," Columbia Business School, The W. Edwards Deming Center for Quality, Productivity and Competitiveness, undated, http://tinyurl.com/oqlgv79.

62. Hart, "Capitalism at the Crossroads: Next Generation Business Strategies," op. cit., pp. 24-26; Shelly F. Fust and Lisa L. Walker, "Corporate Sustainability Initiatives: The Next TQM?" Korn Ferry Institute, 2007, http://tinyurl.com/mljle7u.

63. "1984: Hundreds Die in Bhopal Chemical Accident," BBC News, undated, http://tinyurl.com/6a499; Sanjoy Hazarika, "Gas Leak in India Kills at least 410 in City of Bhopal," The New York Times, Dec. 4, 1984, http://tinyurl.com/o62tnyh.

64. "Toxics Release Inventory (TRI) Program," U.S. Environmental Protection Agency, updated Jan. 28, 2015, http://tinyurl.com/pcfmenp.

65. Hart, "Capitalism at the Crossroads: Next Generation Business Strategies," op. cit., p. 27.

66. Ibid.

67. Magali A. Delmas, "Barriers and Incentive to the Adoption of ISO 14001 by Firms in the United States," Duke Environmental Law & Policy Forum, Fall 2000, http://tinyurl.com/mscq383.

68. Ibid.

69. "What Is GRI?" Global Reporting Initiative, http://tinyurl.com/7oeu2dg.

70. "William McDonough: Cradle to Cradle Design," TED Talks (YouTube), May 17, 2007, http://tinyurl.com/kfkv529; Oliver Balch, "C-suite interview: Rob Boogaard, Interface – Red carpet corporate sustainability," Ethical Corp., May 8, 2014, http://tinyurl.com/mrnfbhj; and Hanh Nguyen, et al., "Remaking the Industrial Economy," McKinsey Quarterly, February 2014, http://tinyurl.com/ly8kvwr.

71. "Our Story: Post-Consumer Carpet Recycling," Shaw Floors, http://tinyurl.com/lnnd9lo.

72. Jennifer Kesik, "Ethics of Sweatshops: Managing Global Labor Standards in the Sporting Goods Industry," Dec. 1. 2013, http://tinyurl.com/mkjnhwy; John Braddock, "Nike faces allegations of worker abuse in Indonesia," World Socialist Web Site, Sept. 8, 2011, http://tinyurl.com/m9vanpe; David Teather, "Nike lists abuses at Asian factories," The Guardian, April 14, 2005, http://tinyurl.com/kbjsrm7.

73. Max Nisen, "How Nike Solved Its Sweatshop Problem," Business Insider, May 9, 2013, http://tinyurl.com/cydqacl; James Epstein-Reeves, "The Parents of CSR: Nike and Kathie-Lee Gifford," Forbes, June 8, 2010, http://tinyurl.com/cpu97f4.

74. Peter Lacy, et al., "A New Era of Sustainability UN Global Compact-Accenture CEO Study 2010," Accenture, June 2010, http://tinyurl.com/pmyhgwl.

75. "The 17th Annual Global CEO Survey, Fit for the future Capitalising on global trends," PricewaterhouseCoopers, Jan. 20, 2015, p. 35 http://tinyurl.com/puwsxqp.

76. "Integrated reporting," Ernst & Young, June 30, 2013, http://tinyurl.com/kufm726.

77. Ibid.; David Kiron, "Get Ready: Mandated Integrated Reporting Is The Future of Corporate Reporting," MIT Sloan Management Review, March, 13, 2012, http://tinyurl.com/kclbmwx.

78. "GRI & SASB: An Understanding of Alignment," BrownFlynn, May 21, 2014, http://tinyurl.com/kzj33fo.

79. "Integrated reporting," op. cit.; Dunstan Allison-Hope and Guy Morgan, "Navigating the Materiality Muddle," Business for Social Responsibility (BSR) Insight, Aug. 13, 2013, http://tinyurl.com/m88e8ga.

80. Rena Dietrich, "The Role of FASB to Business," The Houston Chronicle, undated, http://tinyurl.com/lkaekxh.

81. "The Hershey Company Joins Sustainability Accounting Standards Board (SASB) Advisory Council," Business Wire, Dec. 4, 2012, http://tinyurl.com/ks6gw97.

82. "2013 six growing trends in corporate sustainability," Ernst & Young and Greenbiz Survey, 2013, http://tinyurl.com/o6u87u3.

83. Paul Polman, "Paul Polman: The remedies for capitalism," op. cit.

84. "GM, Honda to collaborate on the next-generation fuel cell technologies; targeting commercial feasibility in 2020 time frame," Green Car Congress, July 2, 2013, http://tinyurl.com/mfctm75.

85. Justin Gerdes, "Shared shipping is slowly gaining ground between market rivals," The Guardian, Aug. 11, 2014, http://tinyurl.com/q5ubb2l.

86. Karel Beckman, "Perspectives on Obama's clean power plan: small step for US, big step for mankind?" Energy Post, June 11, 2014, http://tinyurl.com/lpz2l96.

87. "FACT SHEET: Administration Takes Steps Forward on Climate Action Plan by Announcing Actions to Cut Methane Emissions," White House, Jan. 14, 2015, http://tinyurl.com/kbpnwf8.

88. Ben Wolfgang, "Obama targets oil and gas industry, demands massive reduction in methane emissions," Jan. 14, 2015, The Washington Times, http://tinyurl.com/k8lnt8p.

89. Denise Robbins, "Myths And Facts About The Koch Brothers," Media Matters for America, Aug. 27, 2014, http://tinyurl.com/kxkwltg.

90. Michael B. Gerrard, "Obama's New Emission Rules: Will They Survive Challenges?" Yale Environment 360, June 16, 2014, http://tinyurl.com/p9jmewp.

91. Jennifer Kho, "Report: More Corporations Turn To Sustainability For Competitive Edge and Profits," Forbes, Jan. 24, 2012, http://tinyurl.com/7na4vkt.

92. Karen E. Klein, "How to Keep Millennials from Getting Bored and Leaving," Bloomberg, Aug. 22, 2014, http://tinyurl.com/pqbcrdo; Steve Cody, "Five Tricks for Working with Millennials," Inc., updated April 18, 2013, http://tinyurl.com/al4x3w9; and Julie Honeywell and Brad Pease, "Attract and Retain Millennials with your Green Building," Paladino, undated, http://tinyurl.com/mvzwcro.

93. "What is Business For? The Millennial Survey 2011," Deloitte, January 2012, http://tinyurl.com/myg2a6d.

94. "Millennials Survey, Millennials at work: Reshaping the workplace," PricewaterhouseCoopers, 2015, http://tinyurl.com/yjdt4k8; for background, see Vickie Elmer, "Work-Life Balance," SAGE Business Researcher, Jan. 12, 2015.

95. "10 Leading Sustainability Innovations," The Guardian, June 16, 2014, http://tinyurl.com/mcuc2rt.

96. "The UN Global Compact-Accenture CEO Study on Sustainability 2013," op. cit., p. 49; "Computing sustainability," The Economist, June 19, 2008, http://tinyurl.com/lbszkoc.

97. Thom Patterson, "Amazing machines poised to fly travelers into a new era," CNN, Nov. 16, 2014, http://tinyurl.com/mp7cn6n.

98. Heather Clancy, "How GE generates $1 billion from data," Fortune, Oct. 10, 2014, http://tinyurl.com/kdf9qns.

CHAPTER 12

1. Quinn Klinefelter, "The Story of Detroit's Bankruptcy: A 'Takeover' or an Inevitable Financial Crisis?" WDET, Nov. 9, 2015, http://tinyurl.com/q4trpqs.

2. Brian Vander Ark, "Failure: Lab Grand Rapids," via YouTube, June 4, 2013, http://tinyurl.com/z9hu28h.

3. Vickie Elmer, "Putting unvarnished failure on stage, in Michigan and beyond," Fortune, Jan. 5, 2015, http://tinyurl.com/gvz2gpp.

4. Sheryl Connelly, "Looking Further with Ford: 2015 Trends," Ford Motor Co., Dec. 29, 2014, http://tinyurl.com/glyflut.

5. Richard Feloni, "LinkedIn founder Reid Hoffman shares 3 lessons he learned from the failure of his first company," Business Insider, July 29, 2015, http://tinyurl.com/zcg5mxs.

6. Sue Shellenbarger, "Better Ideas Through Failure," The Wall Street Journal, Sept. 27, 2011, http://tinyurl.com/j9cugpm.

7. David Grossman, "Secret Google lab 'rewards staff for failure'," BBC News, Jan. 24, 2014, http://tinyurl.com/hqvac8t.

8. Shellenbarger, op. cit.

9. Rick Wartzman, "Drucker's Take on Making Mistakes," Bloomberg Business, June 19, 2008, http://tinyurl.com/hwaqtc7.

10. Amy C. Edmondson, "Strategies for Learning from Failure," Harvard Business Review, April 2011, http://tinyurl.com/peme4pu.

11. "Why Do So Many Mergers Fail?" Knowledge@Wharton, March 30, 2005, http://tinyurl.com/znw8qn3.

12. Glenn Kessler, "Do nine out of 10 new businesses fail as Rand Paul claims?" The Washington Post, Jan. 27, 2014, http://tinyurl.com/jhfw963; Carmen Nobel, "Why Companies Fail – And How Their Founders Can Bounce Back," Harvard Business School Research & Ideas March, 7, 2011, http://tinyurl.com/ogonbv4.

13. Tyler Atkinson, David Luttrell and Harvey Rosenblum, "How Bad Was It? The Costs and Consequences of the 2007-09 Financial Crisis," Federal Reserve Bank of Dallas, July 2013, http://tinyurl.com/zp55lde.

14. "Georgetown study finds the age at which young adults get traction in their careers has increased from age 26 to 30, and to age 33 for African Americans," news release, Georgetown University, Sept. 30, 2013, http://tinyurl.com/zhsm646.

15. Leah McGrath Goodman, "Millennial College Graduates: Young, Educated, Jobless," Newsweek, May 27, 2015, http://tinyurl.com/phexd3h.

16. "Fiscal Year Bankruptcy Filings Continue Fall," U.S. Courts, Oct. 28, 2015, http://tinyurl.com/py2vsc6.

17. "20 Largest Public Company Bankruptcy Filings 1980-Present," BankruptcyData.com, undated, accessed Dec. 10, 2015, http://tinyurl.com/lphhuu.

18. Benjamin Snyder, "Donald Trump's business fumbles," Fortune, July 6, 2015, http://tinyurl.com/npornjs.

19. Jill Lepore, "The Disruption Machine," The New Yorker, June 23, 2014, http://tinyurl.com/kxrnt34.

20. Rafael Efrat, "The Evolution of Bankruptcy Stigma," Theoretical Inquiries in Law, 2006, http://tinyurl.com/o4qausb.

21. Smita Singh, Patricia Corner and Kathryn Pavlovich, "Self-Stigmatisation of Entrepreneurial Failure," paper at the 25th Australian and New Zealand Academy of Management Conference, 2012, http://tinyurl.com/owwgca7 and http://tinyurl.com/pxdl7cn.

22. Shana Lebowitz, "From the projects to a $2.3 billion fortune—the inspiring rags-to-riches story of Starbucks CEO Howard Schultz," Business Insider, May 30, 2015, http://tinyurl.com/npx6tvc.

23. "Fear of failure affects lifelong learning," news release, the British Psychological Society, Sept. 9, 2014, http://tinyurl.com/nbotopt.

24. Lepore, op. cit.

25. Nancy Hass and Rose DeWolf, "Laventhol & Horwath Collapses: Suits Battered Accounting Giant," The Philadelphia Inquirer, Nov. 20, 1990, http://tinyurl.com/nedecst.

26. Gregory Richards, "1990: The other big accounting firm meltdown," Philadelphia Business Journal, Aug. 5, 2002, http://tinyurl.com/pbeyev5.

27. Luke Kawa, "China Has No Good Plan to Deal With Its Achilles Heel," Bloomberg Business, Oct. 7, 2015, http://tinyurl.com/o4b9ttr.

28. Stuart Gilson, "Coming Through in a Crisis: How Chapter 11 and the Debt Restructuring Industry Are Helping to Revive the U.S. Economy," Journal of Applied Corporate Finance, Fall 2012, http://tinyurl.com/q3r8btt.

29. Farhad Manjoo, "The Upside of a Downturn in Silicon Valley," The New York Times, Aug. 26, 2015, http://tinyurl.com/pmfascl.

30. Seung-Hyun Lee et al., "How do bankruptcy laws affect entrepreneurship development around the world?" Journal of Business Venturing, September 2011, http://tinyurl.com/od62n6r.

31. Robin Sidel, "FDIC's Tab for Failed U.S. Banks Nears $9 Billion," The Wall Street Journal, March 17, 2011, http://tinyurl.com/pgdgjzq.

32. "Table A-12: Unemployed persons by duration of unemployment," Bureau of Labor Statistics, modified Dec. 4, 2015, http://tinyurl.com/3gna7.

33. Aaron Schachter and Clark Boyd, "Update: The history of Hashima, the island in Bond film 'Skyfall,'" PRI's The World, Nov. 23, 2012, http://tinyurl.com/ncex6pl; "Bodie State Historic Park," California Department of Parks and Recreation, undated, accessed Dec. 10, 2015, http://tinyurl.com/kj7bbh.

34. "Financial Crimes Report to the Public; Fiscal Years 2010-2011," FBI, undated, accessed Dec. 10, 2015, http://tinyurl.com/nebmy3r.

35. "Global Economic Crime Survey 2014," PricewaterhouseCoopers, undated, accessed Dec. 10, 2015, http://tinyurl.com/pf8uh6x.

36. "Former Enron CEO Skilling gets 24 years," The Associated Press, NBC News, Oct. 23, 2006, http://tinyurl.com/qywmlla.

37. Gilson, op. cit.

38. William K. Alcorn, "Forum Health gets new name," The Vindicator, March 25, 2011, http://tinyurl.com/of8kxcm.

39. Paul Allen, "My Favorite Mistake," Newsweek, April 24, 2011, http://tinyurl.com/qf25jv3.

40. David Allison, "Bill Gates Interview," National Museum of American History, Smithsonian Institution, undated, accessed Dec. 10, 2015, http://tinyurl.com/nwgn83s.

41. Allen, op. cit.

42. "Business School researcher finds organizations learn more from failure than success," news release, University of Colorado, Denver, Aug. 23, 2010, http://tinyurl.com/37syaqr.

43. Brandon Mueller and Dean A. Shepherd, "Learning from Failure: How Entrepreneurial Failure Aids in the Development of Opportunity Recognition Expertise," Frontiers of Entrepreneurship Research, June 9, 2012, http://tinyurl.com/opsozom.

44. Deniz Ucbasaran, Paul Westhead and Mike Wright, "Why Serial Entrepreneurs Don't Learn from Failure," Harvard Business Review, April 2011, http://tinyurl.com/zxxbuqg.

45. David Brown, "Here's what 'fail fast' really means," VentureBeat, March 15, 2015, http://tinyurl.com/mvbejqr.

46. J.K. Rowling, "The Fringe Benefits of Failure, and the Importance of Imagination," Harvard Magazine, June 8, 2008, http://tinyurl.com/3lgw8ce.

47. Karissa Giuliano and Sarah Whitten, "The world's first billionaire author is cashing in," CNBC, July 31, 2015, http://tinyurl.com/jklgkw5.

48. Paul A. Gompers et al., "Performance Persistence in Entrepreneurship," Harvard Business School working paper, July 2008, http://tinyurl.com/zvqx84e.

49. Jeffrey A. Sonnenfeld and Andrew J. Ward, "Firing Back: How Great Leaders Rebound After Career Disasters," Harvard Business Review, January 2007, http://tinyurl.com/p5jctgf.

50. Geoff Lewis, "Failure porn: There's too much celebration of failure and too little fear," The Washington Post, Dec. 4, 2014, http://tinyurl.com/h2o7jo8.

51. Lydia Saad, "Americans' Money Worries Unchanged From 2014," Gallup, April 20, 2015, http://tinyurl.com/lhjp9jx.

52. Steven Church, "Jefferson County Judge Known for 'Rule-From-the-Bench' Style," Bloomberg Business, Nov. 15, 2011, http://tinyurl.com/hgf39mj.

53. Connelly, op. cit.

54. Slavica Singer, José Ernesto Amorós and Daniel Moska, "Global Entrepreneurship Monitor: 2014 Global Report," Table 2.3, Global Entrepreneurship Research Association, 2015, http://tinyurl.com/j3fn7nb.

55. Alicia Robb, Susan Coleman and Dane Stangler, "Sources of Economic Hope: Women's Entrepreneurship," Ewing Marion Kauffman Foundation, November 2014, http://tinyurl.com/zcnksam.

56. Belinda Luscombe, "Why Failure Is the Key to Success for Women," Time, Aug. 19, 2014, http://tinyurl.com/hmppb9o.

57. Slavica, Amorós and Moska, op. cit.

58. Jessica Lahey, "Why we should let our children fail," The Guardian, Sept. 5, 2015, http://tinyurl.com/ot5fp69.

59. Fons Trompenaars and Peter Woolliams, "Lost in Translation," Harvard Business Review, April 2011, http://tinyurl.com/zmh829p.

60. Louis Edward Levinthal, "The Early History of Bankruptcy Law," University of Pennsylvania Law Review and American Law Register, April 1918, http://tinyurl.com/hnc78ld.

61. Ibid.

62. Efrat, op. cit.

63. Jack Lynch, "Cruel and Unusual: Prisons and Prison Reform" Colonial Williamsburg Journal, Summer 2011, http://tinyurl.com/hrekbcx.

64. Charles Jordan Tabb, "The History of the Bankruptcy Laws in the United States," American Bankruptcy Institute Law Review, 1995, available at SSRN: http://tinyurl.com/jsomu64.

65. "The Evolution of U.S. Bankruptcy Law," Federal Judicial Center, undated, accessed Dec. 10, 2015, http://tinyurl.com/o89cgvy.

66. James Narron, David Skeie and Don Morgan, "Crisis Chronicles: The Panic of 1819—America's First Great Economic Crisis," Liberty Street Economics, Federal Reserve Bank of New York, Dec. 5, 2014, http://tinyurl.com/hakbetw.

67. Quentin R. Skrabec Jr., "100 Most Important American Financial Crises," Greenwood, 2015, pp. 53-58.

68. Scott A. Sandage, "Born Losers: A History of Failure in America," Harvard University Press, 2005, p.14.

69. Edward J. Balleisen, "Navigating Failure: Bankruptcy and Commercial Society in Antebellum America," University of North Carolina Press, 2001, Introduction.

70. Scott Jennings, "Kentucky's tradition of reforming nation's prisons," Louisville Courier Journal, Aug. 6, 2014, http://tinyurl.com/jc74wde; "The Evolution of U.S. Bankruptcy Law," op. cit.

71. Eli Hager, "Debtors Prisons, Then and Now: FAQ," The Marshall Project, Feb. 24, 2015, http://tinyurl.com/q99mvab.

72. Christopher D. Hampson, "The New American Debtors' Prisons," Harvard Law School 2015 Stephen L. Werner Prize: Criminal Justice, Aug. 4, 2015, http://tinyurl.com/hvjlvnn.

73. Balleisen, op. cit.

74. "A Brief History of Bankruptcy," BanruptcyData.com, undated, accessed Dec. 11, 2015, http://tinyurl.com/hmcgm39.

75. Alexis de Tocqueville, "Democracy in America," via University of Virginia American Studies Program, 1835, vol. 2, section 3, chp. 18, http://tinyurl.com/hpchkkm.

76. Sandage, op. cit.

77. "A Life Lived in a Rapidly Changing World: Samuel L. Clemens, 1835-1910," The Mark Twain House and Museum, http://tinyurl.com/ptqcbuh.

78. Rebecca Edwards and Sarah DeFeo, "The Depression of 1893," 1896: The Presidential Campaign, Cartoons & Commentary, Vassar College, 2000, http://tinyurl.com/yzogaa9.

79. "Chapter 13—Bankruptcy Basics," U.S. Courts, undated, accessed Dec. 10, 2015, http://tinyurl.com/kz53tfk.

80. David A. Skeel Jr., "The Genius of the 1898 Bankruptcy Act," University of Pennsylvania, Bankruptcy Developments Journal, January 1999, http://tinyurl.com/pwj93xd.

81. Quentin R. Skrabec Jr., "Rubber: An American Industrial History," 2013, p. 75.

82. Tony Borroz, "June 1, 1849: Stanley Twins Steam into History," Wired, June 1, 2009, http://tinyurl.com/o6s4hmw.

83. Ryan Bradley, "A Brief History of Failure," The New York Times, Nov. 12, 2014, http://tinyurl.com/pagn94e.

84. Anthony Young, "The Rise and Fall of the Edsel," Foundation for Economic Education, Sept. 1, 1989, http://tinyurl.com/nwbzlcg.

85. Ben S. Bernanke, "The Crisis as a Classic Financial Panic," Speech, Board of Governors of the Federal Reserve System, Nov. 8, 2013, http://tinyurl.com/ltx68lf.

86. David B. Ballard et al., "The Great Depression, 1929–1939: A Curriculum for High School Students," Federal Reserve Bank of St. Louis, 2007, http://tinyurl.com/nsvnk35.

87. Gene Smiley, "The American Economy in the 20th Century," 1993, p. 9–1.

88. Thomas A. Durkin, "Credit Cards: Use and Consumer Attitudes, 1970-2000," Federal Reserve Bulletin, September 2000, pp. 623–634, http://tinyurl.com/nzxvu5q.

89. "Equal Credit Opportunity Act (ECOA)," Consumer Financial Protection Bureau, June 2013, http://tinyurl.com/npm7pbg.

90. Viral V. Acharya, Julian Franks and Henri Servaes, "Private Equity: Boom and Bust?" Journal of Applied Corporate Finance, Fall 2007, http://tinyurl.com/pwv6wta.

91. Yuliya Demyanyk and Otto Van Hemert, "Understanding the Subprime Mortgage Crisis," Federal Deposit Insurance Corp., Feb. 4, 2008, http://tinyurl.com/pu58fd5.

92. "Financial Crisis Inquiry Commission Report," Financial Crisis Inquiry Commission, January 2011, pp. xv–xxvii, http://tinyurl.com/c79hfv2.

93. Christopher J. Goodman and Steven M. Mance, "Employment loss and the 2007-09 recession: an overview," Monthly Labor Review, Bureau of Labor Statistics, April 2011, http://tinyurl.com/ps5r99u.

94. "Fiscal Year Bankruptcy Filings Continue Fall," op. cit.

95. Rachel Gillett, "What the Hype Behind Embracing Failure Is Really All About," Fast Company, Sept. 8, 2014, http://tinyurl.com/pxzh5ho.

96. Barrett Watten, "Learning from Detroit: The Poetics of Ruined Space," Detroit Research, Spring/Fall 2014, http://tinyurl.com/och4not.

97. Joel Kurth and Christine MacDonald, "Volume of abandoned homes 'absolutely terrifying,'" The Detroit News, May 14, 2015, http://tinyurl.com/nheaete.

98. Barnini Chakraborty, "Fixing Detroit: America's comeback city?" Fox News, Dec. 18, 2013, http://tinyurl.com/nvmtpr8.

99. Danielle Douglas and Michael A. Fletcher, "Toyota reaches $1.2 billion settlement to end probe of accelerator problems," The Washington Post, March 19, 2014, http://tinyurl.com/qh4sclp.

100. David McHugh, "Volkswagen suffers loss due to scandal but sales hold up," The Associated Press, Oct. 28, 2015, http://tinyurl.com/ncd9gee.

101. L.M. Sixel, "Halliburton pays $18.3 million in back wages after federal inquiry," Houston Chronicle, Sept. 22, 2015, http://tinyurl.com/nz68wew; "Halliburton pays nearly $18.3 million in overtime owed to more than 1,000 employees nationwide after US Labor Department investigation," news release, U.S. Department of Labor, Sept. 22, 2015, http://tinyurl.com/odd68er.

102. "Lenovo: strong quarter hit by one-off costs," Financial Times, Nov.12, 2015, http://tinyurl.com/q2put4h.

103. "Tuck Professor Sydney Finkelstein Announces Best and Worst CEOS of 2014," news release, Tuck/Dartmouth Newsroom, Dec. 17, 2014, http://tinyurl.com/qesn7t6.

104. Katy Stech, "Bankruptcy Law Overhaul Would Mean Big Changes," Bankruptcy Beat, The Wall Street Journal, Dec. 8, 2014, http://tinyurl.com/ojzmj3s.

105. "146 Startup Failure Post-Mortems," CB Insights, Dec. 3, 2015, http://tinyurl.com/ngcfum4.

106. Gillett, op. cit.

107. Rob Asghar, "Why Silicon Valley's 'Fail Fast' Mantra Is Just Hype," Forbes.com blog, July 14, 2014, http://tinyurl.com/no6e67u.

108. "The Joys and Disappointments of Older Part-time Workers," news release, Rutgers, Sept. 3, 2015, http://tinyurl.com/nb2vpav.

109. Larry Hardesty, "Automating big-data analysis," MIT News Office, Oct. 16, 2015, http://tinyurl.com/pqbj5qp.

110. Vickie Elmer, "A new tool tells companies when they're about to lose their best people," Quartz, July 31, 2014, http://tinyurl.com/pytega6.

111. James Sterngold and Matt Wirz, "Financial Crisis Anniversary: For Corporations and Investors, Debt Makes a Comeback," The Wall Street Journal, Sept. 5, 2013, http://tinyurl.com/o35zhoa.

112. Jeanne Harris and Mark McDonald, "What the Companies That Predict the Future Do Differently," Harvard Business Review, Sept. 25, 2014, http://tinyurl.com/gmhurxl.

113. Edmondson, op. cit.

REFERENCES

CHAPTER 1

Books

Ferriss, Timothy, "The 4-Hour Workweek: Escape 9-5, Live Anywhere, and Join the New Rich," Crown Publishing Group, 2007.

An entrepreneur shares tips and tricks for people to make money while working independently.

Schwartz, Morissa, "The Gig Economy: Your Road to Financial Freedom," GenZ Publishing, 2016.

A full-time independent contractor explains how Millennials can thrive in the freelance economy.

Articles

Hook, Leslie, "Year in a word: Gig economy," Financial Times, Dec. 29, 2015, http://tinyurl.com/yaswd5u9.

The business publication recognizes and explores freelancers' impact on the new economy.

Scheiber, Noam, "How Uber Uses Psychological Tricks to Push Its Drivers' Buttons," The New York Times, April 2, 2017, http://tinyurl.com/m8tts6l.

A reporter investigates potentially deceptive practices by one of the largest gig economy platforms.

Tolentino, Jia, "The Gig Economy Celebrates Working Yourself to Death," The New Yorker, March 22, 2017, http://tinyurl.com/m8nouaq.

A writer argues that the new freelance economy exploits the young and the desperate.

Reports and Studies

"The 2017 BridgeWorks 3G Report," BridgeWorks, 2017, http://tinyurl.com/y9s78sa5.

The workplace consulting firm discusses how multiple generations can prosper in organizations.

"The 2017 Deloitte Millennial Survey – Apprehensive millennials: seeking stability and opportunities in an uncertain world," Deloitte, 2017, http://tinyurl.com/h4arf2c.

Analyzing results from a workplace study, the international consultancy reports that Millennials in developing countries are pessimistic about their future.

"America's Families and Living Arrangements: 2011," Housing and Household Economic Statistics Division, Fertility & Family Statistics Branch, U.S. Census Bureau, 2011, http://tinyurl.com/y9ncvadt.

The U.S. Census Bureau presents its annual study on family cohabitation in the United States, reflecting the higher number of Millennials staying at or returning to their parents' home.

"Unemployment Rate," Bureau of Labor Statistics, 2017, http://tinyurl.com/zyq5xlx.

The federal government agency tracks unemployment data from the past decade.

Hathaway, Ian, and Mark Muro, "Tracking the gig economy: New numbers," Brookings Institution, Oct. 13, 2016, http://tinyurl.com/yap56sj2.

A public policy organization examines the growing gig economy.

CHAPTER 2

Books

Botsman, Rachel, and Roo Rogers, "What's Mine Is Yours: The Rise of Collaborative Consumption," HarperCollins, New York, 2010.

Botsman, a business consultant, and Rogers, the founder of several sharing-economy companies, trace the roots of the sharing economy and the changes in how people consume goods and services.

Chase, Robin, "Peers Inc: How People and Platforms Are Inventing the Collaborative Economy and Reinventing Capitalism," PublicAffairs, New York, 2015.

Chase, a co-founder of Zipcar, draws on the relatively short history of the sharing economy and explores how it is changing the broader economy.

Stephany, Alex, "The Business of Sharing: Making It in the Sharing Economy," Palgrave Macmillan, New York, 2015.

Stephany, CEO of JustPark, a sharing-economy company in Great Britain, outlines best practices for succeeding in the sharing economy by examining the experiences of his own firm as well as others.

Articles

Asher-Schapiro, Avi, "The Sharing Economy Is Propaganda," Cato Unbound, Feb. 13, 2015, http://tinyurl.com/o2275be.

As part of a multi-author debate on a libertarian website, a journalist who has written about how Uber drivers see their work argues that much of the "sharing economy" is old-fashioned capitalism in disguise.

Badger, Emily, "Airbnb is about to start collecting hotel taxes in more major cities, including Washington," The Washington Post, Jan. 29, 2015, http://tinyurl.com/nac6kdd.

Airbnb agrees to be the tax collector for some cities to ease regulators' concerns about lost revenue.

Benkler, Yochai, "Sharing Nicely: On Shareable Goods and the Emergence of Sharing as a Modality of Economic Production," Yale Law Journal, 2004, pp. 273-358,http://tinyurl.com/nv384q2.

Harvard law professor's thorough analysis was the first real articulation of the modern sharing economy.

Cannon, Sarah, and Lawrence H. Summers, "How Uber and the Sharing Economy Can Win Over Regulators," Harvard Business Review, Oct. 13, 2014, https://hbr.org/2014/10/how-uber-and-the-sharing-economy-can-win-over-regulators/.

A manager at Google Capital (Cannon) and a former Treasury secretary (Summers) offer detailed advice on how sharing-economy companies can get the best treatment from regulators.

Cohen, Boyd, and Jan Kietzmann, "Ride On! Mobility Business Models for the Sharing Economy," Organization & Environment, Aug. 31, 2014, http://oae.sagepub.com/content/27/3/279.

The authors examine shared transportation business models to find the optimal balance between companies and local governments.

Feeney, Matthew, "Level the Playing Field—by Deregulating," Cato Unbound, Feb. 10, 2015, http://tinyurl.com/onphurf.

A policy analyst at the libertarian Cato Institute argues that new technologies have made much regulation counterproductive.

Kelly, Kevin, "We Are the Web," Wired, August 2005, http://tinyurl.com/p4kjdtj.

Wired magazine's founding executive editor offers a fascinating recounting of the development of the technologies that power the sharing economy.

Shafroth, Frank, "The Unforeseen Fiscal Challenges of Uber-Like Services," Governing, March 20, 2015, http://tinyurl.com/pmh3mlj.

The director of the Center for State and Local Government Leadership at George Mason University illuminates the challenges the sharing economy poses for government.

Sundararajan, Arun, "A Safety Net Fit for the Sharing Economy," Financial Times, June 22, 2015, http://tinyurl.com/qclxwu8.

A professor of information, operations and management sciences at New York University's Stern School of Business argues that benefits such as health coverage, worker's compensation and paid vacations should be available to sharing-economy workers.

Reports and Studies

"Alternative Financial Services: A Primer," FDIC Quarterly, April 27, 2009, http://tinyurl.com/p643omd.

Report from the Federal Deposit Insurance Corp. explains how alternative financial services work, including peer-to-peer lending, and how the services interact.

Krueger, Alan B., and Jonathan V. Hall, "An Analysis of the Labor Market for Uber's Driver-Partners in the United States," Working Paper #587, Princeton University, Jan. 22, 2015, http://tinyurl.com/n5norw8.

A Princeton economist (Krueger) and Uber's head of policy analysis (Hall) examine Uber data and find mostly positive effects for communities and employees.

Schneiderman, Eric T., "Airbnb in the City," New York State Office of the Attorney General, Oct. 14, 2014, http://tinyurl.com/m8pqffb.

Report lays out the New York government's case against Airbnb, finding the rental activities supported by the platform frequently violate state laws and harm communities.

CHAPTER 3

Books

Bamberger, Kenneth A., and Deirdre K. Mulligan, "Privacy on the Ground: Driving Corporate Behavior in the United States and Europe," MIT Press, 2015.

A University of California, Berkeley, law professor (Bamberger) and a professor at Berkeley's School of Information (Mulligan) explain the regulations governing corporate use of consumer data in five countries, including the United States, and how those regulations shape company behavior.

Howard, Philip N., "Pax Technica: How the Internet of Things May Set Us Free or Lock Us Up," Yale University Press, 2015.

A communications professor at the University of Washington outlines the challenges to come in the age of the Internet of Things and suggests measures to ease the way.

Schneier, Bruce, "Data and Goliath: The Hidden Battles to Collect Your Data and Control Your World," W.W. Norton & Co., 2015.

A security expert explores, and explains, the reach and power of surveillance tools that corporations and governments are using.

Articles

Barocas, Solon, and Andrew D. Selbst, "Big Data's Disparate Impact," California Law Review, 2016, http://tinyurl.com/j6ovlkc.

A technologist and a lawyer team up to examine the ways in which algorithms used in big data analytics can discriminate against groups of people.

Hunt, Robert M., "You Can Patent That? Are Patents on Computer Programs and Business Methods Good for the New Economy?" Business Review, Federal Reserve Bank of Philadelphia, First Quarter 2001, http://tinyurl.com/hzao6ga.

A Federal Reserve Bank economist offers a history of patent protection for software and questions whether the current system is a good one.

Richards, Neil M., and Jonathan H. King, "Big Data Ethics," Wake Forest Law Review, May 19, 2014, http://tinyurl.com/hz33hlm.

A law professor (Richards) and a technology company executive (King) examine the ethical issues confronting those performing big data analytics.

Reports and Studies

"Big Data and Privacy: A Technological Perspective," President's Council of Advisers on Science and Technology, May 2014, http://tinyurl.com/p92vpo5.

A report by a White House technology panel recommends that regulators focus on the uses of big data by companies rather than on collection and storage.

"Consumer Data Privacy in a Networked World: A Framework for Protecting Privacy and Promoting Innovation in the Global Digital Economy," White House, Feb. 23, 2012, http://tinyurl.com/judzdv9.

A White House report calls for legislation creating a "Consumer Bill of Rights" that would restrict what companies can do with consumer data.

"Data Brokers: A Call for Transparency and Accountability," Federal Trade Commission, May 2014, http://tinyurl.com/mwury6w.

This 110-page report from the federal agency that oversees consumer protection offers a thorough examination of the data broker industry and finds it lacking in transparency.

"The Latest on Workplace Monitoring and Surveillance," American Management Association, Nov. 17, 2014, http://tinyurl.com/yjb4q4a.

Corporate training group offers a wealth of up-to-date survey data on the surveillance and monitoring practices of U.S. companies.

"A Review of the Data Broker Industry: Collection, Use, and Sale of Consumer Data for Marketing Purposes," Senate Committee on Commerce, Science and Transportation, Office of Oversight and Investigations Majority Staff, Dec. 18, 2013, http://tinyurl.com/h5gvfhw.

A Senate report examines the growth of the multibillion-dollar data broker industry and finds that it operates hidden from consumer view.

Ciocchetti, Corey A., "The Eavesdropping Employer: A Twenty-First Century Framework for Employee Monitoring," May 29, 2010, http://tinyurl.com/jfy8enl.

A professor of ethics and legal studies at the University of Denver's Daniels College of Business says the American legal system has failed to keep up with changes in monitoring technologies.

Furletti, Mark J., "An Overview and History of Credit Reporting," Discussion Paper, Federal Reserve Bank of Philadelphia, June 2002, http://tinyurl.com/gnnlr7g.

An analyst at the Federal Reserve Bank of Philadelphia provides a concise and interesting history of the development of consumer credit databases and reporting services.

CHAPTER 4

Books

Caligiuri, Paula, "Cultural Agility: Building a Pipeline of Successful Global Professionals," Jossey-Bass, 2012.

A Northeastern University professor of international business and strategy discusses the cultural skills needed to succeed in today's international business world.

Caligiuri, Paula, David Lepak and Jaime Bonache, "Managing the Global Workforce," John Wiley & Sons, 2010.

A Northeastern University professor (Caligiuri), a Rutgers University professor of human resource management (Lepak), and a professor in the Department of People Management and Organization at the Spanish university ESADE (Bonache) cover a wide range of topics essential for global human resource managers and others.

Moussa, Mario, Madeline Boyer and Derek Newberry, "Committed Teams: Three Steps to Inspiring Passion and Performance," John Wiley & Sons.

A consultant and faculty member in the Wharton School of the University of Pennsylvania's executive education program (Moussa) and two lecturers in the school's undergraduate programs (Boyer and Newberry) use Wharton research to develop a handbook for building effective teams.

Salomon, Robert, "Global Vision: How Companies Can Overcome the Pitfalls of Globalization," Palgrave Macmillan, 2016.

A New York University associate professor of management and organizations examines the cultural, economic and political risks international expansion can pose to organizations.

Articles

Burnham, Kristin, "Social Business: Slow and Steady Worked for Philips," Information Week, May 20, 2014, http://tinyurl.com/j5zff9z.

Royal Philips Electronics, a health care, lifestyle and lighting business, develops a social networking site for employees to share knowledge.

Griffith, Erin, "Vente-Privée USA to Shut Down," Fortune, Oct. 24, 2014, http://tinyurl.com/z3n8a5x.

A journalist looks at the breakup of the U.S. joint venture between France's e-commerce site Vente-Privée and American Express.

Kalman, Frank, "MetLife's Global Mobility Surge," Talent Management, May 1, 2015, http://tinyurl.com/hozwqnn.

The insurance giant develops an in-depth strategy to give top managers international experience.

Swift, Mike, "At Google Groups are Key to Company Culture," The San Jose Mercury News, June 22, 2011, http://tinyurl.com/6z422zf.

Google turns to employee resource groups to pull together workers from around the world.

Whitney, Kellye, "Special Edition: Executive Education," Chief Learning Officer, Feb. 22, 2016, http://tinyurl.com/j523mxg.

Executive education programs from top-name business schools are thriving.

Reports and Studies

"Global Business Driven HR Transformation," Deloitte, undated, accessed March 9, 2016, http://tinyurl.com/hunrybm.

The consultancy examines necessary changes for human resources managers as the business world evolves.

"Globalization of Management Education. Changing International Structures, Adaptive Strategies, and the Impact on Institutions," Association to Advance Collegiate Schools of Business (AACSB) International, 2011, accessed March 8, 2016, http://tinyurl.com/jb4enfn.

The nonprofit seeking to foster the development of top-quality management education worldwide examines management education at business schools.

"Ready-Now Leaders: 25 Findings to Meet Tomorrow's Business Challenges. Global Leadership Forecast 2014-2015," The Conference Board and Development Dimensions International, undated, accessed March 8, 2016, http://tinyurl.com/hwqpuwy.

The Conference Board, an independent business membership and research organization, and DDI, a human resources consultancy, survey corporate leaders about their top challenges.

"Talent mobility: 2020 and beyond," PwC, undated, accessed March 8, 2016, http://tinyurl.com/z29cshd.

The consultancy looks at changes in employee mobility, along with expected trends for the future.

"What's Next: Future Global Trends Affecting Your Organization," The Economist Intelligence Unit, undated, accessed March 9, 2016, http://tinyurl.com/jtafcmo.

The research arm of The Economist examines forces driving workforce globalization.

"The World in 2050: Will the Shift in Global Economic Power Continue?" PwC, undated, accessed March 9, 2016, http://tinyurl.com/ojomu5d.

The consultancy considers economic changes in the world's largest economies by 2050.

Daniel, Shirley J., Fujiao Xie and Ben L. Kedia,, "2014 U.S. Business Needs for Employees with International Expertise," for the Internationalization of U.S. Education in the 21st Century conference, April 2014, http://tinyurl.com/hftpezd.

A University of Hawaii at Manoa accounting professor (Daniel), a Ph.D. student at the same school (Xie) and a University of Memphis professor of management (Kedia) survey more than 800 companies about their international business and the need for employees with international skills.

CHAPTER 5

Books

Babcock, Linda, and Sara Laschever, "Ask for It: How Women Can Use the Power of Negotiation to Get What They Really Want," Bantam Books, 2009.

An economist (Babcock) and writer (Laschever) discuss negotiation strategies first laid out in their earlier book, "Women Don't Ask: Negotiation and the Gender Divide," Princeton University Press, 2003.

Carter, Jessica Faye, "Double Outsiders, How Women of Color Can Succeed in Corporate America," JIST Works, 2007.

A female African-American entrepreneur dissects the assumptions and cultures that create barriers for women of color seeking to rise to corporate leadership positions.

Hirshman, Linda R., "Get to Work . . . and Get a Life Before It's Too Late," Viking, 2007.

A lawyer writes an impassioned manifesto on work as the cornerstone of a satisfying and self-sufficient life—and a rationale for not scaling back or stepping out.

Slaughter, Anne-Marie, "Unfinished Business," Random House, 2015.

The CEO of think tank New America and former State Department official builds on her controversial 2012 article in The Atlantic, which argued that it is impossible for professional women to balance work and life successfully.

Articles

Lindzon, Jared, "The CEO Gender Gap Is Slowly Closing at Major Public Companies," Fast Company, Oct. 3, 2016, http://tinyurl.com/j7vtd5j.

This article, part of the magazine's ongoing "Strong Female Lead" series, examines the pace of women's advancement and finds it implacably glacial.

Miller, Lisa, "Why We Need Older Women in the Workplace," New York Magazine, Aug. 4, 2015, http://tinyurl.com/pzwa5jk.

A middle manager shares her take on the value of mentors and role models.

Mochari, Ilan, "Glass Ceiling Debate: He Said, She Didn't," Inc. magazine, May 2014, http://tinyurl.com/juhjnjs.

Female entrepreneurs discover bias where they most—and least—expect it.

Reingold, Jennifer, "Why Top Women Are Disappearing from Corporate America," Fortune, Sept. 9. 2016, http://tinyurl.com/hafp9fx.

A senior editor at the business magazine examines why the number of female CEOs of Fortune 500 companies remains small and some female executives do not get second opportunities.

Reports and Studies

"Barriers and Bias: The Status of Women in Leadership," American Association of University Women, March 29, 2016, http://tinyurl.com/jcberkc.

The AAUW has expanded its mission beyond academia to explore root causes of the lack of women in leadership in the workplace.

"Everyday Moments of Truth: Frontline Managers Are Key to Women's Career Aspirations," Bain & Co., June 17, 2014, http://tinyurl.com/o5y8bnm.

The consulting company delves into the disconnects between leaders' intentions to advance women and corporate culture and daily decisions that hold women back.

"Forum W Annual Report," Moss Adams, 2015, http://tinyurl.com/h7drfrh.

A major accounting firm describes its creation of the industry's format for disclosing how well it is advancing women in leadership.

"Gender Pay Inequality: Consequences for Women, Families and the Economy," U.S. Joint Economic Committee, April 2016, http://tinyurl.com/z669qj9.

A bipartisan panel of the U.S. House and Senate studies the entwined economic consequences when women are not paid equitably or lack equitable opportunity for high-paying jobs.

"Pay Equity and Salary Negotiation Resources," University of Minnesota, Office for Equity and Diversity, 2013, http://tinyurl.com/hbsgdgm.

The university provides a list of articles, websites and other resources on pay equity and negotiation.

"Women and Leadership," Pew Research Center, Jan. 14, 2015, http://tinyurl.com/kmtylw9.

Deep analysis grounded in ongoing research frame this Pew report.

"Women CEOS of the S&P 500," Catalyst, Sept. 30, 2016, http://tinyurl.com/oxc43te.

Compiled annually, the Catalyst list and accompanying reports are widely read and extensively quoted.

"Women in Leadership: Why It Matters," the Rockefeller Foundation, May 12, 2016, http://tinyurl.com/zlpjuqg.

The private philanthropy analyzes in multimedia form the cumulative impact of women's accomplishments and crimped earnings.

Hegewisch, Ariane, and Asha DuMonthier, "The Gender Wage Gap 2015: Annual Earnings Differences by Gender, Race and Ethnicity," Institute for Women's Policy Research, September 2016, http://tinyurl.com/h9t9h46.

Researchers examine the gender gap between men's and women's annual earnings and conclude it will take another 45 years to reach parity.

CHAPTER 6

Books

Axtell, Paul, "Meetings Matter: 8 Powerful Strategies for Remarkable Conversations," Jackson Creek Press, 2015.

An executive coach focuses on the organizational purpose of collaboration and outlines the tactics for meeting success.

Baker, Heather, "Successful Minute Taking: Meeting the Challenge," Universe of Learning, 2013.

An executive-secretary-turned-administrative-trainer spells out the minutia of meeting protocol and process.

Field, Bryan, and Peter Kidd, "Powerfully Simple Meetings: Your Guide to Fewer, Faster, More Focused Business Meetings," MeetingResult, 2014.

Two meeting-efficiency consultants examine ways to make meetings more successful.

Heinecke, Stu, "How to Get a Meeting with Anyone: The Untapped Selling Power of Contact Marketing," BenBella Books, 2016.

A sales consultant explains how to win time with top executives—strategies that are especially useful in flat organizations.

Martin, Jeanette S., and Lillian H. Chaney, "Global Business Etiquette: A Guide to International Communication," Praeger, 2012.

Business school professors outline cultural and international differences and similarities in formal business meetings, communication and etiquette.

Schwartzman, Helen B., "The Meeting: Gatherings in Organizations and Communities," Plenum Press, 1989.

A Northwestern University professor of anthropology explores how various cultures conduct and view meetings.

Articles

"Conference Planning Checklists," National Council of Teachers of English, 2015, http://tinyurl.com/h4m6rv2.

The organization details the ingredients of successful meetings, from a timeline for the event to a day-before site inspection.

"Planning Accessible Meetings and Events: A Toolkit," American Bar Association, 2015, http://tinyurl.com/jcx7gnx.

The voluntary association of lawyers and law students outlines ways to include in meetings people who have limited abilities to see, hear, move or speak.

Axelrod, Dick, "How to Change Your Company Culture One Meeting at a Time," SwitchandShift.com, July 10, 2014, http://tinyurl.com/zdz6aue.

An organizational-change consultant illustrates step-by-step methods of how to shift corporate or departmental cultures through structure and communication at meetings.

Barsade, Sigal, and Olivia A. O'Neill, "Quantifying Your Company's Emotional Culture," Harvard Business Review, Jan. 7, 2016, http://tinyurl.com/zmb6pfc.

Professors of organizational behavior at the University of Pennsylvania's Wharton School of Business (Barsade) and George Mason University (O'Neill) discuss how to track the ·otional culture of workplaces.

Gallo, Amy, "The Condensed Guide to Running Meetings," Harvard Business Review, July 6, 2015, http://tinyurl.com/ohcbwan.

A business writer summarizes current wisdom on calling and managing meetings.

Heffernan, Virginia, "Meet Is Murder," The New York Times Magazine, Feb. 25, 2016, http://tinyurl.com/hdeavpv.

An essayist wonders how meetings "can be made bearable" and surveys a variety of experts.

Silverman, Rachel Emma, "Where's the Boss? Trapped in a Meeting," The Wall Street Journal, Feb. 14, 2012, http://tinyurl.com/jtkrgv7.

A reporter describes a study by London School of Economics and Harvard Business School researchers who tracked the schedules of more than 500 CEOs to learn how they spend their time and how that affects their companies' performance and management.

Spiro, Josh, "How to Run an Effective Meeting," Inc., Aug. 4, 2010, http://tinyurl.com/28hr5js.

A reporter delves into best practices for various types of meetings.

Sutton, Robert, "Tips for Better Brainstorming," Bloomberg Businessweek, July 25, 2006, http://tinyurl.com/hx4b4re.

A reporter outlines common pitfalls and assumptions about brainstorming.

Reports and Studies

"American Time Use Survey," U.S. Bureau of Labor Statistics, 2014, http://tinyurl.com/hm2g2a8.

The federal agency charged with compiling workplace statistics measures how much time Americans spend at work as well as on various tasks.

"Guide to Meeting Facilitation, Best Practices and Talking Tips," Strategic Training Solutions, 2010, http://tinyurl.com/gtzoerd.

A consulting firm provides an overview of how to fulfill the intended mission of a meeting.

"Guidelines on Meetings Planning and Coordination," United Nations Conference Services Division, March 2006, http://tinyurl.com/zwfsneb.

The U.N. agency overseeing conferences gives an overview of the aspects of holding an international meeting, including invitations and seating charts.

"Running Meetings with Robert's Rules of Order," Alpha Rho Chi, March 2014, http://tinyurl.com/zmddnlv.

A professional fraternity for architecture simplifies Robert's Rules of Order.

Kim, Been, and Cynthia Rudin, "Learning About Meetings," Massachusetts Institute of Technology, 2013, http://tinyurl.com/zfxkzex.

Two MIT researchers assess ways to understand what happens in meetings and uncover complications that they attribute to contradictions between explicit and hidden agendas.

Rogelberg, Steven, et al., "Lateness to meetings: Examination of an unexplored temporal phenomenon," European Journal of Work and Organizational Psychology, 2013, http://tinyurl.com/zfqtt8g.

Researchers study punctuality at work and say the topic warrants additional exploration.

CHAPTER 7

Books

Brenner, Susan W., "Cybercrime: Criminal Threats From Cyberspace," Praeger, 2010.

A law and technology professor traces the emergence and evolution of cybercrime from 1950 to the present.

Jordan, Tim, "Hacking: Digital Media and Technological Determinism," Polity, 2008.

A university professor provides an introduction to the culture of hackers.

Lapsley, Phil, "Exploding the Phone: The Untold Story of the Teenagers and Outlaws Who Hacked Ma Bell," Grove Press, 2013.

An engineer and author chronicles how Apple founders Steve Wozniak and Steve Jobs were among the early hackers who got their start in the technology field by stealing telephone service from monopoly AT&T.

Articles

"Cybercrime will Cost Businesses $2 Trillion by 2019," Security, May 12, 2015, http://tinyurl.com/q4xdojo.

A technology research company says that by 2019, the global cost of cybercrime will top $2 trillion, or almost four times the estimated cost of breaches in 2015.

"Hackers Inc.," The Economist, July 12, 2014, http://tinyurl.com/jdwamzj.

Hackers now work for corporate-like organizations, with an infrastructure allowing them to be persistent and almost unstoppable.

Ashford, Warwick, "Sony hack exposes poor security practices," Computer Weekly.com, Dec. 4, 2014, http://tinyurl.com/zw49jjx.

A computer-security journalist details how Sony failed to fix problems that led to data breaches.

Boyd, Aaron, "OPM breach a failure on encryption, detection," Federal Times, June 22, 2015, http://tinyurl.com/zde47hs.

A congressional hearing shows that the failure to perform simple updates led to the data breach at the Office of Personnel Management (OPM).

Chacos, Brad, "Meet Darknet, the hidden, anonymous underbelly of the searchable Web," PCWorld, Aug. 12, 2013, http://tinyurl.com/nxh5ou5.

The "Dark Web" has become a playground for hackers of all intentions.

Griffin, Andrew, "Sony hack: Who are the Guardians of Peace, and is North Korea really behind the attack?" The Independent, Dec. 17, 2014, http://tinyurl.com/q56kglo.

A politically motivated hacker organization reportedly based in North Korea takes responsibility for hacking Sony Pictures, but some experts believe the group is not working alone.

Groll, Elias, "The U.S. Hoped Indicting 5 Chinese Hackers Would Deter Beijing's Cyberwarriors. It Hasn't Worked," Foreign Policy, Sept. 2, 2015, http://tinyurl.com/jotp2gz.

The United States pressures China to rein in its cyberespionage activities.

Hesseldahl, Arik, "FireEye Identifies Chinese Group Behind Federal Hack," Re/Code, June 19, 2015, http://tinyurl.com/pcu8te8.

Cybersecurity investigative firm FireEye uncovers the group that hacked OPM.

Krebs, Brian, "Email Attack on Vendor Set Up Breach at Target," Krebs on Security, Feb. 12, 2014, http://tinyurl.com/oab53g7.

The security blogger who first reported the hack at Target reveals that the attackers breached the retailer's network through a vendor's system.

Mathews, Anna Wilde, "Anthem: Hacked Database Included 78.8 Million People," The Wall Street Journal, Feb. 24, 2015, http://tinyurl.com/h59kk5p.

Information on almost 80 million customers and employees was stolen from Anthem, the second-largest U.S. insurer.

Moritz, Bob, and David Burg, "How corporate America can fight cybersecurity threats," Fortune, Feb. 17, 2015, http://tinyurl.com/jhfsxh5.

The chairman of PricewaterhouseCoopers and a global cybersecurity leader outline what companies should do to deter hackers.

Nakashima, Ellen, "Chinese government has arrested hackers it says breached OPM database," The Washington Post, Dec. 2 2015, http://tinyurl.com/hjluugw.

The Chinese government surprises the United States by arresting the people allegedly responsible for the data breach at OPM, indicating that U.S. diplomatic pressure is beginning to yield fruit.

Peterson, Andrea, "The Sony Pictures hack, explained," The Washington Post, Dec. 18, 2014. http://tinyurl.com/hqn9bql.

A timeline of the Sony Pictures data breach.

Riley, Michael, et al., "Missed Alarms and 40 Million Stolen Credit Card Numbers: How Target Blew It," Bloomberg Businessweek, March 13, 2014, http://tinyurl.com/ox6z3sv.

Target was warned about suspicious activity but failed to act just before 40 million credit card numbers were stolen.

Schwartz, Mathew, "Report Claims Russians Hacked Sony," Bank Info Security, Feb. 4, 2015, http://tinyurl.com/z9vkky2.

Cybersecurity investigators say Russian hackers also are behind the Sony Pictures hack, working in concert with the North Koreans or independently piggybacking on their efforts.

Townsend, Matt, Lindsey Rupp and Jeff Green, "Target CEO Ouster Shows New Board Focus on Cyber Attacks," Bloomberg News, May 6, 2014, http://tinyurl.com/gmaah6k.

Several high-ranking executives are losing their jobs in the wake of data breaches.

Reports and Studies

"APT1: Exposing One of China's Cyber Espionage Units," Mandiant, February 2013, http://tinyurl.com/bjnsvjo.

Cybersecurity research firm exposes an operation in Shanghai, believed to be part of the Chinese military, that hacked into many corporate and governmental networks in the United States and other Western nations.

"Car Cybersecurity: What do automakers really think?" The Ponemon Institute, 2015 Survey of Automakers and Suppliers, http://tinyurl.com/gul2sx4.

An information-security research group surveys automakers, developers and engineers about the role of cybersecurity in the design of software for automobiles.

"Comprehensive Study on Cybercrime," United Nations Office of Drugs and Crime, February 2013, http://tinyurl.com/bncy969.

A U.N. report documents how hacking has become an organized activity, particularly in Eastern Europe, Asia and emerging economies.

"Cybersecurity and the Internet of Things," Ernst and Young, March 2015, http://tinyurl.com/hfgd3ar.

A consulting firm investigates the cyber vulnerabilities posed the Internet of Things.

"Forewarned Is Forearmed: 2015 Ponemon Institute of Cyber Crime Study," The Ponemon Institute, http://tinyurl.com/gln32aq.

Survey provides up-to-date costs of cybercrime globally and shows the differences among various regions.

"Net Losses: Estimating the Global Cost of Cybercrime," The Center for Strategic and International Studies, June 2014, http://tinyurl.com/hsfpaca.

A national security think tank looks at the difficulty of quantifying the global cost of cybercrime.

"Security in Development: The IBM Secure Engineering Framework," IBM Redbook, March 18, 2010, http://tinyurl.com/hqxt4yo.

In a guide to software engineering, IBM outlines an approach that encourages developers to design with security in mind and anticipate vulnerabilities.

CHAPTER 8

Books

Murray, Alan, "The Wall Street Journal Essential Guide to Management: Lasting Lessons from the Best Leadership Minds of Our Time," HarperBusiness, 2010.

Management guide by a Wall Street Journal managing editor provides business strategies for being a successful manager and historical context on current management techniques.

Pontefract, Dan, "Flat Army: Creating a Connected and Engaged Organization," Wiley, 2013.

A Canadian telecommunications executive and business speaker offers a guide for creating a culture of collaboration, engagement and employee empowerment by replacing command-and-control management techniques with collaborative methods.

Tapscott, Don, "Wikinomics: How Mass Collaboration Changes Everything," Portfolio Trade, 2010.

A business consultant explains that the use of collaborative processes by employees is spreading to traditional companies.

Articles

Birkinshaw, Julian, "Beware the Next Big Thing," Harvard Business Review, May 2014, http://tinyurl.com/kexgvy8.

A business scholar advises companies on how to evaluate new management theories before implementing them.

Finley, Klint, "Why Workers Can Suffer in Bossless Companies Like GitHub," Wired, March 20, 2014, http://tinyurl.com/obu4gv6.

A technology journalist examines some of the problems experienced by workers in companies using flat management techniques.

Foss, Nicolai J., and Peter G. Klein, "Why Managers Still Matter," MIT Sloan Management Review, Fall 2014, http://tinyurl.com/pzm64b4.

Two business scholars make the case that managers continue to be essential components of business success.

Garvin, David A., "How Google Sold Its Engineers on Management," Harvard Business Review, December 2013, http://tinyurl.com/pe638nl.

A Harvard business professor describes how Google examined the role of its managers and their contributions to the business.

Hamel, Gary, "First, Let's Fire All the Managers," Harvard Business Review, December 2011, http://tinyurl.com/77swj3x.

Management hierarchies have become inefficient, says a management consultant who has written frequently about innovation.

Hamel, Gary, "Moon Shots for Management," Harvard Business Review, February 2009, http://tinyurl.com/o9r89pk.

A leading management consultant lays out a road map for developing new management techniques, saying current structures can no longer be improved.

Kastelle, Tim, "Hierarchy Is Overrated," Harvard Business Review Blog Network, Nov. 20, 2013, http://tinyurl.com/ksaur6h.

A business scholar makes the case that flat organizational structures can work for any business.

Reports and Studies

Courtright, Stephen, G.L. Stewart and M.R. Barrick, "Peer-Based Control in Self-Managing Teams: Linking Rational and Normative Influence With Individual and Group Performance," Journal of Applied Psychology, March 2012, http://tinyurl.com/p3u5e58.

University researchers find that groups that manage themselves can be more productive.

Friesen, Justin P., Aaron C. Kay, Richard P. Eibach and Adam D. Galinsky, "Seeking structure in social organization: Compensatory control and the psychological advantages of hierarchy," Journal of Personality and Social Psychology, April 2014, http://tinyurl.com/px5cgxx.

Researchers argue hierarchies offer structure and satisfy core motivational needs for order and control.

Ronay, Richard, Katharine Greenaway, Eric M. Anicich and Adam D. Galinsky, "The Path to Glory Is Paved With Hierarchy: When Hierarchical Differentiation Increases Group Effectiveness," Psychological Science, June 2012, http://tinyurl.com/p46x6vz.

Hierarchy helps teams work effectively on collaborative tasks, university researchers say.

Seibert, S.E., G. Wang and S.H. Courtright, "Antecedents and consequences of psychological and team empowerment in organizations: a meta-analytic review," Journal of Applied Psychology, September 2011, http://tinyurl.com/pu7edyx.

University researchers find that workers who felt psychologically empowered performed better.

CHAPTER 9

Books

Fried, Jason and David Heinemeier Hansson, "Remote: Office Not Required," Crown Business, 2013.

Founders of software company Basecamp, which sells a product that allows remote team collaboration, explore why employers increasingly want to "move work to the workers" and how to accomplish it.

Friedman, Stewart D., "Leading the Life You Want: Skills for Integrating Work and Life," Harvard Business Review Press, 2014.

Based on his research and earlier books, a Wharton professor shares insights and skills on being whole and innovative in life and work, and profiles Bruce Springsteen, Michelle Obama and Sheryl Sandberg.

Kossek, Ellen Ernst, and Brenda A. Lautsch, "CEO of Me: Creating a Life That Works in the Flexible Job Age," FT Press, 2007.

Drawing on their research in work-life issues, Kossek, a Purdue management professor, and Lautsch, a Simon Fraser management professor, discuss six work-life patterns and the importance of boundaries and habits.

Williams Yost, Cali, "Work + Life: Finding the Fit That's Right for You," Riverhead, 2004.

A work/life consultant with an MBA from Columbia advises individuals on how to create a vision, develop clarity, plan for child-and elder-care and overcome roadblocks.

Articles

Beauregard, T. Alexandra, "Fairness Perceptions of Work-Life Balance Initiatives: Effects on Counterproductive Work Behavior," British Journal of Management, 2014, http://tinyurl.com/l42emut.

Assistant professor in the management department at the London School of Economics examines array of research workers' perceptions of the fairness of work-life arrangements and the effect of those perceptions on their attitudes and behaviors.

Bernard, Tara Siegel, "For Workers, Less Flexible Companies," The New York Times, May 19, 2014, http://tinyurl.com/p7s2flo.

Although companies say they offer flexible work arrangements, telecommuting and other arrangements sometimes are not available to all employees, but instead to just select professionals.

Berry, Leonard L., Ann M. Mirabito and William B. Baun, "What's the Hard Return on Employer Wellness Programs?" Harvard Business Review, December 2010, http://tinyurl.com/232oxzz.

Workplace wellness programs pay off in savings on medical claims and more, two professors and a wellness program manager write.

Schulte, Brigid, "More than a paycheck: New dads want paid leave to be caregivers," The Washington Post, July 18, 2014, http://tinyurl.com/nrsut8p.

A small but growing number of companies are expanding the paid time that new fathers can take for paternity leave.

Shellenbarger, Sue, "When the Boss Works Long Hours, Must We All?" The Wall Street Journal, Feb. 18, 2014, http://tinyurl.com/oe4pocl.

Shellenbarger, who has written The Wall Street Journal's Work & Family column since 1991, explains how to work for a workaholic boss.

Stone, Brad, "Work-Life Balance and the New Night Shift," Bloomberg Businessweek, Aug. 7, 2014, http://tinyurl.com/k75jjkw.

A journalist considers how and why he and so many professionals end up answering email or otherwise working at midnight.

Weber, Lauren, and Joann S. Lublin, "The Daddy Juggle: Work, Life, Family and Chaos," The Wall Street Journal, June 12, 2014, http://tinyurl.com/ne2g5z4.

As fathers take on a growing role in raising their children, employers are slow to recognize and adapt to the change.

Reports and Studies

"The New Dad Studies," Boston College Center for Work & Family, 2010–14, www.thenewdad.org.

Researchers at Boston College produce a series of studies on fathers' roles, conflict and more; paternity leave, conflict and staying home are among the subjects.

"Survey on Workplace Flexibility 2013," WorldatWork, October 2013, http://tinyurl.com/m74zhxm.

Employers offer between five and eight forms of flexibility, telework and flex time the most prevalent, according to a survey of members of international human resources association.

"2014 Employee Benefits," Society for Human Resource Management, undated, http://tinyurl.com/k28n8ch.

Annual survey of benefits, conducted by the largest professional association for human resources professionals, shows trends over the years.

"Workplace Flexibility Still a Myth to Most," Sloan Center on Aging & Work at Boston College, March 17, 2014, http://tinyurl.com/p37sq5s.

Researchers from Boston College and elsewhere who studied 545 U.S. employers find flexible options aren't available to the majority of workers.

Harter, James K., et al., "The Relationship Between Engagement at Work and Organizational Outcomes," Gallup, February 2013, http://tinyurl.com/pgb7ubm.

Researchers gather results of 263 research studies and conclude that "the relationship between [worker] engagement and performance at the business/work unit level is substantial."

Matos, Kenneth, and Ellen Galinsky, "2014 National Study of Employers," Families and Work Institute, 2014, http://tinyurl.com/kvz2mwt.

Survey of 1,051 employers finds they maintained flexible work options during the recession, and now see such programs as crucial to worker retention.

Van Deusen, Fredric R., et al., "Overcoming the Implementation Gap: How 20 Leading Companies are Making Flexibility Work," Boston College Center for Work & Family, 2007, http://tinyurl.com/qeq9348.

Researchers present case studies from Booz Allen, Intel, KPMG and others on telework, job sharing and ways to implement flexible work arrangements.

Other Resources

Friedman, Stewart, "Work and Life," SiriusXM radio, weekly, http://tinyurl.com/n29tu5z.

Friedman, a Wharton School professor, conducts interviews and moderates call-ins on a live weekly radio show on SiriusXM radio.

Marsh, Nigel, "How to make work-life balance work," Nigel Marsh, TED Talk, May 2010, http://tinyurl.com/o2ekxl9.

A marketer and the author of "Fat, Forty and Fired" talks about the importance of work-life balance—in moderation—and how going to the park and grabbing a pizza may make a big memory for a child.

Sagmeister, Stefan, "The Power of Time Off," TED Talk, July 2009, http://tinyurl.com/qy9s26z.

New York graphic designer who believes in sabbaticals and long vacations shares innovations that came from his yearlong break in Bali. He also discusses stories of others who have taken big breaks.

Weisberg, Anne, "Book Review: All Joy and No Fun," Families and Work Institute, Aug. 26, 2014, http://tinyurl.com/lweoy2s.

First in a series of monthly book reviews from the Families and Work Institute, which will post the reviews on its blog here: http://tinyurl.com/l2nkggo.

CHAPTER 10

Books

Boushey, Heather, "Finding Time: The Economics of Work-Life Conflict," Harvard University Press, 2016.

The executive director of the Washington Center for Equitable Growth, a research and grant-making organization, says a changing economy—one in which women work instead of stay home full time to raise their children—requires employers to provide the resources working mothers need to care for family members.

Gordon, Victoria. "Maternity Leave: Policy and Practice," CRC Press, 2013.

An associate political science professor at Western Kentucky University, who has interviewed women who took maternity leave, says there is a disconnect between policy and practice.

Sholar, Megan, "Getting Paid While Taking Time: The Women's Movement and the Development of Paid Family Leave Policies in the United States," Temple University Press, 2016.

A Loyola University Chicago instructor explains the development of family leave policies in the United States, and notes that most innovations in family policies have originated at the state level.

Articles

Berman, Russell, "A Conservative Push for Paid Family Leave," The Atlantic, Aug. 15, 2016, http://tinyurl.com/kc2x6bc.

A journalist examines the efforts of Republican politicians, including President Trump, and conservative groups to encourage Congress to pass legislation providing for paid family leave.

Bernard, Tara Siegel, "In Paid Family Leave, U.S. Trails Most of the Globe," The New York Times, Feb. 22, 2013, http://tinyurl.com/krbsulm.

The writer explores why the United States is the only industrialized country without a mandatory paid leave law.

Miller, Claire Cain, "Americans Agree on Paid Leave, but Not on Who Should Pay," The New York Times, March 23, 2017, http://tinyurl.com/mm33z7k.

A journalist questions why the nation has not enacted a mandatory paid leave policy when a majority of citizens on both sides of the political spectrum support it.

Murphy, Robert P., " 'Paid Family Leave' Is a Great Way to Hurt Women," Foundation for Economic Education, June 2, 2015, http://tinyurl.com/kqzhyqj.

A Texas Tech University professor argues that paid family-leave policies should be voluntary, not mandatory. Businesses, he said, know better than the government how to structure their employee benefits for recruitment and retention purposes, he writes.

Rogers, Megan, "Why New York businesses oppose paid family leave proposal," Albany Business Review, March 25, 2015, http://tinyurl.com/lnaddno.

A journalist summarizes interviews with business leaders who believe small businesses cannot afford overtime costs associated with mandatory paid family leave.

Warner, Judith, and Danielle Corley, "In the Absence of U.S. Action on Paid Leave, Multinationals Make Their Own Policies," Center for American Progress, Nov. 17, 2016, http://tinyurl.com/jwc26tr.

Researchers at a liberal Washington think tank examine a trend among multinational companies to create policies for paid time off that apply to their employees, no matter where in the world they work.

Reports and Studies

"Americans Widely Support Paid Family and Medical Leave, but Differ Over Specific Policies," Pew Research Center, March 23, 2017, http://tinyurl.com/m7v6tfy.

A nonpartisan "fact tank" finds that most Americans support paid leave but believe that employers, and not the federal or state governments, should pay for it.

"The Economics of Paid and Unpaid Leave," Council of Economic Advisers, June 2014, http://tinyurl.com/mruj93h.

The White House agency dealing with economic policy concludes that businesses would benefit from offering paid family leave to more workers because employees would be more productive on the job and retention of talented workers would increase.

"Employer Costs for Employee Compensation—December 2016," Bureau of Labor Statistics, U.S. Department of Labor, March 17, 2017, http://tinyurl.com/m3y5osc.

In 23 pages of charts, the federal agency reveals the costs of compensation and benefits for employees of private-and public-sector employees. Paid leave, the report notes, accounted for 6.9 percent of private industry compensation.

"Paid Time Off Programs and Practices," WorldatWo` September 2016, http://tinyurl.com/zu8en2c.

In a survey of its members, the human resources trade association discovered that 88 percent believe offering some type of paid time-off program is necessary for an organization to be competitive in the labor market.

"Why Paid Family Leave Is Good Business," Boston Consulting Group, Feb. 7, 2017, http://tinyurl.com/krss4gk.

The management consulting firm reviewed the policies of more than 250 companies and interviewed 25 human resource executives at large organizations. The report's conclusion: Employers espouse a strong business case for paid family leave, which they say helps attract and retain qualified employees.

Gitis, Ben, "The Earned Income Leave Benefit: Rethinking Family Leave for Low-Income Workers," American Action Forum, Aug. 15, 2016, http://tinyurl.com/ly5dbue.

The director of labor market policy for a conservative research group breaks with Republican tradition and proposes a paid-leave benefit for workers with annual incomes lower than $28,000.

Ray, Rebecca, Milla Sanes and John Schmitt, "No-Vacation Nation Revisited," Center for Economic and Policy Institute, May 2013, http://tinyurl.com/mcasupx.

This report reviews laws in 21 "rich" countries that require paid vacations and holidays.

Zagorsky, Jay L., "Divergent Trends in US Maternity and Paternity Leave, 1994-2015," American Journal of Public Health, March 2017, http://tinyurl.com/l29spvb.

An economist and research scientist at Ohio State University's Center for Human Resource Research discovers that the number of women who take maternity leave has not grown in 22 years.

CHAPTER 11

Books

Elkington, John, "The Zeronauts: Breaking the Sustainability Barrier," Routledge, 2012.

The creator of the "triple bottom line" looks at a new five-prong paradigm that moves well beyond incremental change to transformation.

Hart, Stuart L., "Capitalism at the Crossroads: The Unlimited Business Opportunities in Solving the World's Most Difficult Problems," Wharton School Publishing, 2005.

The creator of the Sustainable Entrepreneurship MBA at the University of Vermont explains the history of sustainability and its possibilities.

McDonough, William, and Michael Braungart, "Cradle to Cradle: Remaking the Way We Make Things," North Point ᵉss, 2002.

The originators of circular or closed-loop production describe a seminal process of eliminating waste altogether.

Winston, Andrew S., "The Big Pivot: Radically Practical Strategies for a Hotter, Scarcer, and More Open World," Harvard Business Review Press, 2014.

A business strategist gives a blueprint for how to incorporate sustainability in a business context.

Articles

Bardelline, Jonathan, "How UPS makes the business case for sustainability projects," Greenbiz.com, May 6, 2013, http://tinyurl.com/ofk9xmc.

UPS successfully argued for alternative fuel or advanced technology to power its fleet.

Davis, Grant, "The Triple Bottom Line Goal of Sustainable Business," Entrepreneur, March 2013, http://tinyurl.com/pe36caw.

Entrepreneurs have successfully used the principle of the triple bottom line—profit, planet and people.

Kaye, Leon, "The Business Case for Sustainability Is Becoming Easier to Make," TriplePundit, March 15, 2013, http://tinyurl.com/bb4yy29.

The editor of GreenGoPost, a website devoted to sustainability, describes how "green" efforts have helped the bottom line.

Kelly-Detwiler, Peter, "The Upside and Waging Peace Through Commerce: William McDonough Wants Us to Design Our Way to Abundance," Forbes, Nov. 20, 2013, http://tinyurl.com/mbqet6w.

Architect William McDonough discusses the concept of closed-loop manufacturing, where everything gets recycled.

Kiron, David, et al, "Sustainability's Next Frontier: Walking the Talk on the Sustainability Issues That Matter Most," MIT Sloan Management Review, Dec. 15, 2013, http://tinyurl.com/lxxtfro.

Boston Consulting Group and editors at MIT Sloan Management Review present research on how companies are faring with integrating sustainable values and practices.

Rajaram, Dhiraj, "Making the Business Case for Sustainability," The Harvard Business Review, May 2, 2011, http://tinyurl.com/krn33z8.

CEO of an analytics firm explains companies can measure the financial impact of sustainability strategies.

Scott, Ryan, "The Bottom Line of Corporate Good," Forbes.com, Sept. 14, 2012, http://tinyurl.com/8uy49tk.

CEO of Causecast, a firm that markets a technology platform to social cause-oriented organizations, explains the people, planet, profits framework.

Reports and Studies

"The Business Case for Sustainability," International Finance Corp., 2012, http://tinyurl.com/mhhodsd.

A report from a World Bank affiliate puts the business case for sustainability in an international context.

"Planning for a Sustainable Future," National Association for Environmental Management, 2012, http://tinyurl.com/n364e4g.

Twenty-five sustainability leaders and experts discuss their current thinking about sustainability.

Makower, Joel, et al., "The State of Green Business 2014," GreenBiz and Trucost, 2014, http://tinyurl.com/kqcpcep.

The editors of GreenBiz, a leading website about sustainable business, discuss trends in everything from chemical transparency to corporate leadership.

CHAPTER 12

Books

Gilson, Stuart, "Creating Value Through Corporate Restructuring: Case Studies in Bankruptcies, Buyouts, and Breakups," John Wiley & Sons, 2010.

A Harvard University professor of business administration examines the process of corporate restructuring using case studies of prominent companies, including Delphi, General Motors and Kmart, as well as the Eurotunnel debt restructuring.

Kindleberger, Charles, and Robert Z. Aliber, "Manias, Panics, and Crashes: A History of Financial Crises," Palgrave Macmillan, 2011.

Two academics detail how poor money management historically has given rise to financial crises.

Sandage, Scott, "Born Losers: A History of Failure in America," Harvard University Press, 2005.

A cultural historian at Carnegie Mellon University explains how the meaning of failure changed from a business term to an identity marker for failed businessmen in 19th-century America.

Schoemaker, Paul J.H., "Brilliant Mistakes: Finding Success on the Far Side of Failure," Wharton Digital Press, 2011.

A researcher and business consultant illustrates how many products, from ATMs to smoke-free cigarettes to penicillin, were initially judged as mistakes yet turned out to be money makers.

Skeel, David Jr., "Debt's Dominion: A History of Bankruptcy Law in America," Princeton University Press, 2001.

A professor of corporate law at the University of Pennsylvania shows the political and economic roles in the United States' unique approaches to bankruptcy, from its inception in 1800 to the 1994 bankruptcy reform.

Tugend, Alina, "Better by Mistake," Riverhead Books, 2011.

Drawing on research and behavioral studies, a New York Times columnist shares lessons from aviation and medicine on how to respond to errors, and why it's important yet difficult to accept and learn from mistakes.

Articles

"The Failure Issue—Failure: How to Understand It, Learn from It, and Recover from It," Harvard Business Review, April 2011, http://tinyurl.com/oj235a6.

A collection of articles, many by well-known professors and experts, on aspects of failure in career and business.

Bradley, Ryan, "A Brief History of Failure," The New York Times Magazine, Nov. 12, 2014, http://tinyurl.com/p59yuyu.

A photo gallery of innovative products that never took off, including the pneumatic railroad and a simplified typewriter keyboard.

Bruder, Jessica, "The Psychological Price of Entrepreneurship," Inc. magazine, September 2013, http://tinyurl.com/kht6mzo.

A journalist explains how leading a company through dark times can bring on depression, anxiety, despair and even suicide, leaving founders to feel alone in their emotional and financial battles.

Elmer, Vickie, "A coming-out party for business failures," Fortune, Oct. 21, 2013, http://tinyurl.com/pgct6pk.

FailCon, which started as a storytelling conference for business start-up failures, has grown to 10 cities and now has imitators.

Gillett, Rachel, "What the Hype Behind Embracing Failure Is Really All About," Fast Company, Sept. 8, 2014, http://tinyurl.com/pxzh5ho.

How the movement to celebrate failure began and how those in business should not go overboard in sharing their mistakes.

Lewis, Geoff, "Failure porn: There's too much celebration of failure and too little fear," The Washington Post, Dec. 4, 2014, http://tinyurl.com/h2o7jo8.

A Silicon Valley venture capitalist suggests Americans have swung too far in embracing failure stories while underestimating the risks in new ventures.

Moules, Jonathan, "From failure can come success," The Financial Times, Jan. 24, 2013, http://tinyurl.com/pasvq94.

British start-ups say a fear of failure in that country still holds back entrepreneurs, especially compared with the United States.

Reports and Studies

Altman, Edward I., "Revisiting the Recidivism: Chapter 22 Phenomenon in the U.S. Bankruptcy System." Brooklyn Journal of Corporate, Financial & Commercial Law, 2014, http://tinyurl.com/pkfzhw6.

A New York University professor shows that 15 percent to 18.25 percent of firms that exit Chapter 11 reorganization return to it.

Atkinson, Tyler, David Luttrell and Harvey Rosenblum, "How Bad Was It? The Costs and Consequences of the 2007–09 Financial Crisis," Federal Reserve Bank of Dallas, July 2013, http://tinyurl.com/zp55lde.

Economists review the cost of the financial crisis, and determine that up to $14 trillion was lost or forgone in output, wealth and more.

Gompers, Paul A., et al., "Performance Persistence in Entrepreneurship," Harvard Business School Working Paper, September 2008, http://tinyurl.com/zvqx84e.

Entrepreneurs with a track record of success are more likely to continue succeeding than others. Those with market timing skills also have an edge, researchers found.

Lee, Seung-Hyun, et al., "How do bankruptcy laws affect entrepreneurship development around the world?" Journal of Business Venturing, September 2011, http://tinyurl.com/od62n6r.

Based on analysis of statutes in 29 countries, lenient, business-friendly bankruptcy laws lead to more firms being established.

Sonnenfeld, Jeffrey A., and Andrew J. Ward, "Firing Back: How Great Leaders Rebound after Career Disasters," Harvard Business Review, January 2007, http://tinyurl.com/p5jctgf.

Two business school professors interviewed 300 executives and found that only one-third of ousted CEOs returned to an active executive job, having done so by recovering their "heroic status" and fighting back.

Tian, Xuan, and Yue Wang, Tracy, "Tolerance for Failure and Corporate Innovation," The Review of Financial Studies, Dec. 5, 2011, http://tinyurl.com/zwgdmjd.

Initial public offerings of stock backed by more failure-tolerant venture capitalists are significantly more innovative, and less-experienced VCs are more likely to face capital constraints or career concerns, which may reduce their tolerance of failure.